The attempt to establish [a] 'social contract' between the Go[vernment and the] unions, with a view to stabilizing the economy and restraining industrial militancy, has emerged as the burning issue of contemporary British politics. This study uncovers the roots of this development in the incomes policies of successive post-war Governments, especially of the 1964–70 Labour Government, and traces the way in which wage restraint was secured from the unions, or imposed upon them, in the context of the attempted integration of the unions within the existing economic and political order.

Professor Panitch concentrates on the crucial role of the Labour Party and shows how Labour's incomes policies, and industrial relations generally, have derived less from a concern with socialist economic planning than from the Party's 'integrative' ideology, its rejection of the concept of class struggle in favour of affecting a compromise between the different classes in British society.

While indicating the way in which Labour's close ties with the unions have facilitated union integration, the study reveals how wage restraint, in the absence of effective price and profit controls, has given rise to repeated conflicts within the Labour movement.

In addition to making an important contribution to the understanding of contemporary British politics, the study analyses the underlying tensions between an industrially militant union movement and its political allegiance to social democracy, and casts doubt on the viability of any 'social contract' within the context of the present ailing capitalist economy.

The author is Assistant Professor,
Carleton University, Canada

SOCIAL DEMOCRACY AND INDUSTRIAL
MILITANCY

SOCIAL DEMOCRACY & INDUSTRIAL MILITANCY

The Labour Party, the Trade Unions and
Incomes Policy, 1945–1974

LEO PANITCH
Assistant Professor, Carleton University, Canada

CAMBRIDGE UNIVERSITY PRESS

CAMBRIDGE

LONDON · NEW YORK · MELBOURNE

Published by the Syndics of the Cambridge University Press
The Pitt Building, Trumpington Street, Cambridge CB2 1RP
Bentley House, 200 Euston Road, London NW1 2DB
32 East 57th Street, New York, NY 10022, USA
296 Beaconsfield Parade, Middle Park, Melbourne 3206, Australia

© Cambridge University Press 1976

Library of Congress catalogue card number: 75-16869

ISBN: 0 521 20779 7

First published 1976

Printed in Great Britain by
Hazell Watson & Viney Ltd,
Aylesbury, Bucks

CONTENTS

TO MELANIE

PREFACE

> Recently someone asked, for whom does one write? That is a profound question. One should always dedicate a book. Not that one alters one's thoughts with a change of interlocutor, but because every word, whether we know it or not, is always a word with someone, which presupposes a certain degree of esteem or friendship, the resolution of a certain number of misunderstandings, the transcendence of a certain latent content, and finally, the appearance of part of the truth in the encounters we live.
>
> (Maurice Merleau-Ponty, *Humanism and Terror*)

This book is a product of such encounters with many people in various situations: with my late parents and the social democratic environment of my youth in Winnipeg; with numerous individuals associated with the labour movement in Britain during my years in England from 1967 to 1972; with friends and colleagues on both sides of the Atlantic with whom the ideas contained here were so often discussed. Above all, two people have been most important: Ralph Miliband, my teacher and friend, from whose wisdom, aid and criticism I have benefited greatly; and Melanie Panitch, who has shared these encounters with me, and whose understanding, encouragement and advice have been invaluable. It gives me real pleasure to acknowledge here the debt I owe to both of them.

This study was originally undertaken as a Ph.D. thesis for the London School of Economics and Political Science. For their help, comments and suggestions on the work at that stage and on its elaboration since then, I am particularly grateful to Bob Collison, Avishai Erlich, Sym Gill, Sam Gindin, Ed Harriman, Royden Harrison, Peter Jenkins, Robert McKenzie, Lewis Minkin, Fred Silberman, Don Swartz, Reg Whitaker, Anne Whitehead, and especially John Corina. Many of those involved directly in the events under consideration were kind enough to share their knowledge with me; those who granted formal interviews are listed at the back of this book. The staff at the British Library of Political and Economic Science, at the Labour Party and TUC libraries, and at the research departments of the Labour Party, TUC, TGWU, GMWU, AEU and UPW were always helpful in providing access to relevant material. Social Surveys (Gallup Polls) Ltd opened their files on incomes policy opinion surveys during the 1960s to me, and Dr Jay Blumber of the Centre for Television Research, Leeds University, provided me with unpublished data on a survey of trade union opinion conducted in 1968. H. G. Perry of the Industrial and Commercial Policy Division of the Department of Trade and Industry provided me with unpublished statistics on price control from 1966 to 1970. The National Graphical Association granted me access to the files of Robert Willis, containing memoranda on references and reports of the National Board for Prices and Incomes from 1965 to 1967. The office of the Chief Registrar of Friendly Societies allowed me to consult the Annual Returns of Registered Trade Unions 1960 to 1970. I am also grateful to George Bain of Warwick University and Frank Wilkinson of Cambridge University for making available material in advance of publication.

The Canada Council provided me with generous financial assistance during my years at the London School of Economics, and Carleton University has helped me to undertake further research and prepare the manuscript. Special thanks are also due to Linda Snowden and Dulcie O'Neill, and to the secretaries at the Political Science Department of Carleton University, for their patience and skill in typing the manuscript and to Les MacDonald, my graduate student, for helping me to edit it and prepare the index.

August 1974   Leo Panitch

ABBREVIATIONS

ABCC	Association of British Chambers of Commerce
ACTAT	Association of Cinematographic, Television and Allied Technicians
AEF	Amalgamated Union of Engineering and Foundry Workers (Incorporating AEU)
AEU	Amalgamated Engineering Union
AUEW	Amalgamated Union of Engineering Workers (Incorporating AEU and AEF)
APSR	American Political Science Review
ASLEF	Associated Society of Locomotive Engineers and Firemen
ASSET	Association of Supervisory Staffs, Executives and Technicians
ASTMS	Association of Scientific, Technical and Managerial Staffs (Incorporating ASSET)
BEC	British Employers Confederation
BJIR	British Journal of Industrial Relations
CBI	Confederation of British Industry
CIM	Commission for Industry and Manpower
CIR	Commission on Industrial Relations
CLP	Constituency Labour Party
DATA	Draughtsmen's and Allied Technicians' Association
DEA	Department of Economic Affairs
DEP	Department of Employment and Productivity
EEF	Engineering Employers Federation
ETU	Electrical Trades Union
FBI	Federation of British Industry
GMWU	General and Municipal Workers Union (formerly NUGMW)
ILP	Independent Labour Party
IMF	International Monetary Fund

IRC	Industrial Reorganization Corporation
LPCR	Labour Party Conference Report
OEEC	Organization for European Economic Cooperation
NABM	National Association of British Manufacturers
NALGO	National Association of Local Government Officers
NATSOPA	National Society of Operative Printers and Assistants
NBPI	National Board for Prices and Incomes
NEC	National Executive Committee (Labour Party)
NEDC	National Economic Development Council
NGA	National Graphical Association
NHS	National Health Service
NIC	National Incomes Commission
NIESR	National Institute of Economic and Social Research
NIRC	National Industrial Relations Court
NUGMW	National Union of General and Municipal Workers
NUM	National Union of Mineworkers
NUPE	National Union of Public Employees
NUR	National Union of Railwaymen
NUS	National Union of Seamen
NUVB	National Union of Vehicle Builders
PEP	Political and Economic Planning
PLP	Parliamentary Labour Party
SOGAT	Society of Graphical and Allied Trades
TGWU	Transport and General Workers Union
TUC	Trades Union Congress
UPW	Union of Post Office Workers
USDAW	Union of Shop, Distributive and Allied Workers

INTRODUCTION

Itself a product of the class divisions of capitalist society, the British Labour Party has relied on the support of the working class for its political success. Electorally and organizationally, it was nurtured and has been sustained through its structural ties with the trade union movement from which it derives the vast proportion of its membership and finances. Ideologically, however, the Party has never been exclusively or even primarily a working class party. Ever since its founding conference threw out a motion calling for 'a distinct party . . . based upon the recognition of the class war',[1] the Party has presented itself as a *national* party cast in the historical role of integrating the interests and demands of the working class with those of the British nation as a whole. In this respect, the Party has fitted the mould of what contemporary political sociologists call an integrative political party, fulfilling systemic functions like representation and brokerage, demand conversion and aggregation, imbued with a conception of the social order as being basically unified rather than fissured, and effecting a compromise between the sectional interests of various classes in the society by means of policies 'in the national interest'.[2] This integrative cornerstone of the Labour Party's ideology has shaped its particular socialist orientation, which has been defined not in terms of the conquest of power by the working class, but as the culmination of the development of the whole nation, the product of social harmony and class cooperation. 'Socialism marks the growth of society not the uprising of class. The consciousness it seeks to quicken is not one of economic class solidarity, but one of social unity', Ramsay MacDonald wrote at the turn of the century. 'The watchword of Socialism, therefore, is not class consciousness but community consciousness.'[3]

This ideology has contributed to that aspect of British political culture that portrays the working class as a 'mere' sectional group which by definition is debarred from seeking hegemonic control over

1

British society. To be sure, the internal party conflicts engendered by an ideologically integrative but structurally working class political party have been extant in the Labour Party throughout its history, but to dwell on these exclusively is to obscure the very conditions of the Party's success. For rather than attempt the difficult task of securing working class support by undermining the symbols of national unity which act as a counter to the development of a distinctive political consciousness on the part of the working class, the Labour Party has chosen the easier road of engaging working class allegiance by associating itself with these symbols.

> In reality belief in Labourism does not stand alone . . . It is associated at the deepest level with something else, something positive and far more powerful . . . this is, of course, belief in the nation, in British society, or 'the British way', with its habitual accoutrement of parliament, constitution, monarchy, a certain national political style of conduct and leadership, and so on . . . Labour constitutes, perhaps, the most important element in this astonishing homogeneity of modern Britain. In effect, the most dangerous strain of civil society, the division between classes, runs through it rather than outside it and is constantly 'healed' politically (i.e. kept closed) by the very structure and world view of the party.[4]

If the Labour Party's integrative role is visible from its earliest beginnings, it has become most apparent since World War II. This is in part a product of the fact that for 12 of the 25 years after 1945, Labour Governments had the opportunity of putting the Party's ideology into practice, but also because the British political system in these years exhibited an overriding consensus between the two major parties on what the national interest in fact entailed. This consensus developed in terms of a common response to the difficulties which beset British capitalism. All advanced capitalist societies in the postwar period have experienced the problem of price inflation to which full employment (or rather the Keynesian commitment to much lower levels of unemployment than earlier) combined with the rising wage demands, have made an important contribution. Britain in particular was troubled by this phenomenon due to its heavy dependence on foreign trade and due to the increasing international competition to which it was subject with the decline of the Empire and the rapid economic growth of its competitors, yielding a recurrent series of balance of payments crises. Since both major parties were reluctant to ease the pressure which rising wage demands and international competition had on corporate profit margins by consistently devaluing the currency and undermining the role of sterling and the City of London in the international financial sphere, they tried through intermittent deflationary fiscal policies to limit the incidence of wage pressure. But in addition to the fact that these policies further checked economic growth, their effects were limited because the lessons of the depression suggested that too deep and too persistent a deflation would be politically disastrous and because, as recent experience has shown, increases in unemployment short of a mass depression cannot be relied upon alone to reduce wage pressure significantly. Therefore, in an attempt to control price inflation in the context of managing a predominantly private enterprise economy, both Labour and Conservative Governments turned towards securing – 'in the national interest' – wage restraint from the trade unions, especially although not exclusively, by what was known in the early post-war period as a wages policy and subsequently as an incomes policy. This involved agreement by the organized working class not to seek wage increases in excess of the projected rate of growth of the economy, so that over-all profit levels might be maintained without compensating for wage increases by price increases.

The establishment of a voluntary incomes policy is an integrative operation without peer. Far more than is the case in other fields of state intervention in the economy, it requires the direct cooperation of the organized working class if it is to be successful. Fiscal policy, for instance, is based on taxation which is collected on an individual basis, whether by deduction from the pay slip, or annually via a tax form, or indirectly via the price of goods individuals buy in the shops; in all these ways, the individual worker faces the state atomistically. Incomes policy, however, only operates by acting on workers collectively, in that it seeks to modify the wage bargaining behaviour of the trade unions. The union is the direct object of the incomes policy and it must ultimately be the vehicle for administering the policy to the rank and file. Business groups must in turn agree to at least nominal supervision of prices, profits and dividends in a way consistent with securing trade union cooperation in wage restraint. As such, incomes policy involves the explicit acceptance by the organized working class of the claim that there is a community of interests within existing society, that the harmony between classes posited by a national integrative political party does in fact exist. Andrew Shonfield has observed that:

> what a fully fledged 'incomes policy' really implies is the
> equivalent of a New Social Contract: it presupposes a

society in which the different interest groups have marked
out a sufficient area of agreement about the present
distribution of wealth to deny themselves to try, in future,
to obtain certain advantages at each others expense.
Without this, one or other will surely find sooner or later a
tactical opportunity to redistribute some of the existing
wealth and exploit it – even if that results in inflation.[5]

In Marxist terms, as the Italian trade union leader, Vittoria Foa, has
written, an incomes policy entails: 'the attempt to obtain the working class' consent to more exploitation by means of a communitarian
conception, defining a community of interests between capital and
labour in the name of a supposed interest transcending social
classes.' [6]

It was this central concern of the British state with securing trade
union integration in the economy which underlay the institutionalization of what Samuel Beer has described as *'the new group politics'*
– 'the system of quasi-corporatism bringing government and pro-
ducers' groups into intimate and continuous relationship' in framing,
applying and legitimating state policies.[7] This relationship was based,
according to Beer, on three factors: the need by government of the
advice, information and expertise of trade unions and employer and
trade associations in order to manage the economy and the welfare
state; the need by government for the active cooperation of these
groups in applying policy; the feeling by government that it needed
the approval of these groups to legitimate policy. In exchange for
meeting these needs producer groups acquired the power to influence
policy formation within a common consensus of values, while in turn
'the history of these groups displays the powerful influence of government in calling them into existence, shaping their goals, and endow-
ing them with effective power'.[8] While in broad form this system of
decision-making could be identified in Britain from the early years of
the post-war period, it was characterized primarily by its failure to
operate effectively, especially in the area of economic policy. The
1945 Labour Government successfully obtained trade union cooperation in wages policy in 1948–50, but the policy broke down under
rank and file opposition. In the early sixties the Conservative Government made a concerted attempt to get trade union agreement to an
incomes policy but the roots of the failure continued to hold: the
desire by government to oversee price and profits was very limited;
the extent of consultation was seen by trade unions as defective and
their advice was given less credence than that of business groups;
trade union cooperation in applying policies of wage restraint, while

4

not insignificant, certainly was not extensive and when it was forth-coming was often negatived by their own membership. In large measure, the consensus of values which was required for 'the quasi-corporatist system' to function effectively was absent at least with regard to incomes policy.

It is a measure of the importance of the national integrative political party to this system, that the Labour Party based much of its electoral strategy in 1964 on emphasizing the claim that only a Labour Government could achieve the coordination of government and union policies to a degree that would make the system work. Immediately upon its election on 16 October 1964, albeit with a majority of only four seats, it set about achieving that objective, and within two months, it was able to present its first success: 'The Joint Statement of Intent on Productivity, Prices and Incomes', embodying agreement in principle to, and commitment to the development of, an incomes policy on the part of the Government, TUC and the employers' organizations. The wider implications of the Statement were not passed over: it was presented as a major breakthrough in overcoming class divisions and cementing a national consensus between capital and labour under the auspices of a Labour Government. In a widely publicized ceremony at Lancaster House, a venue usually reserved for diplomatic occasions, Government, union and business leaders signed the Statement, as *The Times* put it, 'with something of the pomp and panoply which accompanies the completion of a state treaty'. The 'treaty' atmosphere of the occasion was heightened when George Brown, speaking for the Government, declared that the document 'heralded the end of the class war'. 'History is being made today', Brown said. 'It is a victory for the nation as a whole, a demonstration to the world that the British people are still prepared to respond to the needs of the country in peacetime no less than in wartime.' [9] The occasion marked not only the formal legitimation of the 'new group politics', but also the apotheosis of the major ideological theme of the Labour Party.

The main expression of class conflict in modern British society has been seen in the industrial sphere, in the form of wage militancy and in the resistance of employers and the state to that militancy. The specific aim of the 1964 Labour Government's incomes policy was to infuse the working class with national considerations at that level where economic class considerations had persisted most stubbornly – at the level of trade union wage bargaining. But as the Labour Party extended and elaborated its national integrative posture to attempt to employ trade unions as agencies of social control in restraining industrial conflict, the main political expressions of class divisions in

British society increasingly took place inside the Labour Movement itself. The one major study of the relationship between the trade unions and the Labour Party, now over a decade old, still drew a clear distinction between political and industrial issues, noting that 'purely political issues' rarely had priority at union conferences and that it was only an industrial issue like wages policy that could endanger the survival of the Labour Movement.[10] If the Labour Government's wages policy of 1948–50 did not quite do so, the incomes policy of the 1964–70 Labour Governments rendered such a distinction much less admissible. The political and industrial became molten into one, and the contradiction raised by an industrially militant working class tied to an ideologically integrative political party assumed an entirely new and critical dimension.

The following analysis of the relationship between the Labour Party and the organized working class with regard to incomes policy proceeds historically, uncovering as it unfolds the dynamic of the contradiction in question. It begins with the 1945 Labour Government which provides an essential focal point for later developments, moves to the establishment of an incomes policy consensus between the Party and the unions in the face of the Conservatives' own attempts at trade union integration, and then turns to full examination of the operation of the 1964–70 incomes policy and the conflicts and other policies engendered by it. The historical approach is made necessary not only by the fact that the political history of incomes policy has not yet been dealt with in sufficient detail to be taken for granted, but also because the contradiction inherent in the Labour Party's incomes policy heightened over time, and only reached its crescendo in the late 1960s. The pattern of conflict we shall be examining is a complex one, and the dividing lines do not fall neatly with the Labour Party on one side and the unions on the other. Because the two are intertwined ideologically as well as structurally, the conflict also takes place within the Labour Party between left and right, Ministers and backbenchers, Conference and PLP, and within the union movement, between radical and moderate union leaders, union officials and militant shop stewards, the TUC and individual unions. The conflict, moreover, does not suddenly end with the Labour Government's defeat on *In Place of Strife* in 1969, but tenaciously persists, underlying the attempts to establish a 'new social contract' in the 1970s. This is the subject of Chapter 8. In the Conclusion, a general analysis of social democracy in modern British society is advanced.

1
The 1945 Labour Government: the mixed economy and wage restraint

Economic planning and wage restraint

World War II is usually marked as a watershed for the ascension of British trade unions to what Churchill termed 'an estate of the realm'. Participation in governmental bodies and agencies, and regular and direct consultation with Departments in matters that affected the unions' interests became accepted as a matter of right.[1] This was a development directly related to the increased intervention by the state in the economy, not least in stabilizing the level and influencing the distribution of wages and salaries. The war-time White Paper, *Price Stabilization and Industrial Policy*[2] of July 1941, was the first of a series of official pronouncements over the next thirty years which was to put the case that wage increases without matched productivity growth would lead to an inflationary spiral detrimental to the 'national interest': apart from increases in productivity, the White Paper, like most of its successors, only allowed for concessions to 'comparatively low paid grades and categories of workers'. The inegalitarian implications of wage restraint in such a class-divided society as Britain's posed real problems for the unions. The TUC's General Secretary said of the White Paper:

> If we were within a society where every section of the
> community had approximately the same standard of life,
> the case would be watertight, perhaps, for a common
> sacrifice by everybody. But nobody can argue, despite the
> shortcomings war has brought, that the richer classes of the
> community, aye, even the comfortable sections of the
> community who are not really rich in the sense of this
> world's goods but have an assured income, are not infinitely
> better off than the working-class people, and have not felt the
> burdens infinitely less. Let us recognize that this claim has
> no social justice behind it which seeks to stabilize wages in
> present conditions. It is basically inequitable.[3]

In the face of such concern and the reluctance of Ernest Bevin, as Minister of Labour in the Coalition Government, to coerce the unions, direct control over wages was not introduced during the War. Nevertheless, the TUC did practice wage restraint during the War as well as accept labour direction, compulsory arbitration and a manipulated cost of living index in return for a widespread system of governmental control over the economy based on price controls and subsidies, rationing, raw-material allocation, low-cost utility goods production, and unprecedented levels of taxation. In the words of one expert on incomes policy, 'it was the TUC's first experience of a total incomes policy, and one which has inspired its vision ever since'.[4]

The question of what trade union functions would be in the post-war period were discussed widely during the War, particularly with regard to a wages policy, with its attendant implications for trade union independence and bargaining power. It is important to recognize there were two bases upon which the demands for a wages policy in peace-time were founded. One emanated from Keynesian principles, the other from socialist economic and political thought. The latter posited the planning of the wage structure in the context of a post-war socialist Britain defined not only by the public ownership of productive and distributive resources but also by a system of detailed economic planning which would supersede the profit motive and the market as the basis for economic decision making. With production for use rather than profit, trade unions would be expected to have new functions in a planned socialist economy as organs of co-operation with the planning authorities.[5] Far more prevalent, however, was the call for a wages policy which emanated from the general acceptance that any post-war government would have to maintain effective demand at a level sufficient to achieve full employment. This commitment was embodied officially in the Coalition Government's White Paper on *Employment Policy* of May 1944,[6] but was in fact recognized much earlier. It involved the introduction of Keynesian modifications to the capitalist system and there were those who foresaw that price stability under this 'reformed capitalism' would be threatened if wage demands were not restrained. Thus in a prescient article in *The Times* of 23 January 1943, an unidentified special correspondent contended that the fear of unemployment was an 'essential mechanism' of the private enterprise economy which maintained 'the authority of master over man'. During the War a substitute for this mechanism was found in 'appeals of patriotism' but

> In peace-time with full employment, the worker would have
> no counterweight against feeling that he is employed merely

to make profits for the firm, and that he is under no
obligation to refrain from using his new found freedom
from fear to snatch every advantage he can . . .

If free wage-bargaining, as we have known it hitherto, is
continued, in conditions of full employment, there would be
a constant upward pressure on money wage-rates. This
phenomenon also exists at the present time, and is also kept
in bounds by the appeal of patriotism. In peace-time the
vicious spiral of wages and prices might become chronic.[7]

As a solution to the problem, the article recommended a 'middle
course' between Fascism and Socialism, whereby a range of policies
including some nationalization, price and profit controls, social
security programmes, and works councils would combine 'to produce
a situation in which workers would be prepared to accept discipline
to a necessary and reasonable extent and to accept an over-all wage
treaty which would prevent the vicious spiral from setting in'. Sir
William Beveridge's influential *Full Employment in a Free Society*
suggested such a range of policies and placed the responsibility for
the avoidance of inflation squarely on the shoulders of the unions.
'The more explicitly that responsibility is stated, the greater can be
the confidence that it will be accepted.'[8] The TUC itself, he suggested, should formulate a 'unified wage policy' which would ensure
that the demands of individual unions would be judged with reference to the economic situation as a whole. To complement this, he
advocated a comprehensive system of arbitration, where wages would
be 'determined according to reason and in light of all the facts and
with some regard to general equities and not simply to the bargaining power of certain groups of men', and which with stable prices
and increased productivity, would make possible, a continuous, if un-
spectacular, rise in money wages to maintain the share of national
product going to the wage earner.

The unenviable economic situation facing the Labour Government
upon its election in 1945 ensured that this question would not long
be avoided. With pent-up consumer demands straining to be released
and a labour shortage, an inflation which could threaten Britain's
export prospects and harm her economic recovery, was a real, if at
first underestimated, prospect. The call for a national wages policy
was therefore not abated in 1945.

A common, but highly misleading, assertion made by certain
students of the 1945 Labour Government is that the Labour Party
took office with a strong commitment to socialist economic planning
including a wages policy but that this was rendered impotent by trade

9

union conservatism and opposition to planning of the labour market. Ben Roberts, for instance, has argued: 'The leaders of the Party saw the dilemma and wanted to do something about it; ... The unions, however, wanted absolutely full employment, cheap money, massive government expenditures, stable prices and freedom to bargain for higher wages as and when they like, without any limits.' [9] Samuel Beer has gone even further and incorrectly identified the union rejection of wages policy with the rejection of socialism and tied this to the subsequent ideological drift of the party toward belief in a mixed market economy. Beer correctly observes that the Attlee Government increasingly

> turned away from direct control by public administration and toward indirect control by manipulation of the market ... This approach to planning is quite compatible with private ownership, competition, and profit-making. Indeed, it depends upon a general pursuit of economic self interest. From the viewpoint of economic planning, in consequence, it makes public ownership superfluous and the whole Socialist conception of the cooperative economy sustained by the public service motive irrelevant.

But Beer's view that the principal cause of this tranformation 'was the resistance of trade-unions to government control over the movement and compensation of labour',[10] is highly divorced from reality, as we shall see.

The election of the first majority Labour Government certainly considerably enhanced the trade unions' new found stature in the British political system. The new Parliament contained 120 trade union sponsored MPs who held 29 of 81 posts in the new Government; six were in the Cabinet including the President of the 1945 TUC, George Isaacs as Minister of Labour, and the leading trade union leader of his time, Ernest Bevin as Foreign Secretary. The General Council met frequently on an official basis with Ministers and informal relations between trade union leaders and Ministers were close.[11] Like earlier Labour Governments however, this one was determined to prove its independence from union control, and that strain in its ideology which had always emphasized the Party's national rather than class role quickly reasserted itself. The point was made with great emphasis before the general election by the Party Secretary, Morgan Phillips: 'Let me remove at the outset', he wrote in an election pamphlet, 'any lingering impression of the outworn idea that the Labour Party is a class party.' [12]

Although a considerable amount was written by Party leaders during the 1930s on the subject of economic planning, surprisingly little consideration had been given to the planning of wages or to the role of the unions in a socialist planned economy. Hugh Dalton, who went to the Treasury in 1945, devoted only two paragraphs of his 400-page *Practical Socialism for Britain* (1935) to the question of 'the future place of Trade Unionism in a Socialist society'. He expected that the unions' function of protecting their members against exploitation would continue, although he imagined that this task would become much easier and thus that the unions would become more like professional associations concerned with maintaining a high level of qualification and public service and promoting research and training. Douglas Jay's *The Socialist Case* (1937), which Attlee in 1946 extolled for setting out 'the basic philosophic arguments for collective management of our economic resources', expected wages to remain stable during the 'transitional period to socialism' and for real income to be raised by broad provision of social services. His rationale for wage restraint, however, was not the prerequisites of planning, but the threat rising wages imposed on entrepreneurial profits which would have to be retained in the transitional period. It was only Evan Durbin, who, while emphatically expressing in the 1930s the theme of class harmony within capitalism, nevertheless expected a major change in union functions under socialism. 'No one with a knowledge of Trade Union opinions and practices will doubt that this is one of the real problems of Socialist Planning', he wrote in 1935.[13] In this singular respect, Durbin was not representative of the mainstream of the Party's thought. This was evident from the fact that one of the arguments used by Labour Party leaders in favour of the Morrisonian public corporations was that the trade unions would lose their role if worker control of the boards of the nationalized industries were adopted. Indeed, to have foreseen basic changes in the functions of the unions, the Party would have needed a much clearer and more doctrinaire conception of the kind of economic system it was going to introduce than it had. It is of course true that running through its history, and especially in the Fabian wing of the Party, a dislike for the 'class war' methods of industrial bargaining had been exhibited, but this had not developed, by 1945, into any sort of coherent theory about a transformation of trade unions under economic planning.[14]

The Election Manifesto, *Let Us Face the Future*, despite its overriding emphasis on planning, was vague with regard to what planning might entail. It was framed largely as an attack on 'sectional vested interests', and as such an affirmation of national goals above such interests. But the implication was that it was private industry – 'the profiteering interests and the privileged rich' – not the trade unions that fitted this description. The only mention of the unions in the manifesto came in a pledge to restore, not limit, trade union freedom denied by the Trade Disputes and Trade Unions Act of 1927, and to legislate for the 40 hour week, paid holidays and workmen's compensation. No concession was made by the Party during the election to the view that trade union bargaining freedoms would have to be curtailed by a wages policy. The solution to inflation was to be found in price and rent controls.

This is not to say that the Government did not expect – or did not receive – concessions from the unions. Compulsory arbitration (Order 1305) was kept in force with the consent of the unions, and despite growing union membership, only seven million working days were lost in industrial disputes in the three years after the end of the war; well over ten times that had been lost in the three years after World War I.

Although exhortations to restraint were numerous and the union response substantial, there were no immediate demands from the Government for a wages policy. With regard to manpower distribution, the Government recognized the importance of moving labour into essential industries, but it was not prepared to involve itself in the onerous task of establishing a policy for wages which would alter relative differentials so as to guide labour distribution. Comprehensive labour direction, on the other hand, was ruled out from the beginning and it was the first war-time control the Government dropped. Manpower planning itself lay in abeyance for the first two years until the Economic Survey of 1947, and Ernest Bevin himself complained of this lack of planning in the early days of the Government.[15] When a manpower budget was at last introduced in 1947, the Government indicated its doubts about the effectiveness of a wages policy for the distribution of labour.[16]

In fact, the Government did not want to regulate wage claims for the purposes of manpower allocation. The Prime Minister was opposed to it,[17] as were most leading figures in the Government. Its general attitude to wage policy was clearly enunciated at a closed meeting with the executives of the trade unions, in March 1946, called at the Government's request to enlist support for a productivity drive. Ernest Bevin spoke for the Government:

> He had met many people who had the idea that somehow wages ought to be fixed at a certain limit by the State. In his view this would be fatal . . . The Government's policy was

to leave the trade unions and the State to settle wages where
the State was the employer; and to leave trade unions to
settle wages with private employers; and to create
conciliation, arbitration or anything else they like in order
to settle wages. He thought that the more the trade unions
relied on arbitration courts instead of settling these things
themselves with employers, the more they undermined
their own authority.[18]

At the 1946 Party Conference, Herbert Morrison saw it as part of the
'business of Government' to provide general economic background
information to negotiators, but he rejected both labour direction and
wages policy.[19] The 1947 Conference did pass with NEC support a
Miners' resolution advocating higher wages to attract labour to the
undermanned industries but the NEC successfully urged the Conference to defeat another resolution explicitly calling for a policy on
wages, hours and the distribution of income to prevent inflation and
meet the needs of manpower allocation.[20]

This lack of interest in planning the labour market was in fact
determined by the Government's approach to economic planning in
general, which was founded on a simplistic distinction between 'democratic' and 'totalitarian' planning, the former relying on voluntary
cooperation between 'Government, industry and the people', the
latter subordinating 'all individual desires and preferences to the
demands of the State'.[21] The essence of Governmental planning was
its allowance of considerable freedom of action for both private enterprise and the unions, what is today called its indicative nature.
Labour had inherited extensive war-time controls and retained most
of these at first in the face of continued shortages and the immense
task of reconstruction. But as Attlee said in 1946: 'We are not in
favour of controls for their own sake ... while there are shortages
there must be controls in the interests not of sections of our people,
but of the whole nation ... as these shortages disappear so controls
can be relaxed.' [22] In the early years, these inherited physical controls
were given greater emphasis than the techniques of fiscal and monetary policy, but even in these years there was no attempt to plan the
whole of the country's industrial output. As shortages diminished,
planning came increasingly to mean the maintenance of full employment, balance of payments controls, and the preparation of annual
Economic Surveys with influence being exerted through the market
mechanism. Even the indicative nature of Governmental planning in
forecasting and providing information was distinctly limited. 'In
general', wrote two Oxford economists:

the Government has been content to state early in the year
what needs doing, and then to leave the public without
further detailed guidance until the following year is well
under way. The whole approach to the interim period
between Surveys implies a scepticism as to the influence of
the Survey's plans on economic developments, which may
well be justified, but which is somewhat at variance with the
declared philosophy of democratic . . . planning. Basing
policy on someone's appreciation of what must be done,
means taking care to keep him fully informed of what is
happening and what is expected from him in the near
future.[23]

The implications of the theory (and practice) of 'democratic planning' for wage bargaining were drawn at the time of its enunciation
by Douglas Jay:

It follows from this [theory], I believe, that where manpower
is concerned we should normally prefer the uncontrolled
price process to any positive compulsion. That is to say, we
should, in general, allow wages to be determined by the
strength of the demand for manpower in different industries
as reflected in the collective bargaining process . . . the 'wage
policy' problem is, in fact, a problem not of Socialism but of
inflation. Remove the inflation and free bargaining over
wages, without the limitation on personal freedom, and with
the minimum provided by the social services will give us the
best practical solution.[24]

The TUC, for its part, was very much committed to economic planning in 1945. Indeed, Martin Harrison's study indicated that during
the 1945–50 period, 'The unions were further to the left than usual
– perhaps even slightly to the left of the local parties',[25] and this ideological stance was reflected in trade union demands for controls, planning and public ownership. It was expected that planning would
entail new responsibilities for the unions but would also give new
opportunities for union leaders to take an active part in decision
making at the highest levels. Criticism by American labour leaders
of the servile role of trade unions under Soviet planning was at this
stage met with impatience among British union leaders. The General
Secretary of the TUC, Sir Walter Citrine, told the 1945 Congress that

whilst there are no private employers, and whilst the State
is the sole employer, the Russian unions must in their
essential structure differ somewhat from unions and other
organizations in other countries. They have different kinds

of problems with which to deal . . . I think it would be an
excellent thing if British Governments were able so to plan
the production, the consumption and the general economic
life of the country in the way in which it is done in Soviet
Russia.[26]

Whether or not this view was based on a misconception of the actual
role of trade unions in Russia – and it was a view that was to change
considerably in later years – it indicated at that time a strong belief
in a publicly-owned and state-planned economy.

The TUC's *Reconstruction Report*, adopted overwhelmingly by
the 1944 Congress, testified to this belief. The Keynesian economic
policy outlined by the Coalition Government was deemed inadequate
and the TUC urged on the Government the Manpower Budget which
was finally produced by Labour in 1947. It was felt that for Government to act merely as a flywheel to counter-balance fluctuations in
private investment was not enough and it proposed a National Investment Board 'to ensure that there is comprehensive planning of all
forms of investment', which the public ownership of the greater part
of industry would make possible. Appreciating that war-time economic arrangements had brought about a redistribution of income in
favour of the working class, the TUC sought the continuation of
rationing, and the perpetuation of subsidies, utility goods schemes
and price and profit controls. It recommended the purchase and distribution of a wide range of products through government agencies
as a means of assuring demand and controlling prices, standards,
profit margins and advertising costs. In making these recommendations, the TUC was challenging the conventional economic theory of
consumer sovereignty in a free enterprise economy – a theory to
which the Labour Government, on the other hand, was not unsym-
pathetic in the formulation of its approach to planning.[27] 'The
alleged control by the consumer over the producer', the Report
stated, 'is very unreal; it is the manufacturer or distributor who often
persuades the public what they should buy rather than the latter who
through their purchases persuade the former what they should produce.' [28]

To secure these demands the TUC was prepared to make considerable concessions on its part. In response to solicitations from
Beveridge with regard to what trade unions would be prepared to do
to achieve wage and price stability and labour mobility in conditions
of full employment, the TUC indicated a concern to preserve the
unions' position as representative organizations, a fear that unions
might become agencies of the government, but also pledged:

> if the Government can convince the Movement that in
> genuine pursuit of a policy of full employment it is
> determined to take all other steps that are necessary to
> control prices and can convince the Trade Union Movement
> of the need to secure equivalent guarantees that wage
> movements will not be such as to upset the system of price
> control . . . it would be the duty of the Trade Union
> Movement to give suitable guarantees about wage
> settlements and reasonable assurances that such guarantees
> would be generally observed.[29]

But such undertakings would only be made on a voluntary basis and the possibility of small groups of workers refusing to follow the general settlement, must not be made the basis for the imposition of legislative sanctions.

The TUC's response to early post-war suggestions for a national wages policy was on the whole negative. Its position was based officially on its long-standing opposition to legal intervention in the field of wage bargaining. The TUC was adamant that it would 'neither seek nor agree to the imposition of legal restraints upon the rights of trade unions to formulate their wage policies and to pursue their activities in support of those policies'.[30] Nevertheless, the TUC showed it was prepared to breach the principle of voluntarism when it accepted the continuation during peace-time of Order 1305 on the grounds that its withdrawal 'might well have lent support to the demands which were circulating at that time for the complete elimination of [price] controls'.[31] There were, in fact, other factors involved in the opposition to wages policy. First of all, as TUC spokesmen constantly reiterated, the Labour Government itself was not asking it to approve a wages policy. Secondly, the General Council, and especially that element of the union leadership closest to the Government, like the TGWU's Arthur Deakin, shared the Government's doubts about the efficacy of a wages policy designed to achieve labour mobility, and moreover feared the consequence for wage differentials of such a policy. It was in this context that Deakin made his famous remark at the 1947 Labour Party Conference that: 'the question of wages and conditions of employment, are questions for the trade unions, and the sooner some of the people on the political side appreciate that and leave the job to the unions the better for production'.[32]

Finally, the General Council was doubtful that the calls for a wages policy really emanated from those concerned with economic planning. It appeared to many union leaders now that they had grown in power and labour was in short supply, unions were being asked to behave in their wage bargaining as they had during the depression. Many felt that a wages policy was merely the basis for an attack on the working class and an attempt to bolster profits by enlisting the support of the Government to this end. The thesis that trade unions should restrain wage claims on the ground that prices would inevitably rise to compensate rising costs and thus make futile any increases in money wage rates, was a comfortable doctrine for employers who could use it to refuse wage increases 'in the national interest', and this was bound to increase trade union hostility to the idea.[33] For this was not the first time that an economic theory had warned the unions of the futility of their efforts. The Iron Law of Wages had told workers that there was an inexorable subsistence level which they could only breach at the peril of ruthless national decimation of the working population. The Wage Fund Theory had posited that there was a definite limit to the resources of employers for wage purposes and that unions were only acting irrationally if they tried to expand it. Finally, between the wars, unions had been told that by resisting cuts in wages they were primarily responsible for unemployment. Trade union action was in each case, however, vindicated. Keynes had saluted their persistence: 'They are instinctively more reasonable economists than the classical school.' And Edgworth had argued: 'In the matter of Unionism ... The untutored mind of the workman had gone more straight to the point than economic intelligence misled by a bad method.' [34] The state had often appeared to trade unionists to be less an impartial arbiter of a 'national interest' than a representative of employers' interests, and it was hardly likely that this suspicion would entirely disappear simply because union leaders were now being consulted by government, or because pledges were being made to maintain high employment levels or even because a Labour Government, of which the unions had some unsavoury experience in the past, had come to power. The entry of the state, as a third party, into wage negotiations raised the spectre of the unions having to face two opponents instead of one.

It is important to note, however, that the TUC itself was not at all unanimous in its opposition to a wages policy, a point often overlooked by analysts of the trade union attitude in the immediate postwar period. On the wings of the popular radicalism that swept the country in 1945, many unions looked forward to a system of comprehensive economic planning and demanded trade union action which would be consistent with this development. From 1945 to 1947, leftwing unions, who were to be the most vociferous critics of the wage restraint policy introduced in 1948, urged the General Council to accept a national wages policy to facilitate socialist economic planning by the Government. At the 1945 Congress the Electrical Trade Union asked the General Council to further develop its policy for wages, production and prices on the lines of the Reconstruction Report,[35] and followed this up with a statement forwarded to the General Council which elaborated the ETU position and asked for a special conference of trade union executives to introduce the policy. The General Council refused the request on the grounds that it was opposed to a wages policy and that there had been no Government request for such a policy.[36] At the 1946 Congress, the National Union of Vehicle Builders put a resolution which would have required the General Council to prepare a report on a national wages policy. It was especially concerned with the incompatability of the preservation of traditional differentials and the equalitarian ideals of the movement, as well as with economic planning and full employment. The resolution, opposed by the General Council and particularly by Arthur Deakin, was defeated by 3,522,000 votes to 2,657,000 votes. The large amount of support it received was no doubt influenced by its incorporation of a demand for a national minimum wage, but even this reflected a flexibility on the question of state intervention in wage bargaining. At the 1947 Congress, another ETU resolution was passed without a card vote which welcomed the creation of the Economic Planning Board, but urged upon the Government an overall plan for industry.[37]

There can be no doubt that the intransigence of many union leaders to diminution of their authority by state interference with collective bargaining was a limiting factor on economic planning. But it is incorrect to attribute the failure of the Labour Government to engage in comprehensive economic planning to this one limitation. For planning was faced with even more serious barriers: the power of private capital, both positive and negative (positive in the sense of political influence, negative in the sense of abstaining from productive investment or the transfer of capital abroad); the technical and administrative costs and problems of planning the economy; the difficulties of planning an economy as reliant on foreign trade and foreign loans as Britain in the post-war period; the belief in departmental autonomy and the independence of the nationalized boards. In the face of all these difficulties, the pragmatic, undoctrinaire philosophy of the Labour Party had no diffculty in asserting itself. The idea of planning was not abandoned but was starved of both the fervour and the resources it needed if it was to be more than the basis for a loose and haphazard exercise. And the planning of incomes, that is, the determination of new criteria of economic reward for all classes and occupations – unskilled, skilled, salaried, managerial and entrepreneurial – was the last task in which the Government was prepared to engage. It would exhort, guide, tax and subsidize, but it was not prepared to take upon itself the powers to determine incomes directly.

Indeed, had the Labour Government committed itself in 1945 to a programme of overcoming all these obstacles to introduce a system of economic planning that involved also the planning of wages and other incomes, it is possible that it would have been able to draw on a considerable body of support in the trade unions, as well as the loyalty of the movement in general, to overcome union hostility to state interference in wage bargaining. This was at least the argument of the group of MPs who published the *Keep Left* Pamphlet early in 1947. They drew a distinction between 'real' and 'bogus' planning and were critical of the Government's conception of 'democratic planning' which they saw as a refusal to take any decisions at all without the consent of everyone affected. They were, above all, critical of the way the Government appealed to the trade unions, which they saw as a failure of 'public relations'. These MPs stressed the damaging psychological effect on workers' motivations of the continuing existence of rent, interest, profit and speculative incomes. They felt, moreover, that the Labour Ministers' approach to the trade unions, especially at the March 1946 Conference of Executives, was indecisive, and a product of the Government's unwillingness to depart from its national position to enlist the labour movement in a socialist crusade.

> It is not democratic to make decisions without saying why, but equally it's half-hearted to ask for heroic individual effort without the lead of heroic measures by the Government. A clear-cut decision can easily be dramatized; indeed it dramatizes itself. But only a Tcheckov or a Shakespeare can dramatize indecision and even they, though they can make of it a tragedy or a comedy, could certainly not transmute it to a clarion call.[38]

It is in this regard that the debates within the TUC over wages and economic planning in the first years of the Government, take on their significance. It was the left-wing unions which supported a national wages policy while ranked against them were the 'moderate' unions, who had the closest relationship with the Government. When the Government finally introduced a wages policy in 1948, which was primarily a policy of restraint, the stand of the two sides was almost completely reversed. These divisions indicate that those union leaders in closest contact with the Government and best able to gauge its intentions in these early years realized that it was not so much for the purpose of economic planning that the Government was likely to introduce a wages policy, but for purposes of wage restraint. This form of wages policy had not commended itself, however, to the left wing unions whose commitment was not to the Labour Party *per se*, but to a given set of socialist principles which they wanted to see activated. The moderate union leaders, deeply loyal to a Labour Government, were at the time prepared to accept such a policy when the Government deemed it necessary.

The wages policy of 1948-50

In January 1947, the Government issued a White Paper, endorsed by the union and employer representatives on the NJAC, which outlined the economic problems facing Britain, especially the manpower shortage and the need to increase production and exports.[39] Its basic prognosis was that the economy was faced with a demand inflation in a period of shortages, a situation of 'too much money chasing after too few goods', and that is was essential to hold costs, and especially wages, steady. As for prices and the two main governmental means of stabilizing them, price controls and subsidies, regulation over the prices of essential goods and services would be maintained but the Government would no longer guarantee that subsidies would receive the same support from the Treasury. It was clear that wage restraint was seen as desirable, but the tone remained exhortative.

The harsh winter of 1947 increased the Government's anxieties and forced it into taking new initiatives. The fuel shortage in February led to the temporary closure of many industries, unemployment quadrupled over its December 1946 figure to reach almost two million, and production fell badly. A mounting balance of payments deficit was propelled by the convertibility crisis in the summer.[40] These developments shook the faith of many in the effectiveness of the Government's economic planning, but confirmed the Government's own belief that inflation was its major problem, and provided a new impetus for the Government to act more directly to restrain wage increases as part of its austerity efforts. At the same time, they led the trade union leadership to rally to Labour's support and modify their earlier position.

An important contributing factor to the shift in the response of the TUC was a change in the composition of the General Council, which clearly established the dominance of the 'moderates' over the 'left' in the TUC. Sir Walter Citrine left his post in 1946 to become a member of the National Coal Board and between 1945 and 1947 the

General Council lost ten of its members. In 1947, this fluid situation was succeeded by the emergence of a group of trade union leaders, led by Arthur Deakin of the TGWU (and including Tom Williamson of the NUGMW and Will Lawther of the NUM), who were not only intensely loyal to the Government but who shared the Government's approach to economic planning. This group, whose unions accounted for almost half of the total affiliated membership of the TUC, could usually dictate the decisions of the Congress and exert strong influence on the General Council's Special Economic Committee which was created to deal with the Government during the fuel crisis.[41]

Beginning in August 1947, there was a movement away from exhortation in relation to the unions towards direct Government involvement. The Government enacted the *Control of Engagements Order*, which marked a partial return to direction of labour; Attlee made a formal statement appealing to workers not to press for increases, especially those involving the maintenance of differentials; and the Minister of Labour in September sent letters to both sides of a number of negotiating bodies (mainly Wage Councils) asking them to keep in mind the Prime Minister's statement. On 14 October, at a special meeting convened by the Government, the General Council was asked to give serious consideration to developing a formal wage restraint policy.[42]

The General Council responded to this pressure by promising its first post-war report on the question of wages policy. *The Interim Report on the Economic Situation*,[43] circulated to all affiliated unions in December 1947, was to serve as a vehicle both for securing union support for the Government's policy, as well as for urging on the Government certain actions which it saw as necessary if wage restraint was to be practised by the unions. It was, however, a timorous and vague document. It urged the retention of subsidies, but on the burning question of whether subsidies should be pegged at their existing level, allowed to rise or be reduced, the report was silent. A necessary condition for wage restraint was said to be equivalent profit restraint, but the Report also accepted the Government's argument that specific controls on profits were liable to create the same difficulties or limitations on wages – i.e. 'inequities and bitterness' – and thus be harmful to maximum productive effort. Similarly, while the Report urged the unions 'to exercise even greater moderation and restraint than hitherto', it nevertheless indicated that the TUC was not prepared to introduce a wage restraint policy on its own, and as such fell far short of meeting the Government's requirements. In the absence of the will to formulate a centralized policy for wages for the

TUC as a whole, the General Council's appeal to the unions remained exhortative at a time when the Government expected more convincing means of control over wage increases.

The stage was thus set for action by the Government. On 4 February 1948, it produced a new White Paper, the *Statement on Personal Incomes, Costs and Prices* which marked the beginning of the Labour Government's wages policy.[44] The *Statement* (widely recognized as having been inspired, and probably penned, by Sir Stafford Cripps, who took over from Dalton as Chancellor of the Exchequer in December 1947) declared that there was 'no justification for any general increase of individual money incomes unless accompanied by a substantial increase in production'. The only wage or salary increases it would countenance 'in the national interest' were where only an increase would suffice to attract labour to undermanned industries. The *Statement* fell short of being an incomes policy, as that term is understood today. Although it related wage increase to productivity growth, it set out no allowable rate of increase (no guiding norm), and provided no criteria whereby conflicting claims might be measured. It spoke in terms of personal incomes in general, but it made scant mention of profits and rents and no mention of price control. Nor was an exception made for the lower paid: only if at some future time a marked rise in the cost of living made their incomes inadequate would these need 'reconsideration'.

This was not a wages policy which set out to establish wage differentials as part of a programme of manpower planning. It was expressly a policy of wage restraint. Indeed the Government remained sceptical of the efficacy of a wages policy for manpower distribution, as Attlee made clear in reply to questions from the House about the *Statement*.[45] It was emphasized that it was 'not desirable for the Government to interfere directly with the incomes of individuals except by taxation. To go on further would mean that the Government would be forced itself to assess and regulate all personal incomes according to some scale which would have to be determined.' This was not a task which the Government coveted. The Tory MP, Oliver Lyttleton, was only too happy to point out that 'The White Paper nails the coffin of Economic Planning by admitting that it does not want to interfere with individual incomes except by taxation – a sound Tory doctrine.'[46]

Nevertheless, in making its case for a wage freeze the *Statement* was unmistakably clear and forceful. And it was reinforced by a note of compulsion. First, the Government would be guided by the principles of the *Statement* in its position as an employer. Secondly, increased costs of production occasioned by wage and salary increases might not be taken into account any longer in settling controlled prices. Thirdly, although no direct mention of this was made in the White Paper, it was generally presumed that arbitrators and Wage Councils would take account of the Government's policy. The *Economist* marked the new departure:

> The Government has issued a warning more serious, more forthright, and more determined than any of its earlier statements. It has indeed gone to the practical limit of what would be expected of a popular democratic Government . . . the Government has forced upon the trade unions the responsibility for accepting a policy on wages which is inimicable to the whole tradition and outlook of the movement.[47]

The events which followed the enunciation of this policy are significant for what they illuminate about the decision-making process in post-war Britain. For there was to follow a series of negotiations with the TUC, the FBI, and the BEC as to the means of application of the policy. 'The principle negotiators were three – the Government, organized labour, and organized capital. The bargain was not itself embodied in any legislative instrument as a statute or statutory order. Yet it achieved a regulation of an important aspect of the British economy, that no such legislative instrument by itself could have done. Indeed one may think of it as a kind of extra-governmental legislation.'[48] This description is perhaps slightly less apt for this episode in incomes policy than for the 1964 events. In contrast with the latter period, the Government acted unilaterally in drawing up and issuing its *Statement*. But consultations with both groups followed immediately, modifications in the policy were made to meet their objections, and the policy was applied through their organizations.

The response of the General Council to the *Statement* was entirely a cooperative one.[49] Its objections related to the lack of prior consultation, which it saw as a challenge to its newly-achieved position *vis-à-vis* government, and to the difficulties the policy entailed for them in its application by one-sided concern with wages to the exclusion of profits and prices of the *Statement*. At meetings with Ministers on 5 and 11 February many of the questions by the TUC's Economic Committee concerned the machinery and the method of carrying out the policy. Who was to decide whether conditions had been met for wage increases to take place? Who was to decide to what 'reasonable' level real wages might fall before demands could be made? How was the principle that wage increases should depend on increased productivity to be applied to occupations where productivity could not be measured? [50] Questions of this sort, which continued to plague those who would develop a policy for wages in years to come, remained unanswered in the 1948–50 period. But on the question of prices and profits, the Government saw the necessity of making some response, particularly in view of the TUC's concern that the application of the policy to those seven million workers with claims already in the pipe-line would lead to serious industrial unrest.

On 12 February, Cripps announced to the Commons that he had asked the FBI to study the question of making voluntary proposals within a month to obtain a reduction of prices and accept the consequences of this on the level of profits. He stressed the psychological effect a limitation on dividend increases might have in moderating wage demands. All goods under price control would not be allowed to rise above their January levels and additional price control orders would be issued.[51] Cripps had made it clear at the meeting with the Economic Committee that his purpose in giving the FBI only a month to put forward its proposals was to ensure that if the proposals were inadequate, the Chancellor could himself take action in the Budget, in six weeks time.[52]

The FBI, in conjunction with the National Union of Manufacturers and the Association of British Chambers of Commerce, presented its report to Cripps on 11 March 1948. It recommended to its membership that subject to discretion in exceptional cases, the gross amount of dividends distributed by a business in the year should not exceed the gross amount in the previous year; and that manufacturers' prices be frozen without any reduction in quality and the consequence in reduced profits. It combined these concessions with demands that the Government freeze the prices of basic commodities, like fuel and transport and local rates, and that the Government reduce its expediture and capital investment. It expressed its opposition to governmental controls of prices and profits and to centrally controlled wages.[53] Cripps responded with a cordial letter expressing his view that if carried out, the recommendations 'will be of greatest value to the country'.

In the event, these business organizations were less able or willing to guarantee the compliance of their member firms than the TUC of its affiliated unions. Although dividends were for the most part kept down, exceptions were plentiful, while on prices individual firms were even less forthcoming and the consequences of rising prices were indeed faced as profits – mainly undistributed – continued to rise throughout the period. As a commentator sympathetic to the policy noted: 'Distributed profits have been limited by many firms, but on balance the appeal has made little difference to the movement of profits, since it was more difficult to exercise moral pressure on industrialists than on wage earners'.[54] The Governmental new measures to control prices also turned out to be of little consequence. Although fourteen new price control orders were announced by the Board of Trade on 24 February, none of them affected food or other goods figuring substantially in working class budgets, and the ceilings placed on prices already under control were relaxed by April, in response to pressure from business.[55] J. C. R. Dow's conclusion was that the effectiveness of the Government's policy was not due to its disallowing controlled prices to rise when costs increased because of wage demands, since this proved 'too difficult to enforce. It was effective because of restraint of the unions.'[56]

But the actions taken in February and March 1948 by the Government and by business organizations, although largely symbolic rather than effective, considerably influenced the positive response of the trade unions. On 18 February, the General Council endorsed the White Paper's policy of stabilization as applied to wages on the condition that the Government pursued a vigorous policy to reduce profits and prices. To make the policy more palatable to its members, the General Council sought 'to give more precise and more practical definitions of the limited and exceptional circumstances in which ... it might still be in the national interest for trade unions to proceed with claims . . .' These principles of the White Paper were acceptable to the trade union movement to the extent that they:

> (a) recognize the necessity of retaining unimpaired the system of free collective bargaining and free negotiations; (b) admit the justification for claims for increased wages where those claims are based upon the fact of increased output; (c) admit the necessity of adjusting the wages of workers whose incomes are below a reasonable standard of subsistence; (d) affirm that it is in the national interest to establish standards of wages and conditions in undermanned essential industries in order to attract sufficient manpower; and (e) recognize the need to safeguard those wage differentials which are an essential element in the wage structures of many important industries and are required to sustain those standards of craftsmanship, training and experience that contribute directly to industrial efficiency and higher productivity.'[57]

Analysts of the wage restraint policy have usually contended that these five points 'left the gate wide open for wage increases in that they could be used to justify almost any wage claim', but that the TUC used its influence to ensure that unions did not 'walk through it at all'.[58] This ignores, however, that the last of the five points concerns only intra-industry differentials and does not allow for inter-industry differentials to be taken into consideration. This was an important modification in the TUC's position and was duly noted at the time. *The Times* saw this as 'remarkable evidence of the courage of trade union leaders and of their loyalty to the Labour Government'.[59]

The White Paper was endorsed at a special conference of trade union executives on 24 March, strategically held just two weeks before the 1948 budget speech, (the vote was 5,421,000 for to 2,032,000 against, a majority of 3,389,000) and was re-endorsed by substantial margins at the 1948 and 1949 annual congresses. The self-imposed restraint was in fact remarkable in its application. From a base rate of 100 for wage rates and retail prices in June 1947, wage rates and prices both stood at 104 in January 1948; when the policy broke down in September 1950, wage rates stood at 110, retail prices at 114. Thus, whereas real wage rates had risen from a base rate of 100 in 1938 to 106 in 1946, by 1950 they had fallen back to 101. It was only increased earnings – less subject to union control – which compensated for rising prices, but whereas average weekly earnings had increased by 11s 6d between April 1947 and April 1948, they rose between April 1948 and April 1949 by only 5s 4d, and between April 1949 and April 1950, by 4s 9d. As one Oxford economist noted at the time: 'The fashion has grown up in some publications of referring to wage stabilization in inverted commas, or with the epithet "so-called" as if it were unreal. The implication is as incorrect as it is injudicious ... the data show that wage-earners' organizations themselves acted in a way which happened to check the egalitarian tendencies in the economy.'[60]

The policy's success with regard to wages was the direct result of the unions acting not as representatives but as agents of control over their members' demands. It was, moreover, a task which only the unions themselves could have undertaken; direct application by the Government of such a policy, in conditions of rising prices and profits, would certainly have led to massive industrial unrest. The trade union leadership realized this and continued to insist that the policy be one of voluntary action. They were especially concerned lest the Government try to apply its policy through the Minister of Labour's power of veto over Wage Council proposals or through his influence on arbitrators, and were in fact able to get assurances from the Prime Minister on the day before the special conference that new directives to wage councils issued by the Ministry of Labour would be withdrawn. Notably, the Government subsequently continued to demand that Wage Councils take account of the White Paper.[61]

Apart from this insistence on the voluntary principle, however, the General Council completely reversed its earlier position on wages policy and economic planning. Tom Williamson, General Secretary of the NUGMW, proposed in his union's journal in March 1948, that a national wages commission be established by the trade unions to coordinate the wage claims of different unions. 'We are entering upon a new chapter in industrial negotiations', he wrote. 'The old pull-devil-pull-baker method of deciding wage claims is inconsistent with a policy of full employment.' [62] Arthur Deakin, whose earlier opposition to a wage policy of any sort had been unmistakable, now accepted the Government's argument that wages had to come first in a general attack on inflation, and spoke in favour of proposals for preferential wage treatment for workers in undermanned industries.[63] These union leaders were acting as the administrators of the Government's economic policy and therefore increasingly reflected the Government's attitude, not least its pragmatic approach to profits in an economy still predominantly capitalist. Speaking for the General Council at the 1948 Congress, Sir George Chester told the delegates:

> Few of us realize that marginal surplus or profit is essential
> to the conduct of British industry, whether it be nation-
> alized or in private hands. The position you and I occupy
> as industry is now organized depends on that one incentive.
> It is an unfortunate circumstance, but it is absolutely true
> and it is inescapable until we can alter the whole structure
> of industry and replace the incentive of profit with another
> incentive. I say to you in no unmistakable [*sic*] terms that
> if you had statutory control of profits ... you would be
> doing a graver disservice to British industry and to the
> British people at the present time ... than by any other
> action that you could take.[64]

What these statements by trade union leaders indicate is that the socialist as opposed to the Keynesian and Beveridge approach to wages policy and the economy generally, was no longer, if it had been at all, available to the unions. The preconception that the creation of a socialist commonwealth and a classless society would by definition alter the determinants of economic motivation and thus enable the state to plan without conflict, had been set aside. In its place, a wages policy had been introduced in a society still divided by class and with an economy where private enterprise, profit and the market mechanism (combined with a considerable degree of state intervention), continued to exist. This did not mean that no justification could be offered within the labour movement for a wages policy, but it did mean that the justification had to proceed from different premises. As we have seen, a dearly held tenet of the labour movement was that a wages policy could only succeed on the basis of the voluntary agreement of the organized working class. This was in fact the view of all those who advocated such a policy. And it was clear that such voluntary agreement was only possible if a consensus would be reached on the distribution of income and power in the society. The Labour Government had by 1948 come to believe that the social, political and economic conditions of Britain at the time all provided a foundation for this necessary consensus, and was able to carry the top levels of the trade union leadership with it in this belief.

The first premise from which this belief proceeded was that redistribution of income had gone as far as it could, that the share of the national income going to the working class had reached its upper level, and that any further increase in its reward had to come from productivity growth. 'Believe me,' Morrison appealed to the delegates at the 1947 Party Conference, 'there is little or no more to be got toward a better standard of living by squeezing the incomes of the rich . . . From now on what we get in social benefits and higher wages we shall, broadly speaking, have to earn by higher production.' The half-century-long struggle by the labour movement for social justice was over, he said. Success had brought a new task.[65] At the 1948 TUC, Cripps similarly argued that there was no relief for wages to be had from profits. Retained profits were needed for reinvestment and distributed profits, even if reduced by the 'drastic amount' of one-quarter, would only yield 4d on the pound if distributed among all wage and salary earners. 'What it comes to is this, there is only a certain sized cake to be divided up and if a lot of people want a larger slice they can only get it by taking it from others. There is only one way by which we can, with a given volume of employment increase our real standard of living and that is by each of us producing more.' [66] For Labour leaders of both the left and right wings of the Party, in other words, the economic basis for a consensus on the distribution of income had been achieved. In the face of recurring rank and file demands for more, they concluded that the problem was not economic but moral. For Morrison, the workers were too conservative and clung to patterns of behaviour appropriate to a time before social justice was achieved. For Cripps, they had lost the Christian values of self-examination and duty, which could alone solve Britain's and the world's difficulties.[67]

The belief in the consensus stemmed not only from this first premise, however. Equally important was Labour's changing conception of the role of private enterprise and entrepreneurial profits. In 1945, it may have been contended that in the transitional period to socialism, profits could not be too heavily squeezed if the economy was to continue functioning. By 1948, however, it was clear that private enterprise was not merely a transitional phenomenon. The 'revisionist' argument in the Labour Party that was elaborated in the 1950s, was evident among the leadership in the late 1940s. As R. A. Brady noted at the time:

> The thesis of Burnham's *Managerial Revolution* seems to
> have been taken over by Labour spokesmen and Labour
> theoreticians, lock, stock and barrel. References to Burnham
> are scattered through Labour literature, and find their way
> into Labour speeches on the floor of Parliament. One would
> gather from these references that businessmen in Britain
> are being led, as though by the unseen hand of technological
> logos, to encompass broad social ends which are not only no
> part of, but are actually contrary to, narrow objectives of
> their early entrepreneurial intentions.[68]

Within this context the conflict of interest between labour and capital had been overcome. The implication for a wage policy was that in the interests of equality of sacrifice, entrepreneurs should be asked to undertake restraint as well, but that unnecessary interference with their ways of production would be harmful to production in a mixed economy.

This philosophy determined many of the Government's actions during the period that the wages policy was in effect. The Government turned from reliance on physical controls to economic management through budgetary policy. In November 1948, it introduced its 'bonfire of controls' initiating the removal of a massive range of commodities from price control, and the gradual disengagement from rationing and utility schemes. As part of its concessions to the unions, the Government did not place a ceiling on subsidies until April 1949 and continued to press for voluntary dividend limitation, but those policies were maintained against the tide of increased reliance on the market and freedom of action for private enterprise. The Government was, with the cooperation of the TUC, operating a policy of indirect control on wages, at the same time as it was moving in the opposite direction with regard to other economic factors.

Opposition in the labour movement and the breakdown of wages policy

Although the Labour Government's wages policy was supported until mid 1950 by the three main central bodies of the labour movement – the annual TUC, the Labour Party Conference, and the Parliamentary Labour Party – there was significant opposition to the policy from the beginning. That the Government would not be able to rely solely on the traditional loyalty of its backbenches on this issue was seen when the trade union MP, William Monslow, immediately labelled the White Paper as a 'psychological disaster', which was 'insiduously directed primarily against the wage-earning sections of the community',[69] reminiscent of the 1931 betrayal. Conservative MPs lauded the 'extraordinary sense of restraint' of the General Council. 'Sometimes, indeed, we could hardly believe the printed reports . . .', Macmillan said of the union leaders' speeches, 'when we are warned that the profit motive is essential to all industry, nationalized or unnationalized, and that statutory contol of profits would be the greatest disservice to the British people, we may gasp a little, but we approve'.[70] But to delegates to the TUC and Party Conferences, who were used to hearing from their leaders that profits were an unmitigated evil, the defense of profits sounded as though their leaders had become 'the gramophones of the FBI'.[71] And Cripps' ascetic appeal to Christian values, while not without effect, also produced the acid remark that Cripps (a vegetarian) might 'live on orange juice and radish tops, . . . [but] the workers of Great Britain cannot be expected to follow his example to that extent'.[72]

The main factor which preserved the wages policy against this opposition was the unflinching support of the trade union leadership. Undoubtedly an important reason for their willingness to withstand the demands of their rank and file was that a large part of the wartime bargain had yet to be dismantled at the beginning of 1948, but this could not have been enough in itself as the Government's 'bonfire of controls' erased most of the remaining vestiges of that bargain and the General Council's proposals for the Budget were hardly at all accepted by the Government. The real reason was political, and was based on the loyalty these leaders felt for the Labour Government and its ideological position. In most analyses of the relationship between the unions and the Labour Party, it is argued that while unions can directly influence party policy, the Party has no analogous means of influencing the unions.[73] But to look for direct means of control is to misunderstand the relationship; the main points of contact are informal, but close and continuous. Labour Party representatives sat on the General Council's Economic Committee throughout 1948–50. The Party and the TUC and the TGWU shared the same building; leading trade unionists were in the Cabinet. Attlee and Cripps were invited to address the annual Congress, a forum denied Conservative Ministers.[74] The means of influence of the Labour Government over the unions were considerable. Like any Government, it could threaten the unions with unemployment, if they did not comply with the policy. But unlike an alternative Government, it can also warn the unions that the preservation of the Government itself was at stake. In the late 1940s, this proved to be very effective. 'If I were confronted with the defeat of the Government or the reduction of wages,' said Sam Watson, the miners' leader and a member of the Party NEC, 'then I would advocate a reduction of wages to save the Labour Government.' [75]

The General Council's support meant that the executives of the largest unions would use their block votes both at the Trade Union Congresses and Labour Party Conferences to back wage restraint. It also meant that these votes would be used in support of the Government on resolutions which touched on wider questions of economic policy, from which wages policy could not be isolated. At the Congress the two biggest unions, the TGWU and NUGMW had more than one quarter of the votes at their disposal and the six largest (TGWU, NUGMW, NUM, USDAW, NUR, AEU) more than half the votes. At the Party Conference, the six largest unions commanded two-thirds of the total trade union vote and almost 50% of the total Conference vote.[76] These six were, of course, not always in agreement on the question. Both the USDAW and the AEU voted against the policy at the March 1948 Special Conference, and the USDAW voted against the policy at the 1948 Party Conference, although both unions supported the General Council on the issue at the 1948 and 1949 Trade Union Congresses. But the combination of the voting power of the TGWU, NGMWU, NUM and NUR, together with the support the policy was able to get from some smaller unions, and some constituency parties in the case of Party Conferences, guaranteed the policy against defeat throughout 1948 and 1949.

Within the Parliamentary Labour Party, the effect of the General Council's support was no less important. For the first challenge to the White Paper came from the PLP and was led, moreover, by trade union-sponsored MPs. A letter signed by sixty Labour MPs expressed their support for the White Paper but asked that more emphasis be put on the limitation of profits.[77] On 10 February 1948, 21 Labour MPs introduced a critical motion demanding that the Government withdraw the White Paper.[78] The real significance of this revolt lay in the fact that ten of its sponsors were members of the Trade Union Group, including the Chairman of the Group, as well as both the treasurer and the secretary of the Miners' Group, which itself held considerable status within the PLP. Dissension within the ranks of trade union MPs was a novel occurence, for they rarely acted as an economic interest bloc within Parliament and left, after 1945 at least, high policy matters to the leaders of the TUC to take up directly with the Government. They were noted for their traditional discipline and solidarity with the Party in Parliament and in fact, as James Mac-Gregor Burns has observed, were 'at least as much instruments of the Government as they are vehicles of economic self expression'.[79] Any possible danger was averted in two ways: first, by Cripps's guarantees that effective action would be taken to restrain prices and profits; and secondly by a meeting held by Deakin with the TGWU Group in the House, where he asked them not to take precipitate action in view of the discussions going on between the TUC and the Government. Trade union action in Parliament against the White Paper would only have embarrassed the General Council at this juncture and would, at any rate, have challenged the procedure of keeping discussions of wage policy outside the precincts of the House of Commons, and within the extra-parliamentary system of direct consultations, which Deakin particularly favoured. The crisis subsided as a number of the sponsors of the motion, including the Chairman of the Trade Union Group, withdrew their names, and on the night before the debate in the House on the White Paper, it was understood that the Speaker would not call the motion.[80]

On all fronts therefore, the General Council's active support was able to overcome opposition to the policy. The union leaders' actions were all the more remarkable because it placed them in a position of potential conflict with their own members. For as one union leader after another attested at the Congresses of 1948 and 1949 'it is a fact that in factories and workshops all over the country today workers are demanding effective action in regard to the question of wages'.[81] Union leaders were in danger of being seen by their rank and file as agents of the Government. Deakin's TGWU was especially singled out, and suffered widespread revolts within its ranks during this period.[82]

Since the Labour Government was self-admittedly pursuing a 'national' rather than a 'class' policy, and the TUC was advocating support for this policy, it inevitably appeared to many trade unionists that the unions were abandoning their class role. The unions' self-abnegation was therefore subject to strong internal criticism. 'This question of loyalty,' a USDAW delegate told the 1948 Congress, 'it seems, is being somewhat prostituted . . . the first loyalty of every trade unionist is to his or her class. Loyalty is a class question.' [83] The fears of many moderate union leaders were expressed by NUPE's Bryn Roberts, himself a strong supporter of centralized bargaining through the TUC:

> An indefinitely prolonged policy of restraint will create conflict within the unions and create conflict between the unions. It will transform the old class struggle. The struggle now will not be between the workers and the employer: the struggle will be between the trade unionist and his own executive council, and I know no policy better calculated to create dissension within the unions, to undermine the position of the leader and to provide glorious opportunities for disruptive elements to exploit. Indeed, the remedy may prove worse than the disease.[84]

Because its support for the policy was essentially political, the General Council interpreted this dissent as also being politically motivated. Whereas earlier, leaders like Deakin had seen agitators as merely acting to intensify unrest that arose from social conditions, they now ascribed all opposition and unrest to the activities of the Communist Party,[85] as part of an attempt to destroy the Labour Government. Indeed, Communist influence was significant in this period and Communist trade union leaders were vociferous in their opposition to wage restraint. The ETU and AEU were led by Communists and Communist influence was appreciable in the TGWU, NUM, NUR and USDAW. But opposition to the General Council on the issue of wage restaint can by no means be attributed entirely to Communist opposition. Opposition in the TUC to the wages policy was swollen by over a million votes which usually supported the platform.[86]

If the tactics of the General Council had rested solely on an anti-Communist crusade, it is unlikely that it would have secured support for the policy for well over two years. In fact, their tactics were carefully designed to obtain the necessary support. The General Council and the union executives that supported the policy continued to act at Congress and at Party Conferences in the nominal role of pressure groups. At the 1948 and 1949 Congresses, resolutions supporting the wage restraint policy were framed in terms of general demands upon the Government to maintain the purchasing power of wages by taking more effective action to control prices, to extend cost of living subsidies and to impose stricter limitations on profits. By putting such resolutions, trade union leaders were able to appear before their members in a more favourable light, but in speaking to these resolutions, the General Council leaders invariably defended the Government's economic policy, denied that prices and profits had risen substantially and opposed statutory controls and limitations of profits. Delegates who voted for the resolutions often made it clear they did so because of the text and complained of the speeches by the resolutions' movers.

These resolutions served to undercut an opposition which itself was not intractably hostile to a wages policy *per se*. Of a barrage of resolutions submitted by constituency parties and unions to the Labour Party Conferences on the issue of wages, prices, and profits (ranging from 39 resolutions in 1948 to 44 in 1950 [87]), very few indicated explicit disapproval of wage restraint, but almost all demanded increased controls of profits and prices. What these resolutions invariably proposed was that wage restraint be made conditional upon the introduction of an economic plan covering prices and profits and essential commodities, upon statutory controls on profits, a wealth tax and the maintenance of subsidies. Yet the official resolutions were in general terms no less demanding (except that they did not make support for the wages policy 'conditional') and thus were able to secure support from both those sections which favoured a 'mixed economy' and those who were opposed to it but unwilling to embarrass the Government.

The 1949 TUC gave the wage policy a majority of almost 5 million votes, but a gap was clearly developing between the way they voted – to show their loyalty to the Labour Government – and their actions in the wage bargaining sphere. Immediately after the Congress, the Confederation of Shipbuilding and Engineering Unions' General Council voted to seek a £1 a week rise (considered a colossal demand at the time), although a week earlier most of the executives of the unions in the Confederation had voted for the policy. Other unions, including the NUR, followed suit. Speaking at the Party Conference, Barbara Castle suggested that 'once it begins to dawn on the minds of ordinary people that price mechanism is coming increasingly into operation as the instrument of distribution, then we undermine our policy of wage stability . . . and we tend to undermine the morale of our workers without which we shall not get the productivity we need so urgently'.[88]

The immediate cause of the breakdown of the wages policy lay in the Government's and TUC's attempt to extend it in the context of the Government's continuing economic difficulties. On 18 September 1949, the Government announced a devaluation of the pound by 40%. This came as a shock to the TUC, but in the interests of restraining costs and thus maintaining the competitive advantage which devaluation gave to British exports, it went further than before in its advocacy of restraint, and stated publicly that the Government could not be expected to maintain general stability of prices. TUC officials drew up a plan for a complete wage freeze to apply to all workers without exception. This was, however, too much for the TUC's Economic Committee and even the staunchest backers of the restraint policy baulked. A member of the Committee told the press their problem was 'not so much what we would like to do, but just what our members will willingly support'.[89] After long and heated meetings a policy was hammered out and was accepted by the General Council on 9 November. It asked member unions to reconsider existing wage claims and to forgo increases afforded by sliding-scale cost-of-living arrangements in their contracts. This policy of freezing wages was to apply so long as retail prices did not rise by more than 5%. It recognized that consideration in certain cases might be given to low-paid workers, but nevertheless urged that 'in consideration of even such cases regard be had to the general economic problems necessitating rigorous restraint'. As Allan Flanders wrote at the time, 'this was restraint with a vengeance which avoided the problem of distinguishing between justified and unjustified wage increases by having none at all'.[90]

The recommendations were put to another Special Conference of Executives in January 1950, shortly before the 1950 General Election. This had an important effect on the conference in that the executives were concerned that a large vote against the policy would harm the Party electorally. The General Council insisted on the vote, but the result was inevitably disappointing to it. The miners had voted in December by an overwhelming majority to reject the wage policy of the TUC on the advice of their National Executive which had supported wage restraint from its inception in 1948. They were joined in opposition at the conference by the AEU and NUR. With these giants against them, the General Council could not hope to secure the kinds of majorities they had received earlier. The vote was 4,260,000 to 3,606,000, a majority of only 657,000 votes, a stark contrast to the majority at the Congress four months earlier. Opposition centred on the lack of restraint of profits. The engineering, foundry and building workers argued that rising profits in their industries were more than large enough to absorb wage increases. There was general resentment against the abandonment of physical controls and the Government's reliance on the management of demand through the budget. 'Keynes's economics', said one delegate, 'are not working-class economics.'[91] Throughout the debate the Labour Government's wage policy was repeatedly painted as being anti-working class in its conception. Unofficially, at least, the policy had broken down.

Throughout 1950, the trend against wage restraint was maintained. The TGWU continued to follow its hard line (in May, Deakin indicated that he was favorable to the idea of a National Tribunal being set up to consider claims from the unions),[92] but after the April union delegates' conferences, the writing was on the wall for the official TUC policy. Among others, the USDAW conference overthrew its executives' support of the policy, and with this one blow, involving 342,000 votes at the TUC, the slender unworkable majority was gone. When, in addition, rearmament for the Korean War occasioned further price and profit rises, the General Council had no alternative but to relax its own position. In June it issued a new statement in which it did not leave off advocating restraint but did recognize that 'there must be greater flexibility of wage movements in the future, than was envisaged in the policy approved in January'.[93] Even this moderate wage restraint policy was not acceptable to the unions. At the 1950 Congress in September they vented their wrath for the earlier policy on the General Council by taking the very rare action of defeating the platform on a major policy issue (the first time since 1945). A composite resolution moved by Walter Stevens of the ETU, the most vociferous opponent of the wage restraint policy since 1948, declared that 'Congress is of the opinion that until such time as there is a reasonable limitation of profits, a positive planning of our British economy, and prices are subject to such control as will maintain the purchasing power of wages at a level affording to every worker a reasonable standard of living, there can be no basis for a restraint on wage applications.' [94] The General Council, led by Deakin, stood fast in its condemnation of 'this policy of smash and grab', but the resolution was carried and the General Council's Report rejected by 3,949,000 and 3,727,000 votes. The Government itself was less bold than the General Council in facing the Labour Party Conference a month later. The NEC recommended the unanimous acceptance of a vague, but critical resolution, which called upon the Government to reduce prices and control and reduce profits and make allowances for low wages. However, James Griffith, speaking for the NEC, combined this acquiescence with the demand that 'the policy of restraint should be continued as far as ever it is possible'.[95] In fact, both the General Council and the Government continued to express their concern for the consequences of uncontrolled wage increases, and continued to advocate restraint.

These appeals fell on deaf ears, however. It was not only that unions were now making claims (for claims had been introduced from 1948 to 1950), but that they were no longer tolerating the delays they had accepted previously in negotiations.[96] Various factors contributed to the breakdown of wage restraint. Certainly rising prices and profits was one of them. Wage rates had lagged behind prices throughout the period and although, in general, earnings were able to keep pace with price rises, the increase in the cost of living was much more marked for the working class than the middle class, as the heaviest increases were in food and clothing prices, the items that figured most in working class budgets. At the same time, there occurred in the latter years of the Labour Government's period in office, a clear tendency for property incomes to gain at the expense of working class incomes. The share of wages in the gross national income rose (mainly at the expense of profit and interest) from 33.6% in 1938 to 39.3% in 1948, then fell back to 38% in 1949, and this trend acelerated in 1950.[97] This is not to underestimate the substantial impositions Labour made on the higher income brackets. Although the progressiveness of the income tax did not increase after the war, combined income and surtax rates were 19 shillings in the pound in 1949 and 1950. Taxes on distributed profits, and luxury goods were heavily increased. As we have seen, however, the Government was constricted by the inherent dilemma of applying a 'fair shares' policy within the confines of a capitalist economy. Insofar as Labour relied mainly on private enterprise (which occupied 80% of the field in 1950) to increase exports, expand investment and improve productivity it felt private enterprise had to be given its reward in the form of profits. This limited the ability of the Government to accede to demands for higher profits taxation, or even for a wealth tax (the capital levy) for which the TUC had repeatedly called since 1940. Yet the Government's taxation policy was the ethical foundation, not only for wage restraint, but for its exhortations for the abandonment of traditional wage differentials. It was neither equipped nor prepared, as we have seen, to determine centrally all incomes; therefore the large pre-tax and post-tax differentials between managerial and entrepreneurial incomes on the one hand, and wage incomes on the other, largely undermined the consensus which the wages policy required for its success. Increased profits, combined with capital gains and known tax evasion, were bound to provide a source of malaise for wage-earners. The dissension produced went beyond disagreement over the relative shares of increased productivity to disagreement over the more stable shares of the national income itself. Nor could a solution be found in overcoming traditional differentials within the working class to the benefit of the lower paid so long as the even wider income differentials and the status associated with them were being called into question.

An underlying cause of the breakdown was the threat to the stability of the trade unions themselves. The most influential section of the union hierarchy in fact seemed to accept the given social order, but where a wider consensus on the legitimacy of economic rewards does not exist, the trade unions can only engage in wage restraint for a very limited period if their organizations are to remain intact and their hold over their membership to be maintained. Total union membership which had risen constantly since 1945 to a high point of over 9 million in 1948, declined in 1949 and 1950 by 0.8%.[98] Moreover, as many workers increasingly relied on total earnings – overtime, payments by results systems, etc. – to keep pace with the cost of living, trade unionists became restive about the gap between wage rates and earnings as well as about the effects of this 'wage-drift' in disturbing both intra-industry and inter-industry differentials. They consequently put heavy pressure on union leaders to pursue wage claims. The inability of union leaders to withstand these pressures without the ensuing disruption of their organizations, was another major factor in the demise of the wages policy.[99]

Overtly political factors contributed as well to the breakdown, just as they had been indispensable to the policy's introduction in the first place. The close ties between the Labour Party and the trade unions remained intact, but the Labour Party increasingly presented itself as an integrative party which was much more than the political arm of the labour movement. The significance of this posture should not be under-estimated as it naturally led trade unionists to expect their industrial organizations to continue to press their class interests. There was a slight but perceptible feeling of estrangement from the Labour Party by 1950. A survey carried out in the Manchester Docks in 1950–1 indicated that of the 17% of the dockers who were opposed to the relationship between the unions and the Party, almost all attributed this opposition to the policy of wage restraint.[100] But the unease was deepened in the last years of the Government by the declining trade union influence in the Cabinet and especially by the death of Ernest Bevin, 'the key link with the trade union movement'.[101] Trade union sponsored MPs held two less Cabinet positions in 1951 than they did in 1945, and they bore the brunt of the reduction in the total number of Government posts. This was not due to any discrimination on the part of the Prime Minister, but reflected the rise to prominence of the young intellectuals who had come in to the PLP in 1945. The growth in the number of middle class MPs – an essential element in the Party's integrative posture – led to a growing feeling 'that the Labour Party is ceasing to be a *"labour"* party. The reason why the unions are so concerned to keep their strength in the House is that they want to ensure that the atmosphere and outlook of the Parliamentary party are constantly influenced from within by working class thoughts and reactions'.[102]

The breakdown of wage restraint did not produce a rift between the trade union leadership and the leadership of the Labour Party. On the contrary, they both joined together to face the 'Bevanite' revolt. The roots of this revolt lay not only in rearmament, but also in opposition to the Government's economic policy and soon after the resignation of Bevan, Wilson and Freeman from the Government in April 1951 they took up the cry for increased controls, subsidies, a capital levy and increased profits taxation.[103] Despite the fact that trade union leaders were making many of the same demands themselves – and were being asked by the Bevanites to 'accept the logical consequences of those arguments',[104] their opposition to Bevan was based on the fact that he was challenging their claims to speak for the rank and file trade unionist in the Party and was spearheading the very dissent that had defeated the General Council at the 1950 TUC.

Faced with this challenge, and challenges to their leadership from within the unions, the trade union leaders sought to maintain their authority by turning their backs completely on the idea of union participation in a wages policy. Although careful not to rekindle antagonism by using the phrase 'national wages policy', Party leaders maintained their interest in wage restraint policies. To re-establish the bargain, Cripps suggested to the unions that they might negotiate price increases with the employers, and indicated that he was prepared to allow a total increase in the wage bill of £50m to be distributed by the TUC among its member unions.[105] This would have involved the General Council itself having to discriminate between the validity of various claims – a role which it refused to take up and for which, after three years of advocating restraint, it did not have its members' confidence. Reeling under the Korean inflation in the summer of 1951, Gaitskell, who had taken over from Cripps at the Treasury, proposed to introduce legislation to impose a statutory limitation on dividends as a gesture to the unions for renewed restraint.[106] Before a bill was introduced to this effect, however, the Labour Government was defeated at the October 1951 General Election.

It was in any event unlikely, given the spate of wage claims at the time, that the unions would have agreed to a resurrection of the policy. Gaitskell's speech to the TUC in September 1951, in which he appealed for restraint and attempted to account for rises in prices, profits and dividends, was, as *The Times* reported, 'heard in silence'. The only response of the Congress was to pass resolutions urging more effective controls of prices and profits. A resolution calling upon the General Council to examine the possibilities for formulating a planned wage policy, was rejected overwhelmingly. The General Council's new position in fact was enunciated clearly as early as November 1950 in response to proposals for a Government-appointed National Wages Board, which would supervise the decisions of the Wage Councils and all voluntary collective agreements. 'The demand for a national wages policy which has been revived again', the TUC now said, 'does not come from those who would be most directly affected by it . . . However independent a central commission sought to be, it would inevitably turn to the Government for guidance on such problems as the national importance of one industry relative to another, and of all wage-earners relative to other sections of the community.' Having been burned once, 'voluntarily' so to speak, the TUC was in no mood for 'planning' the wage structure either by itself or by any other body. 'After 150 years of a pattern of industrial relations which is flexible and wide in its coverage, such a scheme is unthinkable.' [107]

It was a view that would guide the British trade union movement well into the 1960s, in fact until the next Labour Government made cooperation in an incomes policy the test of trade union loyalty to the Labour Party.[108]

2
Incomes policy and Labour in opposition

1951–9: a policy in search of support

The political significance of the breakdown of the wages policy in 1950 was that the ability of the Labour Party, as a national party, to integrate the unions with regard to the most difficult structural problem facing the British economy was considerably diminished. Party manifestos during the 1950s did not resurrect wages policy proposals and Party leaders themselves generally avoided specific reference to a revival of the policy. This was an indication of the differential power the trade unions have *vis-à-vis* the Labour Party: their influence is greater in framing an electoral programme than in determining the actual policy of a Labour Government. Although many of the conflicts that divided the Party during this period in opposition were not unconnected with the questions the wages policy had raised, differences on this issue were not a prime focus of controversy themselves. The reasons for this were not only the result of factors internal to the Party and the unions; in part it was attributable to the fact that, in general, Conservative Governments in the 1950s were agnostic about a national wages policy, and thus external pressure on the Party to develop a counter-policy in opposition was not great. It was only when the Conservatives experienced in the early sixties their own 'conversion' to indicative planning and incomes policy that Labour returned to the question with some relish, offering the electorate an incomes policy which, ironically in view of both earlier and later developments, was presented as a showpiece of Party–union concord.

Officially the General Council's policy was that Tory policies of decontrol and the effect on prices of a gradual removal of subsidies made it impossible for the TUC even to consider suggestions for a wages policy. This was not simple posturing. An examination of the TUC budget proposals and post-budget statements throughout the 1950s shows that the trade unions had very little effective influence

over the Government's economic policy.[1] In taking this stand, however, the General Council was not by any means reneging on its
long-standing policy of cooperation with non-Labour Governments.
Despite the fact that the new administration generally disposed of
governmental committees on planning and controls, it extended if
anything the system of consultation with the unions.[2] Nor did the
General Council so easily unlearn the lessons in the 'national interest' they had been taught by the Labour Government. The Council's leading members personally held the view that the decision of
the 1950 Congress had been a mistake and that the wage restraint of
1948–50 had been 'a remarkable contribution in the fight against
inflation in a difficult period of history'.[3] The General Council
vociferously opposed resolutions at successive Congresses until 1956
which called for the TUC 'to support efforts of the Unions to defend
the living standards of their members by the submission of wage
claims', and in general terms instead urged 'the observance of
reasonableness in the formulation of wage claims'.[4]

The Labour Party, on its part, did not upset this carefully balanced
position of the TUC and remained noticeably demure in its pronouncements on the question of wages and wage restraint in the early
1950s. This was, after all, one of the luxuries of the opposition and
there was, at any rate, a widespread belief in the Party in its first
years out of office that the next Labour Government would be elected
during a period of depression and stagnation, not one where excess
demand would be the problem. Moreover, the trade union leaders,
on whom the Party leadership was relying as their bulwark against
the Bevanites, were in no mood to recommit themselves to the Party
on the question. Speaking directly on the question of a national
wages policy at the 1952 Party Conference, Deakin warned the Party
off this track: '... the unions have experienced difficulties and criticisms from their members by reason of the suggestion that we have
been more concerned with our own Party in Government than in the
handling of our industrial problems'.[5] The struggle that Deakin and
his followers were waging against the left in the Party was in fact
closely connected with the 'difficulties and criticisms' the trade union
leadership was experiencing within their own organizations and the
TUC against their continued advocacy of wage moderation. 'They
are afraid of Bevanism,' G. D. H. Cole wrote at the time of the trade
union leadership, 'not without reason, as calculated to strengthen
opposition to "wage restraint" and to collaboration in measures
designed to increase productivity ... But most of them are at the same
time conscious of the need to walk warily lest they be repudiated by
their own followers and forced to adopt industrial policies which

they believe would be disastrous in the present economic situation.'[6] The Party therefore confined itself to reaffirming its unshakable belief in free collective bargaining, and to passing resolutions pledging a Labour Government to control rising prices.[7]

Nevertheless, as the economy continued to experience rising prices and money wages, a growth rate slower than that of other European countries and recurring balance of payments problems, it became increasingly *de rigueur* to lament the bargaining power of the unions under full employment. Not only in the popular press, but among economists and industrial relations experts there was broad agreement that 'the balance of industrial power has swung decisively in favour of the unions'.[8] The problem facing the Government, however, was that although the major question asked by these writers was how to deal with increased power of the trade unions, the intractable difficulty of 1948–50 of how to 'plan' wages without 'planning' the whole range of income distribution, stood out clearly.

The Conservative Government in its first term of office was not above raising the idea of a wages policy with the TUC from time to time, but in general it tended not to press the matter.[9] In 1956, however, the Government issued *The Economic Implications of Full Employment*, its own sequel to the 1948 White Paper.[10] It accompanied this with a 'price plateau' policy whereby it asked for wage restraint in exchange for the Government holding down prices in the nationalized industries and appealing to the private sector for price and profit restraint. In view of the fact that the Government's appeal to the national interest was the same as that made in 1948, the General Council acrimoniously split over whether or not to meet the Government's request for cooperation, even though its first response was to refuse to circulate the White Paper among the affiliated unions. Its final decision, which was a negative one, was largely influenced by the fact that the demands made upon the Government by business organizations in exchange for restraint were incompatible with demands being made by the unions. The FBI wanted substantial reductions in Government expenditure and taxation, whereas the TUC asked for maintained or increased food subsidies. The Government undertook a deflationary policy which included abolishing the bread subsidy and increasing charges for school meals. In these conditions, while some cooperation was secured from the employers, a similar response by the General Council could not have been carried at the 1956 Congress.[11]

In the absence of an agreement with the unions, Conservative policy changed, first in the direction of direct encouragement of employer resistance to wage claims, and then, fearing the consequences of large strikes on the economy, in the direction of an even more severe policy of deflation, increasing unemployment to a level of 2.8% in January 1959. In August 1957, the Government established the Council on Productivity, Prices and Incomes (The Cohen Council) which, due to its 'impartial' composition was expected to be able to outline the national interest with respect to wage claims. This was less a wages policy than an attempt to avoid one. The Government held that state action could not solve the wage–price spiral 'without measures intolerable in a free society' and that in any case, 'Ministers change and Governments change and perhaps the conception of the national interest changes with them'.[12] TUC endorsement of the Council was not sought and consultations were only held with respect to the details of its composition and activities. The TUC, for its part, argued that the Council's members, appointed by the Government alone, would not be impartial but merely defend the Government's deflationary policies and act as an additional voice for wage restraint. When the first report of the Council contended that a measure of unemployment was healthy and necessary to lower wage increases, and rejected the TUC's advice to it for dividend limitation, price controls, subsidies, and controls on raw materials, the TUC felt this was a confirmation of its suspicions and boycotted the Council for the rest of its short existence.[13]

Nevertheless, as the Conservative Government began to concern itself with measures of wage restraint, if not a wages policy *per se*, so did the Labour Party. In 1957, Harold Wilson, then Shadow Chancellor of the Exchequer, affirmed that 'wages were at the centre of the cost-push spiral', and began examining 'the conditions in which wage restraint could once again become a reality'. This could not be achieved by 'force, threats or bluster', Wilson believed: 'For a **Labour** government no less than the Conservatives, success or failure in the battle against inflation would depend on its ability to secure an understanding with the unions which would make wage restraint possible.'[14] Labour's major economic policy document, *Plan for Progress* (1958) came as close to outlining the skeleton of a wages policy as is possible without mentioning the name. It contended that 'the growth of money incomes must broadly keep pace with higher productivity, taking the economy as a whole . . . A Government which is determined to restore a climate of expansion, maintain fair play between different sections of the community, promote greater equality and create a price-freeze, has the right to rely on the goodwill and cooperation of the trade union movement as of every other responsible organization in the country'.[15] It argued that increases in productivity need not necessarily precede pay rises since the pressure for wage increases often was instrumental in bringing about greater efficiency and higher productivity; nor should increases be related exclusively to productivity in any particular industry, since the scope for raising productivity differed as between industries. And 'whilst some measure of restraint on demands for higher incomes will be needed, it will be clear that no kind of wages freeze is envisaged.' These qualifications were clearly designed to overcome union anxiety about this section of the document.

The first opening towards a resurrection of agreement with the unions on this matter in fact came from the TUC at the 1956 Congress, in the context of a shift *against* the TUC policy of wage moderation under a Conservative Government. For it was at this Congress that the TGWU under Frank Cousins (elected General Secretary after the deaths of both Deakin and his hand-picked successor, Jock Tiffin) first made its influence felt on the left of the labour movement. The delicate balance the General Council had maintained between officially opposing a wages policy and yet at the same time opposing wage militancy could no longer be sustained. The wages policy question became a more political one than it had been earlier in the decade, as the TUC now explicitly tied rejection of wages policy to the absence of economic planning.[16] In moving this resolution, Cousins explained:

> We do not share the view that it is not of any great consequence which political party is in power when you are facing an economic problem. We think it matters very much. We think that a Government which by its very nature represents labouring groups and is pledged by its election policies to look after the interests of the working class and in making these policies intends to carry them out, is more ready to discuss and examine with us the effects of those policies.[17]

Neither the Party nor the unions were prepared, however, for an agreement on wages policy at this time. Whereas Cousins's formulations of support for the Party on this question were not only general, but also phrased in explicit class terms, the Party leadership was for its part concerned to diminish the class basis of its appeal. This was perhaps its foremost concern after the late 1940s, as NEC documents of that period reveal. At the request of Herbert Morrison, a memorandum by Richard Crossman was circulated to the NEC in early 1950, which suggested that the main cause of the failure to achieve a working majority at the 1950 election was that the Party was divided 'between those who favoured consolidation and wooing the middle classes on the one side, and those who wanted more nationalization and the mobilization of the working class vote, on the other'. Crossman argued that this could only lead to a compromise between false alternatives. He suggested that class and nationalization be played down and the Party concentrate on emphasizing limited controls and planning 'as essential for full employment and fair shares'.[18] Although *Plan for Progress* had tried to follow up this approach, the questions of class and nationalization remained in fact the dominant ones for the Party in this period. As a result the Party could not take advantage of its special relationship with the unions to claim, as it did in 1964, that it alone could guarantee economic growth because of its ability to integrate union demands in a mixed economy. Instead, Gaitskell, and the revisionist wing of the Party generally, were considerably embarrassed by strikes and wage demands and some held an unstated but firm belief that the trade union association with the Party was its prime electoral liability.[19]

Trade union resentment to this attitude was seen in a motion at the 1956 TUC by ASLEF which expressed its 'profound dissatisfaction with the lack of policy displayed by the Labour Party in face of the attacks made on the workers' standards by the present Government',[20] and in the occasional left-wing motions at Party Conferences which expressed similar sentiments.[21] The divergence in approach between union and Party leaders was clear from an important confrontation between Gaitskell and Cousins in a Labour Party television broadcast in April 1958, where Cousins would not commit himself to Gaitskell's position that restraint would be required from the unions, apart from saying that the unions would cooperate more easily with a Government whose class interest reflected their own.[22] And whereas Harold Wilson repeatedly proclaimed that only a Crippsean package could solve the problem,[23] trade unionists for their part after the fall of the 'triumvirate', never defended the 1948–50 policy. The Trade Union MP, Charles Pannell, genuinely reflected trade union opinion when he said: 'After Sir Stafford Cripps in 1949 . . . the wage freeze became as dead as a dodo; it is out, never to return.'[24] At the 1958 Conference, Cousins himself squashed any hopes he might earlier have raised about the possibility of resurrecting an agreement on wages policy in time for the 1959 election.

> We have said that we do not accept and would not accept a policy of wage restraint, a transference of the economic problems of the community on to the shoulders of the organized and unorganized workers merely as a means by which the economy could be balanced . . . we do not change our views on the entitlement of the workers by the transference

> of Government from one Party to another. If we did, we
> would be entitled to be accused, as certain sections of the
> community do describe us, as an adjunct, an industrial
> mouthpiece, of a political party. We are not that at all.[25]

It required a very different conjuncture of events before the Party in
1964 could face the electorate as a national party whose link with the
trade unions was held to be not a liability, but an asset, by virtue of
the fact that it alone could secure trade union agreement to voluntary
wage restraint.

Conservative planning and incomes policy

Just as the decade of the 1950s was marked by the absence of a distinct national wages policy on the part of the government and opposition in Britain, so the decade of the 1960s was distinguished by the
attempt to use wages policy as an instrument of economic management. This necessarily involved an attempt to secure a greater degree
of state–union engagement than had heretofore been achieved. The
integration of the trade unions which had emerged during World
War II had for some time been seen to be inadequate; the British
political and economic system now needed a further development in
this sphere. Unofficial strikes, especially in the motor industry, became fairly common in the 1950s, and unions increasingly tended
to pursue an annual wage claim. Moreover, company profits were
generally declining relative to wages in the last years of the decade.[26]
Although the rate of economic growth (and real wages) had risen
substantially, other capitalist countries had fared appreciably better
in this regard. Almost immediately upon the return of the Conservative Party to Government in the 1959 general election, pressures built
up for a new attempt to solve Britain's recurrent balance of payments
problems in a way less detrimental to economic growth than the
traditional policy of 'stop–go' combined with official exhortations for
wage restraint. Increasingly, in official circles fiscal policy came to be
seen as incomplete in itself and Government thinking began to turn
towards an incomes policy.[27] (The terminology with regard to wages
policy showed a change at this time, reflecting the desire to present
such policies as not only concerned with working class incomes.)

These developments in the Government's own thinking were
strengthened by the publication in early 1961 of the OEEC's *The
Problem of Rising Prices*.[28] The report contended that for the UK,
as well as other countries, excessive wage increases were 'both an
important and independent inflationary force' and that the increase

of wages in the 1950s was less due to excess demand for labour than to the strength of organized labour. This being the case, simple demand management could not be expected to solve the inflationary problem. Since the reduction of the organizational strength of the unions was seen as technically difficult and politically undesirable in that union power was still needed to counterbalance the power of employers, the report diagnosed wages policy as a cure. The Government would establish a wage 'norm', and the burden of proof would be upon any labour or management group which wanted to deviate from it; only this specific action could be considered a wage policy. Apart from applying the norm to the public sector, the Government was not expected to regulate individual wages or prices; the report relied on the 'sanction of public opinion' for the effectiveness of the norm. Significantly, in an important 'reservation' to the report, two of the six authors advocated the alternative approach of altering the organizational basis of the unions – 'modifying the size and function of the organizational units on both sides of the bargaining table'.[29] This alternative idea for dealing with the power of organized labour was to run concurrently with the voluntary incomes policy approach throughout the decade.

In the twelve months between July 1961 and June 1962, the Conservative Government successively introduced the pay pause, the 'guiding light' wage norm, and the National Incomes Commission. The pause, which applied a wage freeze in the public sector and asked that the same line be followed in the private sector, was supplanted in April 1962 by a 'guiding light' wage norm of 2 to 2.5% as the upper limit for wage increases, including wage drift. In June 1962, the Government established the NIC as an independent body charged with looking into pay claims referred to it by the Government, although neither the Government nor the NIC would be empowered to alter a settlement. This particular attempt at an incomes policy was combined with a commitment by the Government to indicative economic planning and the establishment of the consultative planning body, the National Economic Development Council (NEDC). By adopting a favourable attitude to 'planning', the Government reasoned it would meet the unions on their own ground when putting forward policies for wage restraint. Such was the importance attached to achieving some direct control over wage movements, that it appears that this sharp shift in policy was largely taken for this reason alone: 'It is surprising, and completely substantiated by the documentary evidence, that the Government envisaged the NEDC as a way of involving the unions in an incomes policy.'[30]

Although the TUC did join NEDC, in terms of its immediate results this approach failed in that union agreement to an incomes policy was not secured during the life of the Government. The General Council did not in principle deny the need for an incomes policy, and it agreed that it was 'a condition of price stability that increases in income should keep in step with the growth of real output'.[31] It continued to reject the Government's overtures, however. Although its new General Secretary, George Woodcock, was personally very much in favour of union engagement in this sphere, the TUC doubted the actual commitment of the Government to tripartite economic planning, and was particularly influenced by the fact that the pay pause had been introduced without consultation with the unions. That the Government could have taken such drastic action without prior notice to the General Council itself, undermined the TUC's claims to member unions that it could influence the nation's economic policy through its numerous points of contact with the Government.

The TUC's main substantive attack was that the Government was asking that wages rise to match the growth in output at the same time as it was holding output down in yet another phase of the stop–go cycle. The cornerstone of TUC economic policy in the previous decade had been the advocacy of measures to stimulate expansion. It had been the major institutional advocate of the need for higher productivity based on greater investment to solve Britain's economic problems and the major critic of 'stop-go'. But from July 1961 it was faced with a situation in which the Government combined general policies of restraint with more direct action on wages than it had ever taken. And they were convinced that the reason lay in the Government's belief 'that the main need is to reassure foreign speculators that the value of their sterling holdings will be maintained whatever the cost in terms of lower living standards and the sacrifice of economic growth'.[32] To this was added the traditional union hostility to interference with collective bargaining *per se*, especially with regard to the postponement of negotiated agreements in the public service, arbitration awards and wage council awards. Finally, the measures were seen as inequitable in their application. They were manifestly discriminatory against public employees and as an 'incomes' policy, it was particularly narrowly applied to wages. The Treasury ruled out the application of any general 'norm' of restraint to be applied to distributed profits, and throughout the whole period the Government limited itself to general exhortations of restraint for profits and dividends. As for the NIC, the TUC was critical of the idea that 'independent experts' could define the national interest in a way acceptable to workers.[33] It boycotted the NIC from the beginning and although provision was made in NIC's terms of reference for joint submission of claims by the parties concerned, no joint references were made.

The TUC's refusal to endorse the incomes policy of the Conservative Government did not rest solely on these well-versed arguments, which often sounded hollow in the mouths of moderate trade union leaders. Factors internal to trade union politics were no less important. As the General Council repeatedly contended, it would not have carried the unions with it had it chosen another course. The pay pause had engendered a militant response from individual unions, and in these circumstances the General Council was being nothing less than truthful when it said that the Chancellor was 'asking trade unions to accept wage restraint . . . in circumstances when they would be least likely to be able to secure the assent of their members. In a democracy wage restraint is difficult to apply in any circumstances. Without the willing cooperation of workpeople any agreement on the part of executives on the General Council themselves would be worth little'.[34] But while the General Council was unwilling to expose itself to certain defeat by endorsing the incomes policy in either its short- or long-term stages, it is important to recognize that the pause did not lead the TUC to retreat from its long standing moderate policy of consultation with the Government of the day. In 1961 union leaders did seriously consider political resistance to the pause, including withdrawing from existing consultative machinery and directly supporting a number of unions affected by the freeze. But the moderates prevailed, and the TUC 'exercised a massive moderating influence whilst awaiting the lifting of the pause'.[35] The General Council refused demands to call a special conference of executives (this would be 'a propaganda conference only'), to organize mass demonstrations (this would 'create a political atmosphere'), or to coordinate joint strike action (this would involve coordinating claims and procedures which was 'neither possible nor desirable').[36] The thinking of the General Council in this matter was reflected in Woodcock's address to the 1963 Congress: 'We left Trafalgar Square a long time ago . . . we have to deal with the affairs of the moment in committee rooms with people who have power . . . The whole work of the TUC in my time has been centred on developing this process'.[37] The General Council was not going to allow the pay pause, whatever its dislike of it, to push it out of Whitehall into Trafalgar Square. It was this same consideration which had led the General Council to decide to join NEDC. The moderate wing of the General Council reasoned that insofar as the pay pause had proved that trade union penetration of the state's decision making processes was in-effective, the answer lay, not in mobilizing mass support for union demands, but in more consultation. Men who had spent their lives developing government–union consultations, who spoke with pride of being able to ring up a Minister at any time, were hardly likely to abandon this approach with ease. Woodcock, having spent his career within the TUC bureaucracy, was particularly committed to this approach. He now readily admitted that consultations with the Government in the past had been more formal than effective,[38] but he had 'every reason to believe' that the NEDC would change this situation.

Given the hostility in the unions to the Government and its in-comes policy, the support of Congress for joining NEDC could only have been secured by combining it with the promise that 'this deci-sion does not imply acceptance of the Chancellor's view that the solution to Britain's economic difficulties is to be found in wage re-straint'.[39] The General Council at first insisted that an incomes policy would not be seriously discussed by the Council. This was, of course, an unrealistic posture given the Government's aims and Woodcock's intention to use the Council to bargain with the Government for economic and social policies desired by the TUC. In fact, prices and incomes policies were discussed and the second NEDC Report ex-plicitly stated that 'a necessary part of its task' was to develop 'policies to ensure that money incomes (wages, salaries, profits) as a whole rise substantially less rapidly than in the past'.[40] TUC participation in a voluntary incomes policy, however, had to await the election of a Labour Government. The 1963 and 1964 Congresses exhibited un-diminished hostility to an incomes policy under the Conservatives, and in informal sessions during the 1963 Congress, the General Coun-cil was forced, on Cousins' emphatic insistence, to amend its major report, *Economic Development and Planning*, to omit explicit ac-ceptance of the NEDC's views on the need for an incomes policy and to put greater emphasis on the fact that the NEDC had failed to examine directly 'the inequitable distribution of the nation's wealth'.[41] This stance was reinforced by the FBI's indication that it had by no means accepted the argument that similar considerations ought to apply to profits and dividends as to wages and salaries as part of an incomes policy; it also opposed various schemes of price regulation.[42] In January 1964, the employers did put forward a pro-posal for taxing profits if they should rise by a greater percentage than wages, but these proposals were rejected by the TUC represen-tatives as being too vague to provide a *quid pro quo* for advising member unions to restrain wage claims, and in any case, 'any general statement on prices and incomes by NEDC would at that stage be undesirable'.[43] Nevertheless, within two months of its election in October 1964 a Labour Government was able to secure just such a general statement. The factors that contributed to this agreement on a voluntary incomes policy were not only a product of the events during these early months of Labour Government, but also of the relationship between the Party and the unions with regard to incomes policy during its last years in opposition.

The Labour Party–trade union agreement on incomes policy

The 1963 Labour Party Conference passed a resolution on economic planning by a vote of 6,090,000 to 40,000 which called upon the Party, in consultation with the trade union movement, to develop 'an incomes policy to include salaries, wages, dividends and profits (including speculative profits) and social security benefits'.[44] The resolution, moved by Jack Cooper of the GMWU, was supported by every union affiliated to the Party, and the most vociferous opponents of the Conservative policy, including Cousins and the Boilermakers' Ted Hill, spoke in support of the motion. The significance of this resolution was that it was more than a policy statement; it was a massive demonstration of Party–union solidarity, to which Party leaders attached no little importance with an eye to the coming election. It was important that the resolution came from the floor – normally such basic policy resolutions are moved by the NEC itself – for it allowed the Party to be able to claim that the unions desired an incomes policy under a Labour Government. And the fact that a card vote was taken when the outcome was so decisive, reflected exactly the 'demonstrative' nature of the exercise.

Trade union response to the pay pause and its aftermath had indeed been highly political. A Gallup Poll in December 1961 found that 56% of the respondents thought there was a class struggle in Britain.[45] The pause marked the exact point where Labour went ahead of the Conservatives in the opinion polls, a situation not reversed again until after 1964. Trade union contributions to the Labour Party election fund in 1964 were almost £600,000, the largest amount ever contributed, and an increase of 84% over 1959.[46] At every TUC from 1961, the resolution which rejected the Government's wages policy contained an overtly political call for the return of a Labour Government or the defeat of the Conservative Government. This posture in fact led the Civil Service Clerical Association in 1962 to put down its own motion condemning wage restraint, on the grounds that the main resolution 'politicized' the TUC.[47]

These developments did not mean that the Labour Party had suddenly become content to present itself as a trade union or as a working class party. It appealed directly to middle class voters, to the professionals, the scientists, the managers and even set about to achieve an understanding with those 'progressive' elements in the City of London and among industrialists who were looking for a dynamic capitalism.[48] It saw the main affiliation to the Party of manual workers as now 'obsolete' and urged the unions to undertake a membership drive among traditionally middle class employees.[49] The concern to stress the Party's national rather than class nature remained a preoccupation of the revisionist wing, which adopted the theme that the aim of the Party was still the creation of a classless society, but that only an integrative political party could bring this about. Gaitskell argued that '. . . you want to build your classless society not by the class war but by a party drawn from all classes as ours is'.[50] But this theme was not exclusive to the revisionist leadership of the Party. Harold Wilson warned the 1961 Conference: 'We shall . . . as a national Party and a nationally based Government, be frank in condemning all who shirk their duty to the nation. The professional fomentors of unofficial strikes and those who easily follow them, equally with businessmen who cling to out of date methods and out of date machinery because it yields them a profit . . .'[51] He maintained and elaborated this theme after his election to the leadership, after Gaitskell's death in 1963. On the other hand, left wing union leaders consistently argued that the Labour Party must remain a socialist and working class party. That was the touchstone of the unions' successful opposition to Gaitskell's attempt after the 1959 election to write out the commitment to 'the common ownership of the means of production, distribution and exchange' from clause four of the Party Constitution. Frank Cousins was no less critical, in the midst of the intra-party controversy over unilateralism, of the leadership's attitude to trade union wage demands and strikes. He told the 1961 Party Conference: 'I would like to hear more and more of my Parliamentary colleagues every time they get the chance to do so, warning the Government that head-on clashes will come and that the Parliamentary Party will be on the side of the workers and not trying to find a solution to it and get them back to work quickly.'[52]

How then did the union–Party agreement on incomes policy come about in this period, when it had failed to be established meaningfully earlier? One major factor was that the Conservatives' own conversion to planning in 1961, combined with a renewed bout of deflation in the 'stop–go' cycle, finally led Labour to accept the strategy canvassed by Wilson and Crossman in the 1950s and adopt the theme of a plan for economic expansion as the Party's policy touchstone. Reversing priorities established but a year earlier, the NEC's *Signposts for the Sixties* adopted by the 1961 Conference, listed the plan for growth as Labour's first priority.[53] The attraction of this theme as an electoral platform was that it was so comprehensive in its promise to make every section of society better off. The various elements of the Party, which remained divided over questions of public ownership, income distribution and wage restraint, could bury their differences beneath a common commitment to harnessing 'the white heat of the technological revolution' to a plan for economic growth. It allowed the Party, moreover, while retaining its national image, to present the close liaison with the unions to advantage. Instead of responding defensively to press and governmental attacks on the unions, the Party took on the role of being the sole agent which could coordinate union wage policies with an indicative plan. The Party was able to appear not merely as the political arm of the labour movement, but as a national party which could exert social control over trade union demands and moreover do this without legal controls but with the voluntary cooperation of the unions. This strategy was most clearly enunciated in *Socialist Commentary*. It accepted that economic expansion should be made the overriding target of election propaganda but noted that both the Conservatives and Liberals would take the same approach. What was required was that Labour's claim to be the party of economic growth carry conviction; and here Labour had a ready-made advantage: 'The appeal can only prove superior if Labour can show that its close alliance with the unions is an asset, *which it alone enjoys*, and not a liability. It must be able to show, by working out a joint policy now, that the unions will cooperate wholeheartedly only if Labour is in office.' [54]

In a brilliant speech immediately after the 1959 election, Aneurin Bevan had made the same point: 'I would describe the central problem falling upon representative government in the Western world as how to persuade the people to forego immediate satisfactions in order to build up the economic resources of the country . . . How can we persuade the ordinary men and women that it is worth while making sacrifices in their immediate standards or foregoing substantial rising standards to extend fixed capital equipment throughout the country? This is the problem and it has not been solved yet.' But Bevan was less sure whether the Labour Party, as a national and integrative party, could promise a solution:

it is the function of democratic politics to try to raise the
stresses and strains of society to a level where they can be
solved politically. But if it does not represent them ade-
quately, bring to the floor of the House of Commons the
stresses, problems and strains of contemporary society, people
will seek to solve them elsewhere . . . They will essentially
find expression in attempts to raise the standards of living
by direct action by the trade unions themselves.[55]

Other Labour Party leaders, however, believed that it was necessary
to show the electorate that they would solve the problem, and hence
the emphasis given by them to securing a symbolic agreement on
incomes policy before the 1964 election. In this at least they were
successful, largely because the unions responded to this electoral
strategy. 'We are meeting at a time when we are conscious of the
possibility of the electoral success of the Party', Jack Cooper told the
1963 Party Conference as mover of the planning and incomes policy
resolution. 'I firmly believe that one of the best guarantees of
success would be for a clear understanding to be achieved between the
Party and the Trade Union Movement before the election takes
place.'[56]

Union loyalty to the Party was an important factor in making this
a viable electoral strategy, but it was not the only one. By the early
sixties, the General Council – to use the phrase of one TUC official –
'had caught its breath' after the 1948–50 wages policy, as was indicated by its preparedness to engage in incomes policy discussions on
the NEDC, as well as by the TUC's first major post-war inquiry into
trade union structure and function.[57] There was, moreover, a growing
awareness inside the trade union movement that traditional collective bargaining had proved extremely limited in itself in effecting
changes in income distribution and pay relativities. Within the
working class, wage differentials had only slightly altered as between
the higher and low paid since the beginning of the century.[58] And as
between the classes, increasing doubt was being cast upon the claim
that significant income and wealth equalization had taken place.[59]
R. J. Nicholson, by studying Family Expenditure Surveys during the
1950s, found that income distribution (pre- and post-tax) showed the
same degree of inequality in 1959 as in 1953. And when he later
examined the national incomes and expenditure accounts, he found
that the overall distribution of pre-tax incomes showed no significant
change between 1957 and 1963, indeed the proportion going to the
bottom 30% of income recipients decreased slightly; in post-tax
incomes he found a marked shift towards more inequality after 1957.

Moreover, income from rents, dividends and interest had shown an accelerating rate of growth since the war, and after 1957 emerged as the most rapidly-growing sector of personal incomes.[60] In these circumstances some unions began to look favourably on suggestions for, incomes policies that would be redistributive in their effect, particularly as regards lower-paid workers.[61]

Therefore, when the Labour Party put their own version of the incomes policy to the unions it was unlikely to meet with immediate hostility; the form which it took would govern its acceptability. During the duration of the pause the Party limited itself to joining the unions in attacking the Government's action for its damage to established forms of negotiation and arbitration, for unfairly singling out the public sector and for combining the policy with general deflation. The most oft-repeated accusation was that the pay pause 'was calculated to divide rather than unite the nation', by not applying the policy to rents, profits and dividends as well as wages.[62] Positive support for the idea of an incomes policy did not really come until July 1962 when Gaitskell told the House of Commons that the pay pause had at least 'brought out into the foreground again, that there is a problem of an incomes policy. We all knew that there was in the 1940s until the problem was swept under the rug by the . . . [Conservative Government] who pretended that it had not existed for all these years.'[63] From this point forward the Party placed no little emphasis on coming to an agreement with the unions on the question.

The form which Labour's incomes policy proposals would take were outlined at this time by Gaitskell. He saw four essential conditions which had to be fulfilled if an incomes policy was to be successfully established. It had to be based on expanding production and productivity; it had to emerge from a voluntary agreement between both sides of industry; it had to be comprehensive, covering all sources of spending power; and it had to be applied fairly to all sections of the community.[64] Here was the foundation upon which James Callaghan, as Shadow Chancellor of the Exchequer, called for an incomes policy, at the 1962 Party Conference, as one of the pillars of Labour's plan for economic growth. It was a proposal which in its very conception was designed to secure trade union support. And the fact that Wilson, Callaghan, Brown and Peter Shore (Head of Research at Transport House at the time) sat on the Economic Committee of the TUC when it was responding to the Tory incomes policy gestures, gave them a 'feel' for the TUC position, a sense of what would be needed to appeal to the unions. Party leaders repeatedly guaranteed that the unions would have a real influence on policy formation under a

Labour Government [65] whose incomes policy, in any case, would emphatically not be one of wage restraint, but of keeping rising incomes in step with increasing production while at the same time achieving a fair distribution of the national income. Significantly, Callaghan assured union leaders that a Labour Government would not ask them to endanger themselves with their members:

> Trade union leaders can agree with the Government to try to restrain incomes . . . but there is no union leader in this country who can, in the end, override the basic wishes of those who elect him to his job. Therefore, what we have to do – and this is a gigantic essay in persuasion and cooperation – is to secure the assent of the whole nation to the idea of an incomes policy, that it is fair and that it will be equally applied, and then the trade union leaders of this country will find it possible to really represent as they will need to do, the views of their own members in cooperating with a Labour Government.[66]

The 1962 Conference was not asked to endorse an incomes policy. But immediately after this Conference the party set about consideration of the problem in earnest. Inside the Party, the Finance and Economic Policy Sub-committee of the NEC concerned itself with questions of economic policy and planning and discussed in this context the need for an incomes policy.[67] The Party also sponsored a number of informal 'experts' conferences for economists, businessmen, trade unionists and shadow Cabinet members, and one of these, in March 1963, considered the question of incomes policy. It is worth noting, in view of later developments, that Len Murray, then the head of the TUC's Economic Department and a co-opted member of the Party's Finance and Economic Policy Sub-committee, took the approach at these meetings that Party leaders and advisors were overrating the economic significance of an incomes policy, in terms of its possible short-term contribution to the balance of payments. He suggested as well that the problems which such a policy would create for the unions in terms of wage negotiations, had to be faced. If an incomes policy was desirable immediately, it was for political reasons, Murray argued. The trade unions did not deny the validity of these political reasons, but they would expect the Party to meet certain conditions of 'social justice' on its part.[68]

Not surprisingly, the Party leadership was primarily concerned with the political considerations. In discussions with union leaders they decided not to concentrate on the details of incomes policy, but on receiving agreement in principle on the need for a policy and a commitment from the unions to join with a Labour Government and employers organizations to work out an incomes policy. In March 1963 the Party issued an invitation to the TUC's Economic Committee to send representatives for a general exchange of views on economic matters with Party representatives. The first main topic of conversation concerned the machinery of planning itself, particularly the question of whether Labour's planning would emanate from an NEDC-type structure or whether it would be centred in a Government department. A meeting in July concerned itself with incomes policy. Although no formal agreement was reached, it was out of these discussions that acceptance of the 1963 Party Conference resolution on planning and incomes policy grew. The idea was floated at the meeting that what would be needed was agreement between Government, employers and unions on a norm which would then be adopted by the Government. But it was agreed that even this general formula begged more questions than it answered: criteria for exceptional cases and mechanisms for applying the criteria had to be developed. No specific *quid pro quos* in exchange for union participation were discussed.[69] But on the principle itself, the Labour Party secured from the unions the political agreement on incomes policy it needed for electoral purposes, and as a basis for discussion should it form the next Government. Labour's incomes policy was defined only in that it would apply to all incomes and that it meant not wage restraint, but 'the planned growth of incomes'. The latter phrase, coined by Cousins, was particularly important, and it reflected the assumption underlying the agreement that a Labour Government would introduce a period of rapid economic growth and expansion under which real wages would rise much faster than previously. It was carefully enshrined in the 1964 election manifesto.[70]

Party leaders used the agreement to good effect to demonstrate the influence a Labour Government would have over the unions. In a highly publicized address to the 1963 TGWU delegates conference, Harold Wilson said the next Labour Government would 'have to ask for restraint on the matter of incomes'. In as much as he reiterated that this would be combined with 'social justice' in taxation and social policies and would involve a rise in real wages, his statement was received with applause at what *The Times* called 'the high citadel of opposition to wage restraint'.[71] Repeatedly, Party leaders belaboured the point that the 'party of the pay-pause' could never secure union agreement to an incomes policy. 'The great weakness of the Conservatives is their failure to try to represent the nation.'[72] Wilson added to this image when he intervened with some success to help end the Port Talbot steel strike and the electricity supply strike in early 1964. 'To put it mildly,' *The Times* conceded, 'all this represents a fairly significant exercise when we remember how much importance Mr Wilson will be obliged to place, as Prime Minister, on trade union cooperation in the economic policies of his Administration.' [73]

Any attempt by the Party to have developed a deeper and more detailed agreement on incomes policy would have run the risk of endangering this political capital. Although a paper was presented to the NEC's Finance and Economic Policy Sub-committee in October 1963 which went into some detail on a norm and an Incomes Board, the ideas were not put to the unions, nor adopted for the Manifesto. And although several trade union leaders favoured a conference of trade union executives to work out the details of an incomes policy, this was not encouraged by Wilson.[74] For the agreement on principle in fact masked considerable differences. The debates on incomes policy at the 1963 and 1964 TUC suggested that a considerable body of trade union opinion understood the words 'measures of price control', which the 1963 TUC set down as one of the conditions for an incomes policy,[75] to involve much more than the promise in the Party Manifesto to strengthen the Monopolies Commission and review unjustified price increases. There was also an inherent contradiction in the definition of incomes policy adopted by the Party, (that equal treatment would be accorded to all forms of income, which would each rise broadly in accordance with productivity growth – this would obviously freeze the structure of income distribution) and the redistributive objectives of the Party and the TUC (particularly that wages be 'not only dependent on the level of productivity but also take cognizance of any effect resulting from the cost of living and the level of profits').[76] The Party, of course, included redistributive measures in its programme, particularly a capital gains tax and measures to block tax evasion, but these would be, as the Party Manifesto pointed out, supportive of an incomes policy, and not part of one.[77] The trade unions expected such limited measures from a Labour Government apart from any consideration of incomes policy and certainly did not regard them as *quid pro quos*. Moreover, if the incomes policy was going to be used to limit consumer demands, a redistribution of income to low-paid groups with a high propensity to consume would frustrate that purpose. As for specific measures within an incomes policy, a working party on taxation for the NEC's Finance and Economic Policy Sub-committee proposed in April 1964 an 'excess dividends levy' which would siphon off any increases in dividends greater than the percentage increase in wages and salaries after a given base year. This statutory scheme would have solved the problem, evident in 1948–50, that dividend increases can be postponed while wage claims, once foregone, are not recoverable.[78] But Wilson had made it clear in a TV Broadcast with five leading industrialists in January 1964 that he was opposed to statutory dividend limitation.[79]

Perhaps most significant were the differences *among* Party leaders about the voluntary nature of the proposed incomes policy and any changes in trade union functions that would have to accompany it. On his part, Wilson, in promising to change the Trade Disputes Act to protect the unions from the effects of the *Rookes v. Barnard* decision in 1964, publicly disparaged the idea of a Royal Commission to enquire into trade union functions, (which the TUC had indicated to the Conservative Government it would accept in exchange for action on *Rookes v. Barnard*).[80] Ray Gunter, the Shadow Minister of Labour, on the other hand, warned the trade unions that unless the required centralization of the trade union movement came about to bring authority and discipline, 'in seven to ten years time the State will have to intervene. Industrial courts with the authority of judicial courts, will be created and any dispute will have to be referred to them'.[81] This statement produced a very hostile reaction even among traditionally loyalist trade union leaders, usually careful of their criticisms of the Party in an election year.[82]

Given these differences, the political agreement on incomes policy between the Party and the unions was no mean accomplishment. It was founded largely on the ability of the Party leadership to convince union leaders, particularly Frank Cousins of the TGWU and others who shared his views, that a Labour Government would be involved in comprehensive planning of the economy in close consultation with the working class organizations. One of the two arguments for wages policy which appeared during World War II – a system of detailed economic planning which would supersede the profit motive and the market as a basis for economic decision-making – which was abandoned by 1948 in favour of the 'inflation under full employment' argument, now again served to attract union support for the planning of wages. A new leader of the Labour Party now came to the TUC and spoke of replacing 'a system of society where making money by whatever means is lauded as the highest service',[83] and argued elsewhere that the 'fundamental inspiration of our social life should be the age-old Socialist principle: from each according to his means, to each according to his needs'.[84] For union leaders like Cousins, as for the left wing group of MPs,[85] this meant that the question of a change in trade union functions could again be put on the agenda. Cousins told the 1963 Party Conference:

There is nobody here who can say what a level of wages is
for an individual worker, or the comparison between two
groups of workers, or the relative importance of a collective
group of workers to the community. We do not determine
them here, we determine them sitting opposite the employers; and we shall continue to do that until such time
as the system changes to ensure that we do get a better rate
of return for the labour that we put in, and nobody has any
doubt about this. Harold Wilson knows this: Harold says
this every time he gets the opportunity. He is wanting to be
part of a team that is going to change the system, and the
function of a trade union will change along with a change in
political function; it is bound to do so. I would suggest to
you, that one of the things we should always remember, is
that when we are putting a government in, as we are intending to do, to help us to plan the economy, we have the trust
that it is the same kind of economy they are helping to
create.[86]

These last words, coming, as they did, with the distinct prospect of
a return of a Labour Government, seemed at the time less important
than the unity the Conference displayed on incomes policy. Beneath
the surface, however, wide and important differences both within the
Party and within the TUC remained, and these differences could not
be ignored for the sake of unity for too long after a Labour Government took office. The 1964 TUC, less than two months before the
General Election, gave overwhelming support to an incomes policy
under a planned economy introduced by a Labour Government, but
it explicitly opposed an incomes policy which had wage restraint or
limitations on collective bargaining as its aim. It laid down the
further condition that a planned economy must include 'the extension of public ownership based on popular control on a democratic
basis at all levels'.[87] The economic growth theme that the Party had
adopted effectively covered over the split between the Party leadership and the unions that had developed over clause four and public
ownership after the 1959 election. But beneath a common acceptance
of economic planning and growth as a platform, the fundamental
differences that the clause four issue had revealed continued to persist. In sharp contrast with Cousins' concern with imperative planning, public ownership and 'changing the system', was the
Economist's support of Labour in 1964 on the basis of 'the need for
a central drive to make all firms much more profit conscious and
profit-seeking'.[88] The Labour Party had not in fact found a solution

61

to the problem that it faced in 1948–50, that of meeting demands to restrain profits, while at the same time trying to encourage private industry to greater investment. This point was made by the only speaker at the 1963 Conference who opposed the incomes policy demonstration but he was promptly silenced by Frank Cousins himself.[89] The function of an integrative political party is not to resolve the differences between the various demands it reflects, but to aggregate these demands in a way convincing enough to secure its objective of achieving political power. Any individual group which it integrates into the political system is likely to accept this aggregation on the premise that once the party secures power, its own demands will take precedence over conflicting demands to which the party is committed. This expectation was especially strongly felt by the British trade unions in the 1963–4 period.

3
The voluntary incomes policy agreement

Labour's 'new group politics'

Elected with a bare majority, the 1964 Labour Government inherited a balance of payments deficit of some £800 million, and a severe sterling crisis. The crisis strengthened the Government's resolve with regard to incomes policy. The key to faster economic growth was the competitiveness of Britain's exports; while no western economy had been successful in combining stable prices with a high level of economic growth and full employment, the problem for Britain, with its dependence on international trade, was particularly serious. A policy to check the rise in prices to improve Britain's trade position was thus essential to the Government's growth plans as well as to maintaining the value of sterling. The nature of such a policy was conditioned by the Government's view that the main cause of rising prices was 'the excessive expansion of money incomes'.[1] The Government was aware, of course, that this was too 'simpliste' an analysis. Since 1958, annual average wage earnings in manufacturing in Britain had risen more slowly than in any other western European country. The problem was that output also had risen more slowly than in these countries, a factor which made the increase in unit labour costs comparatively high.[2] The Government therefore also put considerable emphasis on the need for greater productivity, not as a substitute for wage restraint, but as a supplement to it.[3]

The Government ruled out devaluation and extensive deflation as immediate responses to the economic crisis and sought to rely on international loans to guarantee the value of the currency until the deficit could be overcome. It also ruled out a wage freeze, although five days after the election George Woodcock told the Government that he would be prepared to put the idea to the General Council and ventured the opinion that this would have a good chance of being accepted. He accompanied this offer, however, with his belief that the freeze would begin to erode immediately under the injustices it would cause and would kill any chance of securing TUC agreement to a long-term incomes policy.[4] The Government took note of this advice and opted instead for a permanent incomes policy developed in agreement with the Trade Union Congress and the employers organizations. Responsibility for the negotiations and for the incomes policy in general was assumed by the newly created Department of Economic Affairs with George Brown, the deputy leader of the Labour Party, at its head as First Secretary of State. The DEA was a product of the widespread feeling in the Labour Party (and particularly strongly shared by the unions) that economic policy had been too much subordinated in the past to orthodox Treasury concern with sterling and the balance of payments to the detriment of economic growth.[5] Of particular concern was the belief that the Treasury was unsuited by temperament and tradition, as well as by the Chancellor's already heavy burdens, for the close contact with industry which was considered a 'sine qua non' of both indicative economic planning and incomes policy. The hallmark of the DEA on the other hand, was to be 'good communications and mutual understanding' with industrialists and trade unions on economic planning, regional policy and the promotion of productivity.[6] The dividing line between the DEA's functions and those of the Treasury were vague, however, despite a 'concordat' between the two departments drawn up six weeks after the election. Control over public expenditure, monetary policy and the balance of payments remained with the Treasury, and since the Government intended to 'plan' mainly through financial inducements rather than use direct controls, this meant that effective control over policy remained with the Treasury, while the channels of contact between industry and government were developed via the DEA. Nevertheless, the influence of the DEA did not seem inconsiderable at the outset; it was responsible for 'coordinating the work of other Departments in relation to the plan',[7] and Brown at least saw the DEA as charged with developing the broad outlines and principles on which policy would be based; and even if the Prime Minister's interpretation – that of 'creative tension' between the two departments – was adopted, it was expected that the DEA would at least be equal to the Treasury (headed by Callaghan) in putting the case for growth inside the Government.[8]

Discussion on the development of the incomes policy began in early November. For the unions, the TUC alone was engaged, primarily the Economic Committee, and even more singularly, Woodcock himself. For private industry, the main bodies involved were the Federation of British Industry and the British Employers Confederation and, to a lesser extent, the National Association of British Manufac-

turers and the Association of British Chambers of Commerce. The
four men most intimately involved on the negotiations were Brown,
Woodcock, Sir Norman Kipping (FBI) and Sir George Pollock (BEC).
Immediately after the election, Woodcock had expressed the fear
that it would be 'very difficult, if not impossible', to establish an
effective incomes policy because business response to incomes policy
proposals was bound to be conditioned by uncertainty aroused by
the Government's small majority.[9] But these fears were unfounded.
The likelihood of any divided response by four business organizations
was lessened by the merger between the FBI, BEC and NABM into
one organization, the Confederation of British Industry, which took
place in June 1965, and which by late 1964 had already been set in
motion.[10] Moreover, as H. A. Clegg has noted of employer associations: 'When a pay policy is being introduced there is generally not
too much difficulty in persuading them to accept.' They are particularly attracted to an incomes policy because it is designed to lower
their labour costs. In addition, winning their consent is a simpler
matter technically than is the case with the unions: 'Far fewer people
are directly involved and most of the decisions are taken in private,
protected from the searchlight of publicity.'[11] These organizations
had supported the Conservative Government's attempts to secure
an incomes policy and in 1963–4 even made some concessions with
regard to the marginal inclusion of profits in the policy.[12]

The main obstacle to their agreement was Labour's commitment to
include prices, profits and dividends in the policy. But on closer
examination this proved to be not a very great barrier to business
agreement. For Brown immediately made it clear that the Government was not returning to an 'elaborate system of price control'. A
'more sensible way' of dealing with prices, as far as this Government
was concerned, was to establish an independent price review body to
report on a 'small and identifiable number' of key consumer prices
and manufacturing costs. As for profits and dividends, the price review body might also deal with cases where restraint on wages and
salaries was resulting in 'excessive growth of profits', but in general
the Government indicated that it intended to deal with them as had
the Conservative Government – not within the rubric of the incomes
policy, but by fiscal measures: 'We have to recognize that profits
differ in character from earned incomes since they arise as a residual
rather than a main element in costs, and therefore, are not the subject
of negotiation.'[13] This aversion to direct controls, evident in most
fields of policy, was welcome to private industry. Although some ill
feeling was created by Callaghan's announcement that the Government would go ahead with a capital gains tax and a reformed Cor-

poration Tax to encourage retained profits at the expense of dividends, the first effects of these changes were still eighteen months off in November 1964 and relations between business and the 1964 Labour Government were generally very good indeed.[14] Employers associations experienced more direct consultation with this Government than before,[15] and when they met with the DEA ministers they faced three eminently respectable Gaitskellites, all on the right of the Labour Party (Brown, Anthony Crosland and William Rodgers). Moreover, a number of leading industrialists went to work for the DEA immediately after the election, and had part of their salaries paid by their firms. The major point of criticism levelled by the business organizations at the time was that the economy was being run at a level of 'over-full employment', and that 'an incomes policy, though helpful, cannot be completely effective in an overheated economy'.[16] But this was a concern with regard to the maximum impact of the policy on wages, and did not affect the chances of employer agreement to it, although it was used to effect in their discussions with the DEA.

The main challenge for the Government, therefore, lay not in securing the agreement of the employers' organizations to an incomes policy, but in obtaining the cooperation of the TUC. The Government was aided by the same strong sense of trade union loyalty to the Labour Party that had been the basis of the pre-election incomes policy agreement. That this loyalty should have persisted despite the elaboration of Labour's national orientation is perhaps less paradoxical than it might seem at first sight. For although in terms of ideology and policy, the Labour Government could not be described as working class, particularly in view of the party's pointed appeal in 1964 to middle class voters, the Labour Government in a purely psephological sense was as much a working class government as were its predecessors. In 1964 social class remained the prime determinant of voting behaviour as between the parties.[17] There was an evident feeling on the part of the trade union leadership that it was trade unionists who had voted a Labour Government back into power and the Chairman of the TUC's Economic Committee was echoing the sentiments of his colleagues when he said: 'I believe we put the Labour Government back because we trusted it to do a job.'[18] In the sense of recruitment to political leadership, the working class element in the Parliamentary Labour Party had declined from 92% in 1918 to 32% in 1964.[19] But the major influx of middle class MPs came not in 1964 but in 1945 and the decline since then could simply have reflected the more general decline of manual as opposed to white-collar occupations and the greater availability of secondary education. The number of union sponsored MPs rose from 93 to 120 at the 1964 election and although some of these new recruits had little union experience as the GMWU and the TGWU broadened their sponsorship to include people without manual backgrounds, this was offset by the fact that the Trade Union Group remained the largest and potentially most powerful group in the PLP and included at least four MPs who combined major status in their unions with being an MP.[20] Of more significance was the marked declining trend in working class Cabinet membership. Out of a Cabinet of 18 in 1945, 9 Ministers were of working class occupational background, while out of a Cabinet of 21 in 1964 only 6 fell into this category.[21] In 1964, however, statistics of this sort were misleading. The really important decline occurred during the years after 1964 when working class Cabinet membership fell to 4 in 1966, 2 in 1967 and only 1 in 1968. The 1964 Cabinet at least maintained the tradition of working class recruitment, most significantly by including Frank Cousins as Minister of Technology. Brown himself had been a TGWU official until 1945 and a former chairman of the Trade Union Group of MPs, and while his 'credentials' as a trade union colleague were somewhat suspect in the eyes of the General Council, his persuasiveness lay in his ability to 'speak their language', as one TUC official put it, a trait the General Council found uniformly lacking in later Ministers responsible for the incomes policy.

The really important factor leading to the General Council's agreement lay not in the influence they expected to exert through the PLP or even through the Cabinet, but in the belief that the Labour Government finally would give effect to full TUC participation in policy making. This philosophy was developed most cogently by Woodcock. He believed the working class had gained more from the activity of the state in the economic and social field than by anything trade unions did themselves and his main interest was to secure a strong voice for the TUC in managing the economy, not so much in terms of detailed economic planning, as in the maintenance of full employment and the expansion of the welfare state. He held that such trade union influence would only be possible if they used their strongest bargaining card with the state, i.e. accepted responsibility to limit wage claims. Woodcock saw his job at the TUC as 'educating' member unions to this effect and his enthusiasm for income policy and for a Royal Commission on trade unions was based on his hope that it would redefine the functions of the trade unions in terms of participation in, and responsibility for, national economic and social policy.[22] The member of the General Council who had had most doubts about this approach (both in terms of questioning the benevolence of the state towards the working class in a capitalist society and in terms of the effects of collaboration with the state on trade union freedom) was Frank Cousins who was now a senior member of the Government and not directly involved in the incomes policy discussions. Now the General Council accepted Woodcock's approach almost to a man and there was a distinct hope on the part of the TUC hierarchy that the DEA would become the instrument of the trade unions inside the Government, not in the sense that all union views would be channelled through just this one Department, but in that they expected the DEA to be instinctively and temperamentally on the side of the trade unions in contrast to their experience with the Treasury.

Given this background, the incomes policy discussions were initiated with the best prospects of success. The General Council's predisposition to cooperate was strengthened moreover by the immediate economic crisis which created what John Corina has suggested is a pre-condition for such discussions – 'an extreme sense of incomes policy urgency'.[23] The way the Government responded to this crisis (in contrast to later responses) made a substantial impact on the General Council. Callaghan's autumn budget committed the Government to raise pensions and abolish NHS charges by April 1965 and to introduce a capital gains tax which Callaghan hoped would 'have a substantial effect on helping wage and salary earners in this country to accept the need for an incomes and prices policy'.[24] But these gestures were less important to the General Council than the fact that the Government had avoided a general deflation and rejected Woodcock's offer of a wage freeze. This seemed an important indication to the General Council of the difference between a Labour Government and a Conservative Government which the General Council believed would have jumped at the chance of a wage freeze endorsed by the TUC. In these circumstances Woodcock described the atmosphere at the November meeting of the General Council as one of 'enormous goodwill' towards the Government's bid for an incomes policy, combined with 'a willingness, perhaps an anxiety, to cooperate with the Government'.[25]

The development of the policy

The development of Labour's incomes policy proceeded in three stages: first, discussions on the principle of the policy, leading to an agreement embodied in the *Joint Statement of Intent* of 16 December 1964; second, discussions on the machinery under which the policy would operate, culminating in the White Paper, *Machinery of Prices and Incomes Policy* of 11 February 1965; and finally, discussions on the criteria of the policy, established in yet another White Paper, *Prices and Incomes Policy* of 8 April 1965. The whole process was completed in less than six months. These statements of Government policy were drafted in a unique way, which indicated the extra-parliamentary nature of the exercise. Whereas in the case of legislation, employers associations and the TUC were barred from seeing a draft of a Bill before publication and only the general content of the Bill would be indicated to them, both the employers associations and the TUC took part in the actual drafting of the Prices and Incomes White Papers, and although the first drafts were the DEA's, there were actual negotiations over whether particular phrases and provisions should be included. An introductory paragraph was inserted specifically noting that, while issued by the Government, the White Paper was the product of agreement with the TUC and the employers associations.

The *Statement of Intent* did not itself establish an incomes policy, but was the basis from which the policy grew. The Government, the TUC and 'Management' all agreed to 'take urgent and vigorous action to raise productivity throughout industry and commerce, to keep increases in money incomes in line with increases in real national output, and to maintain a stable general price level'. As a policy statement, the declaration of intent was too general to have much economic significance. As a publicity exercise, however, designed to launch the Labour Government's 'educational' campaign to persuade the trade union rank and file that their wage demands had to be moderated to take account of national economic objectives, to stress cooperation rather than conflict between employers and unions, it was unparalleled in its sphere. The Lancaster House ceremony where George Brown heralded the end of the class war, was broadcast on national television and featured in the press; 50,000 copies of the Statement, neatly set out in 'treaty' format, were dispatched immediately around the country to hang in factories and union offices. Sir George Pollock later referred to it as 'one of the most powerful propaganda weapons ever put in the hands of a government'.[26]

Immediately after the signing of the Statement of Intent, discussions began on the machinery of the policy. The General Council would have preferred this matter to have been left until 'the heart of the matter'[27] – the criteria of the policy – had been settled. Discussion of the machinery inevitably involved the question of the powers of the prices and incomes body, a question the General Council were reluctant to discuss before the body's functions and objectives were known. Brown, however, told them that he wanted to reach agreement on machinery first because he was anxious that investigations of particular price increases should begin as quickly as possible and that no complex terms of reference were needed for such investigations by the price review body.[28] Brown would argue at this time that 'the only point at which the endless circle of inflation can be broken is at the point of prices',[29] and in early January the Government wrote to a number of trade associations expressing their anxiety about price increases and, with an enthusiasm that marked his tenure at the DEA, Brown personally contacted the Chairmen of a few retail chains. The possibility of exerting some influence on prices on a less *ad hoc* basis by immediately putting a price review body into operation was of considerable appeal to the General Council. It would clearly be difficult for them to commit the trade unions to wage demands that matched the growth in productivity, if their real earnings were eroded by a rising cost of living. In the event, however, the General Council's expectations in this regard were unfulfilled and although the White Paper on Machinery was published on 11 February, the National Board for Prices and Incomes was not established until April when the criteria White Paper was published and the first price references did not go to the Board until May. 'On prices the Government appears to have had second thoughts about referring some increases to the board before criteria are agreed', the *Financial Times* reported on 12 February. 'The employers associations are understood to have swiftly put paid to that idea.'

The White Paper [30] announced that the Government would establish a National Board for Prices and Incomes which would investigate particular cases through a Price Review Division and an Incomes Review Division; the Government would retain direct responsibility for references to the Board. The Board was expected to avoid the pitfalls of its predecessor, the National Incomes Commission: it would report within two or three months on any reference, and instead of being composed solely of 'independent experts' expected to define the 'national interest', of which the TUC was highly suspicious in the past, it would include, apart from an independent chairman and a number of independent members, a businessman and a trade unionist and would also be assisted by panels of businessmen and trade unionists. The Board would be asked to examine cases of price rises and also cases where *prima facie* grounds for expecting price reductions existed both in the private and public sector; it would investigate claims and settlements relating to wage and salary increases, hours reductions and other conditions of work, and, more generally, cases where an overhaul of the pay structure seemed to be indicated for economic or social reasons, as well as the level of earnings in a whole industry or sector. Its functions *vis-à-vis* profits and dividends were left vague; it would be asked to investigate 'where appropriate, cases of increases in money incomes other than wages and salaries'.

The most important topic covered by the White Paper was that concerned with the question of whether the Government or the Board should have powers of compulsion in securing evidence or in enforcing its recommendations. In the case of wage restraint, the state can secure the response it desires in three ways: it can obtain voluntary cooperation of the unions; it can apply legal directives and sanctions with regard to their wage policies; or it can place legal restrictions on the general operations of the unions, either by strengthening them *vis-à-vis* their membership or by limiting the right to strike. The Labour Government at first accepted the voluntary approach.[31] This was partly a matter of Party doctrine, infused by the British trade union movement's philosophy of voluntarism and belief in the right to free collective bargaining. The small majority of the Government in any case made a policy that involved legislation risky. Moreover, there were distinct limits to what legal sanctions could be expected to achieve, at least in a society which continued to permit certain basic political freedoms. A mass strike in defiance of the law is always difficult to deal with and fining or gaoling strike leaders does not guarantee the end of a strike nor prevent emergence of sympathetic strikes. In order for legal sanctions to operate effectively, mass acquiescence is required and for this to be secured an invaluable ally is the TUC itself which can give legitimation to such sanctions.[32]

The Government did not rule out, however, the possibility of legislative sanctions in the future. Indeed, Government spokesmen at times adopted a rather novel interpretation of the term 'voluntary'. It sometimes was defined as a policy without any government sanctions at all while at other times as a policy with government controls and sanctions, but endorsed by the TUC and thus 'voluntary'.

> It is possible that as times goes by, if the policy is not working on a voluntary basis [Definition One], both sides of industry may think there is some further step which could be taken which was not so contrary to the whole spirit and principle of the way things have been done in this country that they would rule it out. But this is quite a way off at the moment, and in the present position I do not see any prospect of continuing a voluntary policy – and by voluntary I mean a

policy by agreement [Definition Two] – which contained the power to fix wages absolutely.[33]

Thus even a policy with powers to 'fix wages absolutely' might have been presented by the Government as a 'voluntary' policy, provided the TUC agreed to such powers. In fact the Government was at no time interested in such powers (except temporarily during a wage freeze); this would have involved a return to direct controls which it had already abjured in the field of prices. It was later to use this definition of 'voluntary', however, with regard to statutory powers to *delay* wage settlements.

Nevertheless, at the beginning of 1965, the Government employed the first definition of the term voluntary and proposed moreover to give the policy a chance to operate on that basis. The Board itself would not be set up as a statutory body, but by Royal Warrant as a Royal Commission and both the CBI and the TUC would be expected to secure the voluntary cooperation of their members with Board investigations and to advise them on the application of the policy.[34] The White Paper was based on the principle of equality of treatment for prices in this regard. The General Council realized, of course, that if the Board were established by statute it could have been given substantial powers in the collection of evidence, for instance, to compel a firm to produce its accounts.[35] The employers organizations, however, were vehemently opposed to giving the Board such powers [36] and the Government, despite war-time and post-war precedents, was not prepared to differentiate between prices and wages. In what was perhaps the most significant of its decisions, the General Council, despite the TUC's traditional refusal to consider prices and wages comparable with regard to state control and its consistent demands for price controls throughout the post-war period, accepted this equality of treatment, although it did look to future price controls if voluntary price restraint did not work.[37] But the White Paper itself made no such differentiation between prices and wages with regard to future developments.

Rather prophetically, Peter Jenkins at the time was moved to quote Schopenhauer: 'It is wise to anticipate compulsion by self control'.[38] But there is little doubt that the General Council was convinced of the Government's commitment to the voluntary approach. The key to future policy lay in the definition of the word 'failed' and the White Paper seemed to give the TUC an entirely new basis of power with regard to determining the success or failure of the voluntary policy. The General Council were adamant that this task should fall to the NEDC, which it saw as 'sufficiently representative of the various interests within the community to be able, whenever necessary, to define the national interest'.[39] And in this respect, the White Paper seemed to meet the General Council's demands by assigning to the NEDC the function of 'ascertainment, interpretation and assessment of the relevant facts about general price and income behaviour' and of considering 'their implications for the national interest'.[40] It was to prove one of the bitterest sources of disenchantment for the TUC that the NEDC never did acquire this directive function over the incomes policy. It was perhaps one of the fundamental misconceptions of the General Council's belief in 'the new group politics' to expect a body like the NEDC to play such a role. The NEDC might indeed attempt to 'define the national interest' but it lacked the power to implement its decisions, which the Government might choose to either accept or ignore. A much more accurate description of where the final power of decision lay with regard to the assessment of the policy's operations was found in that line of the *Statement of Intent* which referred to 'the national interest as defined by the Government after consultation with Management and Unions'. Thus, the influence of the TUC would not rest on the functions the NEDC assumed in relation to incomes policy, but on the importance the Government attached to the TUC's advice and cooperation.

At this point, however, the Government were indeed stressing the importance of the NEDC's role and when Brown made it clear to the February meeting of the Council that it would be the chief forum for evolving the criteria of the policy in the next stage of the discussions,[41] it was perhaps not surprising that the General Council expected this role to be a permanent one. The White Paper, *Prices and Incomes Policy* [42] was published on 8 April and with its publication, the incomes policy edifice was complete. Its first concern was to establish a national 'norm' for wage increases. Using the National Plan's target figure of 25% for the growth of real output by 1970, the White Paper assumed an annual rate of growth of $3\frac{1}{2}\%$, although during the early years the rate was expected to be somewhat below this figure. The norm for increases in incomes was therefore set at 3 to $3\frac{1}{2}\%$. Given perfect price stability, a rise in incomes of this order would compare favourably with the rise of about 2% in real incomes during the 1950s. The norm was expected to apply not just to wage rates but to total earnings and it was to be given more weight in the determination of wages and salaries than considerations of changes in supply and demand for labour, trends in productivity and profits, comparisons with other incomes and changes in the cost of living. Obviously such a major transformation in bargaining habits would not only be impossible overnight, but also would be patently unjust by freezing the distribution of income. It might also, as the White Paper suggested, inhibit structural changes necessary for faster growth. The White Paper therefore laid down a number of grounds for increases in pay above the norm, 'bearing in mind that they will need to be balanced by lower than average increases to other groups if the increases in wages and salaries over the economy as a whole is to be kept within the norm'. Exceptional pay increases were confined to the following circumstances:

> (i) where the employees concerned, for example by accepting more exacting work or a major change in working practice, make a direct contribution towards increasing productivity in the particular firm or industry. Even in such cases some of the benefit should accrue to the community as a whole in the form of lower prices.
> (ii) where it is essential in the national interest to secure a change in the distribution of manpower ... and a pay increase would be both necessary and effective for this purpose;
> (iii) where there is general recognition that existing wage and salary levels are too low to maintain a reasonable standard of living;
> (iv) where there is widespread recognition that the pay of a certain group of workers has fallen seriously out of line with the level of remuneration for similar work and needs in the national interest to be improved.[43]

What was significant about these criteria was that, apart from the rather vague exceptions for the low paid, the question of a more egalitarian distribution between earned and unearned income was entirely left out of the scope of the policy.[44] Dividends went unmentioned, and fiscal policy was called upon to deal with 'any excessive growth of aggregate profits'. Insofar as the policy was expected to impinge on profits, it was through the prices side. The considerations affecting prices were not meant to lay down detailed rules governing price behaviour but to provide 'general guidance . . . for deciding whether individual price decisions are consistent with national objectives'. Individual enterprises were expected not to raise their prices except where there had been an increase in total costs per unit of output (including increases in labour costs consistent with the incomes criteria) and these increases could not be offset by a reduction of other costs or in the return sought on investment. If any of these costs were falling per unit of output or if profits and dividends were based on excessive market power, firms would be expected to reduce their prices. At the same time, however, the White Paper provided that price rises would be justified where an enterprise was unable to secure the capital required to meet home and overseas demand 'after every effort had been made to reduce costs', and that the 'vigorous and efficient enterprise' could reasonably expect a higher level of profit than one that was not. In the case of prices and profits, therefore, the White Paper did not establish a 'norm' for the rate of return on investment which would provide a standard for conduct. It left a wider scope than for wages for corporate self-justification for its voluntary behaviour and a more difficult task of definition for the NBPI on those price references sent to it. Although the TUC had expressed its concern from the beginning on this, the Labour Government nevertheless managed to secure its consent to an incomes policy with surprisingly few concessions to traditional demands from the labour movement for restrictions on prices and profits. 'As long ahead as we can see', Brown told an Institute of Directors meeting, 'Britain is going to have a mixed economy with a very large private enterprise sector. Therefore the profit motive has a very important role to play. It is time we stopped being silly or doctrinaire on all this.' [45]

The final touches to the policy were added by the Government's appointments to the NBPI. Most significant was the appointment of Aubrey Jones as Chairman.[46] Jones had been a Conservative MP since 1950 and a Conservative Minister in the 1955 Government; he was a Director of Guest, Keen and Nettlefolds (GKN) and Chairman of Stovely Industries. The appointment did produce some opposition in the labour movement, notably from one of the Government's staunchest supporters, John Boyd of the AEU, who at the March meeting of the Labour Party NEC described Jones as 'an enemy of the Party and of the working class'.[47] But as a member of the Bow Group, with a widespread image in Whitehall as a 'progressive' and a 'radical', and with views in the early sixties which markedly paralleled that of the Labour Party leadership on the value of indicative planning and a state-induced 'technological breakthrough', Jones was not at all an unlikely candidate for the appointment.[48]

Aubrey Jones had maintained a remarkable consistency over the years with regard to the neo-corporatist philosophy upon which an incomes policy is based. In view of his importance to Labour's incomes policy, his views deserve to be quoted at length:

> The classic remedy for the labourer's plight, trade unionism, in fact solves only part of his troubles . . . It was never calculated to bridge the gap that had grown between employers and employed; it served rather to widen it and to exacerbate

the strife between the two sides. For trade unionism itself
became infested with the doctrine that the struggle of the
classes was something inevitable; this struggle was looked
upon – wrongly – as scrawling itself across the whole of
history; and the more inevitable it is accepted to be, the more
implacable and inevitable does it become.

... [Union] irresponsibility can be overcome only if labour
is made to feel that it has the same purpose as capital, and
that, while they remain rivals, their rivalry is subordinated
to a unity. That, after all, is the first condition of a healthy
society – that there is unity, that within it there are rivalries,
but that they do not disrupt it.[49]

When this was written in 1950, Jones had hoped to find a solution
to conflict in joint production committees: 'Authority remains with
the employer; it is he who still controls. But those who are controlled
are taken into his confidence; their views are solicited; and so the
control, by becoming less of an imposition, is made to operate more
effectively.' By 1965 he saw a solution in union–employer cooperation
in a productivity, prices and incomes policy. In 1950, Aubrey Jones
believed that only a Conservative Government with 'the key to Conservative doctrine – to uphold the unity of the nation', could overcome class conflict, at least until 'the traditional Socialist attitude
towards the private employer [had been] reversed'.[50] But by 1965,
while not relinquishing his membership of the Conservative Party,
he had come to believe that a Labour Government had proved deserving of support in its efforts to subordinate conflict to national unity.
As he explainted upon his appointment:

The party system which we have inherited in this country is
unfortunately founded on class. As a result it is difficult for a
Conservative government to speak to the trade unions and
difficult for a Labour government to speak to employers. I
was being called upon, it seemed to me, as one who might
overcome the rigidities in the present party system and if I
were able to do this, I might be able to deflect British politics
on to a new course.[51]

Trade union support and opposition

The assent the General Council had given to the incomes policy was
of considerable importance to its implementation but, given the
absence of centralized power in the TUC, was not enough. What the

policy now needed was the assent of those who were expected to apply the policy to themselves – the individual trade unions. Ministers embarked on a series of addresses to trade union conferences, the common theme being 'this is no longer the era for trade union militancy'.[52]

In the six months during which the incomes policy discussions were held, there had been virtually no public opposition from individual unions. Even those unions most critical of wage restraint adopted a wait and see attitude. In January the TGWU executive decided to reserve its position regarding the development of the policy, and although reaffirming 'complete opposition to wage restraint', the union featured a front page photo of Brown holding the *Statement of Intent* in the February issue of the *Record*, combined with a laudatory lead editorial.[53] At a conference of forty-six white collar unions in February an attempt by ACTAT to begin a critical discussion of the General Council's support for the policy was supported by neither DATA nor ASSET, and was quickly snuffed out.[54] The first main test of union reaction was the Conference of Executive Committees of unions affiliated to the TUC on 30 April 1965, the first such conference since the one in 1950 which scuttled the last instance of TUC cooperation in a wage restraint policy.

The conference revealed widespread trade union support for the policy, and endorsed the General Council's report by 6,649,000 votes to 1,811,000 votes. The AEU, GMWU, NALGO, NUM, ETU, NUR, the Woodworkers, Printers and Seamen, all voted for the policy. The TGWU alone contributed two-thirds of the votes against, although it was joined by a number of smaller unions including the Boilermakers, ASLEF, Civil Service Union, Sheet Metal Workers and a group of white collar unions, (ASSET, DATA, ACTAT, and the Scientific Workers and the Technical Civil Servants). Moreover, the conference marked the emergence of a new 'triumvirate' in the trade union movement made up of William Carron of the AEU, Jack Cooper of the GMWU and Les Cannon of the ETU. Without the TGWU in its ranks, this 'triumvirate' was obviously less powerful than its predecessor, but it was, if anything, even more strongly committed to ensuring that trade union conference votes should show unqualified support for the Labour Government. The assertion that predominance be given to loyalty to the Government was particularly evident in the AEU. At the beginning of April a circular was sent to all union branches and district committees reminding them of a 1949 union ruling that 'any expression of the view of the union must emanate from the executive' on the grounds that in the event of direct branch or rank and file communication with Ministers, the

Government 'would receive many conflicting ideas on policy'.[55] During the thirteen years of Conservative Government the ruling had been ignored by the executive. The pattern for AEU votes at TUC and Labour Party conferences was set at the April 1965 National Committee (the union's annual conference) when support for the incomes policy was obtained not from a resolution in favour of the policy itself but by a resolution pledging 100% support for the Labour Government.[56] Cooper placed a similar premium on loyalty and when he was later elevated to the House of Lords, he became known among critics of the policy as the first 'Incomes Policy Peer'. Cannon, a vociferous opponent of the 1948–50 wages policy when a young Communist militant,[57] had, after spearheading the attack on the Communist leadership of the ETU in 1962 for ballot rigging, emerged as a strident proponent of both incomes policy and anti-communism. Without fail he looked upon incomes policy votes at union conferences as votes of confidence in the Government.

The concern with loyalty to the Labour Government, and through it to the nation, was clear from the speeches at the Conference of Executives. The Chairman, Lord Collison, urged unions to respond to 'the most significant [conference] the unions have ever held' by 'recognizing that trade unionism is an important and indispensable part of the nation'. The tone was set by John Boyd: 'I was glad when George Brown said that what our Government needs is loyalty; not blind loyalty, let me add, but intelligent loyalty, imagination and faith.' [58] So widespread was this feeling that Woodcock was concerned that the vote should not be seen as merely an expression of loyalty but as a commitment to the terms and conditions of the policy itself: 'an incomes policy must be seen to be and accepted as being a natural and sensible thing to do, not as something artificial drawn out by loyalty to a political party'.[59]

There was indeed evidence that the unions were supporting the policy on these other grounds as well. Speaker after speaker spoke of their desire to break out of the circular experience of wage increases chasing price increases. What they wanted, they said, were increases in real wages and this Brown was offering them. At a GMWU meeting a few days before the conference, he had spoken as if price stability were assured: 'Achievement of the national growth target combined with price stability will mean that a man earning £16 a week in 1964 will be able to earn £20 a week in 1970. The extra £4 will be not simply a paper increase which enables him to maintain his standard in the face of rising prices, but an increase of 25% in his real spending power.' [60] He assured the Executives that this was not a policy of wage restraint: 'It has nothing in common with the wage restraint policies of previous Conservative Governments.' [61] And apart from the general appeal this had for all unions, there was the specific appeal of the 'social justice' aspect of the policy to unions with large numbers of low paid members.

Most important perhaps were the guarantees the unions thought they had that the policy would not impinge on their bargaining freedom. Brown told the conference that the policy's impact would be gradual and that the Government would only look at sanctions if there was a widespread flaunting of the Board's advice; this, given the fact that no references had yet been made, implied a considerable period of grace. Woodcock admitted that employers would use the norm against the unions in bargaining but beyond that the only sanctions brought against those who exceeded the norm 'excessively' would be public pressure.

> This, Mr Chairman, is not a plan; it is not even a policy; let us not make any false claims for what we are about. These words 'plan' and even 'policy' are much too grandiloquent to describe what we have been about and what we are putting before you today. A policy may come out in time but this is only the first cautious, tentative step in that direction.[62]

He did not expect, he said, wages to be kept down to $3\frac{1}{2}\%$ in 1965. All the norm immediately involved was 'a standard of good conduct' which the General Council itself would use to test 'good trade unionists'. 'Nobody should think that we will attempt to impose sanctions on any trade union officers who go on for a claim above the norm. We are not going to fine them or send them to prison. We cannot do that.' If the question of sanctions had been of any importance in the earlier discussions with the Government, there was no hint of it here.

The support given by the conference to the policy marked, ironically, the high water mark of trade union *voting* support. (The height of practical industrial compliance with the policy came later, during the wage freeze of 1966.) It is therefore particularly important to understand the grounds on which the policy was opposed by those unions voting against it at the conference. For these unions formed the bedrock of opposition to which was added eventually the votes of the other unions. The TGWU's position was by far the most significant. Although the union's Acting General Secretary, Harry Nicholas, had reflected his executive's disquiet with the policy at the March meeting of the General Council,[63] the union's executive did not actually decide to vote against the policy until the conference itself, when an open exchange between Nicholas and Woodcock sealed the executive's inclination to oppose. Ever since Cousins' election in 1956, the TGWU had led the TUC's opposition to wage restraint and had been the most sceptical about Woodcock's belief in indicative planning and the TUC's potential power via consultation. Nevertheless the union's opposition to incomes policy had softened, albeit reluctantly, as the prospect of the return of a Labour Government loomed larger and Cousins himself had coined the phrase 'the planned growth of incomes'. As Cousins' successor, Nicholas did not share Cousins' position on the left of the Labour Movement; also, the executive was deeply loyal to the Labour Government (all the more so now that Cousins was a Minister), and a majority of the union's officials, mostly appointed by Deakin, were in favour of supporting the policy.[64] It was, therefore, by no means clear at the outset that the TGWU would refuse to give the incomes policy its blessing.

The most influential figure in the union, however, was not Nicholas, but Jack Jones although he did not actually succeed to the leadership until 1969. Jones shared Cousins' scepticism about indicative planning and his total opposition to wage restraint. His political ideas had been formed as a political education officer in the Attlee Brigade in Spain and by a close association with the Marxist-oriented National Council of Labour Colleges during the 1940s. Although never a member of the Communist Party, he was identifiably on the left of the Labour Party and, unlike Cousins, closely associated with *Tribune*. Most important, however, was his experience as Union District Secretary in Coventry and later as Regional Secretary in the Midlands car industry where during the 1940s he had been closely involved in establishing a strong element of shop steward control over piece rates, overtime and the work process. For Jack Jones, the test of effective trade union action was the extent to which it did not hamper the conduct of this shop-floor bargaining.

The TGWU's opposition reflected this view in stressing that the central function of trade unions – wage bargaining – must not be diminished. But this 'economist' conception was buttressed with a political theory (rarely developed elaborately but which consistently came to the surface) of the role of the trade union and of the state in a capitalist society. Essentially the theory was that propounded by Cousins at the TUC since 1956 – that wages could not be planned outside a planned economy, and that the latter meant not indicative planning but a considerable extension of public ownership and control. The maxim most often quoted at Transport House (the TGWU wing, that is) was the question Bevin used to oppose wage controls during the war: 'Can you fix maximum wages whilst one section works for another's profits?'[65] The TGWU was unimpressed by the

Labour Government's essay in indicative planning. Nicholas was reflecting this aspect of the union's approach when he told the Donovan Commission:

> We could see that if there happened to be an extension of public ownership then the power to determine incomes quite fairly and accurately would have been a starter, but you have no control . . . over certain people's incomes whatsoever . . . if we were given the opportunity of having a completely planned economy, if in this way prices could be rigidily controlled . . . we would be facing completely different circumstances, and we would have a different attitude.[66]

In the existing economic structure, the TGWU held, in direct contrast to Woodcock, that the State had not been impartial as between capital and labour in the post-war period. Jack Jones believed that the State, through its role as an employer of labour and through the coverage of some $4\frac{1}{2}$ million workers via the Wage Councils, already controlled the level of wages of the lowest-paid workers and had been found wanting in its benevolence.

It is important to recognize that this political theory did not provide the grounds for political militancy; what it did do was provide the ideological justification for economic militancy. In other words, its effect on union policy was not to give first priority to a political campaign for public ownership and economic planning, but, given the absence of these political conditions, to encourage the strengthening of trade union organization and the spread of collective bargaining as 'the surest way to establish social justice in this country and to remove the inequalities in earnings between one group of workers and another'.[67] Therefore the first political demand of the union was to abolish the incomes policy which obstructed trade union militancy:

> The one hope for the low-paid workers was that a Labour Government would use its powers and prestige to help extend trade union organization. Instead of doing this, both post-war Labour Governments have imposed incomes policies, which, far from extending trade union organization, have positively discouraged it . . . Who, after all, wants to join a union when it is no longer free to bargain for higher wages? One of the most pernicious effects of Government-controlled incomes policies is that at the end of them, the workers are worse organized than before, and the low paid

workers remain more dependent still on the cold charity of Whitehall bureaucracy.[68]

This low-level political strategy was a product both of the fact that trade union leaders saw themselves first as trade unionists and only second as political actors, and of their pessimistic view of the possibilities of converting the Labour Government (to which they remained loyal) to socialist economic planning in the foreseeable future. And remaining loyal to the Labour Government, they stressed the importance of its abandoning the incomes policy in the Government's own interest. Thus they combined a concern that the effects of the 1948 policy on TGWU organization should not be repeated, with a concern that the Labour Government should not suffer the same defeat it did in 1951, a defeat which they attributed to its wages policy.[69]

Given the fact that the TGWU was attacking the incomes policy, and not the Labour Government itself, the union's criticisms of the policy at the conference were particularly specific: a high wage economy, it was argued, would provide the incentive towards the greater productivity the Government wanted; if the norm applied to total labour costs, including fringe benefits, those who already had good fringe schemes would have an advantage; the cost of living increase ought to be added to the norm if real wages were to increase by 3 to $3\frac{1}{2}\%$ in 1965; dividends were left out of the policy; price increases would be examined by the Board after the fact, while wage claims would be referred before a settlement was reached. Nor was the TGWU impressed with the 'social justice' aspect of the policy, as Nicholas pointed out: 'If the workers in the higher-paid industries accept the need to restrain wage advances, how does the money saved become transferred to workers in the lower-paid industries to enable them to remove some of the wage disparities that exist? Does the Government possess the means to direct finance, say, from the car industry to the bus industry to subsidize the low earnings in that industry?'[70] All the points were put as specific questions to Woodcock, who of course could not answer them except to say that the policy would work flexibly and to argue that the TGWU were not themselves offering an alternative way to get off the wage–price treadmill.[71]

In contrast to these specific criticisms made by the TGWU, the leaders of those white collar unions opposed to the policy dwelt on the more general policies of the Labour Government: the continuing high level of military expenditure, the unequal distribution of wealth, the commitment to maintain a predominantly private-enterprise economy.[72] They took the position that it was not so much the incomes policy to which they were objecting as to the effects it would inevitably have on wages and salaries in a capitalist economy. Their opposition more than in the case of the TGWU, was related to the fact that they were organizing and representing the technical and managerial sectors for which the novel attraction of trade unionism was an economic militancy which could find little place inside the incomes policy. But an explanation of these unions' dissent which stopped at this structural explanation would be inadequate. NALGO, in much the same position structurally, felt able to endorse the policy, while adding the proviso that they expected their members to qualify for exception.[73] The main factor here was that NALGO was prepared to endorse the political nature of the agreement, while these other white collar unions were not. In the case of the latter an important conjunction of factors has to be considered. First, these unions did not have to take account of the strong pull which the appeal to loyalty to a Labour Government exercised over the members of the manual unions. But at the same time, they had thrown up a leadership which was in British terms highly politically conscious, on the left of the Labour Party (and in DATA's case often outside the Labour Party on the left), and not itself conventionally loyal to the moderate Labour Party leadership. Thus the low levels of Labour Party commitment on the part of their members was *combined* with a markedly left-wing ideology on the part of the leadership and produced particularly fertile ground for opposition to the incomes policy. They could argue, as DATA did, that their first concern was political and their industrial concerns were secondary: '*Our primary argument,* and one that is maintained consistently, is that frankly we honestly believe, and with integrity, that in the present economic conditions with the present distribution of ownership, of responsibility for industry, it would not be in the interests of our members to support an incomes policy.' It was only '*a secondary point,* but one of some importance, that our members' position is still unsatisfactory, the position of the technician is unsatisfactory'.[74] No doubt, a government which had met their counter-proposals but still stressed a narrowing of differentials would have posed problems for these white collar trade union leaders. But as matters stood, they felt they faced no dilemma.

Despite this opposition, the Conference of Executives launched the voluntary incomes policy with a significant political victory. Of course, while voting in favour of the policy, many of the trade unions also endorsed a number of criticisms levelled against it, particularly the specific criticisms made by the TGWU, but they assumed that the flexibility of the policy would allow them to overcome those elements of the policy they disliked. Industrially, in other words, the voluntary policy had still to be tested. But few union leaders expected that by the time of the annual Congress, just four months later, they would be asked to endorse a statutory policy.

4
The devaluation of voluntarism

The move towards statutory powers

The voluntary incomes policy was marked, from the beginning, by an inherent instability. The Retail Price Index in mid-April 1965 had shown a rise of four points since the election, the largest rise for a half-year since 1952.[1] Moreover, the Chancellor's April budget substantially increased indirect taxation which gave a further impetus to price increases. Insofar as Brown was correct in his expectation that price stability could create 'the only climate in which we can hope to get an incomes policy'[2] the policy was beginning to operate in inauspicious circumstances. An additional justification for wage claims above the norm lay in the fact that dividend payments, the fastest growing sector of incomes since the war, had increased in the first quarter of 1965 by 28% above the previous year as companies anticipated the effects of the new corporation and capital gains taxes.[3] Finally, apart from the effects of these developments on newly-framed wage claims, there were before April 1965 wage commitments and settlements for some 10 million workers which had not been governed by the norm; these forward commitments accounted for about half of the total increase in hourly wage rates in 1965.[4] In these circumstances, many of the policy's trade union adherents submitted claims for increases above the norm. Indeed, the NUR's President, S. J. Greene, later told the Donovan Commission that the trade union movement had never accepted the $3\frac{1}{2}$% norm. If he voted for it, it was only 'because some experts told me it is mathematically correct to get a 25% growth by 1970'.[5] And as the NBPI later commented: 'Events since the Statement of Intent was formulated have shown . . . that there was a wide gulf between the leaders of the representative organizations and their constituents about the real implications of the undertakings which were signed on their behalf.'[6] The Board was referring here to the behaviour of individual unions and firms, but the statement was true of Government itself which justified a pay award to post-office workers in April 1965 on the grounds that it allowed postmen to catch up with comparable wages in other industries, and which increased the pay of judges by 25% in July on the same grounds despite their already high incomes.

The Government, however, did not itself expect, as the policy went into operation, that pay increases in 1965 would be limited to $3\frac{1}{2}\%$. Roy Jenkins, in a speech a few days before the April Conference of Executives said the policy was never expected to deal with wage settlements already 'in the pipeline'.[7] Indeed the DEA indicated that it had 'not expected that the policy would have much effect on the level of pay settlements in 1965'.[8] Moreover, had the Government chosen to dwell on it, there was some important evidence that the policy was affecting the level of wage claims. While union leaders may have felt unable to make wage demands consistent with the norm, the policy often had a bearing on the extent to which they exceeded the norm, and on their readiness to accept delays in prosecuting a claim. The policy achieved one of the first successes at the April 1965 USDAW annual conference where a resolution for an immediate pay claim of £2 was defeated.[9] Nor was this kind of response confined only to those unions in favour of the policy. The TGWU's opposition, for instance, was by no means total. It decided to cooperate with the NBPI on references, and moreover, since it conducted much of its bargaining in conjunction with unions in favour of the policy, it was influenced by their attitude in framing wage claims, particularly since the the majority of its officials privately supported the policy. In fact, the TGWU was supported by the Minister of Labour, Ray Gunter, in its opposition to an unofficial strike at London Airport against the union's wage moderation:

> These men have flatly contradicted their own union and they pour their spleen on ordinary folk. This is just irresponsibility. This is sheer viciousness. These men have the power to disrupt the lives of good people. These good people may, ere long, say they have had enough and are not going to be pushed around any longer, and they will have all my support.[10]

The threat implicit in Gunter's attack was first directly related to the incomes policy immediately after Callaghan returned from a meeting with Joe Fowler, the American Secretary of the Treasury, on 29 June in Washington where new stand-by credits for sterling were discussed. Callaghan said: 'So far this year, incomes have gone up far too fast, and I want to warn the country about it; they are going up faster than productivity. The $3\frac{1}{2}\%$ normal increase agreed in the

86

declaration of intent is as much as we can afford. But it is being exceeded, and if pressure for higher increases is successful then higher prices will follow in due course as surely as night follows day.'[11] On 22 July, Brown revealed that he was holding discussions with management and unions with a view to strengthening the existing policy, but by the end of July, Ministers were suggesting that, while the voluntary policy could not yet be said to have failed, statutory controls were being considered. Gunter told the House of Commons on 28 July that statutory 'alternatives' were in store if the voluntary system failed, although 'that is unpleasant action within a free society'.[12] On 2 August, Wilson went into greater detail. He pointed to Swedish incomes policy which 'took twenty years to evolve', refused to 'dismiss ours as a failure after only three months', and admitted the 'enormous political difficulties involved in placing statutory limitations on free collective bargaining'. But he warned that if the voluntary system did fail, the Government 'might have to provide for statutory reference of every claim for increased incomes to an expanded and strengthened Prices and Incomes Board'.[13]

By the end of August the Government asked the TUC and CBI to endorse legislation to introduce statutory controls. Yet, as Wilson indicated, the policy could hardly have been adjudged a failure at this stage. When the Government began publicly entertaining the idea of legislation the NBPI had reported on only one reference, an interim Report on Road Haulage Rates on 28 June,[14] and Brown had been successful in persuading the Road Haulage Association to accept the Board's main recommendations. The Board did indeed experience in this case a degree of non-cooperation from firms in replying to its requests for information and the Government itself was finding it difficult to secure adequate information on price decisions with a view to possible reference to the Board (it was in fact largely relying on press reports at this stage).[15] But this seemed to suggest a strengthening of the system with regard to prices alone. The Government had intended that the Board's judgements should establish a body of 'case law' which would serve as a guide for voluntary self-restraint by the unions,[16] but as yet not one wages precedent was on the books.

In fact when the Government came to consider legislation to strengthen the incomes policy, it was mainly (although not publicly) questioning not the success or failure of the voluntary policy in the few months of its operation, but the wisdom of its original decision to seek a voluntary policy at all. In a sense the statutory development was implicit in the voluntary policy from the beginning, as we have seen, but the fact that this development came so early was directly related to the fact that British policy decisions were, in this period of large balance of payments deficits and reliance on foreign loans to maintain the value of sterling, heavily subject to influence from those Governments and Central Banks which were Britain's creditors. Wilson himself had realized this would be the case: 'You can get into pawn, but don't then talk about an independent foreign policy, or an independent defence policy . . . If you borrow from some of the world's bankers you will quickly find you lose another kind of independence because of the deflationary policies and the cuts on social services that will be imposed on a government that has got itself into that position.'[17] It was one of the deeper ironies of the Labour Government that it did place itself in this position: in seeking to maintain the value of the pound by relying on foreign loans and abjuring a radical departure from previous form to deal with the pound's weakness, Wilson's warning, issued before the election, became a fair characterization of the Labour Government itself. This is not to say that foreign creditors continually dictated British policy in any crude way. Indeed, it would be more accurate to say that the Government eventually came to share the diagnosis and cure proffered by its creditors.

The external pressure generally took the form of demands on the Government to introduce deflationary measures to facilitate its goal of balance of payments equilibrium by the end of 1966. These demands were reflected inside the administration by both the Treasury and the Bank of England which were responsible for sterling and closest in their thinking and contacts with British and foreign financial opinion. Amidst heavy criticism in financial circles and from the CBI that the April Budget was insufficiently deflationary, the Government immediately began to reconsider its strategy. In order to impress speculators, it announced steps to liquefy gradually the Government's own dollar portfolio, although it refused to touch the bulk of Britain's foreign assets, which were in private hands. But with bad trade figures published in June and with a further round of negotiations for stand-by credits for the pound imminent as Callaghan went to Washington in late June, there was another wave of speculation against sterling which produced further demands at home and abroad for an extensive deflation. The Government responded on 27 July with a severe economic package which postponed many of the public expenditure programmes promised during the election. Callaghan told the House that 'it was vital to reassure the world trading community and the holders of sterling balances of our utter determination to make Britain strong and sterling strong'.[18]

Although this deflationary policy involved a return to 'stop–go' and invalidated the forecasts of the National Plan some six weeks before they were published, it did not end the speculation on sterling, nor in itself convince Britain's creditors to provide further needed stand-by loans. The American Treasury, which, in conjunction with European financial opinion, had counselled deflation, had also privately begun in June expressing its views with regard to making the wage restraint aspect of the incomes policy more effective. Reliance on deflation alone had drawbacks not only for Britain but also for her main allies and trading partners. It might have entailed large cuts in military expenditure, particularly the withdrawal of British troops east of Suez at a time when America was itself at war in South-East Asia, and meant that the import surcharge imposed in November 1964 would be maintained while it was in the interest of her trading partners to have it removed. The American Government preferred that Britain seek balance of payments equilibrium through wage restraint rather than by such measures, and it offered to mount an immediate rescue operation for sterling among the Central Banks in exchange for a British commitment to introduce incomes legislation by the end of the year. It was primarily this that spurred the Government to turn to a statutory policy before the voluntary approach had even been tried.[19]

The Treasury developed a proposal for compulsory early warning legislation by which the Government would have to be notified of any intention to increase prices or pursue wage claims, which the Government could then refer to the Board if it chose and require that any proposed price or wage increase be deferred until the Board reported. The DEA reluctantly accepted these proposals, and on 26 August Brown informed the TUC and CBI of the Government's intentions. In seeking the consent of the CBI and the TUC for the introduction of legislation, the Government now adopted the second interpretation of the term 'voluntary' – the policy itself would contain statutory controls but would still be 'voluntary' in that these would be agreed to by the central trade union and employers organizations. The CBI found the proposals acceptable, not as a legitimate extension of the voluntary policy, but due to the necessity of a positive response to the critical situation which Brown had outlined. Woodcock for the TUC, however, despite dramatic appeals by Brown that without the TUC's agreement that very day the support operation would be called off by the Americans, maintained that the General Council would have to be consulted first, and invited Brown to put the Government's case to the General Council himself. On 1 September, the Cabinet formally made the decision to legislate, and on 2 September, as the General Council met in Brighton to prepare the agenda for the 1965 Congress, they were joined by Brown who put to them the Government's decision.

The General Council's twelve hour meeting with Brown was a unique affirmation of the special relationship Labour Governments have with the British trade union movement.[20] The direct appeal Brown made for loyalty to the nation and to 'their' Government probably was unmatched since the 1931 crisis, certainly surpassing the more 'distant' stance of Cripps in 1948 and 1949. In the morning session Brown had little difficulty in convincing the General Council that the Government's economic strategy was correct, that drastic steps had to be taken to obtain international support for the pound, that the proposals he was putting to them were the only way of avoiding a return to massive unemployment. As a rule most of the General Council did not question Brown's analysis of the economic situation: any possible alternatives to the Government's strategy – devaluation, physical controls on imports, nationalization of privately-held securities abroad, large cuts in existing military expenditure – they deemed to be outside their immediate province. Indeed, the one member who claimed expertise in the field of foreign exchange markets was Carron who, as a part-time Governor of the Bank of England, reflected the Bank's orthodox views. There was even surprisingly little hostility expressed at being left out of the picture until then, for they accepted, despite their claims to be partners in economic decision-making, that the 'delicateness' of international financial negotiations could be dealt with by the Government alone. If anything, they were flattered that even now they were being taken into the Government's confidence with regard to the 'rescue operation'; it was more than the Tories had done.

Nevertheless, the General Council were obviously in a difficult position. Unlike the six months of negotiation on the voluntary policy, and despite their previous belief that the NEDC would decide on the 'success' or 'failure' of the policy, they now were being asked to endorse a major extension which their representatives had not been involved in developing at all. Moreover, they were being asked to do so at the very time when they were most subject to democratic pressures, on the eve of the annual TUC, with little time available to prepare their own executives or delegations for this new departure. In January, the General Council had 'refused to countenance' compulsion with regard to wage claims, and it is difficult to overestimate how powerful is this feeling among Britain's trade union leadership. It rests on the desire for maximum freedom of action in their bargaining activities, but it has gone beyond this and become a cornerstone of their ideology. Their immediate and genuine response to legislation in this field is that it is 'dangerous to democracy', that free trade unionsm is as much a crucial element in democracy as is freedom of the press, speech or assembly. This aspect of British trade union ideology extends across the political spectrum although it is more pronounced on the left. Of course, this doctrine is not the only aspect of the ideology and can be – and was – overcome at times by appeals to patriotism and party loyalty, or by threats of mass unemployment; but it is abandoned only reluctantly and usually only temporarily. In most cases the General Council would rather have agreed themselves to take the actions sought by legislation, than agree to legislation itself.

In addition, there was the feeling – some said the knowledge – that this legislation could not work in practice. Brown indicated that there would be two legal requirements: one to notify the Government of all claims, the other to delay a settlement until the Government decided whether to refer a claim to the NBPI (about a month), and then if the claim was referred, until the Board had reported (he estimated a further two months). There were few objections to compulsory notification, since claims are often vague in the first instance and are rarely settled within a month of being framed in any case. But the possibility of a further delay while the PIB considered a reference was 'a matter of very great argument'.[21] If some unions complied, while others did not, the former would be at a disadvantage. Moreover, even if most union officials did comply, they could hardly guarantee compliance on the part of shop stewards. Were they expected, they asked, to endorse fines or even prison against their members when they practised what was considered to be traditional bargaining? And what about those 15 million employees who were not in trade unions – would it not be a disadvantage to be a member of a trade union subject to such laws? Once these questions were raised, the arguments followed that, while the legislation might be needed for the loan, it would really not help the incomes policy itself, but might discredit it – and with it the Government and the General Council.

Despite Brown's assurances that the policy would remain 'basically voluntary', that the powers would be used sparingly, if at all, the General Council hesitated. His argument that the legislation would give the Government powers over prices had an impact, but not enough to overcome the General Council's main concern with its implications for wages. But Brown made it clear that the Government was going ahead with legislation in any case: the Government – not the TUC – would govern. In these circumstances the General Council seriously considered a suggestion by Woodcock that it merely issue a statement indicating that it 'noted' the Government's intention, thereby passively acquiescing in the action, rather than sticking their collective neck out to support it. Brown, however, remained adamant. Only if the TUC was seen to be behind the proposals, he said, in the form of another 'joint statement', could the Government obtain the loan from American and European Bankers at their meeting in Basel in a few days time. In face of such disloyalty, he said, he was ashamed to be a member of the trade union movement.

At the twelfth hour, literally, the General Council relented. They would recommend that Congress agree to the legislation. But they also decided that they would present this endorsement to the TUC as having won a concession from the Government. Brown had explained that the legislation could not be passed by Parliament until December at the earliest; until then he wanted the cooperation of the unions to operate an 'early warning system' voluntarily. Woodcock therefore suggested that the TUC would agree to this voluntary interim action, if the Government on its part indicated that it would refrain from introducing legislation until it was convinced that the voluntary early warning system was inadequate. Brown refused to go so far – the Government was legislating in December come what may. But he had fought within the Government to make the legislation permissive, i.e. to leave its application to the discretion of Ministers. Apart from making the NBPI a statutory body, the legislation would only give the Ministers the power to bring the rest of its provisions – compulsory notification and powers to compel delay in pursuing wage claims and price increases – into effect by an Order in Council. Brown was prepared to state publicly that the Government would introduce these Orders only if the Government were convinced they were necessary to make the policy effective, and after further consultations with the TUC and CBI. In return, the General Council gave Brown the vote he wanted, with only six votes against.

After the Government's plans and the TUC's approval were announced, Britain's creditors held to their part of the bargain. The following day, Fowler issued a statement saying that the indications were that Britain would reach balance of payments equilibrium by the second half of 1966: 'As planned, the newly announced programme not only strengthens these indications but provides the basis for long-run stability in costs and prices which is a major factor in combining sound economic growth with balance of payments equilibrium'.[22] On 10 September, the Bank of England announced that a $1,000m loan from ten central banks had been arranged to support sterling. Throughout the autumn and winter it gave the Labour Government a respite from severe speculation against the pound.

The General Council, however, was 'left holding the baby'. They still had to face Congress, and remembering the 1950 repudiation, were aware that they might get their hands sullied. They could argue that they had won a concession from the Government, but few of them were convinced that a compromise had been achieved at all. Woodcock decided to proceed as though there was a real chance that, if the TUC undertook a centralized supervision of wage claims, the Government might not bring into force the penal sections of the legislation. Unions would be asked to provide the TUC with information on impending wage claims, and to agree to refraining from proceeding with them until the General Council had an opportunity of examining them, and if necessary, discussing them with the unions concerned. The TUC would thus institutionalize the role it had played more generally in 1948–50 and in the early 1950s when it counselled wage restraint: as well as representing the trade union movement to government, it would also present 'the national interest' to the trade unions. Woodcock now argued that 'we ought to have known all along that developments were implicit . . . and so we ought not to get up on our hind legs because there has been a proposal from the Government'.[23] But when he had told the Conference of Executives that this was 'not even a policy', he had not warned them of statutory developments. He had been thinking more of developments in the form of an increased role for the TUC, such as the February White Paper hinted at in suggesting that it would be 'helpful' if the TUC and CBI could advise their members on the application of the policy. Now, two days before Congress, he was able to seize the opportunity to get overwhelming General Council agreement to TUC vetting of individual wage claims.

Resolutions at the annual Trade Union Congress are composed as much with an eye to tactical considerations as are statements of policy. The composite resolution in favour of the incomes policy at the 1965 Congress, as had been the case in 1948 and 1949, included criticisms of the prices and profits aspect of the incomes policy so that delegations committed by their annual conferences to critical resolutions on those grounds could still vote in favour of the policy as a whole.[24] The resolution was passed without a card vote. A composite motion which rejected the incomes policy outright while reaffirming the TUC's support for a planned economy based upon public ownership was defeated by 6,131,000 to 2,212,000, showing an increase in the opposition since April of less than half a million. Nevertheless, Congress support for the General Council's Supplementary Report which outlined the new developments was a much closer affair. Two of the largest unions who had supported the incomes policy in April and still did so, NALGO and the ETU, were not prepared to support TUC wage vetting and preferred instead to face up to the legislation. With these unions voting against, the Supplementary Report – and thus both the Government's legislative proposals and the TUC scheme – was passed by only 5,251,000 to 3,313,000 votes, a majority of under two million. The key delegation was that of the AEU. At a $2\frac{1}{2}$ hour meeting the night before the vote, the 32-man delegation had been evenly split for and against and the Chairman, William Tallon, acting in Carron's absence, had to use his casting vote three times before the delegation finally decided by 19 to 12 to support the General Council. Had the AEU's 1 million votes gone the other way, the Report would have been defeated. John Boyd proudly told the press later: 'we in the AEU are the saviours of the Labour Government'.[25]

The extent of the opposition among AEU activists was revealed again the following month at the Labour Party Conference where another AEU delegation voted by 17 to 14 to cast its 750,000 votes in favour of ASSET's emergency resolution against the legislation.[26] Carron was again absent from the Conference, and thus was not able to override the delegation by invoking the National Committee's '100 per cent support' resolution. Nevertheless, with the ETU voting for the legislation (NALGO is not affiliated to the Labour Party) and with the votes of the constituency parties, the emergency resolution was defeated by 3,635,000 to 2,540,000. As had been the case in 1948–50, the major concern of the constituency parties seemed to be that wage restrictions were not being matched by economic controls over private industry. Of 14 CLP resolutions on incomes policy on the Conference agenda, 13 demanded price controls and/or extensive public ownership and control over private industry in conjunction with the incomes policy. The Government, via the NEC, was able to overcome this pressure by accepting a composite resolution which called for 'effective controls to limit prices', by which the mover, Royden Harrison, meant a system of licensing for key prices, but by which the Government and the NEC meant prior notification of a few price increases and in select cases reference to the NBPI to give 'embarrassing publicity to firms making upward price changes'.[27] The Government had emerged victorious in the first confrontation on its statutory incomes policy.

Voluntary 'early warning' and the operation of incomes policy

A White Paper [28] on 11 November 1965 outlined the new early warning system to operate before legislation was passed. For prices, the White Paper claimed it was 'neither necessary nor practicable' to require notification of a large number of price changes; it limited itself to a list of some 75 mainly consumer goods in addition to those goods and services (mainly food and public enterprise services or products) which were already subject to public supervision. For wages, the system directly incorporated the TUC's new wage vetting scheme by which the TUC would 'keep the Government informed of developments', and in addition provided that the CBI would collect information from its member companies on negotiations involving over 1,000 employees and pass them to the Ministry of Labour. The standstill on proceeding with a wage or price increase would be either one or four months, depending on whether the case was referred to the NBPI. The White Paper did not require enterprises to supply information on profits or dividends; and it largely ignored capital goods prices and export prices, in a sense the object of the whole exercise.

What was significant about this system was that while the TUC was now directly involved in vetting wage claims, the CBI refused to engage in supervising either the wage or price decisions of its members. The CBI's Director-General argued: 'I do not think that the CBI, which is after all a voluntary organization of which membership is by no means obligatory, could pretend to exercise a degree of discipline on those people who are voluntarily its members and not have the least effect on those who are not. This would seem to me entirely anomalous and undesirable.' [29] Although the CBI engaged in intense bargaining with the Government with regard to limiting the number of commodities subject to notification, it would go no further than recommend to its members to comply voluntarily with the scheme.[30] And even in this respect its support was limited. It sent the list of commodities to its 13,000 member firms and associations, but attached a covering letter suggesting that companies with an annual turnover of less than £100,000 ignore the requirements and that the others need not notify price increases of $\frac{1}{4}$ per cent or less a month (as much as 3 per cent a year) on those increases involving an increase in sales revenue of less than £25,000. The White Paper itself made no such exceptions. Even to this extent, the CBI leadership described its cooperation with the scheme as that of 'military volunteers'.[31]

In direct contrast was the TUC's response. By the end of September the General Council had established an Incomes Policy Committee, consisting of 21 members (one General Council member from each trade group), which, aided by a Secretariat of four, would meet monthly to express its views on claims. It immediately asked all affiliated unions to supply the Committee with information on all claims. By October the scheme was in operation and by December 174 claims had been considered by the Committee. In its first year of operation the Committee received from some 75 unions 686 claims both national and local, covering at least six million workers.[32] Moreover, the unions opposed to the Government's incomes policy showed a surprising willingness to cooperate with the TUC. The TGWU alone supplied the Committee with from one-half to one-third of the total notifications received.[33] The Committee took one of four courses of action with regard to a claim: it informed the union concerned that it did not want to make any observation; it asked the union in general terms to bear in mind the White Paper criteria during the course of negotiations; it made specific comments on claims which were regarded as conflicting with the incomes policy and sometimes asked the union to reconsider the claim before submitting it to the employers; or, in the case of claims considered particularly important, it asked the union to meet a panel of the Committee to discuss the claim in greater detail. Most of the claims fell into the second and third categories; only 18 went to a panel during the first year, although 14 of these occurred in the first four months of the Committee's existence, at the time when the TUC was still hoping to convince the Government to refrain from legislation.[34] Callaghan told the General Council in January that their scheme was remarkably successful as a *technical* operation, but whether it would contribute to his main concern to get balance of payments equilibrium by the end of 1966, by effectively inducing wage restraint, was another matter.[35]

In undertaking their new role, the TUC had not adopted centralized bargaining in the Swedish style. A more apt description of its activities in this sphere is what H. A. Turner has called 'centrally moderated sectional bargaining'.[36] Although there was a lot of talk at the TUC of 'coordinating' wage claims, in fact virtually no coordination was attempted. The main problem for the Committee was to decide what criteria to use in seeking to moderate sectional wage demands. The Committee did not explicitly adopt the $3\frac{1}{2}\%$ norm in the White Paper criteria. Woodcock took the view, even when a claim went to a panel, that the individual unions themselves knew their own industries best, and he refrained from questioning their reasons for putting a claim. He would therefore only make observations on the claim in light of its effects on the economy in general. Implicitly, however, the Committee was guided by a number of considerations: narrowing wage differentials, twelve month delays be-

tween claims, and productivity rather than comparability demands
in bargaining. In this last respect the Committee achieved its greatest
success, and after the first six months found that productivity did
become the major ground on which unions would argue for increases
before the Committee, although the Committee itself rarely went into
the question of the extent to which productivity arguments were
'genuine'.

But in general, the Incomes Policy Committee had no direct means
of guaranteeing union adherence to its pronouncements.[37] Had it
been prepared to endorse the claims it favoured, unions might have
placed emphasis on getting TUC approval, but the General Council
was not prepared to raise again the spectre of the 'Triple Alliance'.
Nevertheless the Committee was not without authority completely.
There was some moral sanction involved in the TUC telling an individual union that it was acting contrary to the interests of the trade
union movement and 'the national interest'. Further, it could use the
argument that unless a claim was modified it would not get past the
Government and might be referred to the NBPI. On one level, the
TUC was here offering advice to the unions, and on this basis it was
able to convince the unions that they should more often justify claims
in terms of productivity. On another level, the Committee was able
to apply a real sanction at this point. It could – and did – say that if
a claim was not notified to the TUC or had been found 'incompatible', and the union went ahead and met Government resistance, the
TUC would not argue the union's case with the Government. It was
in this way that the TUC was in fact operating to some extent as a
punitive arm of the Government. There was close contact between
the Secretariat and Ministry of Labour and DEA Civil Servants.
Often this contact simply involved clarifying a claim, but at other
times the Government would try to get the TUC to ask a particular
union to modify or delay a claim. Conversely, the TUC had some
success in getting the Government to change its mind on a number of
claims which they at first intended to refer to the Board. As such, the
TUC was able to offer unions an additional means of influencing the
Government, a 'bonus' which small or weak unions would try to get
if possible. Thus insofar as the TUC's own scheme was at all effective
it was mainly through its integration with the Government's
machinery, not as a substitute for it.

It was through the operation of this machinery that the voluntary
policy had really to be tested. Between May 1965 and March 1966,
the Government made 19 references to the NBPI. When handling a
claim, the DEA was guided by a number of principles.[38] It laid particular stress on the 'case law' aspect of the policy, since the Board's

capacity was limited (the DEA operated on the assumption that the Board could handle about thirty references a year). It therefore tried to single out for reference cases which were capable of wide application, particularly those where comparability was involved or where the Board would have an opportunity of establishing what were to be considered 'genuine exceptions' to the norm, which would not lead to 'repercussions'. Another consideration was the availability of ready means of settling a dispute; on this ground, wage claims in both the Electrical Supply Industry and the Bakery Industry were referred in June and December, 1965 respectively.[39] Finally the DEA also took into consideration 'the preference of the parties, because all the references which we made have been made with the agreement of the parties concerned after a certain amount of discussion with them'.[40] In getting this agreement, the TUC played an instrumental role, particularly in overcoming the reluctance of the Bakers and the Railwaymen to have their claims referred.

Two other principles which the DEA had proposed to use at the outset in deciding on references were quickly put aside. At the beginning of the year the Government had wanted to concentrate on private sector price references. Brown had argued that it would be 'very silly' to refer the prices of the nationalized industries to the Board and that if private industry already had to go 'through the hoops' which public industry did, there might not be a need for prices and incomes policy machinery at all.[41] But this created a furore in private industry and the press, and 100 Conservative MPs signed a Commons motion deploring this approach.[42] The Government responded by almost going full circle. After the first three price references in May, which all concerned the private sector, four of the next six before the March 1966 election concerned nationalized industries (an imbalance duplicated with wage references). In addition none of the price references enabled the Board to apply the considerations of the White Papers on price reductions. 'The price references made to us', the Board reported, 'were thus concerned, not with whether prices should be reduced, but whether or not prices should have been increased or should be increased against a background of rising costs.'[43]

The Board itself tried to perform three functions through its reports: an 'educative' function, concerned with convincing public opinion of the need for restraint; a 'consultancy' function to encourage change in industry; and the 'judicial' function involved in testing the cases before it against the White Paper criteria.[44] Rather than operate in separate Price and Incomes Divisions as the February White Paper had suggested, it decided that these matters were bound together too inextricably for such a separation to be useful. The Reports displayed a number of themes which were closely related to the Government's own approach. The Board consistently emphasized the need for more critical methods in determining the use of existing capital and new investment, and for adopting new working practices (especially ending craft/non-craft demarcations) which would allow capital to be used more efficiently. With specific regard to wages, the Board considered it essential to reduce the disparity between low basic wage rates and a pay structure which via supplements and over-time often yielded relatively high total earnings. But it took the view that total earnings – regardless of hours worked – had to be the prime factor to be taken into consideration in determining whether a claim qualified under the low pay criteria. Thus it ruled out low pay as a justification for increases for either the bakers or the railwaymen.[45]

The major concern of the Board, however, was to undermine the comparability approach to wage decisions. This approach, built directly into many negotiating agreements in the public sector, allowed unions to follow a breakthrough made by one group of workers in a particular firm or industry. But for the Board, endea-vouring to reduce the increases before it to the order of $3\frac{1}{2}\%$, and concentrating on the productivity criterion as the main ground for exception to the norm, these comparison formulas were anathema.[46] On these grounds, it rejected in January 1966 an NUR claim for 8% which was based on the accepted use of comparability in the railway industry. Harold Wilson later described it as 'an austere, almost un-feeling report': 'the Board was interpreting its terms of reference tightly and applying the most severe of norms in this case, which covered some of the lowest paid workers in Britain'.[47] But in subse-quent negotiations with the NUR, the Government stuck closely to the Board's recommendations, and in fact the Board had merely been following the Government's own prescription: a DEA brief on another reference at the time urged the Board to take great care to guard against 'circular increases' and suggested particularly rigid guidelines for the Board to follow.[48]

An indication that these considerations were being applied with-out much regard to the redistributive aspect of the incomes policy was to be found in the only Board report on high income recipients during the period of the 1964 Government, published only a week after the railways report, when the Board endorsed substantial in-creases for high ranking civil servants.[49] The Standing Advisory Com-mittee on the Pay of the Higher Civil Service (the Franks Committee) had recommended increases ranging from 3.5 to 11.7% backdated to September 1965 on incomes ranging from £3,500 to £9,200. The

Board endorsed these increases on the grounds that, as it was the first increase for 18 months to two years, it fell close to $3\frac{1}{2}\%$ per year; that narrowing differentials were harming recruitment prospects at the top; and that increases for broadly comparable employment in private industry were appreciably greater than this increase. The Board, of course, had 'special knowledge' of this situation since members of its secretariat, including the powerful Secretary to the Board, A. A. Jarratt, were themselves in this class of civil servants. The Government accepted the recommendations, but in doing so inevitably brought into focus the difficulty of applying a $3\frac{1}{2}\%$ norm across the board to grossly dissimilar incomes: $3\frac{1}{2}\%$ for railwaymen amounted to some £35 a year; $3\frac{1}{2}\%$ for higher civil servants involved an increase of as much as as ten times that figure.

The main theme of the Board's reports on prices was that managements should refrain from their normal practice of automatically passing on wage increases in the form of price increases, at least in the first instance, and undertake instead to introduce methods for increased efficiency and tighter control over labour costs. One of the Board's successes in this field was in securing, in September 1965, a pledge from flour milling and baking firms not to raise the price of bread for three months (the Board had recommended six).[50] But this very success in turn pointed out another major defect in a prices and incomes policy that did not set national guidelines for profits or the rate of return on capital invested. For the firms refused to allow the price delay to cut into the profits and immediately rejected a pay claim which led to sporadic strike action in November and the threat of a national strike in December. Under severe pressure from the Government, the Bakers' Union agreed to suspend strike action and accept a reference to the Board, but clearly felt at the time that they were facing the state as well as the employers. 'The employers who criticized the board's report when it suited them are now hiding behind this body to deny our members their just claim . . . We are dismayed to see our Government – because we are lifelong socialists – ranged on the side of big business against our tiny union.' [51]

The Board's report on prices had shown that the large combines which dominated both the flour milling and baking industry were obtaining a return on investment well below the national average in baking, but in flour milling (which accounted for a much larger proportion of total profits, and itself accounted for 40% of the cost of producing bread), were earning a return on investment of $17\frac{1}{2}\%$, well above the national average.[52] But in its subsequent reports it refused to take into account the total profits situation, as it was taking into account total earnings in the case of wage incomes, and recommended increases in the price of bread in order to raise profits in the baking industry.[53] It did not accompany this with the recommendation that prices and profits in flour milling be correspondingly reduced. Indeed, throughout its life, the NBPI consistently concentrated on recommending cost reductions rather than profit reductions as a means of avoiding price increases. As one student of the Board has suggested, there was 'a political advantage' in this:

> The need for greater managerial efficiency was a subject around which the various elements amongst the Board Membership could unite; it might have split if its only concern in price references was with profits. If the revenue sought by price increases could instead be obtained by greater efficiency, this avoided asking difficult, controversial questions on whether the return on investment could be lowered.[54]

Legislation delayed

Insofar as it had not been clear earlier, it was certainly clear by the beginning of 1966 that the incomes policy was concerned primarily with securing wage restraint to the exclusion of using the policy for redistributive purposes. Where the Government had specifically applied the policy to individual wage claims, it had in fact achieved considerable success. As the Board noted, those recommendations 'concerned with the immediate situation – whether a particular proposal relating to prices or wages was justified or not – ... have in the main been accepted by the parties concerned'.[55] Usually, however, this was achieved only after considerable effort by Ministers themselves. After the report on the railways, for instance, the NUR Executive had voted to take strike action and only after a series of long meetings with Brown, Gunter and the Minister of Transport, Barbara Castle, and finally the direct intervention of the Prime Minister himself at an all-night meeting at 10 Downing Street, were the Government able to convince the NUR to accept the report.[56] Although the Government told the NUR that the whole incomes policy 'could be fatally prejudiced' [57] unless the union gave way, it was in fact aware that railway settlements rarely set a pattern for other settlements.[58] The Government's real concern, however, was to evolve a situation whereby individual cases of restraint would have an effect on other claims by convincing unions generally that their own claims might be referred.

The proposals the Government had produced in August 1965 for legislation had been presented on the grounds that the threat of sanctions contained therein might have this effect. But the Government did not introduce the legislation as soon as Parliament reassembled in October, as it had indicated it would. In fact the Prices and Incomes Bill was not introduced until 24 February when the Government knew it would not get beyond First Reading. For it had already decided to announce only four days later the dissolution of the 1964 Parliament and a general election on 31 March.[59] The reason for the delay was that incomes policy was no longer a matter of 'extra-paliamentary legislation' by the Administration and the central bodies of business and labour, but required the direct involvement of Parliament, and most significantly, the Parliamentary Labour Party. In assessing the relationship of the PLP to the policy, it must first be noted that the vast majority of Labour MPs, including most of the Trade Union Group, would have supported the legislation at this stage and in fact later did so. Indeed, Labour MPs played an active role in promoting the policy among the unions. Rather than the unions 'lobbying' MPs for changes in the policy, many MPs 'lobbied' the unions, urging them to change their wage practices and calling for their votes in favour of the policy at union conferences and among delegations at the TUC and Labour Party Conference.[60] Given the 1964 Government's bare majority of three, however, only a few abstentions on the Labour side in the House of Commons were needed to bring the Government down. Therefore, the attitude the left wing of the PLP assumed towards the policy and the proposed legislation became crucial.

The PLP left was mainly centred in the Tribune Group of MPs, which grew out of discussions before the 1964 election among old Bevanites both inside and outside Parliament at the time. The Group's first meeting was held some two weeks after the election and it immediately began attracting some 25–30 MPs to its meetings. In the period before the 1964 election, the Labour left had supported the idea of an incomes policy. But by the fall of 1965 the Tribune Group was divided in its attitude to the specific policy that had been developed. Some leading members of the Group, especially James Dickens (and to a lesser extent, Michael Foot), were in favour of the policy and not opposed in principle to the legislation.[61] But the Tribune Group differed from the Bevanites in that almost half of its members were trade union sponsored MPs, mostly newly-elected in 1964 and with considerable sympathy for, and personal experience of, industrial militancy. These MPs, led by Stanley Orme, Eric Heffer and Norman Atkinson, had become increasingly critical of the policy as it developed. Shortly after the Government announced its intentions to introduce the legislation, they led a deputation of twelve to

see the Chief Whip, Edward Short, and told him that they were prepared to abstain and bring the Government down rather than support legislation containing penal provisions against trade unionists.[62]

This stand by the Labour left did not shake the Government's
determination to legislate. Instead, when taken together with the
difficult negotiations with the railwaymen (which convinced the
Prime Minister that sooner or later there would have to be a 'confrontation' with the unions), it led the Government to go to the
country in early 1966 for a bigger majority rather than 'yield in-
continently to strike threats', as Wilson has put it.[63] The only reason
the Government actually bothered to introduce the incomes legislation in February, when it already knew it would not pass before the
election, was to reassure Britain's foreign creditors that the Government was not going back on its commitment. The rise in unemployment and the cut-back in general demand that had been expected
after the July deflationary package had not materialized, and foreign
governments and central banks were beginning to get restive once
again.[64]

Part I of the Prices and Incomes Bill reconstituted the NBPI on
a statutory basis, thus empowering the Board to call witnesses and
require evidence. Part II, which could be brought into effect by an
annually renewable Order-in-Council, required that wage claims and
settlements and those price increases subject to early warning (but
not dividend increases) should be notified to the Government subject
to a maximum fine of £50 on the union, employer or firm responsible
for notification. A standstill of thirty days or, where there was a reference to the Board, of four months, would then be in force, again
subject to penalty. It provided for fines of up to £500,

> If any person takes, or threatens to take any action, and in
> particular any action by way of taking part, or persuading
> others to take part, in a strike with a view to compel, induce
> or influence any employer to implement an award or settle-
> ment in respect of employment at a time when the implemen-
> tation of the award or settlement is forbidden under
> the foregoing provisions.[65]

But if the Government considered the introduction of the Bill
to be tactically important in relation to Britain's commitments
abroad, it was also dangerous to Cabinet and Party unity at the time
of an election. The main danger was that the Bill's publication, and
particularly the penal provisions against strikers, would lead Frank
Cousins to resign from the Cabinet. 'Cousins is the one Minister
Mr Wilson can least afford to have resigning', *The Times* wrote just

three weeks before the election, 'to become the standard bearer for a coalition of left-wing critics, and the Minister who would have least to lose by resigning, because he is not a professional politician and could go back to union leadership.'[66] Cousins had not at all played a role similar to that of Bevin in promoting trade union support of the Government on the issue of wage restraint. For although he refrained from criticizing the incomes policy in public, neither did he promote it. On the one occasion on which he responded to a challenge in the House on the consistency between his membership of the Government and his union's opposition to the policy, he reiterated his belief in the 'planned growth of incomes'.[67] But when he addressed the TGWU conference in July he expressed 'delight' that the conference had 'registered some firm views on some matters of real concern' and did not dissociate himself from the conference resolutions against the incomes policy and the Government's Vietnam policy: 'If anyone suggests that the way to prove I could be a good Cabinet Minister is to pretend that I did not, and do not, belong to the Transport and General Workers Union, and that I am not part of the same struggle, then all I can say is that they will never understand us.'[68] He saw his contribution not in promoting an incomes policy (or a foreign policy) which he did not believe in, but in convincing trade unionists and industrialists of the necessity for adapting flexibly to technological change and automation.[69] In the Cabinet, Cousins made it clear that he was not opposed to a prices and incomes policy in principle but he wanted the Government to introduce strict controls on prices, which would both make firms more resistant to wage claims and produce voluntary cooperation from the rank and file.[70] He made no secret of his intention to resign if the Government introduced penal sanctions against trade unionists. The majority of the Cabinet, and Wilson himself, had no interest in price controls, however, and looked to wage restraint and the legislation to achieve their aims in this field.

That the Government was able to maintain Cabinet and Party unity at this time, despite the introduction of the legislation, was due to both the response the labour movement traditionally shows to the principle of solidarity at election time, and to the Government's own attempt to play down the incomes policy issue. A PLP meeting called to air a critical discussion of the legislation became an occasion for the Tribune Group, no less than the rest of the MPs, to display party unity.[71] No doubt the fact that Cousins did not resign at the time was partly out of loyalty. But Cousins was also convinced that the legislation, or at least the penal provisions, would not be reintroduced after the election when a stronger Labour Government could withstand more easily foreign pressure, and he subsequently contended that the Prime Minister himself had assured him on this.[72] To be sure, Labour Ministers did not emphasize this aspect of the incomes policy in the election campaign and the Election Manifesto made no mention of the Bill, nor of penal sanctions to enforce the early warnings system.[73] And in a television interview on 10 March, the Prime Minister said that 'once you have law prescribing wages I think you are on a very slippery slope. It would be repugnant I think to all parties of the country'. Nor, he added, could unofficial strikes be outlawed by legislation.[74]

The Labour Party was able to face the 1966 election as a united party because all sides were anxious to employ a language that masked the policy differences that separated them. There had emerged during the brief term of office of the 1964 Labour Government a yawning gap within the labour movement with regard to the effective meaning of words used to describe the incomes policy. The Government sincerely had no intention of introducing a law prescribing wages (such centralized economic controls were exactly what it did not want), but it did not see as incompatible with 'free collective bargaining' a law that provided penalties for workers who refused to accept a delay in negotiations long enough for the state to bring its influence to bear for wage restraint through its appointed agency, the NBPI. Most of the trade union movement, however, thought even the latter action to be a very great infringement on 'free collective bargaining'. Whereas the Government meant by 'voluntary' the agreement of the unions to a policy with statutory elements to delay wage settlements, large parts of the labour movement understood 'voluntary' to mean a policy without legal penalties of any kind, with or without official trade union endorsement. Whereas the Government meant 'effective measures to limit prices' to be a system of notification of a very limited number of consumer goods, significant sections of the movement meant by these words that a large number of key prices should be subject to state control and only increased under licence. Whereas the Government understood by 'planning' a programme of economic forecasts, exhortations and fiscal inducements, another part of the labour movement thought planning meant direct government controls over investment and an extension of public ownership. All these policy divisions were overcome at the time of the 1966 election by a verbal and symbolic unity although it was now a more difficult operation than at the time of the 1964 election. But the next Labour Government was to learn to its cost that when phrases inevitably take form as policy instruments, meanings become less obscure and divisions bite deep.

5

The politics of wage freeze

The prelude to the freeze

At the 1966 General Election Labour was returned with a bigger increase in its parliamentary majority than any party in Britain had ever won after a term of office: it gained forty-nine seats and lost only one and its majority was transformed from one of the most precarious under which a government could operate to one of the safest for which a government could hope. The parliamentary constraints which had impeded its plans for incomes policy since the fall of 1965 were thus removed overnight. Moreover, the Government, whatever its equivocations on the question during the election campaign, could reasonably interpret its victory as a vote of confidence in its incomes policy and face union opposition to the policy with more confidence than before. In a major policy speech at the Scottish Trades Union Congress three weeks after the election, and the day after that body had voted overwhelmingly against the reintroduction of the incomes policy legislation, the Prime Minister now boldly stated that the Government's economic strategy would not be settled 'by a card vote which ever way it goes', but by an unpalatable choice between wage restraint and unemployment:

> We cannot compromise on our programme to get into
> balance by the end of this year. And speaking with all the
> authority at my command I have to tell you that the one
> thing that can stop us is a rise in industrial costs ... So
> be clear, the Prices and Incomes Policy is not a whim of a
> Government Department, not a bright idea that has occurred
> to George Brown and me. It is a necessary condition of main-
> taining full employment.[1]

The Government's parliamentary problems may have been solved by the election, but as Wilson made clear, the prime objective of economic policy – achieving balance of payments equilibrium without devaluation – was as pressing as ever. The deficit had been more than halved in 1965, but the improvement did not continue in early 1966. As far as the Government were concerned the incomes policy had failed to contribute sufficiently to this main aim of economic policy. The policy did have the effect of restraining wage increases: according to one econometric analysis, the rate of increase of weekly wage rates between the first quarter of 1965 and the second quarter of 1966 was 'significantly below the expected by about one percentage point'.[2] But this restraining effect diminished in late 1965 and early 1966, and whatever the effect of the policy on weekly rates and total earnings, the growth in hourly earnings of 9.6% between April 1965 and April 1966 (reflecting a decline in hours worked in the period) looked too high to the Government, particularly since the rate of growth of output in 1965 had fallen to 2.7% from 5.5% in 1964, and seemed further endangered by the fall in company profits of 6% in the first half of 1966.[3]

Essentially, the Government decided to pursue the same approach it had adopted earlier: a combination of mildly deflationary fiscal policy with increased tightening of the incomes policy, the latter reflected in three decisions shortly after the election. First, the Cabinet confirmed its intention to go ahead with legislation, and after consultations with the TUC and CBI beginning in May, the Prices and Incomes Bill was redrafted and ready for publication by the end of June. Secondly, the functions of Government Departments *vis-à-vis* the policy were rearranged to help overcome the undue concentration Brown and the DEA had given to individual wage and price cases. The DEA remained responsible for the development of the policy in general and for framing the legislation. But the examination of individual cases passed to the Ministry of Labour for wages, and to the various 'sponsoring' Ministries (mainly Agriculture and the Board of Trade) for prices; reference to the NBPI became the joint responsibility of the DEA and the relevant Ministry. This change had the effect of further steering the policy towards wage restraint. For while the Ministry of Labour had been closely involved in the development of the policy as a whole and was prepared to limit its conciliatory functions in the interest of securing wage settlements in line with the norm, the sponsoring Ministries among which responsibility for prices was dispensed, had no direct interest in the policy, and were reluctant to see 'their' industries subjected to an inquiry by the Board. The result, as one Member of the Board later wrote, was that 'Incomes cases come more readily and rationally through the machinery, as far as the PIB, where necessary'.[4]

The third decision was both more momentous and more spectacular in that it reflected the Government's determination, evident with regard to the railwaymen in January but strengthened by the election victory, to engage in a direct confrontation with the unions to keep wage increases within the norm. The Government decided to treat as a test case a claim by the historically moderate National Union of Seamen for a forty hour week at sea and a basic rate of pay of £60 a month. In March, on the same day as the union executive voted £3,500 to the Labour Party General Election Fund, it had rejected an employers' pay offer of 3%, as it did a 'final offer' in April involving an hours reduction alone equivalent to a 5% increase in wages in 1966. On 2 May, the union's annual conference, reflecting a groundswell of rank and file militancy, unanimously endorsed strike action beginning on 16 May. In meetings with the union executive in early May, Gunter and Wilson urged the union to accept the employers' 3% offer of March, in exchange for which the Government would set up a full-scale inquiry into the shipping industry. The union, however, had no intention of calling off the strike on the basis of an offer consistent with the incomes policy norm but even below the employers' 'final offer'.[5]

The Government was aware that a prolonged seamen's strike would have an immediate effect on the Trade balance, but since it was concerned primarily to prevent speculation against the pound, it reckoned that foreign confidence would respond to a strong stand against wage increases.[6] Speaking on television the night the strike began, the Prime Minister characterized it as 'a strike against the state, against the community', with the main issue being the credibility of the incomes policy as an instrument designed to help correct the payments deficit.[7] A week after the strike began the Government declared a State of Emergency, but rather than risk the odium which would have been attached to a Labour Government breaking a strike by the use of troops, concentrated on appeals to the national interest in the hope of undermining public support for the seamen, and on pressure on the union directly and through the TUC. On 26 May, it set up a Court of Inquiry under Lord Pearson with Hugh Clegg, a newly-appointed member of the NBPI, as a member to emphasize the relationship between the dispute and the incomes policy. The Court produced an interim report on 8 June which, while condemning the decision to strike, nevertheless recommended a substantial improvement on the employers' 'final offer'. The NUS, believing that they could get the employers to improve on the Pearson Report, decided to hold out, but on 14 June the Prime Minister indicated to the House of Commons that the cost of any settlement would have to be within the limits set by the Pearson inquiry, a statement which the union believed was a deliberate attempt to steel the employers' resistance.[8]

As the strike wore on, the Government widened its attack. On 20 June, the Prime Minister claimed that pressures were being put on the NUS executive by a 'tightly knit group of politically motivated men who, as the last General Election showed, utterly failed to secure acceptance of their views by the British electorate, but who are now determined to exercise back-stage pressures, forcing great hardship on the members of the union, and endangering the security of the industry and the economic welfare of the nation'.[9] Since no member of the executive was actually a member of the Communist Party, Wilson explained a week later that his charge had been based mainly on the fact that two non-Communist militants on the executive had stayed, while in London, at the same flat as the Communist chairman of the London Strike Committee and that the flat had been visited while they were there by the Communist Party's industrial organizer. The strike was being used, he claimed, 'to secure what is at present the main political and industrial objective of the Communist Party – the destruction of the Government's prices and incomes policy'.[10]

On 29 June, the NUS executive, without funds to continue any longer, decided to call off the strike on the basis of an employers' offer along the lines of the Pearson Report but which increased slightly the number of days paid leave. An attempt by the militants on the executive to submit the question of calling off the strike to a Special General Meeting of the union (which would almost certainly have voted to stay out, given the militancy among the rank and file), was defeated by 29 votes to 16.[11] The Prime Minister saw this attempt to consult the membership as further evidence of the 'undemocratic pressures' which he had 'revealed'.[12] Although the press, which was hostile to the Seamen throughout the dispute, had a field day with the Prime Minister's charges, this was not the decisive factor in leading the union to call off the strike, except as an indictaion of the lengths to which the Government was prepared to go in discrediting the union. The executive unanimously passed a resolution condemning the Prime Minister's 'innuendo' and the right wing General Secretary of the union, William Hogarth later wrote: 'Some of the things being said would be laughable and deserving only to be ignored were it not that some misguided folk believe them.'[13] Public opinion, probably influenced by the Government's decision in April to grant an increase to doctors of 30% over a two year period, was clearly sympathetic to the seamen and remained so after the Prime Minister made his allegations. Indeed, the Gallup poll showed that 50% of Labour Party supporters and 51% of trade unionists took the strikers' side, while only 13% and 17% respectively sympathized with the employers.[14] And although George Woodcock, who had stood by the Government throughout the strike, added to the press barrage by saying at first that if the allegations were true, it would be 'a crime against trade unionism',[15] he indicated a more general feeling on the part of the unions when he said: 'The Communist Party's interest in the strike is something I am prepared to spend a lot of time not bothering about', and he subsequently characterized the Prime Minister's 'evidence' as having amounted to 'damn all'.[16] The main factor that led the union to call off the strike was the perilous state of its finances, combined with the tepid support it received from the other unions. The General Council advised member unions not to extend the dispute,[17] and the unions, perhaps moved by appeals for loyalty to the Labour Government and the nation, and certainly fearful of inducing the dreaded and much threatened alternative of unemployment, steered clear of the strike.

The six-week-long Seamen's strike had the immediate effect of severely worsening the balance of payments situation. The Government's expectation that the short-term effect on trade would be matched by renewed confidence in the pound once the Government's determination was clearly seen, did not materialise, and in the beginning of July the pound fell to its lowest level since November 1964. The Government's first reaction, however, was to stick to the policy it had evolved before the election. On 4 July the Prices and Incomes Bill was re-introduced. Although the General Council's attitude to this was mild,[18] Frank Cousins, who had made a final effort to persuade the Cabinet against it during June, immediately resigned from the Government. In his resignation letter to the Prime Minister, Cousins contended that the Government had slipped back to the usual position of Treasury dominance and that this had 'obviously driven us to the position where our international monetary transactions have been based on assurances of our intention to restrict internal demand'. He indicted the Government for abandoning a policy of promoting economic growth and productivity and substituting in its stead wage restraint, which he believed had made the seamen's strike inevitable, had undermined the Ministry of Labour's conciliatory role and which would involve using the NBPI to 'create a pretext of adjudication whilst they would really be a rubber-stamping authority for previously determined Government decisions'.[19] His action had the effect of bringing the basic ideological differences that separated Cousins from the Cabinet into the open. In his first speech as a backbencher, he explained that his difference with the Government was not in principle over the 'planning' of wages but over the fact that to his mind the Government was not involved in economic planning at all. Cousins had always had doubts about indicative planning; his experience in office confirmed them:

> I saw the type of planning we did ... I could get more in-
> formation from outside than I could get from inside. I could
> get better facts related to the growth prospects of some of the
> major companies through my position as General Secretary
> of the Transport and General Workers' Union ...
>
> If you are to have controls, and if you assume that we want
> controls ... there is a way to get them. Take into public
> ownership the major sections of industry. If this is the theme
> and purpose I withdraw any opposition. I would say, 'go
> ahead with the Bill', accepting that it includes the policy of
> public ownership within it. But it does not. Its main pro-
> vision is to control the power and authority of the voluntary
> system which has been created by understanding between
> employers and employees on what wages should be.[20]

Cousins' resignation meant that the direct integration of the lead-ing trade unionist in the Cabinet, which had been hailed with such enthusiasm in 1964, had failed. The Cabinet was left without a major figure from the trade union hierarchy even of the standing of George Isaacs, let alone Bevin. *The Times* called it 'the most politically significant resignation since Aneurin Bevan's in 1951'.[21] Cousins immediately resumed his position as General Secretary of the TGWU, and although the executive of the union required him to resign as an MP, he stayed on in the House until November, with the express purpose of fighting the legislation. The large majority of the PLP, including most of the Trade Union Group, stood by the Government. Nevertheless, fifty Labour MPs signed a reasoned amendment, sponsored by six trade union Tribune MPs, which rejected the Bill, and called instead for a productivity drive linked to higher wages; an extension of public ownership; stringent controls on prices, dividends, imports and overseas capital investment; and a drastic reduction in defence expenditure. Significantly, in view of later developments, twenty-two of the fifty signatories were trade-union-sponsored, a higher proportion than the numbers of trade union MPs in the PLP as a whole (44% as against 36%).[22] Outside of Parliament, trade union disaffection was seen when the tradition-ally loyal miners, at their annual conference two days after the Bill was published, voted by 243,000 to 241,000 to oppose the Bill, against their executive's recommendation.[23]

The seamen's strike, Cousins' resignation and the increased PLP and trade union opposition to the legislation all indicated that the Government–union consensus on the incomes policy would be subject to severe pressures under the 1966 Government. But to this point, the policy was still mainly a continuation of the approach taken by the 1964 Government. The statutory delaying provisions of the Bill, even the confrontation with the seamen had been a culmination of the strategy adopted at the beginning of the year, and the wage norm and the criteria of the policy remained those established in the tripartite discussions before April 1965. The attempt to limit general demand and thus the rate of growth in the interests of the balance of payments was part of this approach, but the Government had so far refrained from reverting to a 'full stop' including abandoning full employment. But if to some extent the original basis of the consensus still obtained, it was by this time extremely unstable. For the introduction of the Bill did nothing to quell the run on sterling, which indeed reached massive proportions by mid July. Treasury forecasts began indicating that balance of payments equilibrium could not be achieved either by the end of 1966 nor indeed by the end of 1967. The Bank of England made it clear to the Government that without an unequivocal deflationary programme the Central Banks could not be expected to continue their support of sterling.[24] In an attempt to salvage what remained of the Government's growth objectives, a number of Ministers (including Brown, Jenkins, Crosland, Crossman, Benn and Castle) tried to raise the devaluation alternative, but the Prime Minister adamantly held to the view that devaluation would not solve Britain's underlying problems of economic structure, would itself necessitate a heavy deflation, and since the pound was the main 'line of defence' for the dollar, would endanger the international monetary system.[25] Reliance on import controls and restrictions on overseas private investment does not seem to have been considered as a sufficient alternative in itself and had the additional disadvantage of further upsetting monetary allies. The Government turned instead to a massive deflationary programme, designed to further reduce domestic demand by over £500m. As for the incomes policy, it was turned into a wage freeze.

Inside the Government there were three distinct views with regard to a freeze.[26] The Treasury's main interest was in the increased taxation and public expenditure cuts; it took the view, most commonly associated with Professor Paish, that the wage inflation problem would be solved by the deflationary package – by running the economy at a level of unemployment of 2 to $2\frac{1}{2}\%$. A freeze would be an additional 'bonus' to which it was not opposed.[27] The DEA, which saw both its incomes policy and the National Plan being destroyed, had urged a lesser degree of deflation together with the replacement of the $3\frac{1}{2}\%$ norm by a zero norm, but with the retention of some of the exceptions embodied in the incomes policy to retain its original structure. The Ministry of Labour, however, and particularly its Deputy Secretary, Sir Denis Barnes, with whom the Prime Minister had developed a close relationship during the seamen's strike, advocated a complete twelve month wage freeze without exceptions of any kind. The final package reflected all three positions, but leaned heavily to the Treasury and Ministry of Labour plans.

On 20 July the Prime Minister outlined the measures the Government was taking to deal with the short-run pressure on sterling and with the 'underlying problem' of money incomes increasing faster than production.[28] The measures included a £150m cut in public investment programmes; a 10% surcharge on purchase tax and excise duties; increased postal charges; tightened controls on building; restrictions on hire purchase; a cut of £100m in Government overseas expenditure; and a £50 limitation of travel outside the sterling area. Henceforward a level of up to 2% unemployment would not be 'unacceptable'. There would be a six month 'standstill' on the payment of wage and salary increases from 20 July, followed by a further six months of 'severe restraint'. Companies would have to 'hold down' their dividends during the twelve month period. The Government also called for a similar standstill on prices, but since one of the main purposes of the deflation was to raise prices by indirect taxation, prices would be allowed to increase to cover these, as well as increased import costs and seasonal factors. For the DEA, the measures constituted a particularly heavy loss of credibility, and George Brown reacted by submitting his resignation, only to withdraw it again after his supporters urged him to stay on. (He remained at the DEA, however, only long enough to see the Prices and Incomes Bill through Parliament and on 10 August he moved to the Foreign Office and Michael Stewart became Secretary of State for Economic Affairs.[29]) Frank Cousins announced that if he had not already resigned, he would have done so on 20 July.[30]

In its extensiveness and rigid implementation the freeze was designed to be far more severe than its predecessors of 1948 and 1961. Rather than follow the 1961 precedent and allow payment of increases due after 20 July under agreements already made (this involved some six million workers, most of them covered by long-term contracts), the Government required employers to renege on their contracts and defer payment for six months. Although the arbitrary nature of this was evident in that workers lucky enough to have had increases paid on 19 July escaped the freeze, the Government reasoned it was less arbitrary (and certainly more comprehensive) than allowing six million workers to escape the freeze.[31] It extended it as well to cost of living arrangements, standing commitments for periodic review and Wage Council proposals, and it prohibited any retrospective payments covering the standstill period. There was, in addition, no question of the freeze being 'voluntary' this time, not only because statutory powers were already at hand, but also because employers had to be protected at law for reneging on contracts. Although the Prices and Incomes Bill introduced on 4 July was now inadequate (it provided statutory delays only for those increases referred to the NBPI whereas the freeze ruled out all increases *a priori*), the Government took advantage of the fact that the Bill had already received its second reading, and appended as an amendment a completely new section (Part IV) empowering the Government to make an order enforcing the freeze on the basis of the same penalties as in Part II. Part IV, unlike the rest of the Bill, would lapse automatically after twelve months. Its powers did not apply to dividends or profits. It did permit the Government to make an order holding any price or reducing it to the level prevailing on 20 July, but the prices criteria established in April 1965 still applied during the freeze except for the one which allowed for an increase in the rate of return on capital. The major change with regard to supervision over prices was that the Government promised to extend the early warning system to cover a wider field of items and until that was done any manufacturing (but not wholesaling and retailing) enterprise with over 100 workers was expected to notify the Government of price increases and to refrain from introducing the increase until it received Government approval.

These cold details were all set out in a new White Paper [32] released on 29 July, coincident with the date of Wilson's visit to Washington where he received American support for the measures (President Johnson hailed Wilson as a 'man of mettle' comparable to Churchill).[33] Meanwhile, the Prices and Incomes Bill was being rushed through Parliament with great haste to ensure that the new freeze powers were available by the time Parliament rose for the summer recess on 11 August. First and Second Readings of Part IV were taken not on the floor of the House but in the Standing Committee to which the original Bill had been sent after its Second Reading, which now sat virtually without break, often throughout the night, until it finished its work. The Opposition and the PLP Left were incensed at the way the Bill was being handled. Since the Committee stage of legislation is designed to deal with the details of legislation after it is passed in principle on Second Reading, this meant

that the principle of the statutory freeze could not be discussed properly by Parliament. A Conservative motion that the Bill be brought
to a Committee of the Whole House was debated on 3 August. While
the Government maintained that, since the penalty clauses of Part
IV were the same as in Part II, there was nothing in principle new in
the Bill, the Opposition argued that the penalties might be the same,
but the crimes were different.[34] The motion was defeated by 277 to
255 votes. The Government set aside only one day respectively for
the Report Stage debates and Third Reading (9 and 10 August);
and the Lords were required to deal with all the stages of the Bill on
11 August. The Prices and Incomes Act was given Royal Assent on the
following day.

What exactly had happened to the Labour Government's incomes
policy as a result of the 20 July measures? The first and main effect
was the abandonment of full employment. Unemployment rose from
1.1% in July to 2.3% in November and to a high of 2.6% in February,
1967; from 260,000 registered unemployed to over 600,000.[35] Secondly,
Labour's essay in economic planning, which with full employment,
had been the basis upon which the incomes policy was presented to
and found acceptable by the party and the unions, came to an end.
Virtually every assumption underlying the forecasting exercise called
the National Plan was swept away on 20 July. Thirdly, 20 July laid
bare the fallacy of the 'partners in economic decision-making' approach. The possibility of a freeze was not raised with the General
Council before the measures were announced and that body could
only regret 'that the Government felt compelled to announce publicly, without prior consultation with those who had signed the Joint
Statement of Intent on Productivity, Prices and Incomes, so violent a
departure from the principles on which the Joint Statement was
based'.[36] Finally, the freeze marked the clear end of the voluntary
incomes policy. In the first instance the Government tried to maintain
that the voluntary policy was still in operation in that the implementation of Part IV was discretionary: it would only bring it into effect
by Order in Council if the freeze was not being observed. But the
double-edged definition of voluntarism was particularly difficult to
maintain when it was made clear at the same time that if anyone
could not be persuaded by the threat of powers to accept the freeze,
the powers would be applied.[37] In any event, there was little prospect
that this verbal tightrope would have to be walked for long. When
Michael Stewart took over the DEA on the day the Act was passed,
he had no doubt that Part IV would be invoked.[38] By the time the
House reassembled on 18 October, an order had been made bringing
Part IV into effect.

The total result was that the four main pillars with which union agreement to the incomes policy had been secured – full employment, economic planning, tripartite economic decision-making and voluntarism – had all been broken. Although 20 July 1966 is usually portrayed as the turning point for the Labour Government in this respect, it is important to recognize that these pillars – with the important exception of full employment – had already begun to show cracks by this time. The National Plan as a viable blueprint for economic growth, the extent of the TUC's influence on the Government, the voluntary nature of the incomes policy, had all been brought into question as early as the summer of 1965. What 20 July 1966 did was to give a harsh and conclusive answer to these questions, and inevitably raised again the older question, of in what sense Labour could continue to present itself as a socialist and working class party.[39]

The labour movement and the freeze

The reaction of the Parliamentary Labour Party to the freeze and Part IV was remarkably mild, and despite the reversal of the policies on which they had been elected, Labour MPs reflected a desire to rally behind the Government in the crisis. Two right-wing MPs, Roy Hattersley and Ivor Richards, organized a note of support among backbenchers for the wage freeze,[40] and although at a meeting of the PLP on 25 July the Prime Minister faced a barrage of hostile questions, the situation indicated that the PLP's opposition to the incomes policy had not grown significantly beyond the number which signed the amendment against the Bill on 14 July. To be sure, the freeze finally erased any differences within the Tribune Group on the question of opposing the incomes policy and they led forty-seven MPs in issuing a long statement condemning the Government's action and urging an alternative policy on the Government along the lines of the 14 July amendment.[41] But not all the signatories of the 14 July amendment and the 25 July statement were the same, only thirty-one having signed both times. Significantly, only sixteen union sponsored MPs signed the latter (34%), suggesting that the hard core opposition had greater difficulty making recruits among the normally loyalist trade union MPs after the economic crisis. Moreover, not all the forty-seven were prepared to abstain either on the Conservative motion of 3 August to commit the Bill to a Committee of the Whole House, or on the divisions during the Report Stage and Third Reading. Under a directive from the Prime Minister for strict whipping to prevent Labour abstentions and fervid demands from right wing

MPs that the Chief Whip threaten abstainers with expulsion from the Parliamentary Party, the number of abstainers was held to thirty on 3 August and twenty-two on Third Reading.[42] Although one of the signatories of the 25 July statement, John Rankin, had announced to the Speaker on 20 July 'that opposite us there is the Official Opposition, there is the Liberal Opposition, and now there is a Third Oppositon on the other side',[43] he and seven other of the 25 July signatories voted with the Government in the 3 August division. The hard core PLP opposition to the incomes policy was made up of the twenty-seven MPs who signed both on 14 and 25 July and abstained on 3 August (most were members of the Tribune Group, thirteen were trade union sponsored, seven were elected in 1966 and over half (fifteen) were elected since 1964). But this opposition was itself highly limited. On two Labour left amendments during the Report Stage to delete the penal clauses from Parts II and IV of the Bill, the Government majority was cut to thirty-nine and forty-two respectively, but while roughly twenty Labour MPs abstained, they refused to vote against the Government even to support their own amendments.[44]

In view of the limited debate allowed in the House, the main burden of the Labour opposition was carried by Frank Cousins in the Standing Committee. To Cousins, this was 'the most important Bill that has been put before a Labour Government and probably the most important that has been before any Government in this century',[45] and as one Tory MP commented on Cousins' absence from one of the Committee's sessions: 'without the right honourable member for Nuneaton in his place today, this is rather like acting Hamlet without the Ghost'.[46] Cousins' main attack on the Bill was that it sought to make the trade union movement 'an adjunct of Government' in a capitalist society, with voluntarism coming to mean 'freedom only to do as it is told by the Government to do'.[47] In fact, however, most of the amendments to the Bill put by Cousins (which constituted the vast majority of all amendments put in Committee) were concerned with an attempt to make the Bill's control of profits at least slightly more commensurate with its control of wages. And it was in this respect that some of the basic differences between the Labour left and the Government came to the fore. The difference was not one, as it has so often been portrayed, of the Government favouring the planning of wage increases in principle, and the left opposing it in principle. The difference was that where Brown argued[48] that both Conservative and Labour Governments in the sixties were 'planning' but maintained at the same time that profits had to remain the 'motive power' for most of the economy, Cousins would not accept this as planning. 'I am not against profits – they can be a stimulus in the society in which we are living – but I have said many times that there are alternatives to this system. I am not advocating that we should have Communism, but if we are to have a system that takes out by profits we cannot at the same time say that we have not got a free-for-all society. I cannot see why we should have restraint placed upon us by a Labour Government which cannot be placed upon us by a Conservative Government.'[49]

Cousins' role in leading the opposition in Parliament to the Bill was an anomalous one, however, in that he recognized the meagre chances of success on this plane, unless the trade union movement itself came out unequivocally against the freeze.[50] It was here that he believed the crucial battle had to take place, and there is in fact little doubt that the TUC contributed in no small measure to the Bill's easy passage through Parliament. On 27 July, the General Council endorsed the freeze [51] ('at this time the needs of the nation must where necessary override sectional demands'), and thus eased the dilemma before many Labour MPs about divided loyalties. The decision was by no means an easy one for the General Council. They had met the Chancellor on 18 July, but the possibility of a freeze had not been discussed and their suggestion that the Government respond to the sterling crisis by 'direct action' (through restricting private overseas investment and imposing import quotas) had been ignored by the Government.[52] Moreover, despite their protests that the freeze would perpetuate income inequalities, dishonour agreements, hurt the low-paid most, prejudice a return to the voluntary policy and 'most important of all' be unlikely to work anyway, the Government made it clear that they were going ahead with the freeze even without TUC support,[53] however great the difficulties of such a course would be. There was little belief on the part of the TUC that the Government's policy was designed to have a progressive influence on the collective bargaining system: 'To a Government', Vic Feather, then Assistant General Secretary, argued, 'an incomes policy is something which produces quick enough results to impress sceptical foreign creditors.' [54] In this situation, the General Council was sorely tempted at its meeting on 27 July 'to reject . . . or at least wash their hands of the proposal', and this was in fact the course advocated by Woodcock and even strong supporters of the incomes policy like Alf Allen of USDAW, who believed the Government was prepared to condemn the TUC to years of futility in attempting to influence members' wage claims.[55]

The majority, however, favoured supporting the Government, and the General Council decided to do so by a vote of twenty to twelve with two abstentions.[56] There were two main reasons. First, they were moved again by loyalty to, and faith in, the Government, believing the measures 'would not have been introduced by a Labour Government unless it had been overwhelmingly convinced they were necessary . . . There was no question in the General Council's mind of the integrity of the Government's intentions . . .' [57] Secondly, they were truly frightened that the Government might go much further in terms of unemployment if the crisis persisted. Wilson had warned them of a 1931 situation and indicated that if the Government had not acted as it did, it would have precipitated an international crisis with unemployment in Britain reaching, perhaps, two million. Moreover, the Prime Minister told the TUC leaders that he would give consideration to their proposal that the low-paid and those involved in genuine productivity deals should escape the full rigours of the freeze, especially during the period of severe restraint after January 1967. [58] Thus when the General Council issued its statement endorsing the freeze, it went beyond mere 'acquiescence'; it saw its role as mobilizing that 'overwhelming public support' without which it was convinced the 20 July measures would fail: 'if trade unionists are prepared to play their part in helping to moderate the excessive increase that has been taking place in incomes, they will be making a positive contribution to economic expansion and to full employment and thus helping to promote their own real interests'. [59] The Government was not slow to draw the correct implications. George Brown immediately welcomed the TUC's 'cooperation in something that must have gone very deep to its heart, something which means tremendous interference with all its traditional thoughts, habits, beliefs and make-up . . . The TUC, not for the first time is ahead in saying *"we will surrender for the good of the country". This is what this party and this movement is always doing'.* [60]

In industrial terms the freeze was for the most part immediately accepted by the trade unions. Even those unions most opposed to the Government's policy, including the TGWU and ASSET, refrained from using the strike weapon as a means of challenging the freeze. [61] Whether the unions would be prepared to follow the General Council in its political endorsement of the freeze, when they met at the annual Congress in Blackpool at the beginning of September, was another matter, however. In the weeks after 20 July, a number of unions which had earlier supported the incomes policy, including NALGO, USDAW, and NUPE with a combined membership of almost one million, announced their intention to cast their votes against the freeze at Congress, and there was a real possibility that the NUR (whose $3\frac{1}{2}\%$ deal with the Government in February 1966 was due in September but held up by the freeze) would also vent its frus-

tration at Congress. Moreover, the AEU, GMWU and NUM executives, who wanted to support the Government and the General Council, were tied by resolutions passed at their annual conferences which
ruled out support for a general statutory wage freeze. The General
Council and the Government were saved from a repeat of the 1950
repudiation, however, by the readiness of a number of the leaders of
Britain's largest unions to give their support to the freeze by arguing
that the incomes policy decisions of their conferences were not binding in the new situation created by the July economic crisis. The only
union executive which was prepared to put this argument to the test
of a recalled delegate conference was the NUR executive, whose
decision to support the freeze was endorsed by a Special General
Meeting on 21 September which voted by 51 to 26 to 'accept the
unpalatable, but necessary wage standstill in the present situation'.[62]
The NUM and GMWU executives rested their case for support on
their prerogative to administer union policy between annual conferences, although both Cooper of the GMWU and Ford of the NUM
both admitted this support was inconsistent with their conferences'
decisions.[63] The AEU executive again followed Carron's ruling to the
effect that the 1965 National Committee's '100% support for the
Labour Government' resolution overrode all others as a guide for
action; and in face of the possibility that the union's delegation to
the TUC would decide to cast its votes against the freeze (the left in
the union claimed that nineteen of the thirty-five members of the
delegation wanted to oppose the freeze), Carron denied the delegation
the opportunity of coming to a decision on the question, and cast
the AEU's votes at the Congress on his own authority, claiming that
policy decisions between the annual conferences were the prerogative
of the executive alone.[64]

Together these three unions accounted for 2,290,000 votes at the
Congress, more than enough to defeat a motion moved by the TGWU
and seconded by NALGO which called for the withdrawal of the
freeze and the Act by 5,037,000 to 3,903,000 votes. The General
Council's Report was passed by the even narrower margin of 344,000
votes (4,567,000 to 4,223,000).[65] The extent to which even the *original*
policy had been discredited in the eyes of the unions was seen by the
response at Congress to a resolution moved by Cannon and seconded
by Cooper which pledged support for the national plan and the
incomes policy along the lines of the voluntary policy of April 1965,
stressing the low-paid. The resolution was passed by 4,930,000 to
3,814,000 votes, indicating that the union opposition to the original
policy had grown by two million since April 1965 and one-and-a-half
million since September 1966. Moreover, Congress came very close

to placing itself in the anomalous position of endorsing the statutory freeze while at the same time opposing the milder early warning legislation. The NUM had placed a motion on the TUC agenda against this legislation before the freeze, and since the motion formed the basis of a composite resolution on the question at Congress, the NUM was obliged to move it, despite its subsequent endorsement of the freeze. It rationalized its position by arguing at Congress that it supported the Government in the crisis, but opposed legislation in principle.[66] The TUC was saved from taking a similar equivocal stand by the action of USDAW, which adopted the exact opposite approach to the NUM, i.e. it opposed the freeze because it made no special provision for the low-paid, but also opposed the NUM resolution on the grounds that USDAW still supported the earlier incomes policy, even with compulsory powers, because it contained exceptions for the low-paid. By virtue of USDAW's 350,000 votes, the resolution was defeated by 4,683,000 to 4,209,000 votes.[67] In a sense, Clive Jenkins had the last word on the 1966 Congress: 'You can see more acrobatics here than you can at the circus.' [68]

There was no attempt at this Congress to make TUC support conditional upon the Government leaving its powers in reserve. The freeze was generally seen as operating compulsorily on the unions in any case and the Government's distinction between voluntarism and compulsion was hardly taken up by the General Council spokesmen or by the speakers from the floor who supported the policy. But the one union most determined to puncture the freeze, Clive Jenkins' ASSET, decided to challenge in the Courts the right of employers to defer agreements involving breach of contract with no legal basis without benefit of the legal immunity which Part IV was designed to provide.[69] Throughout August and September the union came under heavy pressure from the Government not to proceed with its test case. As we have seen, the Government was convinced that it would have to use these powers at the time the Bill was going through Parliament but it hoped to be able to delay bringing Part IV into effect so that Parliament (scheduled to reconvene on 18 October) could endorse the Order within the twenty-eight days required by the Act without having to be specially recalled, and preferably to delay until after the Party Conference at the beginning of October. Although ASSET sponsored only three Labours MPs, many others, including about ten members of the Government and the Prime Minister, were members of the union and its Parliamentary Committee. Ministers wrote letters to the Committee suggesting it urge the union to reconsider and some wrote directly to Jenkins threatening that prominent Ministers would publicly resign from the union.[70] Nevertheless, the union proceeded with its action and on 29 September the Court ruled in favour of the union's case. Immediately, the Newspaper Publishers Association, which had been calling for Part IV to be invoked since August on the grounds that employers should not bear the opprobrium of the Government's freeze, announced they would pay 25,500 of their employees a cost of living bonus due to them under a 1964 long-term agreement, thus practically inviting the Government to use its compulsory powers not only to protect employers against suit for breach of contract but also to make orders enforcing the freeze in specific cases.[71]

These events took place on the eve of the Labour Party Conference in Brighton where, after a special meeting of Ministers on 1 October, it was announced that Stewart would enter into immediate consultation with the TUC and CBI about the question of bringing Part IV into force. Stewart had expected considerable opposition from the General Council, but when he met the TUC leaders in Brighton on 3 October, he was surprised to find none.[72] They realized that the general trade union acceptance of the freeze might break down under pressure from the rank and file if some groups of workers secured increases either through agreement with their employers or through action in the courts; indeed it was in the interests of the trade union leadership, who might otherwise have been discredited in the eyes of their members by virtue of their passive acceptance, to have the freeze applied rigidly across the board. Meeting in Brighton on 4 October, the Cabinet decided officially to implement Part IV and the necessary Order was made on 5 October, the day the Labour Party Conference itself debated the incomes policy.

One additional consideration led the Government to drop finally and unequivocally the pretence of a voluntary policy. The Government was beginning to turn its thoughts to the period after freeze and severe restraint, and although it was clear that the specific Part IV powers were only relevant to this period, the Government wanted to make it equally clear that there would be no subsequent return to a voluntary system. In September, Ministers close to the incomes policy began to speak, albeit vaguely, of the statutory powers, not as a temporary departure from the normal state of affairs, but as a turning point marking a permanent compulsory role for the State in collective bargaining. The first salvo had come, in fact, in the Prime Minister's address to the TUC. Referring to Bevan's famous last speech in the Commons on the inability of post-war governments to *persuade* the people to forego immediate material satisfactions in the interests of growth, Wilson said that Labour had turned to solving this problem through 'the disciplines of . . . legislative action.' He indicated that this would not be dropped lightly in the future, but attached to the collective bargaining system 'to ensure that the planned increase of incomes is related to the increase in national productivity, *and does not attempt to go beyond it*'.[73]

It was in this context that one of the most ideologically instructive debates ever conducted within the labour movement concerning the relationship between the State and the trade unions took place. On 9 September, Richard Crossman, then Leader of the House and closely involved in the development of the incomes policy, openly stated that the freeze was not merely an interruption of normal practice, but an unprecedented and irrevocable socialist action on which there would be 'no going back': 'The July measures were not a last-ditch defence of Government policy, but a last-minute dash for freedom, a break-through into new patterns of industrial relations and new experiments in cooperation between State planning and collective bargaining.'[74] On the same day, a front page editorial in the *New Statesman* picked up the theme, urging that the Government should immediately introduce Part IV, not only because price increases during the freeze were undermining trade union 'voluntary' compliance, but because:

> far more important – the more thoughtful members of the Labour Movement should look carefully at the political possibilities of Part Four, which may turn out to be far more relevant to the problems of socialist reconstruction than its hallowed predecessor, Clause Four. Much of the debate conducted by the Left on this issue has been lamentably illogical. Since when has free market bargaining been a fundamental principle of socialism? It is, on the contrary, just as inimical to the aims of socialism as syndicalism itself. The essence of social democracy is that the market is an unjust and inefficient method for regulating the economic relationships between citizens; that it must be controlled by the intervention of state machinery which is itself responsible to a parliament elected by universal suffrage. This, in its clumsy way, is precisely what the new Government legislation aims to do.[75]

It was an argument directly aimed at the Left of the Party and the unions by the journal closest to those Bevanites like Wilson, Crossman and Castle who were now in the Cabinet. The *Statesman* shared the Left's view that the Government had not been involved in planning during its first two years in office; it agreed the Government had done everything in its power to avoid using physical controls and upsetting the capitalist system. Nor had the freeze been recognized by the Government as a 'socialist' measure, but had been designed to 'reassure capitalist opinion'. But whereas the *Statesman* had before the freeze called for a price freeze without a wage freeze and for physical import controls, it, together with 'the more thoughtful members of the Government', had begun to realize at the beginning of September that the degree of intervention in the market involved would be seen as 'socialistic': 'Prices and incomes regulation, conceived in ideological confusion, born in panic, defended by ministers with hesitation and shame, may be a foundling, but it has true socialist blood in its veins, and properly nurtured is likely to grow into a powerful champion of social progress.' The more conventional definition of socialism was set aside. 'It is pointless to argue that wage and price regulation is only acceptable as part of a completely socialist structure in which virtually all wealth is publicly owned. This, for the present at least, is a pipe-dream.' Collective bargaining, instead of being presented as a product of capitalism and private property, was now seen as an independent defining characteristic of the system, 'a prime source of social evil', maintaining inequalities among workers. Since the Government had inadvertently 'blundered into socialism', it was up to the 'Left' to consolidate the 'benefits' of this accident, and ensure that this 'major instrument of socialist planning' was used to even differentials between different groups of wage earners.[76] In a society divided by wide differences of wealth and income between the classes, it gave a new twist to socialism: equality within one class.

The Left outside the Government could scarcely credit that this argument was being made at all, let alone by its erstwhile Bevanite colleagues. Since when had free collective bargaining been a fundamental principle of socialism? 'The answer is surprisingly simple: since the emergence of capitalism. And as long as we retain a capitalist economy, the hard-won rights of the unions to conduct wage bargaining with employers will be the surest guarantee of rising living standards for working people.'[77] As for Cousins, he had already answered claims by the Conservatives that the limitation of the freedom of the unions during the freeze was the consequence of socialism: 'That is not socialism. It is far from it. It may be Fascism, but it is not Socialism.'[78] And at the TUC, he had responded to Wilson's 'inference that not at any time in the future are we to have a free negotiating machine. Well, if the trade unions themselves are going to surrender their authority, I suggest they will want to surrender it to this body here . . . modernization of our instruments is not a transference of our power into the corporate body of the State.'[79] Again, differences within the Labour opposition to the incomes policy could be seen in this context. Whereas Ian Mikardo challenged Wilson and Crossman to accept the ownership and control sections of *Keep Left*, in exchange for which he would accept the Government's proposals on wages control, Eric Heffer argued that even in a publicly owned economy trade unions would have to be free 'to defend and develop the interests of their members'.[80] But both recognized that such differences were academic in terms of the argument before them, which *Tribune* saw as an attempt to devise a socialist camouflage for 'an unfair incomes policy in the context of a rampantly capitalist economy', and which Michael Foot called dressing up 'one of the Ugly Sisters as Cinderella'.[81] Had the argument been presented in circumstances other than an indiscriminate wage freeze, deliberately induced price rises for deflationary purposes and rising unemployment, had the legislation been designed to produce greater equality rather than unparalleled wage restraint to 'reassure capitalist opinion', as the *New Statesman* itself put it, the argument might have had some appeal to the Left. In the given situation, it fell on particularly stony ground.

The debate was a clear admission that the Wilsonian 'technological revolution' and economic planning had not laid to rest the conflict which had emerged within the Labour Party after the 1959 election with regard to the meaning of socialism for a party like Labour. The debate centred on the right of trade unions to free collective bargaining rather than clause four, but all the earlier ingredients – class, ownership, equality – were there: 'the milk and honey have proved elusive', *Socialist Commentary*, reflecting the view of the Gaitskellites, gloated, 'and now we suddenly find ourselves plunged right back into the unfinished argument about socialism'.[82] But as *Socialist Commentary* also pointed out, the terms of the debate were such that by identifying socialism with compulsion over trade unions, a split between the Party and the unions was even more likely than before. As such, the argument remained one conducted essentially between those who claimed Bevan's mantle inside and outside the Government, and did not become the central focus of the Labour Party Conference, which rivetted its attention on the narrower question of the rights and wrongs of the freeze. The NEC, which had supported the Government throughout, (15 of the 28 NEC members were Ministers in the Government at the time),[83] issued a document, *Economic Policy*, which affirmed that 'the most urgent aim' of the incomes policy was 'to moderate a rise in prices and restore our international competitiveness', although it added that it supported the Government's intentions to develop the policy in the future 'in such a way that the distribution of incomes is influenced less by the arbitrary forces of *laissez-faire* market forces and more by considerations of social justice and economic efficiency'.[84] Speaking in the debate for the NEC, both Callaghan and Gunter hinted that there would be no return to the voluntary system after Part IV expired, but both explained the introduction of Part IV not in terms of 'socialism' but as due to the intransigence of ASSET and the NPA.[85] The NEC statement was endorsed by 3,836,000 to 2,515,000 votes, and the debate itself indicated that the Part IV decision had caused few unions to change their votes since the TUC. A TGWU resolution specifically against the legislation was defeated by 3,925,000 to 2,471,000 votes and two other critical resolutions against the policy in general also fell, while an NEC-backed composite resolution congratulating the Government and the DEA 'on the singleminded determination with which they have pursued the Prices and Incomes Policy', but which incorporated many of the CLP motions on the Agenda by emphasizing that acceptance of the policy was conditional upon price stability and benefits to the low-paid, was passed by a majority of over two million votes.[86]

Despite these clear victories for the Government, the Conference did provide an important foretaste of the fate of the policy at future Conferences as well as of the Government's independence from Conference in any case. For at this Conference, the AEU proved unable to hold its 768,000 votes in consistent support of the platform, and without this support the 1.5 million vote majority on incomes policy was overcome on two resolutions which had direct bearing on economic policy and the freeze. A TGWU emergency resolution expressed 'its grave concern at the sharp growth in unemployment, particularly in the motor car industry' and proposed work sharing as an alternative to unemployment. This motion placed Carron in a difficult position, not so much because the AEU was committed to the principle of work sharing by its National Committee (Carron had again ruled that the '100% support resolution' overrode all others and denied the delegation a vote on the specific resolutions before the Conference), but because the redundancies in the car industry were affecting many of the union's members, large numbers of whom had been demonstrating outside the conference hall on this very issue. Carron cast the AEU votes in favour of the motion, which was passed against the recommendation of the NEC by 3,289,000 to 3,137,000 votes. The following day, with Conference debating foreign policy, Cousins moved another resolution which contended 'that unless there is a substantial reduction in military expenditure the Labour Government's ability to achieve the national economic recovery, social progress and prosperity to which it is pledged, will be impeded by recurring balance of payments crises'. Cousins explained that the resolution was intended to continue the previous days' debate on economic issues: 'we cannot afford to cut today's wages to provide more money for defence commitments'.[87] Again the AEU's vote was cast with the resolution and against the Government, this time due to a chance occurrence which allowed members of the delegation to make their own decision on the question. With Carron and other AEU leaders absent from the Conference on this day, responsibility for casting the AEU votes fell to Hugh Scanlon, then a member of the executive vying for the succession to the union leadership. Scanlon passed the official voting pad to each member of the delegation, and when it was returned to him, it showed unanimous approval for the TGWU resolution. The resolution was carried by 3,470,000 to 2,933,000 votes.[88] These events suggested that the election for the Presidency of the AEU in 1967, the preparations for which by the various factions in the union had already received widespread national attention, would be of crucial importance in terms of TUC and Party Conference support for the incomes policy. At the same time, however, they also underlined the extent to which the Government saw adverse Conference decisions as not binding. Responding on television to the question of how these votes would affect Government policy, Wilson pointed out that the Government alone had to 'take the decision': 'You take one or two kicks in the teeth, but the Government had said it would govern. It has to go on governing.'[89]

The Government had one remaining political hurdle to clear with regard to its statutory freeze – the Commons debate on the activation of Part IV, on 25 October. By this time criticism of the behaviour of union sponsored MPs had emerged, most notably at a protest rally against the freeze organized in Glasgow by eleven trade unions, where Clive Jenkins had threatened that the unions might 'reselect' their MPs.[90] That there was considerable disquiet among union MPs, particularly in view of the quickly rising unemployment, was clear from the debate. Jack Ashley, a GMWU MP, probably reflected feelings widespread among the loyalists, when he said: 'I must tell the Government they cannot have it both ways. Unless the Government can grapple, and grapple successfully, with this question of unemployment, which no one on this side of the House will tolerate, I very much regret that strong Government supporters like myself will be compelled . . . to consider withdrawing support from the policy.'[91] At the same time, however, many of the loyalist MPs were concerned that those MPs who were not prepared to share the 'sacrifice' of supporting the Government should not go unpunished, and in fact Labour MPs were threatened with the loss of the Whip should they abstain. In the event, 28 Labour backbenchers did abstain, although only 8 of these were trade union sponsored on this occasion. The Part IV order was endorsed by 307 to 239, a majority of 68.[92] The PLP's Liaison Committee, which was responsible for party discipline, decided against taking drastic action against the abstainers, and limited itself to reminding MPs 'that no organized group within the Party is acceptable which is not officially recognized by the Parliamentary Labour Party'.[93] Although aimed directly at the Tribune Group, the limited nature of this action was an indication of their invulnerability so long as they were reflecting criticisms voiced by a large section of the trade union movement. *Tribune* did not miss the opportunity to point out that 'if the widespread opposition to the Government's economic policy as revealed in the factories, in the constituency parties and the Labour Party Conference itself, could find no voice in the House of Commons, then it would not only be the PLP but Parliamentary democracy itself which would be in danger'.[94] To have withdrawn the Whip from these 28 MPs (including Frank Cousins who did not resign his seat until November) might have entailed, as one commentator suggested 'the formation of a Left wing socialist party by courtesy of the Chief Whip! And this would not be another I.L.P. Twenty-eight Left wing rebels, sure of their seats for four years, backed now by the TGWU, and soon perhaps by the AEU could raise a very substantial rumpus.'[95] This was an eventuality desired no less by the 'rebels' than by the leadership of the Party as was seen by their continued refusal actually to vote *against* Part IV. Explaining the reason for the abstentions, Ian Mikardo said they 'were naturally unhappy about adding to the considerable difficulties which the Prime Minister and the economic Ministers already have on their plate. This is no contumacious defiance: there never was a sadder or more regretful revolt.'[96]

From freeze to severe restraint

The political support which the Government obtained from the three main bodies of the labour movement on the statutory wage freeze was not in any sense merely symbolic, but extended to its actual operation. Because of the unwillingness of the unions to enter into a direct confrontation with the State, the Government actually had to enforce the freeze through the imposition of orders in only 14 pay cases during the whole life of the Act. The orders covered some 35,000 workers in all out of a working population of 23 million and only three of the orders concerned more than 1,000 workers. The PLP had the opportunity of rejecting the orders through the negative resolution procedure of Parliamentary control, whereby an order under Part IV could have been annulled by a 'prayer' to that effect being passed within 40 sitting days of the order being laid before Parliament. Prayers to annul the orders were made in fact in 13 of the 14 cases, but it was the Conservative opposition in each case which took the initiative, and although approximately 20 Labour MPs consistently abstained on the votes, 6 of the 28 MPs who abstained on 25 October, voted with the Government on some of the orders.[97]

The TUC, for its part, was closely consulted by the Government on each of the orders. At the request of the Government, the TUC generally asked the union concerned to accept the freeze so the Government would not use its powers, but if the union refused, the TUC tacitly agreed to the imposition of the order, although it did succeed in getting a few of the orders rewritten.[98] In public, the TUC continued to express regret at the need for statutory powers, but it considered that any singular attempt to evade the freeze was against the interests of the rest of the unions which accepted it. The TUC's quiet acceptance of the use of the powers was in marked contrast to that of the CBI. On 21 October, the Government made an order requiring dry cleaners and laundries to freeze their prices. The CBI charged that the Government's action was based on letters from housewives whose complaints were 'groundless', and it claimed there had been 'inadequate consultation' on the order. As a sign of its disapproval, it withdrew from the consultations then in progress on the White Paper for severe restraint and announced that it would re-examine the whole question of its relations with the Government and that it was now for the Government 'to restore industry's confidence'. In a letter to the CBI the Prime Minister conceded that the time allowed for consultation had been too short and promised adequate consultation in the future. In the event, this was the only prices order of any kind made during the whole period of freeze and severe restraint, and most applications for price increases even in this industry after the order was made were permitted by the Government.[99] In the words of the CBI's President: 'The CBI reacted immediately and forcefully as we felt that if we let this incident go by default, our future influence with the Government would be gravely weakened. Subsequent events have, I feel sure, justified our action.' [100] Trade union cooperaion on the other hand meant that the freeze was an unparalleled success in terms of wage restraint. The retail price index rose between July and December by over 1% while weekly wage rates remained static and average earnings increased by less than $\frac{1}{2}\%$.

This close compliance with the policy continued during the following six-month period of severe restraint when, despite the increases then allowed in the way of settlements made before 20 July and deferred for six months (alone involving an increase of approximately 1% in earnings), average earnings of all employees rose by only 1.2%.[101] Nevertheless, it was in this period that the Government, by reverting to two of the exceptions established in the original policy, hoped to lay the foundations for a return to a long term tripartite policy, and it put great stress on consultations with the TUC and CBI which began in late September on the preparation of a White Paper for the severe restraint period.

This approach, however, foundered for two main reasons: first, because the Government was primarily concerned that the exceptions should not become avenues for widespread union avoidance of severe restraint, and secondly, because in these circumstances, the TUC was loath to bear responsibility for what it saw as a too-restrictive incomes policy. The July White Paper had established that the norm would continue to be zero under severe restraint and that any exceptions would be 'much more stringent' than under the original policy; and at the TUC in September, the Prime Minister had indicated that the only exceptions would be for the low-paid and for productivity bargains, but maintained that these would have to be 'real productivity concessions' rather than 'a pious declaration of intent' and that increases for the low-paid would have to be such that they did not become 'stalking horses to enable differentials to be invoked'.[102] Clearly, it would have been most useful to identify the low-paid as all those earning below a particular amount, but both the Government and the TUC backed away from this, although Cousins, back on the General Council and the Economic Committee, himself suggested a £15 minimum for a standard working week. The Government insisted that this figure was far too high and that total earnings including overtime had to be used to identify the lowest paid, not pay for the standard week. Even a figure substantially below this would have led to a general rise in wages inconsistent with 'severe restraint', and the Government refused to go further than to suggest vaguely that only those workers whose total earnings were insufficient to secure more than a subsistence standard of living should be counted as exceptions to the zero norm.[103] For its part, the TUC considered that the stringent terms in which Government insisted on casting the productivity criterion would discourage unions from negotiating productivity bargains and, as for the low-paid criterion, contended that by placing so much emphasis on only aiding the low-paid if wage differentials were reduced, 'the Government appeared to be still concerned exclusively with the redistribution of incomes among workers, as distinct from the redistribution of incomes in general'.[104]

The basis for agreement on the criteria simply did not exist. The Government also proposed, however, that the White Paper should establish a joint TUC–CBI–Government vetting committee which would examine key wage cases during the period of severe restraint and after to adjudicate on increases under the policy. This would have been a major institutional development in the incomes policy and was basically an attempt to give the statutory policy wider legitimacy by indicating that the prohibition of specific increases was the product of 'the national interest' as determined not unilaterally by the Government, but together with the central organizations of business and labour. Such a direct role in decision-making at another time might have appeared most attractive to the TUC, since such a role was one of the main objectives of the TUC throughout the early sixties and since it would have finally laid to rest the determination of national interest by 'independent experts', to which the TUC had objected since the creation of the Cohen Council in 1958. But in the economic and political environment of late 1966, the proposal was particularly unattractive to the TUC. First of all, the TUC had no intention of allowing the CBI a direct say in wage increases unless a similar committee was set up to supervise price increases and this was not included in the Government's proposal. Secondly, and even more important, the General Council drew back from taking even part of the blame for what it saw as a unilateral Government policy, expecting that, although such a committee would take responsibility, the final power of decision would still remain with the Government.[105] One unidentified member of the Economic Committee was quoted as saying: 'We are prepared to advise and do all that sort of thing, but we are damned if we are going to do Harold's job for him and his Government.' [106] At least, not any more than they were already doing.

Thus, despite considerable efforts by Stewart and the DEA, the Government was unable to resurrect an agreed tripartite incomes policy. The White Paper [107] published on 22 November had to admit this failure: the consultation had shown 'a wide measure of agreement about the national need for exceptional restraint although it cannot be said that the criteria . . . have been wholly endorsed'. The policy's main objective remained 'to ensure that any rise in money incomes in the first half of 1967 is kept to a minimum'. Commitments entered into before 20 July 1966 and due to be implemented in the first half of 1967 were to be deferred until 1 July 1967 and the public service was singled out for additional restraint in that substantial payments even after that date would have to be made in instalments.

The two exceptions to the zero norm were vaguely but uninvitingly defined. For increases under productivity agreements, 'employees concerned should make a direct contribution toward increasing productivity, for example, by accepting more exacting work or a major change in working practices . . . Payments of increases on these grounds should be dependent upon a firm assessment of the improvement in productivity and not paid "on account".' As for the low-paid, increases would only be allowed for 'the lowest paid', and 'it will be necessary to ensure that any pay increases justified on this ground are genuinely confined to the lowest paid workers and not passed on to other workers'. On prices, however, the White Paper was far more fatalistic: 'It is admitted . . . that some increases in prices may prove unavoidable.' And it added the one justification for price increases which had been included in the original policy, but omitted in July: 'There may also be exceptional circumstances in which without some increases in price, the receipts of an enterprise are not adequate to maintain efficiency and undertake necessary investment.' The 'return on capital' criteria, suspended for six months, had returned.

Although the CBI's official reaction to the White Paper was quite welcoming, the General Council's Statement was the most critical since the incomes policy had been established. Indeed it now engaged in many of the criticisms of the inequities of the freeze from which it had abstained earlier. At the same time the General Council reconvened its Incomes Policy Committee (whose sittings had been suspended during the freeze) and announced that this was the first step towards a 'coordinated trade union incomes policy' based on annual economic reports which the TUC would issue independently. It opposed the continuation of the statutory policy after July 1967 and offered their own policy as 'a more positive approach'.[108] This was, however, a long range proposal more concerned with incomes policy after July 1967 than with the period of severe restraint. Indeed, despite its critical stance and its adamant feeling that the policy should be seen as having been created by the Government alone, the General Council did not withdraw its practical cooperation during the severe restraint period. Until the end of severe restraint, the Incomes Policy Committee basically accepted the zero norm, and maintained close contacts with the Ministry of Labour and the DEA. The NBPI continued to see the Incomes Policy Committee as one of the bodies 'executing or helping to execute the prices and incomes policy'.[109]

In the absence of tripartite agreement on the criteria, the main burden of definition fell to the NBPI. The importance of the Board as a policy-defining body in this period was seen when the Government referred to the Board a series of test cases on low pay from which some general principles might be distilled, and it found the same can of worms which the Government and the TUC had opened and quickly closed in their discussions on the White Paper. Rather than adopt a precise minimum figure as a standard of need to define 'the lowest paid' and thus be seen it be 'inducing' claims, the Board decided not to define the lowest paid in any general way at all.

It proceeded, therefore, to treat each case as unique: it endorsed an agricultural workers' increase since their earnings were well below those in any other industry; but it recommended for retail drapery that since only a minority of workers were receiving total earnings at the level of the statutory minimum set by the Wages Council, the proposed increase should be reduced and that the lower recommended increase should be 'tapered off' for workers with earnings above the minima.[110] In the case of local authority and NHS manual workers, the Board abandoned the low pay principle entirely: 'The root cause of the problem is low productivity and any remedy must be capable of curing the weakness of low pay and low productivity at the same time. Its aim should be to raise standards of pay ... *because standards of work justify it*.[111]

By refusing to define the lowest paid, the Board considerably diminished the value of the one criterion which permitted the Government to present the incomes policy as one of 'social justice', or as a 'major instrument of socialist planning'. 'The Board's piece-meal approach', Hugh Clegg later admitted, 'meant that no general policy for dealing with low pay emerged from the Board's reports.' [112] Moreover, the Government accepted this approach as the correct one, which meant that its own decisions with regard to claims for the low-paid were based mainly on *ad hoc*, often arbitrary considerations which were not easily discernible to the unions concerned. The main consideration, in fact, was not low pay itself, but the extent to which an increase for the lowest paid might induce other claims, even other claims for low-paid workers. This was seen particularly in the Government's attitude to local authorities and NHS increases during the period of severe restraint, a case which also indicates the degree to which the Board was liable to be influenced by the Government when preparing its Reports. An immediate increase to local authority manual workers on 6 March 1967 was justified under the White Paper's 'existing commitments' as the settlement was made before 20 July 1966 and had been deferred for the maximum six months. The Board had decided in early February that NHS workers, who had not completed their agreement by 20 July, should nevertheless receive the same increase on 6 March since pay in the two services generally moved together and the already low NHS earnings had fallen further behind the rest of industry over the previous five years, and since the unions concerned had fully cooperated with the reference. When informed of the Board's intentions (the DEA generally saw early drafts of the Board's reports a few weeks before publication), the Government indicated to the Board its concern that this decision would create a precedent. In light of this, the Board decided since the NHS unions had been given no grounds for expecting special treatment from the Board anyway, there should be a compromise with the Government's view, and the increase should be deferred until May, six months after the earlier NHS agreement expired.[113] In the absence of clearly defined and promulgated standards such 'compromises' – based on calculations of union expectations and strength – were inevitable.

Insofar as the low pay criterion was devalued by both the Board and the Government, unions naturally looked to the only other exception, the productivity criterion, as a source for increases. Here the Board was less chary about definition. In December it set out stringent guidelines against which all productivity agreements should be tested.[114] The rigid standards produced a flurry of union criticism and led the General Council to attack the principle of the Government transferring the responsibility for determining criteria in the national interest to the Board which, they argued, was no more qualified for this task than the National Incomes Commission had been.[115] The Government, however, endorsed the guidelines. One important case at this time illustrated both the reasons why the Board thought it necessary to define the criterion narrowly and the extent to which even this criterion might in practice be abandoned for other considerations. One week after its report on productivity agreements, the Board reported on a three-year productivity agreement in the electrical contracting industry involving a 13% increase for 1966 (delayed by the freeze) and further sizable increases in 1967 and 1968. The Board found that the increases were unjustified even under the more broadly defined productivity criterion of April 1965, let alone under the stringent severe restraint guidelines. No detailed attempts had been made by the parties to calculate the extent of the productivity gains and there were no controls in the agreement to ensure they were achieved. The Board realized, however, that the agreement had been concluded for other, more compelling, reasons than productivity. The new anti-communist leadership of the ETU had, since coming to power in 1962, established very good relations with the employers, and the union itself submitted evidence to the Board showing how it had opposed local bargaining efforts and strike action. The problem was that the workers in the industry had little benefited from the 1963–6 agreement and the tight union discipline: 'the relative position of contracting electricians was somewhat worsened rather than improved during the three years'.[116] The new agreement, with its large increases in wages, was a product of the need, as employers put it, to maintain 'the new spirit which now exists between the Association and the Unions'.[117] If the ETU leadership 'now failed to deliver the money, their opponents, who retained a considerable following, would have a field day. The Board were aware of these points', Hugh Clegg has written.[118] In order to accept the settlement without undermining its own productivity criteria, the Board 'had recourse to sophistry. The standstill had imposed a delay of six months on increases negotiated but not yet paid. The Board now argued that this meant that the increases had to be paid at the end of the six months, even though the increase was 13% in a period of zero norm.'[119] It did recommend that the subsequent increases due in September 1967 and 1968 should be renegotiated in light of any progress made toward increasing productivity, but the Government itself was less discriminating and allowed all three stages to be implemented without renegotiation.

The Board had recognized the possibility that the full agreement might, despite its reservations, be implemented. It argued, therefore, that 'the employers must be prepared to accept that if productivity does not come up to their expectations, the failure should be reflected in reduced profit margins . . . [rather than] by increasing the level of prices'.[120] In view of this recommendation, it was surprising indeed that the Board did not examine the profit situation of the firms in the industry in any detail. The National Incomes Commission, reporting on the 1963 Agreement, had found that the contracting industry was sheltered from foreign competition and that within the industry there was an absence of 'keen and effective competition' particularly among the large firms. It made 'an urgent case in the national interest' for a survey of price and profit policies in the industry: 'Without proper evidence and findings on profits there is a danger not only that our findings relating to wages will be regarded as one-sided, but that they will, again in terms of an incomes policy, reveal only a part of the picture.'[121] But whereas the NIC had lamented at its lack of powers to collect evidence on profits, these were now in the possession of its successor: that was one of the very purposes of making the Board a statutory body through Part 1 of the Prices and Incomes Act. Yet despite the NIC's strident demands with regard to the analysis of profits in this very industry, the Government did not ask the Board to examine profits when making its reference and the Board itself

did not take any initiative in this matter. It limited itself to an examination of the profit statements in the published accounts of seven
of the 2,650 member companies of the employers federation (even
the NIC looked at more), and although this cursory examination
showed that the rate of profit was higher than in manufacturing
industry generally, and had increased considerably since 1961,[122]
the Report only commented that there was little variation in profit
between 1963 and 1965. It was even more surprising, in view of the
Board's recommendation that profit margins should bear the burden
of any failure to cover increased labour costs by increased productivity during the period of the 1966 agreement, that when the Government asked the Board at the end of 1968 to review the consequences
of that agreement, it did not ask that the performance of prices and
profits be examined, and the Board itself did not do so.

Indeed, the Board generally was lenient with regard to prices and
profits in its reports during the period of severe restraint. It was
given several references raising the question of whether prices should
be increased to cover rising unit costs following the decline in demand
induced by the deflation, and the Board justified price increases in
these cases on the 'efficiency and investment' (i.e. return on capital)
criterion reintroduced in the November White Paper.[123] Where the
Board was critical of price increases during the period of severe
restraint, it was primarily with regard to the Government's policy
of deliberately trying to deflate the economy through price rises
induced by increased taxation, and particularly the Selective Employment Tax introduced in the 1966 Budget.[124] But during the period of
severe restraint, the Board was given only one price reference by the
Government which was open to rejection on SET grounds. Moreover,
the main contributing factor to price rises in this period was not
increased taxation as had been the case during the six month standstill, but increased profit margins and import prices.[125]

Whereas it had been possible for the Government to argue in the
latter half of 1966 that price increases were the result of its deliberately letting through its controls increases due to taxation, the increases in 1967 indicated that there was virtually no control at all.
Indeed, over the whole year of standstill and severe restraint, there
were only some 1,000 notifications of price increases to the Government under the early warning system embodied in the legislation. Of
these, 561 were received by the Board of Trade and 395 accepted as
justified; and 192 were received by the Ministry of Agriculture,
Fisheries and Food of which 87 were accepted as notified, 72 accepted
after modification, only 33 were withdrawn or lapsed.[126] Even more
notably, although the major rises in the retail price index occurred

in housing and transport, the Ministry of Transport received only one price notification (which it permitted) and the Ministry of Housing and Local Government received none.[127] The DEA had estimated in 1965 that there were three million price changes a year in Britain;[128] even if that figure was reduced substantially during the deflation of 1966–7, it is obvious that Labour's 'price control' covered an infinitesimal proportion of the total, less than one-thousandth of 1%. The effects of rising prices in a period of wage freeze and severe restraint was that overall real wage and salary earnings for the twelve month period, fell by almost 1%.[129] For the large majority of workers the fall was much greater since, as the NBPI pointed out, 'while retail prices increased for everyone only a minority of workers received pay increases during the period of severe restraint'.[130] The extent to which manual workers real wages were cut can be seen from the fact that weekly *money* earnings in engineering, ship building, chemicals and iron and steel were between 2 and 5% lower in January 1967 than in June 1966 as a result of less overtime working and the freeze, and only in iron and steel had they risen above the June 1966 level by June 1967.[131] Not surprisingly, the NBPI reached the conclusion that 'a widespread impression exists in the public mind that prices have moved much faster than wages, and this impression increasingly made the standstill less acceptable'.[132] The extent of public disenchantment with the policy could be seen from public opinion surveys which showed that whereas 43% of respondents saw the prices and incomes policy as a 'good thing' in July 1966 rising to 48% in August as the freeze was introduced heralding a freeze on prices as well as wages, this fell to 37% by September and to 33% by July 1967.[133]

As is clear from the statistics on wages for the twelve months after July 1966, this public disenchantment with the incomes policy did not affect trade union compliance during the period. Ironically, at the end of the period in June 1967, it was found that the hastily drafted powers of the 1966 Prices and Incomes Act were in fact less prohibitive than they had seemed, at least with regard to increases due before 20 July 1966. ASSET had continued its challenge in the courts on the grounds that the wording of Part IV was ambiguous and it was not what was actually paid on 20 July which was legally binding, but what was contractually due to be paid according to settlements before that date. In June 1967, the Court of Appeals found in ASSET's favour.[134] *The Times* commented: 'Last year's Prices and Incomes Act has been shown to leak like a sieve ... If all trade union leaders had adopted the litigious militancy of Mr Clive Jenkins the policy would now be in shreds.' [135] Apart from DATA, however, other unions did not seek to escape through this loophole in the Act. Nor was this reluctance to take legal action compensated for by more traditional forms of militancy. Cousins explained to the 1967 TGWU conference his own union's unwillingness to take strike action against the freeze: 'We did not do so because we do not want to destroy the Government; we wanted to persuade them.' [136]

The unions had stood by the Labour Government. But while they did so, it became increasingly clear that this cooperation could not continue without having a permanently damaging effect on trade union organizational strength. Total trade union membership in Britain had been growing steadily in the 1960s, apart from a marginal decline in 1962 after the Conservative Government's pay pause and deflation; in 1964 and 1965 membership grew by 1.5% and 1% respectively. But the sharp rise in unemployment coupled with the difficulty of recruiting new members when wage increases were prohibited led to a fall in membership of 0.7% in 1966, the largest fall in any year since 1958 and before that since 1945. The effect on membership of trade unions affiiliated to the TUC was even more marked, the decline in 1966 being 82,000 in all, almost 1% and, apart from 1958, the largest fall in membership since 1932.[137] Union activists naturally vented their frustration on their leadership. As Woodcock affirmed in March 1967: 'this resentment is building up, it is there – perhaps to the Government it remains hidden below the surface, but to me and the General Council it is hitting us hard frequently as we come against it.' [138]

More significant still were the signs of disaffection from the Labour Party. In response to a freeze order blocking an increase for 1,500 of its members, the National Society of Pottery Workers with 27,600 members announced in February that it was withholding its affiliation fees to the Labour Party because, its General Secretary said: 'This Government is totally anti-trade union, and it is time the rest of the Trade Union movement woke up to the fact. We shall not be making any further payment to the Labour Party for the time being – we are not going to provide the ammunition for the Government to shoot us down with.' [139] In November, a major branch of the NUR, Croydon No. 1, disaffiliated from three local Labour Parties, and calls for similar action at both the local and national level were not infrequently heard from the branches of other unions, although they were generally discouraged by union officials.[140] The most telling action perhaps was taken by individual rank and file members who contracted out of paying into the political funds of their unions. The number of trade unionists paying the political levy fell by 192,000 in 1966, by far the largest fall in any year since 1927 (the decline in

1950 had been 130,000).[141] Labour Party membership, which had reached a peak of 6.5 million in the mid-fifties, declined to 6.3 million by 1962 and then recovered strongly to almost its peak level by the end of 1965, fell by over 100,000 in 1966; trade union membership fell by 63,000 and individual membership by 41,000. The fall in union membership was cushioned by unions maintaining their total affiliations at previous levels, and the Party ascribed the fall in individual membership to the increase in minimum subscriptions in 1966 from 6d to 1s, but the widely reported demoralization of constituency labour parties as well as a further reduction in individual membership of almost 42,000 in 1967, indicated that there was much more involved than the cost of membership.[142] In March 1967, Labour lost two by-elections in traditionally solid working class constituencies (Rhondda West and Glasgow Pollok), and in the local government elections in April and May, the Party lost control of London for the first time since 1934 and was left with fewer seats in the borough elections than in any year since 1945.[143] These electoral defeats cannot be wholly ascribed to the Government's incomes policy and the effects of rising prices on real wages during the freeze and severe restraint, of course. Nevertheless, a survey by Mark Abrams in 1968 found: 'A high proportion of the lost Labour vote is made up of disaffected working class voters, who put "keeping down prices" as a top priority . . . They incline, at least more than the other groups, against interference with the unions or with unofficial strikes.' [144] These clear signs of rank and file disenchantment did not end with the freeze and severe restraint, but were quickened and deepened and eventually taken up by the TUC and the Labour Party Conference as the Labour Government maintained its statutory incomes policy in being after June 1967. It is to this developing conflict between the labour movement and the Labour Government that we now turn.

6
The statutory incomes policy – Labour Government versus labour movement

The 1967 legislation: 'C'est seulement le provisiore qui dure ...'

A fundamental problem facing any Government which has imposed a wage freeze is to guard against a compensatory wage explosion in the following period. To the Labour Government in 1967, this problem was particularly acute in that its entire economic strategy was predicated upon securing a stable balance of payments surplus by early 1968. Thus while an overall surplus in the last quarter of 1966 convinced Ministers that 'the corner had been turned',[1] it was clear that an extensive relaxation of wage restraint and deflation could have the effect of upsetting the fragile renewal of confidence in the future of the pound's stability. Callaghan's 'steady as she goes' April budget saw the contribution of incomes policy as that of keeping the growth of wages to 6% over 1967 as a whole,[2] but a new White Paper[3] in March retained the 'nil' norm (lest any figure above zero might be seen by the unions as a minimum due to them after the freeze and severe restraint) with any increase having to be justified on the grounds of the four exceptions in the original policy. On prices and dividends, on the other hand, there was a complete return to the pre-freeze policy. Callaghan told the House in April of the Government's desire to see 'a recovery from the present low level of profitability', and he pledged: 'I have no intention of killing the goose that lays the golden eggs.'[4] The Government's approach again pleased the CBI ('remarkably close to our original proposals'[5]), but disappointed the TUC. Indeed relations between the Government and the TUC in early 1967 were more strained than at any time since the 1964 election. After the fruitless discussions on the severe restraint White Paper had suggested the chances were slim of resurrecting outright union endorsement of continued wage restraint, the DEA showed little interest in detailed negotiations on the TUC's demands for a 'more radical and progressive' post-freeze policy. The new White

Paper was submitted in draft to the TUC only some ten days before publication in more-or-less non-negotiable form. The Economic Committee responded by refusing to discuss the draft with Stewart in any detail.[6]

Earlier discussions in January and February were concentrated almost exclusively on the question of continued statutory backing for wage restraint after the freeze powers expired in August. In this regard the General Council hoped to resurrect as far as possible its September 1965 agreement with George Brown: the Government would not renew Part IV or replace it with new legislation and refrain from implementing Part II of the 1966 Act, and the TUC would, for its part, strengthen its own wage vetting scheme. The standards by which the General Council examined claims would be set out in annual reports on the economic situation with particular reference to wage developments, and would be specifically endorsed by an annual conference of executives, starting with one in March to inaugurate the policy. But while the General Council hereby was picking up Cousins' suggestion to the 1966 Congress that if the unions gave up powers it would be to the TUC not the state, the Government immediately made it clear to the Economic Committee that it was not interested in a repeat of the 1965 bargain.[7] Stewart did suggest that the one way which the TUC might eventually make its plan a viable alternative to legislation would be to introduce sanctions of its own (i.e. ultimately by threatening 'recalcitrant' unions with expulsion from the TUC), but the General Council, surprised to find themselves rather than the Government on the defensive in the face of their proposal, responded bitterly. They felt that Stewart, unlike Brown, was not prepared to engage in 'horse-trading' with them, and they complained of being 'subjected to the lectures of a schoolmaster'. Woodcock was convinced that legislation would prove to be less effective than TUC wage restraint in the long run:

> The Government say to us: 'Your scheme sounds all right, but what do you do with your recalcitrants?' I ask them: 'What do *you* do with our recalcitrants? Are you going to send them to prison?' This, of course, is the implication of legislation. Well you will not deal with recalcitrants by sending them to prison ... but they might be dealt with either by their own executive, if they are up against their own union policy, or by the TUC if it is the executive that is calling a strike. Without giving any guarantee that we can smooth every difficulty, we offer the best prospect there

is in this democracy of dealing with people who do not conform.[8]

The Government did not minimize the role the TUC could play as an agency of social control against those 'who do not conform': it saw the TUC's Incomes Policy Committee as an important complement to a statutory policy and one of its main aims was to promote the assertion of centralized TUC authority over wage movements.[9] Accordingly, although the Government had made up its mind to activate Part II and also seek new powers in 1967, it refrained from announcing this officially before the 2 March Conference of Executives so as not to jeopardize the prospects of the General Council's plan being endorsed by the unions. But in its discussions with the General Council it refused to be shaken on the need for continued powers, as well. A last-ditch attempt by the General Council to change the Government's mind at a two-hour meeting with the Prime Minister on the eve of the Conference, produced only the suggestion that the Government was prepared to negotiate on the length of the period for which claims and settlements could be delayed (the Government was suggesting 10 to 12 months), but that new legislation in 1967 was inevitable.[10] In these circumstances, the Conference was a particularly inconclusive gathering, despite the fact that with the TGWU voting in favour of the TUC scheme the General Council's new policy was endorsed by 7,604,000 to 963,000 votes. For it was clear from the debate that the vote represented less a positive interest in the TUC scheme than a demonstration against legislation, a desperate grasping of straws in the hope that the Government might yet be persuaded to desist from new legislation, if not from Part II of the 1966 Act.[11]

The extent to which a repeat of the September 1965 bargain was not on the cards as far as the Government was concerned was reflected in the fact that the main division inside the Cabinet did not concern the question of whether new legislation was required or not but whether legislation should be permanent or, like Part IV, of temporary duration.[12] A strong group of Ministers, led by Crossman and Stewart, contended that the freeze should be treated as a watershed as had been suggested in September 1966, and that the freely voluntary principle should be buried once and for all. In the end, however, the Cabinet opted instead for maintaining the voluntary–statutory dichotomy. It introduced new legislation empowering it to delay wage increases referred to the Board for seven months, but it also limited the life of this legislation to one year. There were a number of reasons for this, above all the Government's primary concern with the short-term balance of payments performance. Since the content of the policy was determined by this consideration, it followed that the statutory powers should also be pushed forward a year or so at a time on the grounds that the immediate economic situation made this imperative. While some conflict with the unions was inevitable, it was thought inadvisable to exacerbate this conflict unduly by raising questions of principle at this stage. A twelve month 'transitional' Bill had the support of the CBI and would also be easier for the PLP to accept than permanent legislation. Finally, the Donovan Commission was scheduled to report at the end of 1967, and was expected (indeed being privately urged by the Ministry of Labour [13]) to make wide-ranging proposals with regard to a legal framework for collective bargaining. The Government could reasonably expect, therefore, that Donovan would give the legitimacy to permanent statutory powers which they lacked in early 1967 in the labour movement.

The problem with this approach was that it gave the impression that the Government had taken a clear decision on the voluntary–statutory question and decided to bring all statutory controls to an end when the 1967 Act expired. Indeed, moved by the exigencies of securing union and PLP support, some Ministers spoke as if this was the case. The Prime Minister, for instance, told the UPW executive on 31 March: 'we believe on the whole that it is necessary to keep some reserve powers for a few months longer – this wouldn't go beyond the early months of next year, of 1968'.[14] In fact, however, the Government had merely postponed a final decision on the principle of statutory powers, and the actual position was stated more candidly by Stewart, who repeatedly made the point that, while it was the Government's 'hope and expectation' that no powers would be needed after August 1968, it would not be 'sensible or prudent' to give any definite assurances, and that the question could only be answered in the light of the economic situation in 1968 and the proven effectiveness of TUC wage restraint.[15] As a result, opponents of the Bill, both Conservative and Labour, argued that it was the Government's policy to maintain a permanent statutory policy under the guise of temporary powers. And although the Government had in fact made no clear-cut decision either way, these charges were given added force when Crossman said in July that the 1967 Bill left the Government with a great deal less in the way of powers than he and others had originally thought essential, that an effective TUC scheme could not be established successfully in one year, and that if wages moved ahead of productivity again and economic forces reasserted themselves 'the same sort of medicine' would have to be applied as before.[16] Iain Macleod took this as proof that 'the Government have no intention of relinquishing powers in the real sense this August, next August, or any other August'.[17] And Ian Mikardo suggested: 'The French in their ineffable wisdom have many interesting sayings, one of which is "C'est seulement le provisiore qui dure" . . . I have a horrible feeling that that is what is happening and will happen to the prices and incomes legislation. It will go on being temporary for-ever.' [18]

The 1967 Prices and Incomes Bill was of particular significance because it was the first time – although not the last – that a Labour Government introduced legislation dealing with trade unions with-out the official support of the TUC. This had important implications for the PLP, for when Labour MPs – and particularly trade union MPs – voted for the earlier legislation, even if this put them in con-flict with the policies of the individual unions which sponsored them, they were able to argue that they were acting in accordance not only with the requirements of party discipline but also with the policy of trade union movement as a whole. This situation did not obtain in 1967 and loyalist Labour MPs, led by the Chairman of the Trade Union Group, Ness Edwards, had warned the Government as early as February that they would not support new legislation, with some MPs suggesting that at least sixty of their colleagues were prepared to abstain or vote against.[19] Although the Cabinet's decision to seek temporary powers no doubt mollified some of these MPs, particu-larly since their opposition was seen to be a factor in the decision, they were still faced with the unpalatable fact that one union con-ference after another in the spring of 1967 came out against the legislation, while delegates increasingly questioned the loyalty of sponsored MPs to their unions.[20] In March an NOP national survey found that 70% of respondents (including 76% of Labour supporters) felt that 'before the Government extends its powers until 1968, the trade union leaders should be given a chance to show that they can keep wage claims down to a reasonable level', and 52% thought that the Government would be wrong to continue with wage restraint at all for a further year.[21] Inevitably, a large number of MPs attributed the disastrous results of the local elections in April directly to the incomes policy.[22]

The Government's parliamentary problems were considerably lightened, however, when the General Council made clear that, while it could not endorse the legislation, it would not campaign against it. Although the General Council as a whole, before the Conference of Executives, had joined with Cousins in arguing that it was not pos-sible to have both legislation and TUC wage vetting, in April the

General Council went ahead with its own scheme anyway.[23] This decision to 'ignore the Bill', as the General Council put it, was not based on the belief that the powers would necessarily end in 1968; on this, they adopted a fairly cynical stance.[24] It was instead a re-flection of the extent to which the majority of the General Council were still operating – either because of their own convictions, or out of loyalty to the Government – within the economic policy para-meters laid down by the Government, and of their concern, despite their strained relations with Ministers, to preserve their long-standing policy of accommodation with the government of the day. Woodcock told the Conference of Executives: 'We have to work with them and we want to work with them. We are not seeking to fight the Govern-ment. Let me make this absolutely clear.' And he went on to express the General Council's 'firm belief' that the real threat to the unions was not the legislation but rather 'what the Prime Minister described the other day when talking to us, as those "other measures" which will be necessary if the Government do not get an effective incomes policy . . . greater taxation . . . a slower rate of economic expansion . . . unemployment . . . less expenditure on public services . . . Those are the real alternatives.' [25] The other alternatives that the TUC had itself raised and were to raise again in their Economic Review at the end of the year – effective price control, temporary import quotas, the nationalization of the private foreign investment portfolio – were still in 1967 but window dressing to the General Council's primary, although by this time unofficial, acceptance of the Govern-ment's economic strategy. Growing rank and file resentment made formal endorsement by the General Council impossible, but as in the years after 1950, the General Council continued to counsel wage restraint. As such, an open confrontation with the Government on the Bill was out of the question and the only public demonstrations were mobilized by the newly-organized and Communist-led Liaison Committee for the Defence of Trade Unions.

Indeed, since Labour MPs did not enjoy the equivocal luxury of being able to 'ignore the Bill', Woodcock went out of his way to help the Bill's passage in Parliament, contending when it was published on 5 June: 'We are of course against legislation, but if the Govern-ment want a little bauble or plaything we are not going to stop them.' [26] Addressing a full meeting of the Trade Union Group on 6 June, he described the Bill as 'innocuous', pointed out that the Gov-ernment had considered more extreme measures and assured MPs that the legislation would not hinder the TUC's scheme. Ness Edwards, who had opened the meeting by describing the Bill as one of the most serious problems ever to face union MPs, had to admit after Woodcock's speech that the logic of the situation was that they could not oppose the Bill in the Commons.[27] Although Edwards symbolized the disquiet in the Group by abstaining himself on Second Reading on 13 June, he was joined by only thirty-one other Labour MPs, who were mostly members of the Tribune Group, although fifteen of the abstainers were also trade union sponsored.[28] The Bill passed through the rest of its stages in the House without any difficulty, but trade union MPs were reminded of the bitterness being engendered among union activists when the TGWU conference on the day after the Bill was given Third Reading unanimously decided to introduce new procedures to review and possibly reconstitute its panel of MPs at the end of the 1966 Parliament in the light of their MPs' voting behaviour.[29]

Inevitably, the striking ambivalence of the General Council's stand became the central focus of the 1967 TUC in September. That the Congress would oppose the Government's incomes policy and legislation was in little doubt: the unemployment totals in July and August were the highest since 1940, and although the Government introduced some mildly reflationary measures during the summer, the imposition of a 10% increase in electricity prices on the eve of the Congress further aroused the temper of the delegations.[30] The General Council recognized that it would be unable to stem resolutions critical of the Government's incomes policy, and did not oppose either a resolution from the Boilermakers calling for the repeal of the Acts or one from the TGWU condemning 'restrictive and negative incomes policies'. Both were passed without a card vote, with only Lord Cooper prepared to speak against repeal of the legislation.[31] The General Council was concerned, however, that these expressions of criticism should not go so far as to disturb the prospects of securing a better relationship with the Government (especially since, in August, Stewart was moved from the DEA and responsibility for the policy taken over by Wilson himself and Peter Shore). Woodcock suggested to the press that less attention should be paid to Congress decisions than to the Conferences of Executives which voted solely for or against a report from the General Council and which were not encumbered by critical motions from the floor; and the General Council decided on an 18 to 14 vote to take a strong stand against a motion sponsored by USDAW, ASSET and SOGAT called the 'Plan for Economic Progress' which 'deplored' the deflation and unemployment policies, rejected Government interference in collective bargaining and called, among other things, for an extension of public ownership as vital for planning and real wage growth. Speaking against the motion, Woodcock claimed it was putting into question the TUC's policy of accommodation: the choice between different economic policies, he contended, was a technical rather than a political question, and if the TUC engaged in 'political attacks', it only hindered the process of negotiation on these technical matters. 'You do not tell a man with whom you hope to make a deal, as I do, that he stinks.'[32] The line was not a popular one. Cousins castigated Woodcock for wanting 'the bureaucrats who sit on the platform' to determine by themselves what the TUC ought to be doing and he pointed out that it was not on technical grounds, but on a basis of 'political reasoning' that the General Council itself had decided to oppose the motion.[33] The motion was passed by 4,883,000 to 3,502,000 votes.

The tide clearly had turned inside the trade union movement and in registering its protests Congress sought to remind the Government that, in the words of the mover of the motion 'the mistake should not be made of assuming unquestioning and indefinite support of trade unionists irrespective of policies being followed'.[34] This did not mean that the political accommodation between the TUC and the Government had broken down over incomes policy. Congress did not neglect to pass a motion reaffirming its support for the Labour Government, and at the Labour Party Conference a month later, the unions were prepared to subordinate the role of the Party Conference as a policy-making body to its less abrasive role of giving symbolic support to a Labour Government in office. This was reflected most clearly when the UPW delegation, which had come to the Conference intending to vote against the incomes policy, was moved by an impassioned appeal by Callaghan that the Conference should have the patience to allow the Government to prove the socialist worth of its economic policies, to cast its 200,000 votes in support of the Government. This made just enough difference to enable the Conference to pass a motion which accepted the statutory powers as 'vitally necessary at this time', by 3,213,000 to 3,091,000 votes. When combined with the votes of other unions which were more concerned that the Conference should refrain from criticism rather than give outright support, this resulted in the defeat by majorities of approximately 1.5 million votes of a Boilermakers motion calling for the incomes policy to be withdrawn and an ASSET motion along the lines of the 'Plan for Economic Progress'. Of course, the resources the Party leadership could command under pressure at the Conference were not limited to Callaghan's eloquence. Despite signs of disquiet in the NEC earlier in the year, the Government retained its control over it – and thus of the platform – at the Conference (fourteen of the twenty-eight NEC members were Ministers). The fact that

Communists were debarred from membership in union delegations at Labour Party Conferences but not at the TUC also made a difference in the outcome on a closely-fought issue at the two gatherings. Finally, Ministers were able to make use of the resources available to a Labour Government in office: on the eve of the Conference, the Prime Minister met with the NUM executive and told them that the Government intended to defer sixteen projected colliery closures until the following spring. The NUM, which had opposed the incomes policy at the TUC, voted in favour at the Party Conference.[35] The frustrations inside the Party, which had been reflected in the thirty-nine critical CLP resolutions on the Agenda (mostly condemning the lack of price restraint), were only vented in the passing of a resolution which agreed with the policy in principle, but regretted the lack of restraint on prices, dividends and profits.[36]

The 1967 Conference proved to be the last reprieve on incomes policy which the Party outside Parliament would give the Government. For the process had already been set in train which would tilt the political balance in the trade union movement well to the left of the Party leadership. As the Conference was meeting, the returns were coming in on the final ballot in the election for the Presidency of the AEU, from which Hugh Scanlon emerged victorious over John Boyd in the highest poll ever recorded. The election campaign had developed into a straight left–right contest with Scanlon as the candidate of an unprecedented coalition inside the union of Communist and left-Labour activists, and with incomes policy and 'Carron's Law' as the main issues in the election. Boyd, as Chairman of the Labour Party in 1967 and as Carron's choice for successor, was vulnerable on both issues. He had been given the dubious privilege, moreover, of casting the AEU's vote against the 'Plan for Economic Progress' resolution at the TUC over the heads of the union delegation, and did so amid the shouts, 'This is Carron's vote, not the AEU's'.[37] Scanlon, whose industrial background and attitudes were similar to those of Jack Jones, particularly with regard to promoting shop-floor bargaining, and whose political attitudes were to the left of both Jones and Cousins, was not only committed to turning the TUC and Labour Party against the Government's incomes policy, but also to overcoming the General Council's belief in the need for voluntary wage restraint.[38] Coming at precisely the time when the failure of the Government's economic strategy was pushing it towards increased state controls over the unions, and because it meant that both of Britain's largest unions were led by men on the left of the Labour Party, Scanlon's election eventually proved to be of even greater importance to the relationship between the Labour Party leadership and the unions than Cousins' election as General Secretary of the TGWU in 1956.

Devaluation and the 1968 prices and incomes bill

Although the behaviour of incomes in 1967 was fully consistent with the Government's expectations, the balance of payments position continued to confound the Government. An increase in rank and file militancy in the autumn prompted renewed ministerial alarums of a 'red plot' to disrupt industry and threats of legislation to discipline unofficial strikers,[39] but in terms of their total effect on wage growth, these first signs of renewed militancy did not bring about an increase in wages for 1967 beyond the 6% which the Chancellor had taken account of in his April Budget.[40] But despite the economic success of the incomes policy, reinforced by an unemployment policy designed to provide what Callaghan called 'a somewhat larger margin of unused capacity than we used to try to keep',[41] the main objective of policy, a movement towards balance of payments surplus, did not materialize as imports increased while exports decreased in 1967. A number of unforeseeable factors – the closure of Suez, the autumn dock strikes and a slow growth in world trade – aggravated the problem, but as the NEDC admitted in 1968 'even without these it is unlikely that the desired improvement would have taken place'.[42] By the summer, senior Treasury officials already had come to the conclusion that the parity of sterling could not be held,[43] and when currency speculation turned into another mass run on the pound in November, the Government devalued by 14.3%. The incomes policy, used for so long to avoid devaluation, was transformed immediately into a key element in a new two year strategy to 'make devaluation work', under a new Chancellor of the Exchequer, Roy Jenkins.

The fact that the Government did not devalue earlier meant that it had a much greater deficit to overcome and more accumulated debts to pay off, and this in turn necessitated the achievement of a larger surplus in a shorter space of time than would otherwise have been the case. The Government's strategy – outlined in its Letter of Intent of 23 November to the IMF in exchange for further stand-by credits – was to depress personal consumption drastically in order to shift resources to exports. A £700m cut in public expenditure for 1968–9 was announced in January (including postponement of the raising of the school-leaving age, termination of free milk for secondary schools, introduction of prescription charges as well as eventual cuts in defence expenditure) and this was followed in March by a massively deflationary Budget which involved tax increases, particularly in indirect taxation, which Jenkins himself described as 'the

biggest in our history'.[44] The contribution incomes policy was expected to make was to ensure that wage increases did not negate the
effect of these other policies on personal consumption. The November letter to the IMF pledged the Government to an incomes policy
which 'measures up to the requirements of the new situation . . .
The vetting arrangements will be strengthened in order to ensure
that the rise in wages and salaries does not exceed what the economy
can afford in the next twelve months'.[45] Although it did not explicitly
say so, it implied, as the Prime Minister later put it, 'an incomes
policy which by the very nature of things requires statutory backing'.[46] The Labour Left contended that the publication of the letter
was proof that the IMF was dictating the statutory policy to the
Government, and there can be no doubt that British drawings were
'conditional' upon the Government satisfying the Fund that it was
undertaking measures to guarantee financial stability.[47] But the
charge of 'dictation' involves the assumption that there was in fact
a basic disagreement between the Government and its Treasury
advisors on the one hand and the IMF on the other with regard to
correct economic policy in general and the function of incomes policy
in particular. Such an assumption is unwarranted. While the post-
devaluation measures were no doubt introduced with an eye to
foreign confidence, on the question of statutory wage restraint too
many Ministers over the previous three years had defended this as at
least a necessary crisis measure for it to be seen merely as a product of
IMF demands. The point was that the Government essentially *agreed*
with its creditors that the policy, however unpopular with its supporters, was right in economic terms.[48]

The chances of securing even union acquiescence in, let alone
endorsement of, this strategy were particularly poor. The 1949 devaluation had shown the extent to which the prices and profit increases which follow a devaluation can undermine union cooperation
and the 1966 Labour Government had much less good-will upon
which to draw, lacking the 1945 Government's record in the areas of
full employment, public ownership and the social services. Trade
union membership declined in both periods of cooperation with wage
restraint, but the degree of damage was much greater in the later
period: on top of the fall in membership of 0.7% in 1966, there was
an even more disturbing decline, at a time of rising unemployment,
of 1.4% in 1967.[49] Whereas the call to further wage restraint in 1949
followed a Congress which had endorsed the wage policy, the 1967
Congress had already condemned the incomes policy. The immediate
effects of devaluation were such that although average earnings went
up by 3.5% between the fourth quarter of 1967 and the second quar-

ter of 1968, the retail price index increased by 3.8% producing a fall in real earnings for the third six month period out of four since the 1966 election.[50]

The General Council welcomed the devaluation as the only way to secure balance of payments stability and were prepared to accept a cut in real wages for the first six months,[51] but there was a sharp divergence from the Government on its deflationary strategy for the following eighteen months. The General Council's approach was set out in its first Economic Review, a 44,000 word, wide-ranging document, which in its comprehensiveness was only rivalled by the TUC's 1944 Reconstruction Report. Its main theme concerned the development of a new National Plan, which unlike its predecessor, would treat the balance of payments as a real part of the plan, and embody detailed forecasts and specific requirements for investment decisions down to the level of large firms. Based on an examination of productivity trends, the Review argued that the Government could pursue a target rate of growth from mid 1968 to mid 1969 of 6% without raising the unit cost of labour. The TUC would cooperate by continuing with its own incomes policy which, allowing for increases of $1\frac{1}{2}$% to be absorbed by local bargaining outside TUC control, would allocate the remainder of a 5% general increase on the basis of an across the board 14s a week so the low paid would receive a larger percentage increase. The second theme of the Review concerned the redistribution of income. It contended that recent studies had given the lie to the 'insistent line of propaganda' that there had been a remorseless levelling of incomes by taxation which crippled business initiative since the war and demanded 'a transfer of income and wealth to the worst-off sections of the community from the 10% who own 90% per cent of private property and receive each year 25% of personal incomes after tax'.[52]

The importance of the Review was that it defined more precisely than ever before what exactly the TUC wanted from the Government in exchange for cooperation on incomes policy, and made the General Council more confident in its representations. The problem with it, however, was that it committed the TUC to operating an incomes policy in the context of a total economic policy which the TUC did not have the means to effect by itself. For although the TUC had armed itself better than before to take advantage of the planning institutions which were supposed to give the unions increased influence in the state's councils, these institutions had already been relegated to the wings as effective policy actors. The DEA, which was finally divested of its control over incomes policy in April, was but a shadow of its former self, and the TUC discovered from NEDC meet-

ings in 1968 that that body as well 'no longer appeared to be fulfilling its original functions and was being used more as a sounding
board for Government policies'.[53] It was the Treasury, with its lack
of close contact with the unions and its traditional tendency to over-
look their concerns, which was in firm control of the driver's seat.
Only two meetings between the Economic Committee and Ministers
took place on the Review in December and January and they underlined, rather than resolved, the differences in policy. A 6% rate of
growth would have destroyed the Government's policy of reducing
personal consumption, and while the Government accepted a $3\frac{1}{2}\%$
figure for wage increases, it was as a *maximum* permissible figure, a
ceiling rather than a norm, applicable to the low paid no less than to
other wage earners. The TUC argued that since by the Government's
own calculations prices would rise by at least $4\frac{1}{2}$ to 5% due to devaluation and the Budget, the Government was requiring the incomes
policy to effect a substantial cut in real wages yet again.

After the two meetings with the Economic Committee, the Prime
Minister told the Commons that if the $3\frac{1}{2}\%$ figure was not accepted
as a ceiling the voluntary system 'would have to be substantially
strengthened, if need be, by new powers'.[54] In the meantime, the Part
II powers were used for the first time to impose a standstill order and
a reference to the NBPI of a £1 wage increase in the Municipal Bus
Industry at the end of January. Since the Board had already pronounced against the agreement in an earlier report, the move was
designed not to secure the Board's opinion but to effect a temporary
statutory freeze on busmen's pay.[55] Indeed, even had the General
Council accepted the $3\frac{1}{2}\%$ as a ceiling, this could not have negated
the Government's belief that the severe restraint it sought needed
statutory powers 'by the very nature of things'. The Incomes Policy
Committee had remained a very low priority for General Council
members (at its September 1967 meeting only one of the nineteen
members had bothered to attend), and although the Committee received 441 claims between May 1967 and January 1968 and passed
only 126 of these, unions for the most part ignored the TUC's bland-
ishments except as a guide to the Government's view on a particular
claim.[56]

As in the previous year, the TUC Conference of Executives met
(on 28 February) before the Government's plans were announced,
and this again enabled the impression to be created that unless the
unions endorsed the Economic Review as a whole – including TUC
wage vetting – new legislation would be introduced. Although the
press in February was full of 'inside reports' that the Government's
decision on statutory powers hung on the size of the Conference

majority for TUC wage-vetting, Woodcock admitted that an adverse vote would merely be for the Government 'an excuse for saying that legislation is the only weapon we have', and suggested from his vantage point on the Donovan Commission that it was by then not incomes legislation but more direct statutory controls over union activity that the TUC had to prevent by showing its 'responsibility'.[57] But with new incomes legislation in 1968 seeming a probability with or without TUC vetting, the basis of the overwhelming support shown for TUC vetting at the 1967 conference disappeared in 1968. Cousins explained that his executive had come to the conclusion that the best way to put pressure on the Government was to stop being equivocal on the question of incomes policy:

> What we are saying is, under a circumstance where there is a real approach to a planned economy this document is the first halting step towards defining the measures that we think should be taken. But no one is taking any notice. We go direct to the Government, and they reject our approaches. We are rapidly nearing the stage where the issue is: can we halt the Labour Government from destroying the Labour Movement? We think we are doing the right thing by voting against this because, if not, we connive at, we assist in, and we are ready to accept the pattern that has been set.[58]

Scanlon was even more fundamentally opposed: he expressed the AEU's opposition to giving up any of its autonomy to the TUC and argued that the General Council was effectively saying 'you had better let George Woodcock cut off your head or Roy Jenkins will do it for him'.[59] The Review was passed but only by the small majority of 4,620,000 to 4,084,000 votes.

The Government's plans were first outlined in the Chancellor's Budget speech of 19 March and further detailed in a White Paper in April.[60] With the exception of productivity agreements which conformed with the NBPI guidelines, even justified increases would be subject to a *ceiling* of $3\frac{1}{2}\%$ per annum. The 1967 Act would be replaced by another which would increase the total delaying powers of the Government to twelve months from seven; these powers would last in the first instance until the end of 1969 *but the new Act would include provision for renewal*. To redress the balance, the otherwise regressive and deflationary budget increased family allowances (but confined the increase to the lowest income brackets by means of a tax 'claw-back') and introduced a special one-year-only levy on investment incomes above £3,000 a year; and the legislation applied to dividend incomes, allowed the Government to secure price reductions when recommended by NBPI reports, and required early warning of local authority rent increases. Inevitably, the unions saw these new elements as mere sweeteners to a very bitter pill. The Government itself acknowledged that the investment levy amounted to but a 'small charge on capital' (according to Brittan, 'it was carefully designed to do the least possible damage to the effective functioning of the mixed economy'), and the policy for dividends was less restrictive than for wages, since dividends could be increased in excess of $3\frac{1}{2}\%$ if distributions in the previous two years had been 'abnormally low'. The General Council attacked the budget for cutting personal consumption 'in ways which bear little relation to people's ability to pay . . . when speculators have twice in recent months made vast profits out of the economy's difficulties', and described the incomes policy proposals as 'restrictive and heavily centred on considerations of, at the best, short-term and transient advantage'.[61]

Without changing the substance of the policy as announced, the Prime Minister took two steps at the end of March to quell the hostility of the General Council and aid the 1968 Bill's passage in the Commons. He promised to re-open a series of discussions on the Economic Review and much more significantly he passed responsibility for the incomes policy to the Ministry of Labour, under the new title of Department of Employment and Productivity, with Barbara Castle at its head. Her appointment had manifest political advantages: she was a strong believer in the policy; she could be expected to see the Bill through Parliament with much more authority than Peter Shore; and with her Bevanite past and close relations with members of the Tribune Group and left-wing trade union leaders, her claims that the policy would enter a more socialist phase were more believable than if they came from other Ministers.[62] She immediately embarked on a campaign to outline her new policy to trade union conferences, stressing in particular two themes: first, although the Bill was necessary for the short-term job of making devaluation work, she would emphasise not crude wage restraint, but would promote productivity agreements with the technical aid of her Ministry; and second, there would be a tough prices policy, marked by more references to the Board and the use of the new Bill's powers to compel price reductions.

Mrs Castle's appointment was a sign that the Government was aware of the need to make the incomes policy more acceptable to the unions, but it did not stem the hostility of the movement to the Bill. Despite Castle's speeches to the AEU and USDAW conferences in April, the delegates set the pattern which almost every union conference in the spring and summer was to follow and voted overwhelmingly against the Government's policy and legislation.[63] Indeed Cousins' warning that the problem now was one of saving the labour movement from the Labour Government was in no sense mere rhetoric by the spring of 1968. For the blow of increased statutory powers came at a time when the situation of the Labour Party had reached a truly alarming state. The number of trade unionists paying the political levy had fallen again in 1967, this time by 229,000 which meant that since the end of 1965 the number had fallen by 411,000, over 6%.[64] Moreover, by early 1968, unions began to allow this decline to reflect itself in the numbers on which they affiliated to the Party, leading to a fall of 175,000 in the Labour Party's affiliated union membership in 1968, the largest fall since 1928.[65] A few days before the Budget, the sheet metal workers (in a referendum caused by an amalgamation with a smaller union without a political fund) voted to disaffiliate from the Labour Party against the advice of their left-wing executive, who nevertheless ascribed this 'extreme political disappointment' to the incomes policy.[66] Indeed the agenda of many union conferences in 1968 contained resolutions demanding disaffiliation from the Party, and reports on the morale of the constituency parties showed not only a continuing substantial fall in membership but the same deep sense of malaise as in the unions.[67] In addition to a series of by-election defeats throughout 1967, the Party lost three more seats in March 1968 with average swings of over 18% against Labour. The prospects were, as the 1970 General Election study pointed out, 'a disaster of 1931 proportions if repeated at the general election'.[68]

Inevitably, this crisis was reflected to a certain extent inside the PLP. The 1968 Prices and Incomes Bill clearly was going to be a heavy test to MPs loyalty, and as soon as the Government announced its intentions, Wilson warned the PLP that if it were defeated on the Bill, it might resign.[69] In the absence of any substantive changes in the legislation most PLP opponents of the policy seemed to share the view of Mrs Castle's erstwhile Bevanite colleague, Ian Mikardo, to her appointment: 'Her advent to her new post has brought with it no change of policy, only a change of phraseology ... a change in public relations.'[70] When the PLP first discussed the proposed legislation on 8 May, at the first of two meetings set aside for the purpose, the PLP was rocked by a declaration from Emmanuel Shinwell – the Party's elder statesman who as Chairman of the PLP until 1967 had been a strong disciplinarian and vociferous in his demands for loyalty – that he would not vote for the Bill: 'I am more concerned about saving the party than saving the Government', he explained. His attack on the Bill was endorsed not only by the Tribune Group but by union MPs like Eric Moonman and Tom Dalyell who had voted for the earlier legislation.[71] On 10 May, Labour suffered an unprecedented defeat in the municipal elections in which it lost many of the Party's strongest working class areas and was left with only 450 seats compared to an average of 1200 since 1945. Ministers themselves began to warn against the destruction of the Party: 'Let no-one in the Labour movement think that it can save itself or socialism by overthrowing the Labour Government or its leadership,' Tony Benn declaimed. 'If it did so, on prices and incomes as on any other issue, it would be the final end of the movement itself.'[72]

Despite these forebodings, the Government's hold on the PLP remained just secure enough to ensure the passage of the legislation. This was partly because the alternatives were so limited in the eyes of backbench MPs, who were acutely aware that if the Government were defeated, and carried out its resignation threat, a general election would leave the Party in the wilderness and themselves out of jobs. Moreover, the Cabinet was so united on the need for legislation in 1968, whatever the differences on the question of whether statutory powers should be permanent, that a challenge to the leadership on this issue seemed particularly fruitless, especially to the left-wing opposition for whom Wilson remained preferable to Jenkins or Callaghan. Such were the narrow horizons within which the PLP operated that the leadership question was still seen in terms of Gaitskellites versus anti-Gaitskellites inside the Cabinet, which only left the problem for backbench opponents of the incomes policy of discerning who were the greater enthusiasts for the policy: those old Bevanites like Mrs Castle, Crossman and Wilson, who still tended to speak of the policy as if it had 'true socialist blood in its veins' or those like Jenkins and Callaghan who more pragmatically saw the policy as a useful deflationary tool.

The really crucial element in the Government's stability, however, lay outside of Parliament in the stance of the trade union leadership, who despite their opposition to the legislation, were equally determined that the union alliance with the Labour Party under its existing leadership should not be broken and the Government should not fall. Jack Jones wrote in *Tribune*:

> If we were to allow Government policies to destroy the assumption of working people that Labour is *their* party, then the result would not only put the political clock back a hundred years, but would hinder the well-being and economic progress of working people themselves. The danger is surely there, and results from wrong Government decisions

... The dogmas of incomes policy and the sterile and contradictory edicts of the Prices and Incomes Board were
favoured, while the great resources of loyalty and strength
the Government had among workers and the unions were
squandered. Where does this leave the unions now? Against
Labour? Of course not! For trade unionists to talk of breaking with Labour, or opting out of paying the political levy
is to cut our own throats while giving our Tory opponents
a blood transfusion ... But fear of the Tories is not all. We
have to work through Labour because it remains the only
realistic vehicle for major social and economic progress.
Change its policies we must, but to fail to recognize this
basic fact is to move away from the centre of the battle and
sometimes to turn political activity into a mere hobby.[73]

Contracting out was discouraged and the business of union conferences was usually arranged so that resolutions urging disaffiliation
were not debated in deference to executive backed resolutions reaffirming ties with Labour.[74] The Communist Party also used its
influence in industry to discourage contracting out and held to the
line that the Labour Party remained 'the vehicle of the working
class'.[75] Moreover, the union leadership continued to adhere closely
to constitutional proprieties in respect of union-sponsored MPs.
Scanlon, for instance, in his first meeting with AEU MPs in March
said he recognized that their responsibilities went wider than their
union and made it clear that there would be no attempt to impose the
union's stand on its MPs.[76] And while Woodcock did not this time
actually encourage MPs to vote for the Bill, the General Council
decided again not to campaign against it but 'watch how the Government used its powers' after it was passed.[77]

The signals that the trade union leadership was placing distinct
limits on how far it would carry opposition to the Bill were not likely
to escape a Prime Minister noted for his political acumen, and Wilson, while recognizing that some gesture of compromise was necessary
on the Bill, did not allow himself to be panicked into either abandoning the Bill or turning to a National Government solution (of
which there was no dirth of suggestions in the press at the time).
Wilson continued to believe that the key to Labour's success lay
precisely in its ability to use its ties with the unions as an asset in an
effort to integrate them more fully into the mixed economy. He told
the PLP meeting on 15 May: 'without them [the unions] we could
not continue to exist as the kind of Labour Party which all of us
joined. We would become a reformist party uneasily poised between

the Liberals and the Bow Group. This would destroy the Party.'[78]
At a Trade Union Group meeting two days before, he had already
outlined the extent to which the Government was prepared to retreat: it would drop the renewal provision from the Bill.[79] In other
words the Government was returning to the stance it had adopted in
1967: it postponed the decision on future powers. Wilson emphasized that he was not giving any undertaking on this – no decision
had been made and when the time came to make the decision at the
end of 1969, it would rest, as before, on the proven effectiveness of the
TUC's machinery and the economic and productivity results produced by the policy in the intervening period. What the Government's position would be with regard to the Donovan proposals or
the permanent powers of the 1966 Act (subject only to introduction
by successive Orders in Council) was not mentioned. Although it is
impossible to know just how much effect this 'concession' had on the
PLP, it must have given at least some MPs the ground they needed to
drop their opposition. On 15 May the PLP voted to give 'full support'
to the Bill by 205 to 42 votes, and on 21 May the Bill was given
Second Reading by 290 to 255 votes, a majority of 35 (the Government's over-all majority had fallen by this time to 70). Thirty-four
Labour MPs abstained and one, Peter Jackson, voted against, while
six more potential Labour abstainers were paired with absent opposition MPs.[80]

It was, of course, the Bill's application to wages that provoked
most disquiet both inside and outside Parliament. Gallup polls during the Committee stage of the legislation showed that while a large
majority of respondents approved of the prices, dividends and rents
sections of the Bill, 61% of respondents (including 66% of both trade
unionists and 'lost' Labour voters and 50% of 'loyal' Labour voters)
disapproved the proposals to delay minimum wages.[81] The opposition in the PLP, for its part, was more prepared to test the Government on its threat to resign after the Bill received its crucial Second
Reading by concentrating its attack specifically on the penal clauses
on wages. On a Report Stage amendment moved by the TGWU MP,
Trevor Park, to delete the penal powers over incomes (but not prices)
from the Bill, 23 Labour MPs – almost all of whom were Tribune
Group members and 10 of whom were union MPs – voted for the
amendment and for the first time against the Government on incomes
legislation. At least 20 more Labour MPs abstained. The Government's majority fell to 18, and only the fact that 6 Liberals and 4
Labour rebels were convinced at the last minute by Labour's Chief
Whip to vote against the amendment saved the Government from
possible defeat.[82] The Government's majority reverted to 42 on Third

Reading on 27 June, but the warning was clear. Park predicted: 'If the Government try to seek penal powers ever again, not only will they fail to secure the majority support of the Labour movement, as they already have, but they will not get a majority for it in this House.' [83]

The final breakdown of the incomes policy agreement

The NBPI's *Third General Report* in July 1968 revealed, on the basis of econometric calculations, that incomes policy had succeeded in reducing the rate of increase in incomes by 1% per annum, since its introduction. Although some trade union leaders adduced this as evidence that the policy 'was as irrelevant as the blush on a dead man's cheek',[84] it in fact suggested, when taken as a fraction of the amount by which wages actually increased, that *this* amount had been reduced by from 10% to 30% in any given year. This was no mean reduction as far as workers were concerned, especially since the NBPI's calculations had also revealed a 'perverse tendency' whereby prices rose faster rather than slower in years the incomes policy was in operation.[85] Indeed, Government spokesmen indicated that they would have been more than content with the operation of the policy in 1968 if it produced a similar effect.[86] The deflationary policy together with wage restraint did succeed in considerably restraining wages in the second quarter of 1968, but together with a sharp rise in strikes at a time when unemployment remained high (2.3%) average earnings increased by 4.4% between the second and fourth quarters, and yielded a rise in *real* earnings of 2.7%.[87] Not surprisingly, many trade unionists took this as evidence that militancy pays.

One of Mrs Castle's first successes was to induce Jim Mortimer of DATA, one of the staunchest opponents of the Government's policy since 1965, to join the NBPI. Her influence on the policy was also seen in a reference on top executive salaries to the Board, in a new DEP Manpower and Productivity Service to promote productivity agreements, and in the development of a firm timetable for the introduction of equal pay for women. In the central areas of dispute, however, Mrs Castle did not produce a radical shift of policy. She was not able to overcome the Treasury's interest in using the incomes policy for deflationary purposes nor its concern that the prices policy should not discourage profits, and the DEP proved to have no more influence than the DEA over the sponsoring Ministries responsible for individual price cases. In its General Report, the Board complained that nearly all the price references since the DEP took over the policy had related to the relatively minor issue of distributors margins in the aftermath of devaluation and demanded 'economically more significant' price references.[88] The provisions of the 1968 Act empowering the Government to require price reductions was not used (or indeed recommended by the Board) and the Government's main price success in 1968 was to reduce the size of a proposed increase in the price of hearing-aid batteries. On the other hand, the fact that the Labour Ministry had become fully responsible for administering the incomes policy had the effect of further relegating to the background the conciliation services, particularly since Mrs Castle attempted to influence claims at the earliest stages of negotiation. Since claims for higher wages covering almost nine million workers were in the pipeline in the spring of 1968, this meant that there was considerable friction between the DEP and the unions from the outset. Immediately after the 1968 Act was brought into effect on 11 July, the Government imposed a further six month delay on the municipal busmen's agreement. A busmen's delegate conference called for a nation-wide strike but it was called off three days before it was due to begin on the TGWU executive's advice. In challenging the busmen, the Government had chosen a section of trade unionism where the power of the strike weapon had been diminished by the private car, and the TGWU leadership was not prepared to risk repeating the failure of the 1958 bus strike. The Government was able, therefore, to escape having to make the decision of actually using the penal sanctions against strikers. In other areas of industry, where strike action would have been undertaken more readily and with greater prospect of damage to the economy, agreements were allowed to slip through the incomes policy net. However, rather than mollifying trade union opinion, these particular relaxations of the policy had the effect of convincing trade unionists that the Government's use of the policy was arbitrary and unfair.

Indeed, during the second half of 1968 the incomes policy fell to the nadir of its popularity. In July Gallup found that only 31% of respondents believed 'the trade unions should accept guidance from the present Labour Government limiting the amount of increased pay they try to get for their members', while 51% believed the unions should remain free to negotiate at whatever level the unions think is right', and 63% (including 62% of 'loyal' Labour voters and 72% of 'lost' Labour voters) thought the busmen's award should have been allowed. By December only 26% of respondents thought the incomes policy a 'good thing'.[89] Two surveys of opinion in the summer of 1968 were particularly important because they concentrated on the key groups involved. A survey of 500 business executives found that 72% believed the 'prices and incomes policy is necessary at this time', although 57% thought the policy should not apply to managerial earnings.[90] A survey of 700 trade unionists, on the other hand, found that 57% believed that unions and management alone should decide wages in preference to the Government or the TUC having 'a say in incomes policy as well'. Moreover, it was the rank and file and shop stewards who were more opposed to incomes policy than branch officials and full-time officers, in that the latter were more prepared to accept a TUC operated policy.[91]

The marked decline in working class support for the incomes policy was not only the product of its effects on wages. It was also produced by the fact that the original incomes policy agreement between the Labour Party and trade union leadership had so clearly broken down by 1968. This meant that the legitimacy which official trade union support had imparted to the policy in the eyes of the rank and file was no longer available. If it was hoped that Mortimer's appointment to the Board would re-establish the acceptibility of the policy to some extent, this was more than counterbalanced when Richard Briginshaw, the left-wing SOGAT leader and a member of the General Council, publicly resigned from the Labour Party after the Bill was passed, expressing the belief that 'the time for a fundamental political realignment in Britain has arrived'.[92] The 1968 TUC and Labour Party Conference became just as much demonstrations of union–Government discord over incomes policy as the 1963 Conference had been a demonstration of unity on the question. In the interests of making the protest as clear as possible, the trade union opposition to the policy concentrated on securing large majorities on resolutions calling for the repeal of the legislation. A composite motion by the TGWU (which also rejected in advance 'any further legislation the aim of which would be to curtail basic trade union rights') was passed by 7,746,000 to 1,022,000 votes, with the Chairman unable to find one delegate prepared to speak against the motion. A motion by Jack Peel of the dyers union which pledged its support for the TUC's voluntary policy as the only feasible alternative to legislative interference caused considerable embarrassment to the General Council, and it attempted to induce Peel to withdraw the motion. He refused on the grounds that 'even if it was defeated it would show that had we withdrawn it [TUC] incomes policy was simply a meaningless exercise, that we are playing it out without any real purpose'.[93] The motion was passed by only 4,266,000 to 4,232,000 votes, and as the General Council feared, the derisory majority gave the proof to Peel's words.

Whatever the divisions between the unions on the TUC scheme, the extent of their unity in opposition to the legislation was manifested again at the Party Conference at the end of September. Indeed, the opponents of the policy almost wrested control of the platform from the Party leadership on the issue. The NEC had been divided on the policy throughout 1968 and its inability to bridge this division was seen when the 'Mid-Term Manifesto' prepared by Transport House for the Conference did not even mention incomes policy. At the NEC meeting on the day before Conference, 9 of the 12 union members joined with 3 left-wing MPs from the constituency section in favour of the NEC supporting the TGWU composite calling for repeal of the legislation. This produced a 12–12 deadlock, and the matter was only resolved when the Chairman of the Labour Party in 1968, Jennie Lee, cast her deciding vote with the rest of her Ministerial colleagues.[94] In moving the TGWU motion at the Conference, Cousins concentrated on the 'deep feeling of mistrust' between the Party leadership and the unions and suggested that the Labour Party was 'almost getting to the state of accepting that the workers are on one side and the Government is on the other side', and McGarvey in seconding suggested that the unions' support for the Party in the next election hung in the balance.[95] Although the differences between the union leaders on the acceptability of a voluntary policy was clear (Scanlon damned 'the whole conception', Cousins spoke favourably of the 'planned growth of incomes', and Cooper laid the blame for legislation on the unions' refusal to do the job themselves) each made equally clear his delegation's intentions to vote for the motion. The outcome was not in question, but both Roy Jenkins and Mrs Castle attempted to salvage what they could. Jenkins assured the Conference: 'None of us want to keep the present restrictive legislation a moment longer than we have to. We are not masochists'; and he claimed that the existing legislation was needed in the interests of balance of payments success in 1969, which alone was 'the key to an easier relationship between the trade union movement and the Government'.[96] Mrs Castle opened her speech with the startling statement: 'What we are debating today is how to save our movement from tearing itself apart.' But rather than smooth the waters, she launched into a fulsome defence of the policy as having been beneficial to the working class, and ruled out repeal of the existing Acts: 'The Government cannot repeal its legislation on one part of its policy at the instructions of a Conference that has not got responsibility for what would have to take its place.' [97]

Not surprisingly, Mrs Castle's speech did not go down well with the delegates. Indeed her impassioned question – 'And are we to get no thanks from this audience for the fact that the price of beer has been stabilized in the past two and a half years?' – was greeted with sustained laughter. The TGWU resolution was passed by 5,098,000 to 1,124,000 votes and another which demanded rigorous price control and a return to the Price Regulation Committees of World War II was passed without a card vote.[98] The AEF and TGWU also took the unprecedented action of withdrawing their votes from incumbent but right-wing candidates for the NEC, and this had the effect of putting two more opponents of the policy on the Executive. At the end of the week the Conference passed a motion by Scanlon which pledged support for the Government, but 'subject to the reservations involved in the policy decisions of the TUC'; an amendment to delete the reservations was defeated by 3,287,000 to 2,722,000 votes. It was clear that what Robert McKenzie has called that 'bond of mutual confidence between the parliamentary leaders and a preponderant part of the trade union leadership which is the essential key to the understanding of the functioning of the Labour Party',[99] had broken down, at least with regard to incomes policy, in 1968.

Harold Wilson was correct in seeing the Conference as 'a warning that no one should think . . . the resumption of legislation would be anything but fiercely resisted'.[100] The problem was, however, that the Party leadership was no less committed than it had been in 1963 to the fuller integration of the unions into the mixed economy, believing as much as it did then that its ability to bring this about was a condition of both economic and electoral success. 'Clumsily, perhaps, inadequately no doubt, the Government has been reaching for something better than crude industrial power politics. If you kill that without being clear what you put in its place then you will share a very heavy responsibility', Mrs Castle told the delegates.[101] At least one Minister had come to the conclusion that it would be politically impossible for the Government to continue with statutory controls: Callaghan had told the Fire Brigades Union conference in May that after the end of 1969 the incomes policy would have to be based entirely on voluntary methods. The Prime Minister, however, immediately disassociated the Cabinet from this view and continued to maintain that the decision in 1969 would be conditional upon TUC control having 'proved itself' effective.[102] But the TUC was unable to commit itself to the achievement of incomes policy objectives to the Government's satisfaction; given the opposition in the unions to TUC wage-vetting, the Incomes Policy Committee was careful not to apply its new Economic Review criteria at all strictly after they came into operation in May 1968. Of 327 claims submitted over the subsequent year, 309 were found generally 'non-objectionable' and only 18 were sent to a panel, which itself usually passed the claim.[103] Indeed, the Government's real view, as revealed in an internal

Labour Party document after NEC discussions with Ministers in the aftermath of the Party Conference, was that a return to a voluntary incomes policy would not meet its requirements: 'the argument about legislation is . . . one of theology rather than practical politics where the Government is concerned. It is perfectly possible to devise a voluntary prices and incomes policy but quite impossible to guarantee results. If we require results, then controls are necessary and controls must have some final measure of sanction.' [104]

The Government's dilemma was that a further extension of the incomes legislation was not only unacceptable to the unions, but might endanger the future of the Government and possibly the Labour Party itself. In the autumn of 1968, however, there appeared to the Government one way out of this dilemma. For as was pointed out in the introductory chapter to the 1964 Labour Government's incomes policy, there is a third way of securing the integration of the unions apart from voluntary commitment or legal sanctions over union wage policies: that is, by applying restrictions directly on the unions themselves – by strengthening them *vis-à-vis* their membership and by limiting the right to strike. And after the Donovan Commission reported in June 1968, the Government began to look seriously at this approach. For might not the unions' reaction to penal sanctions be different if they were applied not to wage claims but to unofficial strikes which union leaders themselves found troublesome, and if these sanctions were combined with legislation arising out of Donovan which would formally recognize trade unions as an 'estate of the realm' and seek to extend trade unionism throughout the labour market? It was in this context that Mrs Castle's reference to something 'to put in the place' of incomes legislation was the key statement at the 1968 Party Conference. It inaugurated yet another bitter chapter of conflict in the Labour Party's long history of proving itself a national party without relinquishing its structural ties with the organized working class.

7

'In place of strife'

The Donovan Report and the White Paper

Just a few days before the 1968 Labour Party Conference opened, the business leaders of the motor industry in a meeting with Barbara Castle and trade union leaders in the industry renewed a demand, first put to the Prime Minister in September 1965, that the Government should introduce direct fines on unofficial strikers under a system of making industry-wide collective agreements legally enforceable.[1] Their concern with unofficial strikes was produced by the fact that, whereas the number of strikes officially sanctioned by unions had remained extremely low since 1926, unofficial action had been increasing substantially over the previous decade. These stoppages were almost always 'unconstitutional' – i.e. they took place outside officially negotiated procedure agreements, and although they were characteristically short in duration, they were also often effective in that they were unpredictable and disrupted increasingly integrated production techniques. In industries where this shop floor tactic was used extensively – the docks, shipbuilding, motor-car manufacturing – it had become a strong trade union weapon, the sanction behind the development of shop-steward-led local bargaining, and an important factor in accounting for the phenomen of 'wage-drift' whereby worker earnings ran ahead of wage rates.[2] Although the industrial time lost through strikes was a small fraction of that lost through sickness and injury (not to mention unemployment), the latter did not disrupt production in that they were spread throughout the year and the labour force, could be allowed for by the scale of manning and, above all, did not entail a challenge to managerial authority.

Throughout the period of Labour Government, a close connection was visible between the development of the incomes policy and the question of state action against unofficial strikers. The Ministry of Labour in 1965 had seen 'one obvious general problem' with the incomes policy: 'If trade union leaders accept these wide responsibilities there is a risk that they will cease to be regarded by their membership as representative of their interests and their influence and authority may be transferred to unofficial leaders.' [3] The CBI as well had stressed 'the obvious danger that under pressure to operate an incomes policy unofficial strikes would become even more common than they are at present. Restraint by unions in the official pressing of claims . . . [is] calculated to widen rather than narrow the scope for unofficial action.' [4] And although these effects did not begin to show themselves clearly until 1968 when strikes exceeded their 1964–5 levels for the first time, the dynamic of the situation was that there should be a preventative move by the state. Indeed, the incomes policy legislation had pointed the way, at least as far as the CBI was concerned. At the beginning of 1966, even before this legislation was introduced, the CBI adduced it as 'the most significant factor' in inducing it to endorse the campaign for penal sanctions against unofficial strikes initiated in 1965 by the motor and engineering employers:

> The Government would no doubt differentiate between fining strikers in these circumstances in relation to the question of early warning, and fining in relation to breaches of agreement, but the introduction of such legislation would make it difficult for it to argue that fining of strikers was impracticable. [5]

The question largely lay in abeyance until the Donovan Commission reported in June 1968, although the Conservative Party itself adopted the demand for legally enforceable collective agreements earlier that year. [6] The Ministry of Labour under Ray Gunter, however, made clear to the Commission its own interest in a 'tough' report. It would have been politically advantageous from the Government's perspective to have been able to adopt the role of broker between a tough report on the one hand and trade union opposition on the other, allowing it to claim that it was less influenced by the demands of business and the Conservatives than by the expert opinion of the Royal Commission. [7] The total impact of the Donovan Report, however, was above all inconclusive. Under the strong influence of George Woodcock and Hugh Clegg as Commissioners, the Commission itself tried to find a political formula which would be as acceptable to the unions as to the employers and the Government. It did not condemn the statutory incomes policy, but neither did it accept the CBI's contention that this had laid the basis for legal action against strikers:

> The protection of the Prices and Incomes policy is assumed
> to be of sufficient importance in the national interest to
> justify the possibility of creating additional friction through
> the institution of criminal proceedings . . . It is a unique
> situation without parallel in industrial relations.[8]

The Report fundamentally agreed with the employers and the
Government that unofficial strikes were 'an urgent problem' but it
took the pragmatic view that immediate legal sanctions would not
only divert attention from 'the underlying causes to the symptoms
of the disease', but would not work in any case.[9] Existing legislation
(the 1963 Contracts of Employment Act) already empowered employers to sue workers for breach of contract where strike notice was
not given, but employers tended not to use this device for fear of
prolonging what were usually short strikes by exacerbating the situation. The Commission recognized that employers were seeking to
avoid this difficulty by shifting the burden of disciplining strikers to
the state and the Report contended that this would prove no less
abrasive if adopted, with the additional problem that a resolute body
of strikers who refused to pay fines would only serve to bring the law
into disrepute. A suggestion by the CBI, adopted by the Conservative
Party, that registered unions be required under penalty of deregistration and loss of immunity in tort to exercise discipline over
strikers, was also disparaged by Donovan: lack of union discipline
had played only a 'very secondary part' in unofficial strikes and such
a proposal was 'more likely to lead to internal disruption in the
unions than to a reduction in unofficial strikes'.[10] As for two other
proposals commonly put before it, a 'fixed cooling-off period' along
the lines of the American Taft–Hartley Act, and compulsory strike
ballots, the Commission saw these as likely to impair the flexibility
needed by the Government and the negotiating parties to resolve
disputes.[11]

The Report's main theme was that the underlying cause of unofficial strikes was that the formal but 'empty' system of national
industry-wide negotiations was in conflict with the informal but more
'real' decentralized system of work-place bargaining.[12] This could be
resolved only by a voluntary process of rationalizing the latter into
'an effective and orderly method of regulation'. To this end it recommended that companies and unions encourage factory-wide agreements and formalize the role of the shop steward; that legislation be
introduced obliging companies to register their procedure agreements with the DEP; and that an Industrial Relations Commission
be established to examine disputes procedure in select cases and set

voluntary standards for clear and concise procedures at the work-place level. All this would not only remove many of the causes of unofficial strikes, but also assist in the 'planning of incomes' by enabling companies to exercise effective control over the drift of earnings arising from local bargaining.

Had the Commissioners been consistent in making this voluntary argument, it would have been difficult indeed for the Labour Government to have proposed legal sanctions against strikers as the employers were demanding in the face of both 'expert' and union opposition. The Report as a whole, however, contained a number of contradictions to this general theme which proved to be important in the light of subsequent events. In the first place, the Commission's voluntary approach was weakened in that it was not extended to incomes policy: if penal sanctions were indeed wrong, the attempt to present incomes policy as a unique case looked like, and probably was, mere expedient reasoning. In fact, the Commission was not in principle opposed to legal sanctions. The Report suggested that the Government might follow the approach taken in the case of incomes policy itself, i.e. that the introduction of sanctions might be a second stage which would follow after unions and employers had voluntarily agreed to the introduction of reformed procedures. For once the latter were adopted, it would be possible to identify strikes caused by 'irresponsibility or agitation by eccentrics or subversives', and in that situation 'the threat of legal penalties can create a counter-motive that may influence men's minds and acts and the use of such penalties may command the support of many of the other workers'.[13]

Secondly, the Report made clear that the Commissioners were divided among themselves. Although all twelve Commissioners signed the Report, five of them also added their own 'supplementary notes' in which they argued the case for compulsory powers. The most important of these was Andrew Shonfield's long 'Note of Reservation' which sharply criticized the main Report for not developing a full analysis of 'the long term problem of accommodating bodies with the kind of concentrated power which is possessed by trade unions to the changing needs of an advanced industrial society'. He contended that traditional union rights should be exercised only by those organizations sanctioned by the state itself: 'the distinction between labour organizations which explicitly accept certain responsibilities toward society as a whole, as well as their own members, and those who refuse or are unable to do so, needs to be pressed further . . . by demanding of trade unions the fulfilment of certain minimum standards of behaviour as a condition for being registered'.[14] Indeed in one important respect, this overtly corporatist approach was reflected in the main Report. It recommended that all unions should be required to register with a state agency in order to be considered trade unions for legal purposes, and that unions have specific rules governing matters like admission, elections, discipline, and shop stewards. In itself, this recommendation did not involve a substantial imposition on the unions, because most of them already were registered voluntarily due to certain tax advantages, because the rules suggested did not go beyond what most unions already had, and because refusal to register would not deprive a union or a strike leader of the legal immunities held by virtue of the 1906 and 1965 Trade Disputes Acts. By a majority of 7 to 5, however, the Commission also recommended that this immunity should apply only to registered trade unions and persons acting on their behalf, thus applying a new sanction against unions who refused to meet requirements for union rules set by the state and also depriving unofficial strike leaders of the protection given by the earlier legislation. In Shonfield's view this was 'an essential first step in the process of reform'.[15] The real importance of this majority decision did not lie in the recommendation itself, which was subsequently rejected by the Government, but in the fact that the five members of the Commission who dissented from this recommendation (including the two trade union members, Woodcock and Lord Collison) felt it necessary to suggest an alternative sanction against unions who refused to register. They proposed that this could be done by making the leaders of a body of workers 'which should but does not register' liable to a fine for each day of default.[16] This, as we shall see, could later be taken by the Government to be an endorsement of the principle of fines against workers by the trade union representatives on the Commission.

At the end of July 1968, the DEP forwarded to the TUC and CBI a 'consultative document' which asked for their comments on the Report and indicated that a White Paper would be published before the end of the year outlining the Government's intentions. The response of the two organizations was predictable. The TUC reiterated its commitment to voluntarism, and welcomed the general theme of the Report but opposed any plan for compulsory union registration.[17] The CBI remained adamant that fines by the state be used to enforce agreements and also gave support to other proposals rejected by Donovan, notably the 'cooling-off period' and compulsory strike ballots.[18] The strongest exponents of this view remained the motor companies who described 'the need for action' as 'desperate': 'It would not be overstating matters to say that the economic recovery we are all striving for could be undermined by a continuance of damaging strikes in this our most important exporting industry.' [19]

Harold Wilson carried the same message to the Labour Party Conference in October: 'there is nothing now which can halt the inexorable success of the Labour movement than the Labour movement itself . . . everything we have achieved at so great a cost, can be imperilled by ill-considered industrial action'.[20] Although it was not yet made fully explicit, both the Prime Minister and Mrs Castle believed 'that the confessed failure of the Commission to find any short-term remedy for unofficial strikes could not be accepted'.[21]

Mrs Castle's intentions with regard to the question of legal sanctions were revealed in mid November at the end of a two-day meeting with DEP officials and a select group of academics, employers and union leaders at the Civil Defence College at Sunningdale. A host of legislative alternatives to Donovan were proffered by the DEP and each was meticulously criticized by Hugh Clegg on the basis of Donovan's specific arguments. Mrs Castle indicated, however, her interest in three legal provisions: a 'cooling-off period' in unofficial strikes, restrictions on inter-union disputes, and a compulsory strike ballot.[22] A number of factors appear to have caused Mrs Castle to adopt these provisions – not least the rising trend of strikes in the autumn of 1968 most notably reflected in the refusal of the AEU to join the GMWU in calling a ballot of their membership with regard to a threatened engineering strike, and the demarcation dispute at the Girling brake factory, which directly involved few workers but led to 5,000 workers being laid off by the motor companies. Mrs Castle and other Ministers were convinced that action against strikers would help to resurrect the popularity of the Government.[23] They were encouraged in this by public opinion polls which in the autumn of 1969 indicated that 66% of respondents approved of making unofficial strikes illegal and 75% favoured compulsory strike ballots. (It is important to note, however, that the issue was by no means yet a major one in the public mind at this stage. Only 17% of respondents saw strikes as 'the most urgent problem' facing the unions in the fall of 1968; not until mid 1969, after the Government itself made this its major political priority, did a majority of respondents see strikes as the 'most urgent problem').[24] Finally, Mrs Castle intended to introduce a charter of trade union rights of sufficient magnitude to allow her to obtain union support for something on the other side – i.e. legal sanctions against strikes, for which her officials had pressed Donovan and were still calling. In principle, Mrs Castle remained a strong believer in the right to strike, but she was convinced at the same time that 'disreputable' strikes like inter-union disputes and unofficial strikes were producing a right-wing reaction which she would forestall by limiting 'irresponsible' strikes. Her most important proposal, the cooling-off period, did not deny the right to strike absolutely; as was the case with the incomes legislation, it required workers to accept a state imposed delay during which the cause of the dispute could be investigated. The fact that this also allowed for a period of employer, government and media pressure to be brought upon the strikers, and the fact that it removed the element of surprise which was the main tactical advantage of the sudden unofficial strike, she apparently did not regard as an important infringement on free collective bargaining. Moreover, she could argue that Woodcock and Lord Collison had suggested the use of state-imposed fines as a sanction, albeit in another context. Certainly a careful reading of Donovan allowed her to claim that her difference with the Commission was one of timing rather than principle. Indeed, Woodcock himself later wrote that he had 'always accepted the possibility of some sort of legislation if its purpose is to generalize what had been established as a standard of good conduct', although he believed that this standard should first be established voluntarily and therefore that the Government 'would do well *in the early years* to concentrate on the voluntary approach through the CIR rather than rush precipitately into the use of discretionary powers'.[25] Since it was Mrs Castle's intention to first establish the CIR on a voluntary basis in early 1969 and since she did not envisage that her statutory proposals would be enacted until almost a year later, it was at least arguable, from her perspective, that her differences with the General Secretary of the TUC were not very marked. Mrs Castle's strategy was essentially one of demonstrating her 'socialist' convictions by extending collective bargaining in a capitalist society while expecting of the unions that they prove that they were responsible socialists as well by accepting her anti-strike proposals.

The White Paper, *In Place of Strife*,[26] set out to provide what Mrs Castle saw as 'a coherent philosophy of the relations between management, employers and the Government'.[27] This philosophy was neither particularly imaginative nor new, being basically a combination of modern pluralist social theory together with a strong dose of Fabian state interventionism. 'There are necessarily conflicts of interests in industry', were the White Paper's opening words, and the expression of these conflicts through collective bargaining backed by the right to strike was seen as concomitant with democracy, social justice, economic growth and industrial democracy. As with pluralist theory, however, this conflict of interest was *legitimate* only so long as it was *functional* to the efficient operation of the society as a whole.[28] The second line of *In Place of Strife*, immediately qualified the first: 'The objective of our industrial relations system should be to direct the forces producing conflict towards constructive ends.' The problem was that conflict in British industry was often 'damaging and anti-social', and this is where the state came in. The White Paper's proposals arose out of a long tradition of state intervention 'to contain the disruptive consequences of the struggle for those not immediately affected' and, more generally, where 'it could be shown that certain important economic or social objectives were not sufficiently furthered or were frustrated by collective bargaining'.[29] Thus in a single short paragraph, the White Paper was able to describe the right to strike as one of 'the essential freedoms in a democracy', argue at the same time that 'the growing interdependence of modern industry means that the use of the strike weapon in certain circumstances can inflict disproportionate harm on the rest of society', and express the belief that strikes 'should only be resorted to when all other alternatives have failed'.[30]

It is not necessarily contradictory to speak of essential freedoms and, in the same breath, of restrictions on their use, insofar as the exercise of certain essential freedoms seriously impinges on the integrity or safety of others; as such libel or yelling 'fire' in a crowded theatre are generally legitimately prohibited by the state in the case of freedom of speech. But the blanket caveat that the essential freedom to strike be activated only when 'all other alternatives' have failed, not only implies a much greater *a priori* restriction on this freedom than on others, but immediately raises the questions of who is to decide whether 'other alternatives' are available, what constitutes 'disproportionate harm' on the rest of society, and whose 'economic and social objectives' are frustrated by a strike. These are unavoidable questions in a society where the ability to strike constitutes one of the main sources of power available to those who must sell their labour to others to secure the requisites of material existence. The tightrope walked by the White Paper with regard to the freedom to strike would not have been problematic if British society was characterized unquestionably by a harmony of interests which transcended those conflicts which obtain their expression in strike action; if the state was clearly a neutral referee in industrial conflict; and if the state's economic and social objectives manifestly were arrived at independently of the objectives of those who own and control industry and against whom strikes are directed. The claim that the state's main interest in the prevention of strikes lay in protecting one group of workers from another could not be substantiated insofar as these questions on conflict *between the classes* remained unresolved. It was not at all inconsistent with the Labour Party's ideology that these basic questions on the nature of class conflict and the role of the state in a capitalist society should be glossed over. But, whereas this could have succeeded on other issues and at other times, on the question of the right to strike at a time of protracted disagreement between the state and the unions over economic policy in general and incomes policy in particular, the White Paper's thematic tightrope was bound to strain, and not unlikely to snap.

The White Paper did not concentrate only on the state and the unions, to be sure. A major point, in fact, was that the main responsibility for developing adequate procedures which workers would want to follow in negotiations and disputes lay with management. There would be no 'fundamental solution' to unofficial strikes until management abandoned its 'mistaken belief that it has the right to impose changes on its workpeople without full and adequate consultation and then invite them to go through "procedure" afterwards for the remedy of any grievances'.[31] To encourage the development of adequate procedure agreements, the White Paper proposed to adopt Donovan's suggestion for a Commission on Industrial Relations, to be established without powers of compulsion. The CIR might also endorse trade union claims for recognition, with the Government empowered to enforce its recommendations. In addition, unions would be given the right to obtain from companies information needed for collective bargaining purposes (subject to safeguards to protect 'commercial' interests); legal protection would be given against unfair dismissals of workers; 'experiments' in worker representation on company boards would be encouraged; and state grants and loans would be made available to assist in union mergers and the training of union officials.

These proposals met a number of long-standing trade union demands; indeed, union recognition guarantees and protection against unfair dismissal had been promised in the Labour Party's 1966 election manifesto. What was really new, was the 'something on the other side' which the White Paper gave to employers. In addition to a system of compulsory registration for unions, three main restrictions on free-collective bargaining were proposed: at its own discretion, the Government would be able to impose (*a*) a settlement in inter-union recognition disputes where the TUC and CIR had been unable to secure a voluntary settlement; (*b*) a 28-day 'conciliation pause' (the cooling-off period) in an unconstitutional stoppage during which employers would be required to observe the *status quo* before the stoppage occurred, while workers would be required to return to work; and (*c*) a strike ballot in the case of an official strike which involved 'a serious threat to the economy or public interest'. Failure to comply with statutory orders in any of these areas, would leave union officials and individual strikers open to fines levied by an Industrial Board composed of employer, union and legal members of the Industrial Court. The prospect that strikers might refuse to pay the fines, and that this would result in the imprisonment of trade unionists, could not be ignored by the White Paper, but it saw a way around this dilemma in a proposal for the collection of fines through the compulsory distraint of wages after a return to work. This proposal had an interesting history. The TUC, which traditionally had opposed the attachment of wages under any circumstances, had modified its views on this in 1965 with regard to consumer credit debts. The engineering and motor industry employers, supported by the CBI, seized on this in their evidence before Donovan in early 1966, recommending that attachment of wages be applied under the anti-strike legislation they were proposing;[32] and the Government itself showed real interest in this idea when preparing its incomes policy legislation later in the year.[33] Although Woodcock had made clear that the TUC would never have endorsed attachment of wages if they had known it would be used in this way, and although the motor industry employers themselves had admitted, under questioning from Woodcock before the Commission, that this device would be ineffective if it led to further strike action when the fines were deducted from the pay-packets, the attachment of wages now became one of the central features of the Labour Government's industrial relations proposals.

To be sure, the White Paper saw the total effect of its proposals as designed 'to reinforce, not weaken' the responsibility of the unions. The DEP, in preparing the White Paper, were no less aware than Donovan that as effective deterrents to shop floor militancy, imprisonment or fines were in themselves of minimal use. The difference with the Commission lay in the belief that the existence of legal sanctions was a necessary condition for getting the unions themselves to take action. Thus as with the incomes policy, the White Paper was prepared to suggest that effective union control over their members would leave the law with little actual labour to do, and it even raised the possibility that the powers might be held in abeyance. The White Paper cited a statement by the TUC to the effect that the unions had an 'obligation' to adhere to negotiating procedures they considered satisfactory or seek to negotiate changes to make them satisfactory, and it drew the conclusion that to the extent that this obligation was met the use of the Government's reserve powers would not be necessary. In view of the fact that the controversy over *In Place of Strife* inside the labour movement finally came down to the proposition that if the TUC would 'legislate' against unofficial strikes in its own rules, the Government would not legislate, perhaps the most important line in the White Paper was: 'the trade union movement must show its ability to discharge the obligation referred to in its statement if it rejects every other means of dealing with a problem it has itself recognized'.[34]

In Place of Strife gave full expression to the ideological theme that one of the main functions of a Labour Government is to impose harmony in the national interest over the industrial expression of class conflict. Now that it was directly confronting the trade union movement's commitment to voluntarism, however, by proposing a permanent statutory and penal element in collective bargaining, the Labour Government was also raising the question of whether the labour movement any longer regarded the Government's definition of the national interest as embracing the interest of the working class. On the answer to this question ultimately depended not only the Labour Government's ability to secure trade union voluntary controls over its membership adequate enough from the Government's perspective to drop the legislative proposals, but also the prospect of the labour movement's further acquiescence in legislative controls in the absence of an 'adequate' voluntary response.

The labour movement's response

In the aftermath of its defeat on incomes policy at the 1968 Labour Party Conference, the Government had placed some emphasis on increasing consultations with the TUC. In contrast with the short shrift the TUC's *Economic Review* had received a year earlier, extensive discussions were held in mid December on the 1969 Review. These discussions revealed that the differences with regard to economic policy in general and incomes policy in particular were no less marked than before.[35] Nevertheless, the fact that the Government had shown an interest in consultations, encouraged the General Council in the view that 'the differences related to timing rather than principle',[36] and the discussions took place in an atmosphere free of the emotionally charged debates which had characterized the conferences in the autumn. Although Mrs Castle's main industrial relations proposals were endorsed by the Prime Minister and Roy Jenkins in early December, these Ministers were aware that the White Paper would prove controversial not only within the General Council, but also within the Cabinet itself. On George Woodcock's advice, Mrs Castle decided to put her main proposals to the TUC and CBI at the end of December before they had been ratified by the Cabinet. Although this involved the risk of leaks to the press, it had the advantage that an accommodating response from the General Council would ease the White Paper's endorsement by the Cabinet.[37]

This response was not forthcoming. Woodcock's view that the White Paper set out a 'philosophy more consistent and more acceptable to trade unionism than the [Donovan] Commission's Report',[38] was simply not shared by most of the General Council, who immediately saw the new proposals as putting 'a taint of criminality' on legitimate union activities.[39] There was a general feeling that the White Paper was a crude political ploy to steal the Conservatives' thunder, that Mrs Castle had been 'taken in' by the employers and her DEP advisors, and that the Labour Government was consequently making strikes the main issue in the public mind, when its proper role should be to defend the unions against unfounded charges of union 'irresponsibility'. Although the initial reaction of the more militant union leaders – that the White Paper was corporatist in conception and should be rejected in its entirety – was not widely shared by union moderates, and Woodcock was able to carry the General Council in favour of concentrating their opposition to specific proposals in the interest of maintaining a dialogue with the Government, the General Council showed a degree of unity in opposition to the three penal provisions of *In Place of Strife* which had not been seen with regard to the incomes policy. Cannon and Cooper, who held throughout the ensuing controversy that the union's response was 'unnecessary, melodramatic and negative'[40] often found themselves in subsequent months in a minority of two. A statement adopted by the General Council at a special meeting on 7 January was more strongly worded than any of its earlier incomes policy pronouncements.[41] The Government was being misled by 'outside criticism which is at best misinformed and at worst ill intentioned . . . to impose unreasonable and therefore unworkable constraints on the freedom of working people'. The strike ballot proposal was deemed 'completely misguided and quite unacceptable' designed to diminish confidence in official union leadership. A cooling-off period imposed at the discretion of a Minister was inconsistent with 'democratic procedures' and would lead the unions to seek procedure agreements which were of such a general nature that there could be no claim made that they were not being followed. The General Council accepted that the prevention of inter-union disputes was one of their central responsibilities, but were of the opinion that financial penalties as a sanction would militate against their securing a settlement. The statement reaffirmed the TUC's opposition to compulsory registration and made it clear that they were 'by no means enthusiastic' about state aid to unions, reflecting a fear that this would be used as a lever of state control.

Although the General Council did not publish its statement until the White Paper itself was released on 17 January, the General Council's views were pointedly leaked to the press which headlined the penal sanctions and the unions' opposition to them. This militated against the White Paper's smooth passage through the Cabinet which the authors of the policy had hoped to effect by presenting the proposals to the General Council first. In itself there was little reason for Ministers to object to the procedure adopted in that it was a direct continuation of the approach which had been used in preparing the early incomes policy White Papers. But whereas this procedure had worked smoothly when a consensus had existed on the substance of policy between the TUC and the Government, it exacerbated the situation in the very different conditions obtaining by late 1968. Ministers now complained of being presented with a *fait accompli*, and opposition in the Cabinet extended to those Ministers from whom support might have been expected. Richard Crossman objected to the constitutional impropriety of the procedure (further proof of his theory of drift towards the 'Presidential' status of the Prime Minister) and Anthony Crosland at this late stage suggested the Government should explicitly adopt the approach outlined by Shonfield in his 'Note of Reservation' to the Donovan Report. Callaghan's views, as Party treasurer, that the White Paper would make impossible a reconciliation with the unions necessary to secure adequate financial support for the Party in time for the next general election were endorsed by other Ministers including Richard Marsh and Roy Mason, the only Ministers left in the Cabinet with substantial trade union backgrounds.[42] It took six meetings of the Cabinet before the White Paper was finally endorsed on 14 January. From the beginning, *In Place of Strife* lacked one of the essential conditions that had stymied union and PLP opposition to the incomes legislation – Cabinet unity in the face of this opposition.

One of the crucial questions confronting the Cabinet at this stage was that of legislative timing. Most Ministers implicitly saw *In Place of Strife* as an alternative to a permanent statutory incomes policy with an Industrial Relations Act replacing the 1968 Prices and Incomes Act at the end of 1969. Roy Jenkins, however, urged that the Government should leave its options open to renew the incomes legislation in case the balance of payments situation did not improve as was hoped and it was needed again to underpin international confidence in the pound. Since there was no expectation that the Government could both renew the incomes legislation in late 1969 *and* pass a new Industrial Relations Bill at the same time, he advocated that the anti-strike provisions of *In Place of Strife* should be introduced on their own in the spring, on the grounds of the urgency of the strike problem, allowing the Government to renew incomes legislation in the fall if necessary and secure PLP support for this by introducing the pro-union measures of *In Place of Strife* at that time. Mrs Castle and the Prime Minister were opposed to this strategy, however, and prevailed on the Cabinet to accept a legislative timetable that would allow Mrs Castle to prepare a full Bill which would incorporate the total philosophy of the White Paper as well as allow her time to convince the unions of its desirability.[43] Immediately after the publication of the White Paper on 17 January, Mrs Castle informed the TUC that the DEP would not begin drafting the Industrial Relations Bill until May preparatory to its introduction in November, and that the intervening months would be devoted to consultations on the Government's proposals.[44]

Despite the long time span envisaged before the introduction of legislation, the White Paper's publication produced what Mrs Castle herself has termed as 'a sense of alarm and outrage' from every section of the labour movement.[45] To some extent the General Council's original reaction to her proposals contributed to this: in February she told the PLP that it was a 'tragedy' that the anti-strike parts of her White Paper were leaked before publication, for this gave the movement the 'wrong impression' from the start and left her with a tremendous job in getting her message across.[46] It was not primarily the General Council, however, which mobilized trade union opposition to the White Paper. The CIR was established on a voluntary basis on 1 March, George Woodcock left the TUC to become its Chairman, and the General Council welcomed the appointment and pledged itself to cooperate with the CIR.[47] Indeed, the General Council's approach was initially the same as that pursued on the incomes legislation: concentrating on obtaining union agreement to voluntary reforms in the hope of convincing the Government that legislation would be unnecessary. To this end, the TUC organized a series of 'Post-Donovan Conferences' among the unions in March. Moreover, the General Council maintained this approach in relation to the incomes policy and put extensive emphasis on securing a large majority in favour of its *Economic Review* at the Conference of Executives at the end of February in the hope that this would make it easier for the Government to relax the statutory incomes policy.[48] Although this strategy had failed to prevent the 1968 Act, the executives (including the TGWU) endorsed the *Economic Review* by 6,395,000 to 2,389,000 votes. By committing itself to continuing with its own incomes policy in advance of any promise from the Government not to maintain its statutory powers, the TUC was again abandoning a major bargaining counter with Government and was attacked for this by the AEF and other unions who voted against the Economic Review.

Significantly, the General Council was under considerable pressure to adopt a less equivocal stance in relation to *In Place of Strife*. By the end of February virtually every major union executive had adopted resolutions expressing their determination to resist restrictions on the right to strike, and union journals were replete with attacks on the White Paper. The main line of division inside the movement concerned the question of whether some parts of the White Paper were acceptable while the penal clauses were not, or whether the whole document should be rejected as an unpalatable 'package deal'. But even staunch right-wingers like the AEF's Jim Conway, attacked the penal clauses: 'They sound the death toll of British trade unionism, they drive a wedge between the Labour Party and the Trade Unions.' [49] In February, the General Council received requests from three large unions for a special Congress to mobilize opinion against the White Paper and by April eleven more unions, including the TGWU, had joined in this demand. The Conference of Executives itself was lobbied by a mass demonstration of workers organized by the Liaison Committee for the Defence of Trade Unions, and in Merseyside building workers chose that day to join car workers (already on strike) in a token stoppage against the White Paper.

It was in fact the more militant sections of the rank and file rather than the union leadership that initiated the main challenge to *In Place of Strife*. This was most notably expressed in the Ford strike of February and March. Just as the motor and engineering employers were the most vociferous proponents of legal action against unofficial strikers, so it was the motor and engineering stop stewards who led the opposition within the labour movement to the Government's proposals.[50] On 21 February, car workers at Ford went out on unofficial strike against an agreement reached between the unions and the company involving a 7 to 10% wage increase tied to a penalty clause removing holiday and lay-off bonuses from unofficial strikers. Although the increase was well beyond the incomes policy norm, it was justified by the company (and the Government) on the grounds that the sanctions would reduce strikes and thus raise productivity.[51] The TGWU and AEF made the strike official a week later, which meant that the unions representing most of 41,000 workers involved were backing the strike against an agreement officially concluded between Ford and the eighteen unions in the National Joint Negotiating Committee. A temporary injunction secured by Ford prohibiting the unions from continuing the strike was ignored by the TGWU and AEF leadership and a permanent injunction was refused by the High Court on 6 March. Nine of the other unions followed in making the strike official, virtually isolating the GMWU and ETU in their continued support for the agreement.

The Ford package had been 'deeply coloured by the thinking that had influenced Barbara Castle's White Paper. They were children of the same age'.[52] It was designed to check the power of shop stewards and assert the authority of both management and union national officers on the assumption that the rank and file would forego shop-floor autonomy in favour of the pay increases and that, once the agreement was ratified, the penalty clauses against unconstitutional action would act to divorce militant stewards from the rank and file. In the event, however the strike indicated that the shop stewards were more closely attuned to the membership than the union national officers (not to mention Ford management or DEP officials), as the stewards rallied rank and file support against the principle of penalty clauses.[53] The strike clearly brought to the fore the tension that existed in many unions between 'moderate' national officers and 'militant' stewards. But the support which the TGWU and AEF gave to the stewards indicated that this tension was being resolved, in these unions at least, to the advantage of the stewards. As Huw Benyon has explained: 'The development of shop steward committees during [the 1950s and 1960s] meant that, in particular industries and areas, men were coming forward to full-time union positions with a long experience of shop floor "unofficial" unionism behind them. Men whose political base lay not within the official lay committees of the union but rather on the shop floor with the rank and file ... [This] radical wedge within the trade union bureaucracies ... was beginning to change the nature of national bargaining in the late 1960s, and the nature of politics in the 1970s.'[54]

The strike was intimately connected with the Government's legislative proposals in the minds of all those involved, including the Government. The unions' action in supporting the unofficial strikers was widely taken as a warning of what their response would be to to the use of the legal sanctions proposed by the White Paper, and gave rise to widespread speculation on what would have happened if Ford had been successful in securing a permanent injunction. As one study of the strike has noted: 'Perhaps Jones and Scanlon would have ended in gaol. Perhaps Fords would have got massive damages from TGWU and AEF funds. Such speculation must have had tremendous influence on the opposition to *In Place of Strife*.'[55] Striking car workers joined the demonstration against the White Paper at the Conference of Executives and TGWU shop stewards proclaimed the High Court decision as a first victory against the White Paper.[56] Both the Ford Executive and the GMWU and ETU attacked Jones and Scanlon for engaging in a political strike against the Government, and the architect of the agreement, Ford's Leslie Blakeman who was appointed by the Government to the CIR, saw the union leaders as acting 'in as irresponsible a manner as you would expect from their most militant and revolutionary stewards'.[57] On 14 March, the Prime Minister himself directly connected the strike with the Government's determination to enact *In Place of Strife*'s proposals: 'I want it to be clearly understood that the Government means business about these proposals. All that has happened in these last three weeks provides powerful support for the measures we shall be introducing in Parliament.'[58] And *Socialist Commentary* attacked the 'reckless militancy' of the strikers, suggesting that 'the inevitable backlash' from the Conservatives could only be avoided by the unions accepting *In Place of Strife* which 'despite a few contentious features, has in fact presented the unions with almost a Magna Carta'.[59]

Although Ford threatened to take further legal action and to transfer a projected new plant at Dagenham outside of Britain, it finally accepted on 18 March an agreement which retained the penalty clauses in only a minor form. There was some dissatisfaction on the part of militant shop stewards with Jones and Scanlon for allowing any element of the penal clauses to stand in the final agreement, but this, together with the strike's over-all success, invigorated the militants' opposition to the White Paper and heady talk of a general strike filled the corridors of left-wing gatherings such as the Institute for Workers Control conference in March. In more immediate and pragmatic terms, unofficial strike action began to be prepared for 1 May. The Liverpool Trades Council called for such a strike on 24 March and organizing groups of union officials and stewards were established in major cities by the Liaison Committee for the Defence of Trade Unions.[60] Although this tactic was strongly opposed by the official union leadership, there were significant signs that they too were prepared to adopt a more aggressive stance than they had on the incomes legislation, a necessary condition of reinforcing their authority *vis-à-vis* unofficial elements in 1969. As early as February, Victor Feather outlined the TUC's opposition to the penal clauses to the Trade Union Group of MPs, and the TGWU and AEF held special meetings with their MPs. USDAW's Richard Seabrook demanded: 'The Parliamentary Party and the Movement generally

must assert its sovereignty. The majority in the House, which owes
so much of its existence to the Unions must not desert its responsibilities now.' [61] Other union executives wrote to their MPs urging
them to prevail on the Government to withdraw the penal clauses.

The PLP, for its part, showed itself more responsive to the unions'
feelings than it had been on the incomes legislation. The warning
by Trevor Park that the Government would not get the support of a
majority of the PLP for any penal powers over trade unions after the
1968 incomes Bill, had been given added force in November 1968
when 109 Labour MPs, including forty-five union MPs, had signed a
Commons motion condemning a decision by the Government to refer
a wage award in the building industry to the NBPI.[62] The Trade
Union Group in December, affected by rumours that the Government was considering anti-strike legislation, voted its support for the
voluntary approach of Donovan and the TUC. Tribunite trade
union MPs like Orme, Atkinson and Heffer had by this time acquired
a recognized voice at Trade Union Group meetings and Orme was
asked by the Group in December to prepare a paper on industrial
relations legislation. At Group meetings in January moderate union
MPs who had voted for the incomes legislation added their voices in
opposition to the penal clauses along with the Tribunites.[63] Three
special PLP meetings were held on the White Paper within a month
of its publication, and despite Mrs Castle's assurances that no trade
unionist would actually go to prison by virtue of the attachment of
earnings provision, she was unable to quell disquiet among backbench MPs, who were in any case indicating their independent mood
at the time in opposing a joint Front Bench sponsored Bill on House
of Lords reform.[64] On 20 February the TGWU group of MPs voted
unanimously to support their union's opposition to the penal clauses.
Given this situation, Tribune MPs were able for the first time to leave
the initiative to the Trade Union Group itself to lead PLP opposition to the White Paper, and on 3 March, six moderate trade union
MPs including the Group Chairman sponsored a backbench amendment (to a Government motion to approve the White Paper) in
which they urged the Government not to proceed with strike ballots,
the conciliation pause or the attachment of earnings. Despite a three-
line Whip, fifty-three Labour MPs voted against the Government's
motion and forty more abstained, a revolt unmatched during the
whole Parliament. With the effect of exposing this dissent in the
Labour Party fully, the Conservatives abstained yielding a Government majority of 224 to 62. Significantly the PLP Chairman,
Douglas Houghton, and two of its three vice-chairmen abstained on
the vote.[65]

During this period the Labour Party NEC publicly broke with the Government on both the incomes legislation and *In Place of Strife*. After the 1968 Party Conference, the NEC had turned against the statutory incomes policy with some fervour and asked Ministers whose policies diverged from those established by the Conference to meet with the NEC's Home Policy Subcommittee at Transport House. The Prime Minister responded by forbidding Ministers to appear and informing the NEC that Ministers could not be 'summoned' to Party meetings.[66] The subcommittee consequently met with Mrs Castle in Whitehall in January, there affirming its unanimous opposition to 'any continuance of statutory legislation on incomes with penal clauses',[67] a stand endorsed by the NEC as a whole later in the month. As an internal party document prepared by Terry Pitt made clear, the NEC was above all exercised by the 'real political danger in the present situation . . . that the incomes policy . . . will undermine permanently the crucial pattern of agreement in the Party upon which much of the Party's political strength and unity in the last two elections was based'.[68] The Executive rejected a suggestion by Mrs Castle that a special Party study group be established to help plan the future of incomes policy and was influenced in doing so by 'factors such as the then projected White Paper on Industrial Relations, and the feeling that a study group might appear to imply the Party's acquiescence in continued legislation'.[69]

At the NEC's regular February meeting, a vote on a motion by the NUM's Joe Gormley – to the effect that the NEC could not agree to 'any legislation based on all the suggestions in *In Place of Strife*' – was postponed in order not to prejudice the Commons vote in March. But on 25 March, it passed the Gormley resolution (as amended by Callaghan to exclude the word 'any') by 16 votes to 5, and defeated by 15 to 7 Mrs Castle's motion that it 'welcome the Ministers' assurances that there will be the fullest consultations with the trade unions before legislation is framed'. This placed the NEC in official opposition to the Government's industrial relations proposals, a situation which *The Times* believed 'must be unprecedented'.[70] The meeting had the added effect of reopening publicly the divisions inside the Cabinet on the question. Jennie Lee voted for the Gormley resolution and two other Junior Ministers abstained, but most significant was James Callaghan's equivocal stand of voting for both resolutions. Callaghan's action was interpreted by the press and inside the Party as a direct challenge to Mr Wilson's leadership.[71]

By the end of March, it was abundantly clear that Mrs Castle's hopes of persuading the labour movement of the worth of her total package on industrial relations were not to be fulfilled. Although the Government took courage from public opinion polls which continued to show a high degree of support for anti-strike proposals,[72] this did not translate itself into increased public support for the Government. Three by-elections in March were marked again by massive working class abstentions resulting in a swing to the Conservatives of 16%. If anything, it appeared that the long gestation period between the White Paper and the introduction of legislation was having the desired effect of focusing the public's (and particularly the media's) attention on strikes, but was not contributing, as Ministers had expected it would, to raising the popularity of the Government, while at the same time giving opposition time to solidify inside the Party and the unions. This in turn was encouraging the divisions inside the Cabinet to resurface. Callaghan's action on the NEC expressed the hesitancy and unease with which the Cabinet itself was following the lead of Wilson, Jenkins and Mrs Castle on this issue, in face of the fact that the opposition from the labour movement was itself much less hesitant or uneasy than it had been on the incomes legislation.

The labour movement's 'interim' victory

The response of the Government to this situation was to abandon Mrs Castle's original timetable and adopt instead Roy Jenkins' line that a short bill embodying the major restrictions on strikes be introduced immediately. Jenkins now acquired a strong ally in Richard Crossman who contended that a bill in November, by which time the Labour Party Conference would have met and rejected the Government's proposals, would bring out even more sharply the divergence between Government and Party.[73] But even apart from this concern with minimizing the damage on the Party, the case for immediate legislation had been considerably strengthened, from the Government's perspective, since January. The CBI's response to the White Paper had been quite caustic: it still preferred legal enforcement of collective agreements, and although it was not opposed to Mrs Castle's proposed discretionary sanctions, it believed the Government was offering too much to the unions in exchange.[74] A short, sharp bill that concentrated on the penal sanctions would be sure to have the CBI's support. Similarly, the Conservatives had promised support for the White Paper but demanded that the legislation should be introduced immediately and carried through Parliament as quickly as the Prices and Incomes Bills had been.[75] The Ford Strike and the Prime Minister's expression of determination to legislate in response to it, inevitably raised questions, constantly voiced in the press, of whether a Government so committed to legal sanctions on strikers could justify holding off legislation until the autumn. Poor trade figures in February and March also served to underscore the Treasury's demands that industrial relations legislation be used to serve the Government's deflationary strategy, and particularly to aid the Treasury in negotiations with the IMF in May.

By timing an announcement that it would not renew the powers of 1968 Prices and Incomes Act at the end of the year to coincide with an announcement of a short bill dealing with the anti-strike provisions of *In Place of Strife*, the Government tried to offer a 'sweetener' to the unions and also provide British employers and foreign creditors with a strong alternative to a softer incomes policy. Moreover, since the Government did not intend to abandon its statutory incomes powers completely but to bring into force Part II of the 1966 Act at the end of 1969, it could avoid the difficulty of asking the PLP to give support to both policies at the same time. Announcing the Government's decision at the outset of the Budget Debate in mid April, both Jenkins and Castle stressed the close linkage between the incomes policy and the new legislation. The Government finally had come to a firm decision that the 'stringent statutory powers' of the Prices and Incomes Acts were only effective as temporary measures although they were not prepared to adopt a completely voluntary policy. The Government would therefore return at the end of the year to the statutory policy it had forged before the wage freeze of July 1966 involving powers to impose three month instead of twelve month delays on wage settlements. But this would have to be reinforced by a bill bringing about 'more orderly arrangements' in industrial relations generally, and particularly 'to prevent the occurrence of unnecessary and damaging disputes which are totally incompatible with our economic objectives'.[76]

The proposed bill to serve this purpose was a less carefully constructed package than the White Paper had been. It was an interim bill concentrating only on the main proposals of the White Paper and leaving the others for a subsequent bill in the autumn. The bill would establish the statutory right of every worker to belong to a union, empower the Government to enforce a CIR recommendation for trade union recognition, and remove existing restrictions debarring workers from receiving unemployment benefits when they were laid off due to a strike in which they were not directly involved. On the other hand, the Government would take powers to impose a settlement on inter-union disputes where the TUC and CIR had failed to secure a return to work and to impose a conciliation pause in unconstitutional disputes, restoring the *status quo* before the strike where that was relevant and requiring strikers to return to work for a twenty-eight-day period. Mrs Castle was careful to stress that the strike ballot was omitted because the Government's concern was with unofficial strikes and because time was needed to allow some unions to include provisions for strike ballots in their rules. Moreover, in response to the issue which she saw as having 'caused most heart-burning', Mrs Castle suggested that the Government was prepared to back off on the attachment of wages proposal by allowing the fined striker himself to choose whether he would prefer the normal process of collection of civil debts.[77]

As with the incomes policy earlier, the Government's approach was one of both justifying the need for legislation on the grounds that the unions had not acted voluntarily to thwart industrial militancy, and of using the threat of imminent legislation still to encourage the TUC action by pledging the Government to consider alternatives which met the aims of the proposed bill 'equally effectively and equally urgently'.[78] By this stratagem, the Government left itself crucial room for manoeuvre, room which it increasingly had to occupy in the face of the crisis into which its announcement plunged the Labour Party. At the outset, however, the commitment to legislate was complete. What was expected from the TUC was left characteristically vague and the only indication given of what the Government would 'reconsider' if the TUC came forth with alternatives was in the familiar context of leaving its powers in reserve to be brought into effect should TUC action later be found wanting.[79] Speaking to the PLP on 17 April, Harold Wilson described the bill as 'an essential component in ensuring the economic success of the Government . . . essential to the Government's continuance in office. There can be no going back on that'.[80] This was partly a tactical stance designed to threaten the PLP with the Government's resignation if it defeated the bill, but it also reflected the degree to which the proposed bill was of symbolic importance to the Government as the ultimate expression of its national orientation, of its capacity to 'recognize' that working class 'bloody-mindedness' was the source of Britain's economic difficulties, of its determination to prove that a Labour Government no less than a Conservative one was prepared to deal with strikes, of its ability to put nation before class.[81]

The announcement brought to a head the cleavage between the labour movement and the Government, stripping *In Place of Strife* to its bare essentials and undermining the Government's earlier arguments that the penal clauses were but a small counterweight to a charter of trade union rights. The Scottish TUC on 17 April passed an emergency resolution which said the White Paper could no longer be debated on its merits and therefore 'firmly rejected' it as a whole as well as the 'hasty legislation'.[82] Similarly at the AEU National Committee the Left fought a successful battle to keep Mrs Castle from being invited to address the conference which overwhelmingly voted to reject both the bill and the whole White Paper.[83] By giving the initiative to the more militant sections of the movement, the Government's proposals forced the General Council out of their passive role in the controversy. Its earlier position – that the Government's timetable allowed the White Paper to be considered in a normal way by the annual Congress in September – was now untenable, and on 23 April it decided to call an unprecedented Special Congress for 5 June. At the General Council's 23 April meeting there was virtual unanimous opposition to the proposed bill.[84] The incomes policy 'concession' was seen as the minimum the Government would have opted for in any case, especially since 'the 1966 Act still contained penal clauses to which trade unions are opposed'. The requirement that employers observe the *status quo* during a conciliation pause was desirable but 'would in no way diminish the sense of grievance felt by workpeople if financial penalties were imposed'. Indeed, the *status quo* provision was only useful to workers in cases like dismissals, work speed-ups or the like; on a wage issue or demand by workers for change in work arrangements, the *status quo* automatically applied. As for the flexibility suggested on how fines would be enforced, the General Council refused to 'kid themselves that criminality would not come into this', as one of them put it. Even if treated as a civil debt, refusal to pay fines would lead to distraint of goods, resistance to which was a criminal offence. The spurious position of the Government on this was in fact subsequently revealed by the Lord Chancellor himself, when he told the PLP in May that although 90% of debtors payed up when faced with a bailiff, approximately 3,000 a year went to prison.[85]

The stance adopted by the unions proved to be of critical importance in terms of the Government's inability to carry the PLP with it, in that it permitted centre and right-wing MPs to legitimate their opposition to the bill by identifying themselves with the union position. Indeed, if to the Government the bill was the culmination of Labour's national orientation, to a large part of the Labour Party inside and outside Parliament it was anathema precisely because of its clear expression of the contradiction between the ideology and policies of the Labour leadership and the Party's foundation in the organized working class. Branch resolutions were appearing on the union conference agendas demanding the replacement of the Cabinet with MPs committed to socialism, and the suspension of union financial support or disaffiliation from the Party.[86] Michael Foot, under banner headlines in *Tribune*, attacked the Government for initiating 'the maddest scene in the modern history of Britain' which threatened 'to break the Government and tear the movement to shreds'.[87] Even *Socialist Commentary*, which before the Government's change of pace had described the White Paper as a union 'Magna Carta' amidst its attacks on 'reckless militancy' at Fords, now alleged that although the Government had 'often been accused of flouting basic union sentiments before . . . nothing has cut as deep as this' and recognized the unions' 'legitimate fears that legal curbs might prove to be a wedge towards a progressive loss of their rights and powers'.[88] This view was shared by most of the Trade Union Group of MPs which became obsessed less with the bill itself than what it indicated about the class structure of the PLP. Douglas Houghton, the PLP Chairman, described the mood in these terms:

> What puzzled and angered many of the 'trade union MPs' was how the Government came to reach the conclusions it did . . . The plainest warnings from back-benchers (not to mention the TUC) appeared to make little impression. During many hours in seven meetings of the Parliamentary Labour Party not half a dozen voices were raised to support the Government's so-called penal clauses . . .
> The root of this worrying problem is that too many Labour Ministers are removed by education and life's experience from the great mass of the Movement outside, and from a substantial section of Labour MPs in Parliament. They appear at times to be alienated from working-class thinking.[89]

Paradoxically, the Government's dependence on PLP support for the passage of the bill was less than it had been on the incomes legislation in that it was assured of Conservative support in the House. Indeed Clive Jenkins had initially attacked the Government for its 'sheer, goddamned impudence' in bringing forth the bill in the knowledge that they would have to rely on Tory votes to get the bill through the Commons.[90] The security afforded by Conservative support was only superficial, however, as it soon became apparent that the Conservatives would not vote for a procedural motion after Second Reading to send the bill to a Standing Committee. Without this the Government would have faced, as it had on the House of Lords Reform Bill in February and March, an interminable filibuster on the floor of the House at Committee stage. Despite an attempt by the Prime Minister to strengthen his hold over Labour MPs by appointing Robert Mellish as Chief Whip to signal the end of John Silkin's 'liberal' approach to PLP dissent, backbench opposition continued to mount. Eric Moonman chaired an 'Action Group' of five union MPs which mobilized PLP opposition by canvassing those MPs who had voted against (or abstained) the White Paper in March. By the beginning of May, fifty MPs were pledged to vote against the bill and two weeks later the number had grown to sixty-three with thirteen more committed to abstain.

It is of crucial importance to understand the nature of this opposition emanating from virtually all sections of the Labour Party. It was primarily concerned not to defeat the Government's proposals, but to avoid a split in the labour movement over the penal clauses, to contain rather than encourage militant expressions of dissent. Thus *Socialist Commentary*'s main fear was that the unions would abandon voluntary cooperation on union reform: 'whatever their feelings, however great their sense of outrage, the unions must keep their heads . . . they cannot afford to destroy the Government . . . The Government may have made its greatest blunder but it will be small beer compared with the blunder the unions will make if passion leads them now into total opposition'.[91] And although *Tribune* directed its appeal mainly to the Government rather than the unions, it was mainly concerned to impress upon the Government the need to accept a negotiated settlement with the TUC if a split in the Party was to be avoided. Despite its spirited opposition to the bill, *Tribune* was conspicuously silent on the question of supporting the protest planned for May Day.[92] The Tribune Group did call for the first joint meeting of the PLP and NEC since 1931, but on this the alliance between left wing MPs and NEC trade union representatives broke down, as the NEC defeated the proposal by 13 votes to 7, the main argument against it being the unfavourable publicity to which it would give rise.[93] Pro-Jenkinsite MPs attempted to call a PLP meeting to depose the Prime Minister in the context of the controversy, but this again failed mainly because trade union MPs saw the leadership problem as one involving the whole Cabinet, including Jenkins and Callaghan, and because, as Peter Jenkins has observed, 'a majority in the party was still chiefly concerned with avoiding a disastrous split on the question of trade union reform and still hopeful that Harold Wilson would reach an accommodation with the TUC'.[94] The strength of PLP objections to the bill was dramatized when Houghton on 7 May openly expressed his own opposition to the bill. But Houghton spoke out only after conversations with Feather that indicated that the TUC was preparing its own alternatives to put to the Government, and he urged the PLP to use the TUC's strategy as the basis for their own campaign.[95] Indeed, the importance of the backbench revolt as a factor in securing the eventual withdrawal of the Government's proposals lay not so much in its size (only about 35 Labour MPs were needed to defeat a procedural motion after Second Reading), but in the fact that the TUC by its own actions gave the PLP the opportunity of operating in tandem with the TUC in opposing the bill. If the TUC had indicated a preparedness to acquiesce in the legislation, to see how it operated in practice, or to accept reserve powers while the TUC alternatives were tested, the PLP most likely would have gone along with this. The PLP, in other words, played a role which was mainly supportive of the TUC rather than independent.

The point has been made in earlier chapters that the critical factor which allowed the Labour Government to pass legislation with penal clauses against workers lay in the General Council's placing distinct limits on the extent to which it was prepared to carry its opposition. This factor was by no means absent in the spring of 1969. Indeed one of the major objectives of the trade union leadership, despite the strength of its objections to the bill, was to avoid a situation that might entail an open break with the Government. At its 23 April meeting, the General Council agreed to seek consultations during the drafting of the bill, and to take up the offer to prepare TUC alternatives for the control of strikes. Most of the General Council were concerned that the Special Congress should not merely provide a platform for attacking the Government, but should also endorse 'constructive' TUC action which would permit a negotiated settlement with the Government to take place. The General Council rejected a proposal that the TUC organize a one-day strike to protest against the bill,[96] and there was little dissension among the union leadership with regard to this approach. At the AEU National Committee a few days after the General Council meeting, Hugh Scanlon successfully opposed an attempt to secure the union's official backing for the May Day strikes, suggesting that organized strike action should only be taken if the Government rejected the TUC proposals and actually introduced the legislation.[97] The trade union leadership refused to associate itself in any way with PLP attempts to depose the Prime Minister and strongly opposed demands that unions break with the Labour Party. Indeed, they were working in the opposite direction. Under strong pressure from Victor Feather and Jack Jones, SOGAT leader Richard Briginshaw rejoined the Labour Party in early April, implicitly retracting his call the previous summer for a new political alignment.[98] Cousins emphatically rejected all suggestions from inside his own union for disaffiliation or cutting off financial aid from the Party: 'It is not Harold Wilson's Labour Party', he contended, '– it is ours.' [99]

By preparing its own voluntary action as an alternative to legislation, the General Council seemed to be following a similar strategy to that adopted on the statutory incomes policy. The difference this time was that it was now determined to avoid 'the fiasco which had occurred on incomes policy', as Jack Jones put it, whereby the TUC had committed itself to its own voluntary action without a preliminary guarantee from the Government to drop its legislation, so that the Government had obtained both.[100] Victor Feather's appointment as acting General Secretary, upon Woodcock's departure to the CIR, had an important effect in leading the General Council to adopt a more effective approach than before. Feather was as much committed as Woodcock to maintaining the TUC's engagement with government, and to enlarging the TUC's role *vis-à-vis* individual unions. But he was much less inclined to cast his opposition to statutory controls mainly in terms of the likelihood that they would prove ineffective, as Woodcock had done in inviting the PLP and the unions to 'ignore' the passage of incomes legislation.

> Do not tell me that . . . the law will be ineffective and that
> governments will let it stay ineffective. What governments
> do in those circumstances is not abandon the law . . . They
> try to mend the gap, and there are further amendments
> and further amendments and further amendments. In this
> way the 'teeny bit pregnant' sometimes delivers something.[101]

With particularly intimate and long standing connections with the Labour Party, Feather was also much readier to maintain close ties with the PLP, and in fact kept in very close contact with Douglas Houghton throughout the controversy. His major concern, however, was to ensure that any voluntary alternatives adopted by the TUC should be supported unanimously in order to avoid contentions by the Government that the opposition of a major union rendered the TUC's approach meaningless; as such, he was very much inclined towards accepting TGWU and AEU arguments that the TUC should only undertake its own action once the Government agreed to abandon its penal sanctions.

The General Council took three crucial decisions between 23 April and 15 May when it completed *Programme for Action*, its own statement on industrial relations. First, it decided to allow the Special Congress to vote separately on the TUC proposals, the penal clauses, and the 'acceptable' proposals of the White Paper, thus enabling the

unions to reject the Government's proposals without necessarily endorsing TUC alternatives to them. Secondly, it determined to inform
the Government that the TUC would not cooperate in administering
the penal clauses if they were enacted, suggesting that no 'trade union
representative would be prepared to serve on a body (i.e. the Industrial Court) which was responsible for deciding that trade unionists
should be fined'.[102] Finally it agreed to make 'clear beyond any doubt
that it was the considered opinion of the General Council that the
essential prerequisite for the fulfilment of their proposals for reform
was that there should be no penal sanctions on workpeople or unions
in relation to industrial disputes'.[103] In other words, the TUC would
act voluntarily only if the Government did not legislate; if the
Government put its powers in reserve so would the TUC. Although
this decision was reached only after considerable argument by right-
wing members that this made it appear that the TUC was acting not
out of belief in 'reform', but due to Government pressure, General
Council moderates joined Jones and Scanlon in an adamant 'all or
nothing' approach on the grounds that if the unions were going to
cede powers to the TUC, they would only be able to justify doing so
to their members with proof in hand that this would remove the
legislative threat.[104]

This stand had the effect of changing the nature of the Government's negotiations with the General Council, which took place at
six long meetings between 12 May and 18 June.[105] Instead of the discussions centering around the extent to which the Government
would modify its proposed bill, as had been the Government's original intention, they focused instead on the question of how the TUC
alternatives could be strengthened to serve as an effective substitute
for the Government's legislative objectives, and the Government was
forced to make explicit to a degree unmatched in the incomes policy
discussions, how TUC control over its members could be an adequate
surrogate for the coercive powers of the state. The discussions were
not, as they have often been described, primarily a semantic exercise
in finding a face-saving formula to allow the Government to withdraw the penal clauses 'with honour',[106] but rather a substantive
argument on the fundamental question of whether the TUC and its
affiliated unions could become bodies which would exercise discipline
over their members with the degree of reliability that the state could
expect from one of its own agencies. The TUC itself had invited this
question earlier through its promotion of the idea of TUC wage
restraint in lieu of a statutory incomes policy, but the question had
been raised only implicitly by the Government so long as it was
assured of sufficient TUC cooperation and PLP support to pass the

incomes legislation. But the differences on incomes policy had really gone deeper than disagreements over short-term economic policy to the question of whether the TUC could commit itself completely to meeting the Government's objectives by assuming 'police powers' of its own. Indeed, Woodcock had said exactly this about the incomes policy discussions in an article on the occasion of the TUC centenary in 1968, and he had concluded:

> The TUC cannot become an agent of the Government because the unions cannot become agents of the TUC. Trade unions are essentially representative bodies ultimately responsible to their members. For the response which the Government seems to expect from the TUC it would be necessary completely to transform the ideas of trade unionism as they have developed over the last 100 years.[107]

The TUC's alternative proposals took as their first priority the necessity of developing with employers agreed bargaining procedures at all levels of industry whereby the *status quo* would be maintained during negotiations before changes were introduced by employers, and whereby agreements would be speeded up on union-initiated claims for improved terms and conditions – where the *status quo* automatically applied. Initially, it attempted to engage the CBI in a common effort to this end, but this avenue was quickly closed by the CBI at a meeting on 5 May. The CBI wanted legislation; it was not prepared to aid the TUC in its efforts to avoid it.[108] The General Council was required, therefore, to frame its proposals unilaterally, concentrating on what it alone could do to contain strikes rather than on what could be achieved in conjunction with employers, where it believed the real solution lay. *Programme for Action* admitted that some unofficial strikes were unjustified by being 'unconstitutional', but it defined this more narrowly than the Government had done: only in those cases where there was an established procedure already incorporating a *status quo* provision could a stoppage in defiance of this procedure properly be termed unconstitutional. This was of critical importance because roughly half of what the Government termed unconstitutional strikes did not meet this definition, including the engineering industry which was foremost in the mind of the Government.[109]

The TUC refused to supplement its own 'voluntary' conciliation pause for the Government's. It did propose, however, to extend the powers the General Council already had in this field. It would amend Congress Rule 11 (which empowered the General Council to use their influence in union disputes with employers to affect a 'just settlement') to specifically include unofficial as well as official strikes. On inter-union disputes (where, under Congress Rule 12, the General Council could adjudicate and impose a settlement) it would also prohibit unions authorizing a strike until the General Council considered the dispute and would require a union to take 'immediate and energetic steps' in large unofficial disputes to secure a return to work, while the General Council investigated, under penalty of suspension or expulsion already provided in Congress Rule 13. After the Government's initial reaction that the proposal on unofficial strikes looked like 'a vague, pious hope' [110] in comparison with the action to be taken on inter-union disputes, the General Council added a further section to *Programme for Action* in which it pledged to establish a special TUC disputes committee for unofficial strikes, to issue a recommendation for a settlement and to require unions to do 'all that could reasonably be expected' to secure an immediate return to work. It would also further amend Rule 11 to make it clear that the General Council could take disciplinary action in unofficial strikes, i.e. act under Rule 13 to suspend or recommend the expulsion of unions who did not do all that could 'reasonably' be expected to secure a return to work where the General Council so recommended.[111] It made it clear, however, that the General Council would be concerned with the merits of a dispute rather than with securing a return to work in all cases, as the Government's penal clauses were intended to do. They 'were not trading sanctions with the Government'. They saw their role as helping to secure settlements, not imposing sanctions which would be 'self-defeating' in a situation where all the workers in a particular factory were solidly supporting a strike. This was 'the major fallacy in the Government's thinking' and the TUC was not going to fall for it itself.[112]

The TUC proposals were plainly unacceptable to the Government. Apart from the narrower definition of unconstitutional strikes, the TUC's concern with the merits of a dispute meant it would actually effect a return to work in far fewer cases than the conciliation pause which involved an automatic return to work whatever the merits of the workers' substantive case. A detailed DEP Memorandum to the General Council on 14 May carefully elaborated the Government's requirement that the TUC would have to define precisely the sanctions it would take to ensure a return to work *before a settlement* in lieu of the penal sanctions. But in the context of doing so, it also reflected the extent to which the Government saw the TUC as an agency of the state in this exercise. From the Government's perspective 'equally effective' TUC action would have entailed not only much more frequent TUC intervention in strikes but also much more frequent application of TUC sanctions. Since the only ultimate sanction available to the TUC was expulsion, Mrs Castle had suggested on 12 May that Government fines were a less onerous penalty.[113] The DEP memorandum, however, suggested that the TUC should itself adopt fines as the most appropriate penalty and, in view of the danger it perceived that such action by the General Council might encourage breakaway organizations to be established, it suggested that it might be desirable for the state to back up the TUC by withdrawing legal immunity from prosecution from those officers and members of unions who encouraged a strike in order to bring pressure on an employer to reject a TUC ruling. If the TUC did not have the strength to act as an agency of social control on its own, without causing the disintegration of its organization, the Government was here suggesting it was prepared to employ the state's powers to give it that strength. It would become illegal to strike if the TUC pronounced against a strike.

The Government's position was outlined clearly by the Prime Minister at the 21 May meeting.[114] He saw the TUC proposals as 'a very great step forward' whereby the General Council 'had moved further and faster and more comprehensively than at any time for forty years'. But he saw the proposals, including those on inter-union disputes as valuable only as a supplement to legislation not a substitute for it. Recognizing that it was the hope of averting legislation which made the General Council's proposals acceptable to the unions, the Prime Minister and Mrs Castle promised not to publish the interim bill before the 5 June Congress, but they reiterated their intention to have legislation on the statute book by the summer recess. If the TUC would yet produce something the Government regarded as effective, the Government would amend – not abandon – the bill. The bill itself Wilson still regarded as essential to the continuance in office of the Government, indeed to that of any Labour Government. As for the TUC prerequisite that it would not go forward with its proposals unless the penal clauses were dropped, he regarded this as 'inconsistent and incompatible with good sense': it would destroy the public credibility of the TUC and not be taken seriously. The General Council questioned, however, whether the continuation of the Labour Government was dependent on its taking legislative power to penalize strikers, and affirmed on 21 May that if an impasse was reached, the issue would have to become who was going to back down

Rather than undermine the TUC's position, as the Prime Minister suggested, the 'all or nothing' strategy strengthened its position, at least within the labour movement. In direct contrast with the TUC's earlier stand on incomes policy, the PLP opposition to the bill was reinforced by it. On the night of the 21 May meeting, the Trade Union Group unanimously urged the Government to accept the TUC's alternative proposals as a basis for dropping the penal clauses; and a backbench letter to this effect sponsored by David Winnick, garnered over 60 signatures in a few hours.[115] The General Council's stand, however, was less a product of its own desire to defeat or even embarrass the Government on this issue than of the consistent pressure to which they were subject, from within the trade union movement, where its plan was by no means universally acclaimed. There were strong objections both to the extension of TUC authority over constituent unions and to the General Council's own acceptance of the view that something had to be done about unofficial strikes. The AEU National Committee had voted in April not only to reject the whole White Paper, but also intervention by the TUC itself. Basing himself on these decisions, the AEU's John Boyd was the one member of the General Council who refused to support the TUC plan, and on 20 May he secured the AEU executive's opposition to it by a 4 to 3 vote.[116] It was only with great difficulty that Scanlon was able to reverse this decision at a special AEU National Committee recalled for 3 June, which voted by 30 to 22 to accept the TUC plan.[117] This ensured the virtual unanimous acceptance of the General Council line at the special Congress on 5 June. Without being able to assure his union that the TUC proposals would be dropped if legislation was introduced, Scanlon would not have carried his union with him and this was a major factor in keeping the General Council to its 'all or nothing' position. That there was a significant degree of hostility against the TUC plan well beyond the confines of the AEU was made clear at a large rally in Birmingham a few days earlier organized by the *ad hoc* Committee against Anti-Trade Union Legislation. Many speakers from the floor were as concerned to attack the TUC plan as they were the legislation and many suggested that strike action was what was required to defeat the bill.[118]

Nevertheless, the massive support provided by the Special Congress [119] considerably enhanced the General Council's ability to pursue its 'all or nothing' strategy with the Government. The Government did not immediately accept this as a basis for negotiations, however. On the night of the Congress, Wilson publicly attacked the TUC for asserting a claim 'to power without responsibility' which he pledged himself to reject.[120] At the first meeting with the General Council after the Congress, the Prime Minister said he had meant all along to drop the penal clauses if the TUC further strengthened its disciplinary proposals on unofficial strikes, but he explained that he still meant by this that the Government might legislate reserve penal clauses but never apply them. The General Council responded that if the penal clauses were put in 'cold storage' so would be the TUC proposals and left the meeting in general agreement that although there was no sign that the Prime Minister had modified his views, he could no longer be in any doubt about their determination on the 'all or nothing' position.[121]

At the three final meetings on 11, 12 and 18 June, the Prime Minister and Mrs Castle finally accepted that, as Wilson put it, 'the TUC would not be running in legislative harness with the Government',[122] but turned the 'all or nothing' position back on the General Council as a basis for negotiations: 'If the General Council would agree to legislate, the Government would agree not to legislate.' [123] By asking the TUC to 'legislate itself', it was meant that it would have to change its Rules so that the Government could be satisfied of the 'effectiveness and saleability to the country' of the TUC plan. As Rule 11 stood it was entirely 'permissive' – using words like 'may' instead of 'shall', speaking of 'advice and guidance' rather than positive directives. When he gave advice to one of his staff, the Prime Minister declared, it could be ignored: he therefore gave directives.[124] This comment alone spoke volumes of the way Mr Wilson regarded trade union organization: it suggested that unions in relation to the TUC, and workers in relation to unions, were in a like situation of an employee *vis-à-vis* an employer rather than members of representative democratic organizations. This was highly indicative of the corporatism that prevailed in Government thinking throughout the controversy, indeed throughout the Labour Government's period in office. A draft amendment to Rule 11 was put to the General Council specifying that in those cases where *Programme for Action* defined unconstitutional stoppages as unjustified, the General Council would discipline unions who refused to obey a General Council directive which required unions to take 'immediate and energetic steps to obtain a resumption of work'.[125]

The General Council on 11 and 12 June were prepared to facilitate a compromise by issuing a special 'Note of Clarification' to unions outlining the procedure they intended to follow under Rule 11 as it stood. They refused, however, to adopt the proposed amendment to Rule 11 or to incorporate its wording into their circular. They were agreed that the Prime Minister and Mrs Castle wanted to transfer in some form the penal clauses into the TUC Rules, whereby the General Council would itself become a disciplinary body acting without discretion in unofficial strikes.[126] There was in fact little substantive difference between the Government's phraseology and that which the TUC proposed to use in its circular: both made explicit mention of those paragraphs of *Programme for Action* which outlined whether unconstitutional strikes were justified or not. The problem was that the Government insisted on specifically mentioning unconstitutional strikes, while the TUC wanted to avoid this, for it would give the impression that the TUC would take action against any strike popularly called unconstitutional, i.e. which did not take place until after procedure was exhausted, whether that procedure included a *status quo* obligation on employers or not, and even in those cases where the *status quo* inherently applied, as in a strike over a wage claim. Moreover, even in those cases which *Programme for Action* defined as unconstitutional, the General Council was reluctant to commit itself to automatically requiring a return to work in that it was painfully aware that, while unions and workers might oblige the TUC in this regard in inter-union disputes, they would be unlikely even to contemplate a return to work in a dispute with an employer until there was some promise of a settlement on the issue on which the strike had taken place. To have issued a circular suggesting the TUC would require a strike to be called off without regard to the grievance itself, would have totally undermined the credibility of the union leadership in a union movement as highly mobilized as it was in June 1969. As for attempting to incorporate such an obligation in as symbolic a way as was implied in a Rule change, the General Council told the Prime Minister, in gross understatement, that this would have 'severely prejudiced' the General Council's authority.

The impasse which on 21 May the General Council had warned would come, was therefore reached on 12 June. But it was an impasse which could only be resolved on the General Council's terms given the nature of the situation by this time. For whereas the TUC's stand – we will implement our proposals, only if you completely withdraw the legislation – was one which the General Council and the Government were capable of resolving between themselves, neither of them had the requesite authority to resolve the issue in the terms cast by the Prime Minister – if the TUC changes its Rules, the Government will not legislate. For while the special Congress had given the General Council the authority to carry out its threat not to implement its plan unless the legislation was withdrawn (and no authority to go beyond that), what the Prime Minister and Mrs Castle lacked was precisely the equivalent degree of support from the PLP or the Cabinet to be able to guarantee that the legislation would be either introduced or passed unless the TUC amended its Rules. The PLP Liaison Committee sent a letter to Wilson on 17 June which was endorsed by the Chief Whip, again drawing attention to the state of opinion in the Party and emphasizing that the differences between the Government and the TUC were too small to justify a split in the movement which legislation would entail.[127] More important still, it became clear on the same day that the Prime Minister could not rely on the support of the Cabinet. Fissures in the Cabinet on the proposed bill had emerged publicly as early as 9 May when at a joint annual NEC–Cabinet meeting, Callaghan had bolted once again and opposed the bill.[128] A majority of the Cabinet on 17 June, upon hearing from the Chief Whip that there was no hope of inducing the PLP to support the bill, refused to endorse the Prime Minister's stance in his negotiations with the TUC.[129] At a meeting with the Prime Minister the same evening, the Trade Union Group's opposition reached a peak. By this time, the recurrent talk at Westminster of a 1931 situation was by no means hysterical. Even if the Cabinet had held, there would have been another backbench demand for a PLP meeting on the leadership; Houghton would not have stood in its way – he was prepared to resign as PLP Chairman as soon as the bill was introduced; and the 'Action Group' of union MPs, which had kept clear of the earlier attempted coup, was now ready to join forces with it if necessary. Perhaps most important, Vic Feather, who had informed Houghton of the exact nature of the stalemate in negotiations on 12 June, was himself kept well informed by Houghton of the state of the PLP and the Cabinet. Houghton was emphasizing to Feather that whatever the General Council heard from the Prime Minister on 18 June, they must not abandon the negotiations, because the Prime Minister would have to accept whatever they offered.[130]

However, to concentrate on the Cabinet and the PLP in explaining why the conflict was incapable of resolution on the Prime Minister's terms, as have most interpretations of these events,[131] is fundamentally incorrect. For it involves overlooking the other possibility – that the General Council might have adopted a Rule change. What was exercising most Labour MPs and Ministers was primarily that the legislation would destroy the Labour Party. But Wilson was aware of this danger as much as any of his Parliamentary colleagues. He opened the 18 June meeting by forecasting that a breakdown in the negotiations would mean a deep split in the movement, not only at the top level between Ministers and the General Council but right through the labour movement.[132] Had the General Council alone taken upon itself the burden of avoiding this by transferring the penal clauses to the TUC Rules, this would have been heralded by the Cabinet and most of the PLP with no less, and possibly more, acclaim than the agreement finally reached. Moreover, it is not at all clear that the union leaders did not believe that the Government deserved as much in exchange for withdrawing the legislation. The General Council had gone through these abrasive time-consuming negotiations not only to avoid the bill, but also to avoid what they believed would be a disastrous break with the Labour Government and possibly the Labour Party. They were in fact searching for some political formula whereby the scission between the Government and and movement could be healed. They had no desire to carry any blame for bringing down a Labour Prime Minister, much less a Labour Government. Indeed, some members of the General Council were not fully aware of the state of the Cabinet and many others could not be sure that the Prime Minister's authority might not in the end prevail in Parliament.[133]

The ultimate reason the conflict was not capable of resolution on the Prime Minister's terms was that just as the Prime Minister did not have the requisite authority to introduce legislation, so the General Council did not have the necessary authority in June 1969 to guarantee to the Government that Congress would endorse a Rule change at the behest of the Government. In this sense, it was primarily the militancy on the part of critical sections of the rank and file that dictated the eventual outcome of the negotiations. This militancy was most visible in the AEU, among those workers and their shop stewards whose militancy it had been the overriding objective of both the employers and the Government to curtail by legislation. In order to secure endorsement for the TUC Rule change Scanlon would have had to recall the AEU National Committee once again, and in view of the fact that the original TUC plan had been passed before by only 8 votes it was more than likely that the whole *Programme for Action* would again be rejected by the AEU. Without this union's support any agreement on unofficial strikes entered into by the General Council would have appeared particularly worthless. Nor would opposition have been confined to the engineers. As the Prime Minister himself made clear on 18 June, the Government was seeking to restrict the power of Congress to make and change its own rules, in that any substantive amendments by the 1969 Congress of the Rule 11 changes drafted by the Government would have been unacceptable to the Government.[134] The General Council were extremely concerned that they would suffer a loss of confidence from even the most moderate of union activists if they saw the Government rewriting the TUC's Rules for it. And while a sizable portion of the General Council was prepared to risk this eventuality, an agreement reached on this basis would most decidedly not have had the unanimous support of the General Council. By in-sisting on TUC 'legislation' in lieu of their own, Harold Wilson and Barbara Castle had placed themselves in an impossible position, not so much because of the adamant stand of the General Council or because of the situation in the PLP, but because any agreement reached on this basis at Downing Street would not have closed the issue any more than legislation itself. All the arguments which pre-ceded the Special Congress would have been re-opened and the General Council's authority would have been subject to severe attack from inside the TUC at the very time that the Government had pub-licly accepted that authority as an effective substitute for legislation. The limitations posed to the General Council's authority by its struc-ture as a democratic body at a time when the militancy of activists was very marked, has to be counted as the major factor in leading the Prime Minister and Mrs Castle to accept an agreement on 18 June on the TUC's terms.

The Prime Minister opened the 18 June meeting by immediately retreating from the substantive issue of what action was required of the TUC in unconstitutional strikes. He admitted that if there was any doubt in the General Council's mind that the Government's wording did not allow for discretion on the part of the TUC in applying sanctions, a lot of doubt would exist in other people's minds. He agreed, therefore, to an explicit statement that it would be up to the General Council to decide on the *merits* of any dispute whether or not they would require an immediate return to work rather than on the question of whether a procedure agreement had been followed. On the principle of the TUC implementing its policy through a Rule change there was no immediate retreat, however. Wilson continued to insist that the Government needed TUC legisla-tion to legitimate the withdrawal of its own. The General Council thus concentrated on making the Prime Minister and Mrs Castle see that a Rule change would not end the controversy but rather bring into question the authority of the General Council. Although they were saying nothing that had not been said before, on this occasion (given the desperate need to reach an agreement of some finality and avoid the breaking off of the negotiations) the General Council's arguments, and particularly Scanlon's elaboration of the situation in the AEU, had the effect of leading the Prime Minister and Mrs Castle to accept the validity of this argument.[135] The basis for agree-ment thus reverted to the General Council's offer of a 'Note of Clari-fication'. However, in their own anxiety to reach an agreement and find a political formula to protect the Government (the Prime Minis-ter clearly needed 'something more' than he had rejected at the previous meeting), the General Council suggested that a circular issued unanimously by the General Council would have the accepted status of the Bridlington Principles on inter-union disputes in the annals of the TUC[136] The General Council had no illusion that any such circular would prompt an equal acceptance by unions of TUC interference in strikes between employers and workers as in inter-union disputes. Nevertheless it would be the same form of 'rule clarification' as Bridlington and the General Council were prepared to present it as such in return for an absolute assurance from the Government that the penal clauses would not be introduced during the lifetime of the Government. Thus instead of legislation and instead of a Rule change, the Government accepted a 'unanimous solemn and binding undertaking' on the part of the General Council to govern the operation of Rule 11 according to the circular. The wording was that of the Government's proposed draft amendment to Rule 11, specifically changed however to indicate that the General Council had complete discretion in any case as to whether or not they would require unions to order a return to work.

Notwithstanding the rapturous welcome with which the agreement was received by the PLP and the Cabinet, and Harold Wilson's (now public) declaration that the TUC had moved further in a few weeks than in 40 years, the agreement gave the Labour Government far less than it had wanted or pledged itself to securing, thereby laying itself open to the charges of 'capitulation' with which the Conservatives and most of the national press greeted the announcement. By securing from the TUC another 'declaration of intent' to expand its own role in restraining industrial militancy, the Labour Government had indeed achieved one of its objectives. But the TUC had not gone beyond agreeing to act according to the programme which they had offered to the Government a month earlier. Whereas the Government had obtained in the context of incomes policy both legislation and voluntary TUC action, it now had to settle for the latter alone, with all the indeterminancy that action by a body as decentralized as the TUC entailed. The conditions underlying the ability of the Government to pass the incomes legislation in previous years – the lower levels of industrial militancy, the tendency of the General Council to 'ignore' the legislation as irrelevant, the Government's control over the Party outside Parliament via the NEC, the limited opposition inside the PLP in the face of union hesitation and Cabinet unanimity – all these conditions had begun to fray by the time of the 1968 Prices and Incomes Bill; and the success of the opposition at the 1968 TUC and Party Conference together with the mobilization of the labour movement against *In Place of Strife*, further contributed to their demise by the time the interim industrial relations bill was proposed. When in this situation the TUC adopted a position which forced the Labour Government to make an explicit choice between statutory controls and voluntarism, the labour movement was able to win a significant victory.

It is crucial to reiterate, however, that the 'solemn and binding agreement' not only threw out the penal clauses, but also stood as a political formula designed to protect the Labour Government from an outright challenge to its political authority which the loss of support from the PLP, the Party outside Parliament and the trade unions would otherwise have meant. In other words, the victory secured by the General Council on 18 June, while important, was highly limited by its purely defensive nature: it neither involved a fundamental change in the Party leadership or ideology, nor restored the consensus between the Party and the unions tentatively established on incomes policy five years before. The political formula of June 1969 did not change the nature of the Labour Party, but instead preserved the Party as a viable political force despite the heightening contradiction between its ideology and its working class base.

8
Industrial militancy and political stagnation

The Reassertion of incomes policy

The struggle over *In Place of Strife* brought to a head the contradiction between the dominant class harmony ideology of the Labour Party and contemporary militant trends in the British trade union movement. The resolution of the immediate issue of the penal clauses in the unions' defensive victory of June 1969 did not, however, resolve the underlying contradiction. Indeed in its last year in office, at the very time that the trade union movement was embarking on a period of wage militancy unknown since the early 1920s, the Labour Government remained not only committed to an incomes policy, but to one that contained exactly those statutory and penal elements which had led to Frank Cousins' resignation from the Cabinet in July 1966, *before* the wage freeze. The political formula arrived at between the General Council and the Labour leadership in June 1969, designed as it was to re-establish the Labour leadership's legitimacy's *vis-à-vis* the labour movement, gave the Labour Government the opportunity of restoring its control over the PLP and NEC, of sustaining its independence from the decisions of the Labour Party Conference, and of securing the necessary financial and vocal support from the trade union leadership to enable it to fight the 1970 election effectively. The new element in the situation, however, was that the re-establishment of the political solvency of the Labour Party had little or no immediate effect on the industrial behaviour of the organized working class.

While the interim industrial relations bill occupied the centre of the political stage in the first half of 1969, the incomes policy issue was relegated to the wings, although the substantive questions involved were much the same. Nevertheless, it had become abundantly clear (with the Government's announcement on 15 April 1969 of the activation of Part II of the 1966 Prices and Incomes Act when the 1967 and 1968 legislation expired at the end of the year) that the

Government did not intend to abandon the statutory incomes policy, but that it would attempt to resurrect agreement on it by reverting to an earlier stage of that policy. Part II of the 1966 Act gave the Government the power to impose a three-month delay on a wage increase referred to the NBPI, subject to fines of up to £500 on anyone who attempted to induce an employer to pay (such as by advocating strike action), during this delaying period. The General Council made a conscious decision to defer raising this matter with the Government during the negotiations over the penal clauses in May and June, in the fear that the Government would then use it as a bargaining counter in the negotiations and thus make agreement on the political formula fashioned on the industrial relations proposals more difficult to reach.[1] By leaving the incomes policy legislation aside, however, the General Council was implicitly suggesting that, as Tony Topham pointed out, 'there was a distinction to be drawn between the two types of anti-union restriction'.[2] As a result, the Prime Minister's guarantee of 18 June that there would be no penal sanctions on unions during the rest of the life of the Government, was made without reference by either side to the question of incomes policy. The General Council had used broad enough phraseology in asking for this guarantee to suggest that the statutory incomes policy would be covered by it. It asked that 'there would be no introduction of the proposed penal sanctions, or *any alternative legislative penalties* on workpeople in the lifetime of this Government'.[3] On 25 June, the General Council received the following form of words set out in the Cabinet Office Minutes of the meeting: 'The Government would not proceed with the interim legislation on industrial relations, and they would not include *the so-called penal sanctions* in the legislation to be introduced next session or in any legislation during the lifetime of the present Parliament.'[4] The General Council did not press the issue, and included the Government's words in its circular to the unions on the agreement.

At a meeting with the Economic Committee in July, Mrs Castle explained the Government's intention to reactivate Part II. She admitted that the policy could play only a limited role in influencing current settlements and saw the policy as evolving from one of short-term restraint to having a long-range influence on the pattern of wage negotiations, but the need for the statutory powers of the 1966 Act was not presented by her as temporary, occasioned by the immediate economic situation, or as a bridge to anything else. It was the 'minimum necessary' for the incomes policy to operate and her arguments provided an adequate summary of those adduced by the Government in establishing the statutory incomes policy in the first place.[5] Although Scanlon protested that this was a violation of the 18 June agreement, his interpretation was not endorsed either by Mrs Castle or Vic Feather, and by having abided by the General Council's decision to avoid specific reference to incomes policy in the negotiations, Scanlon had effectively debarred himself from casting his opposition to the incomes legislation on these grounds. He, too, was responsible for the 'political formula' of 18 June. To be sure, the General Council was unanimous in the opinion that Part II should be repealed. Even Les Cannon saw its reactivation as 'a policy of continued intimidation'.[6] The TGWU and AEU also wanted the General Council to follow the 1968 Congress decision in demanding a complete repeal of the incomes legislation, including Part I of the 1966 Act establishing the NBPI as a statutory body, on the grounds that the Board had become, in Scanlon's phrase, 'symbolic of all that we have learnt to resist and detest'.[7] The majority of the General Council, however, led by Feather and Cooper, argued that some of the Board's reports on wages had been helpful to the unions and that the prices aspect of the policy should not be foregone. They were prepared to suggest to the Government that Part I of the 1966 Act alone be retained.[8] The 1969 Congress narrowly rejected this approach, however, by passing by 4,652,000 to 4,307,000 votes a DATA resolution demanding the repeal of the whole 1966 Act and calling on the General Council to lead the unions in 'aggressive opposition' in support of this demand.[9]

The division displayed at the Congress over Part I to some extent concealed the more important unanimous opposition to Part II, and gave some basis to the Government's hopes that the Labour Party Conference, under the pressure of presenting a united front at what was seen as likely to be the last Conference before the election, would be prepared to cloud the statutory issue behind a general commitment to the need for an incomes policy. The danger for the Government, on the other hand, was that the Conference would concentrate on its refusal to adhere to the 1968 Conference's clear demand that the legislation be repealed. At the beginning of 1969, when the NEC decided to confront the Government with this Party decision, this had seemed a real possibility. But the danger was abated when the NEC in the summer of 1969 drew back from its earlier stance by pointedly obscuring the statutory issue. *Agenda for a Generation*, the NEC document on future party policy, endorsed the incomes policy without mentioning at all the legislation. 'We believe in the vital importance of an effective prices and incomes policy,' the NEC affirmed. 'We are convinced that the Government *cannot* abdicate its responsibilities in this field. To allow prices, and the pay of poorer sections of the community to be relegated again to the market place would be folly of the first order.' [10]

The document was introduced to the Conference on 1 October by George Brown, who had a major hand in drafting it, and an observer who had missed the intervening Conferences, might have thought that nothing had changed since 1963. A great deal had changed, however; Scanlon attacked the document in these terms:

> This document is going to be the basis of our future election manifesto. It is going to be read in sheer disbelief by millions of our supporters. They will wonder what has been happening, what it has all been over the last three or four years, when this movement really rent itself in two. We cannot let this situation develop so that we go into the next election split, as we are. [11]

Neither the TGWU or AEU delegations were prepared to accept what Jack Jones termed 'the usual dangerous waffle' on incomes policy, [12] and they demanded a clear reply from the NEC on whether it would join the General Council in pressing the Government to repeal completely the incomes legislation. Tom Bradley, replying for the NEC, refused to give such assurances, and asked that a resolution from Jarrow CLP calling on the Government to adopt a 'genuinely voluntary incomes policy' be remitted on the familiar grounds that the Party needed 'something between a statutory straight jacket and a self-defeating free-for-all'. [13] The resolution was passed, over the NEC's objections, by 3,569,000 to 2,416,000 votes, but such open confrontations were precisely what the Party leadership had sought to avoid. Indeed, the Government's strategy was exactly the same as that adopted in respect of the wages policy at the 1950 Party Conference – one of avoiding embarrassing defeats by accepting resolutions critical of the policy while at the same time reaffirming the Government's commitment to the policy. Two days before the Jarrow resolution was passed, Mrs Castle, speaking for the NEC, had *accepted* a TGWU resolution declaring the Conference's 'unalterable opposition to any legislation that would curtail basic trade union rights including penal sanctions on work people or on trade unions in connection with industrial disputes'. And on this occasion, the mover of the resolution explicitly stated that the meaning of the words included that the penal clauses of the Prices and Incomes Act be removed 'without fail'. [14] In the course of accepting the resolution, however, Mrs Castle cited *Agenda for a Generation* on the incomes policy, proclaimed the Government's refusal to accept that Part II of the 1966 Act constituted any curtailment of basic union rights, and indicated that the Government had 'heard nothing to make it change its mind about the value and necessity for Part II'.[15] But whereas this strategy had worked smoothly in 1950 when Deakin instead of Jack Jones was leader of the TGWU, it proved less effective in 1969. In an angry intervention from the floor, while Mrs Castle was speaking, Jones attacked her interpretation of the resolution and her apparent commitment of the NEC to the Government's position. The Government's cavalier attitude towards Conference resolutions seemed a direct rebuff to the left-wing union leaders' grounds for opposing those militants who had advocated breaking with the Party. 'It is not Harold Wilson's Labour Party', Cousins had said, '– it is ours.' [16] When the NEC refused to dissociate itself clearly from the Government's position, the TGWU and AEU decided to oppose *Agenda for a Generation*, the basis of the 1970 election manifesto, as a whole.

Nevertheless, the Government emerged from the 1969 Conference in a stronger position in relation to the Party than it had in 1968. For although the Party had proclaimed its support for a 'genuinely voluntary incomes policy' and its opposition to the penal clauses of the 1966 Act, it refused to reject *Agenda for a Generation* which was passed by 3,562,000 to 2,272,000 votes, thus endorsing the Party leadership's design to conceal the conflict behind the NEC's 'waffle'.

The opposition to the activation of Part II did produce a shift in the Government's position. Instead of continuing to present Part II as a permanent fixture of Government policy, the Prime Minister announced at the end of October that it would be a 'bridging measure' until a new bill was passed in 1970 which would amalgamate the Monopolies Commission with the NBPI into a new supervisory body, the Commission for Industry and Manpower (CIM). The Government now resurrected the argument that the statutory elements of the policy were temporary, short-term exigencies: where before temporary statutory powers had been needed to 'prevent devaluation' and then to 'make devaluation work', they were now needed *after* devaluation had worked, to protect the balance of payments surplus achieved in 1969. The object of the exercise was to gain time by allaying the unions' opposition with the prospect that the Government's long-term policy would be based on a legislative and institutional framework which would not be prejudiced by the events of the previous years and which would shift the emphasis of policy to prices and the monopoly power of big business when and if the Labour Government was returned after the election. Mrs Castle at least continued to believe in a permanent statutory policy. She told the Commons on 7 November: 'We are always told that voluntary policy could do the job that the prices and incomes legislation was designed to do but I can see no evidence that without the pressures of public opinion that we are able to marshall through prices and incomes legislation there will be any reality in voluntary incomes policy at all.' [17] Nevertheless, the Cabinet had once again come to the conclusion that the safest course was to postpone a decision on the question of a permanently statutory incomes policy. Thus, the Labour Government's last White Paper on incomes policy again expressed the Government's 'hopes that it will not be necessary to perpetuate these delaying powers in setting up the CIM'.[18] But Mrs Castle told the General Council that the question of whether these hopes become a decision 'must depend on the economic circumstances at the time, and particularly on whether there was inflationary pressure'.[19]

Although the General Council looked forward to consultations with the Government on the CIM proposal, there was no question of its endorsing the short-term policy outlined in the White Paper. They were not prepared to walk a bridge, in defiance of the Congress vote, without any definite guarantee that what lay on the other side was substantially different from the previous policy. The White Paper introduced a flexible norm of $2\frac{1}{2}$ to $4\frac{1}{2}\%$ and allowed for increases above the norm for a whole industry with a high proportion of low paid workers and for the introduction of equal pay for women, and suggested that more reliance would be placed on comparability with private industry to overcome low pay in the public service. But it retained the two central tenets of the policy in respect of wages: that productivity improvement should be the main ground for pay increases, and that increases for the low paid could only be justified if their fellow workers accepted a reassessment of differentials, i.e. if it led to redistribution of income *within* the working class. The White Paper contained no reference at all to incomes at the top end of the scale, and the only section dealing with unearned incomes explained that the ceiling on dividends imposed in 1968 was being dropped due to the distortions it was creating on the stock market. The dividends decision particularly upset the General Council who wondered at the Government's audacity in condemning a 'free-for-all' on wages while inviting a 'free-for-all' on dividends. If it was good enough for market forces to operate in the allocation of capital, they told Mrs Castle in an argument reminiscent of the 1948–50 wages policy controversy, it was good enough in the field of labour supply.[20]

The section of the White Paper dealing with prices was remarkably brief, and under heavy pressure from the CBI suggesting it would refuse to cooperate in future policy, the Government also withdrew from this White Paper the list of prices subject to early warning notification.[21] This was in itself a very minor change of policy because it did not involve a change in the actual operation of the price notification system and because price control was virtually non-existant in any case. While the White Paper 'revealed' that 18% of all price increases notified under the early warning system since March 1968 had been modified or withdrawn, what it did not reveal was that over this twenty month period only 854 price increases had in fact been submitted to the Government, even less than the 1,000 submitted during the twelve months of freeze and severe restraint in 1966–7.[22] Nevertheless, in so far as price and dividend control were mainly of symbolic value in order to induce wage restraint, these concessions to the CBI were important. The CBI found the White Paper 'temporarily acceptable'; the TUC pronounced it 'unacceptable to the trade union movement'.[23]

The White Paper was published only six days before the Commons vote on 17 December on the Order to activate Part II. The possibility of another backbench revolt had once again been a major factor in leading the Government to present the Part II powers as temporary rather than permanent. The mood of the PLP had not been much assuaged by this, however, as a large number of backbench MPs doubted the Government's veracity, given their experience with the 'temporary' argument before, and could not convince themselves that such a temporary measure was worth prolonging the political agony which the incomes policy had come to represent for them.[24] Eric Heffer, who led the Tribune Group in its opposition to the Order, had welcomed in October the Prime Minister's 'conversion' to an eventual voluntary policy, but nevertheless warned, 'if the Government tries to activate Part II of the Prices and Incomes Act, we shall vote against'.[25] This was an ominous warning since the only occasion when the Tribune Group had actually *voted against* rather than *abstained* on the incomes legislation (the amendment on the 1968 Bill), the Government had come perilously close to being defeated. In December 1969, the Liberals as well as the Conservatives were pledged to the vote against the Order, the Government's majority had been cut by by-election defeats to sixty-three, and the flu epidemic of that winter was playing havoc with the Whips' calculations. A timely announcement by the TGWU that it was about to review its panel of MPs in time for the general election, added to the Government's discomfort.[26]

Yet, in the event, what the final Parliamentary battle on the incomes policy revealed was the strength of the Government *vis-à-vis* its backbench MPs, particularly in a situation where it was the PLP

opposition that was placed in a position of leading the labour movement in opposition to the Government rather than playing a supportive role to a union campaign, as had been the case with *In Place
of Strife*. The General Council, despite the requirement placed upon
it by Congress that it organize aggressive union action against the
incomes legislation, limited itself to reiterating its opposition at its
one meeting with Mrs Castle and in the TUC statement on the White
Paper. Nor was there much pressure on the General Council, as
militant workers concentrated on pursuing wage demands in defiance
of the policy rather than engaging in the kinds of demonstrations
that had provided much of the impetus to the defeat of the industrial
relations bill in June.[27] Under these conditions the Government was
able to reassert its control over both the NEC and the official PLP
leadership. At an NEC meeting on the day before the Commons vote,
Joe Gormley of the NUM withdrew a resolution against the Order,
allegedly 'in the interests of peace'.[28] And Douglas Houghton on this
occasion entered the debate, at the Prime Minister's and Mrs Castle's
request, on the side of the Government, warning the PLP that the
Order's defeat 'would be the most humiliating experience for the
Labour Party since 1931'.[29] Finally, the Chief Whip conducted what
was generally described as the most furious whipping exercise during
the life of the Government, and sent a letter to all Labour MPs concentrating on making it clear that even abstainers would be subject
to heavy party discipline.[30]

What seems to have most affected Labour MPs, however, were the
Government's arguments that 'giving in' to the unions on this question would harm the Party's electoral chances. At PLP meetings, the
Prime Minister warned MPs against forcing him into calling a pre-
mature election, and joined Mrs Castle and Roy Jenkins in stating
that, while it would be 'neither desirable nor necessary' to include
the delaying powers on wages in the CIM Bill in 1970, without these
interim powers there would be a 'psychological backlash' reflected
in a wage and price explosion which would prevent the Chancellor
from issuing an 'election' Budget.[31] This argument could be counted
to have real effect on backbench MPs since it is conventional wisdom
at Westminster that governments' win elections primarily by granting
pre-election fiscal handouts, a strategy which workers were spoiling
by taking increased purchasing power themselves through their wage
demands and settlements. Thus, George Brown attacked low-paid
striking London dustmen in these terms: 'They will destroy us all
and all that we stand for and all that we were invented for. We were
invented to look after the poorer people.' [32] To this argument was
added the corollary that while the Government might change its

policies in the pre-election period, it had to be seen to do so on its own terms, and not at the behest of its union supporters. Harold Wilson told the PLP on the night before the vote that the Government would put its electoral recovery at risk

> if we give the impression that the Government cannot do
> its job, if we appear to be in pawn. One of our strongest
> assets is that Labour Government does work and looks like a
> government. If we give the impression of having a blind
> spot, of having sacred cows, of being a planning government
> which says there are sacrosanct areas where an unplanned
> scramble and free-for-all must reign, we shall lose.[33]

It was scarcely credible that of all the Government's blind spots, of all the areas it had failed to 'plan', given its own official abandonment of the National Plan as early as July 1966 and its effective abandonment even a year before that, wages might appear to the electorate as one of them. But financial orthodoxy plus statutory regulation over union activities had come to symbolize what 'looking like a government' entailed as far as the Labour leadership was concerned. For the Labour leadership, despite its retreat of June 1969, was still defining the national interest within parameters established by the Conservative Party and the national press as well as its own integrative tradition. Before the 1964 election, when securing voluntary union co-operation in wage restraint was in the forefront of Conservative strategy, the Labour leadership had seen the Labour Party's ties with the union as an electoral asset; and had concentrated on the Conservative Government being 'in pawn' to foreign creditors and their financial orthodoxy. Before the 1970 election, with a Conservative theme of legal controls over unions and Labour's 'capitulation' of June 1969, the Labour Party's ties with the unions were seen as an electoral liability, and Part II of the 1966 incomes legislation was needed as a symbol that the Labour Government was not 'in pawn' to its union supporters.

The Government was right in treating the issue as one of great symbolic importance, although all parties to the controversy recognized that the Part II powers on wages would not be used in a pre-election period. What was involved was the question of whether the political formula of June 1969 had made any substantive change in the Labour Government's relationship to the labour movement. And this time, unlike June 1969, it was left to the body of backbench MPs and particularly the Tribune Group to provide the labour movement with political leadership on the issue. It was not primarily a matter of numbers; a determined group of less than thirty MPs could have defeated the Order by carrying out their threat to vote against the Government, relatively secure in the knowledge that the Prime Minister would neither call an election on a statutory incomes policy issue on which the unions could not have possibly supported the Government, nor attempt to purge a body of MPs who were acting in accordance with Labour Party Conference and TUC decisions. Instead of placing the responsibility for preserving the unity of the Labour Party upon the Government, however, the Tribune Group, like the NEC, the PLP chairman, and most union MPs, took that responsibility upon themselves, and the Order to activate Part II of the 1966 Act passed by 289 to 261 votes with twenty-nine Labour MPs abstaining and only one, Christopher Norwood (who had already announced his intention not to seek re-election), voting against.[34] When the 1966 Bill was first introduced by the Government before the wage freeze, fifty Labour MPs had signed a reasoned amendment urging rejection of a Bill containing penal sanctions against unions. No doubt had it come to signing such declarations in 1969, many more than fifty MPs would have done so. But the intervening years had shown, and December 1969 confirmed, that when it was left to the PLP alone to provide the initiative rather than merely support an explicit trade union political campaign for defeating restrictive union legislation, the Government was able to prevail. The Tribune Group ostentatiously displayed their opposition to the measure by remaining in their seats in the Commons while the House divided on the vote; and the NEC in January 1970 passed its resolution against the Order. These were gestures of defiance, however, which were primarily occasioned by their impotence, protests rather than acts of power.

The new industrial militancy

The final Parliamentary victory scored by the Labour Government on its statutory incomes policy was an attestation to the extreme limitations of the political formula arrived at six months earlier as a harbinger of change in the relationship between the Labour Party and the organized working class. The irony contained in this victory, however, was that it took place at a time when the breakdown of the incomes policy agreement became most apparent in the industrial sphere, when workers openly rejected the Labour Party's contention that they could best improve their lot in capitalist society by fore-going the expression of industrial class conflict in favour of the quasi-corporatism entailed in the new group politics. In the last months of 1969, militant wage demands and strikes by dustmen, teachers, firemen, miners and nurses initiated what has come to be known as the 'wage and strike explosion' which characterized the British economy in the early 1970s. By the end of 1969, 6,800,000 working days were lost in strikes, an increase of 2 million over 1968 and 4 million over 1967. This was the largest consistent expression of wage militancy since the war, and when the strike figure soared to 11 million days in 1970, it was clear that industrial militancy was reaching levels unprecedented since the early 1920s.[35]

This breakthrough to wage militancy must be seen, not in terms of the events of 1969 alone, but in terms of the cumulative frustrations experienced by workers during the years of the Labour Government. As we have seen, the Government's attempt to impose new statutory restrictions on strikes was to a large extent motivated by an anticipation of militant developments, and there can be little doubt that the defeat of the penal clauses invigorated rank and file activists. Yet the *In Place of Strife* episode was in the main a connecting link between the effects of Labour's earlier policies on the working class living standards and the eventual response to this in the wage explosion of 1969–70, rather than an independent cause of it. Average real earnings in the first half of 1969 had again fallen (by 0.4%), which meant that in four of the six half-yearly periods between Labour's 1966 election victory and the summer of 1969, workers had experienced declining real incomes *before tax*.[36] Moreover, the gains secured in the two remaining periods – the second halves of both 1967 and 1968 – had been largely offset by the Government's deflationary fiscal policy, a policy intensified in 1969 to produce what Michael Artis termed 'the largest turnaround in the fiscal balance towards restriction'.[37] On the prices side, the largely symbolic nature of Labour's statutory price control, which had been demonstrated during the period of freeze and severe restraint, was further confirmed over the subsequent three years of the Government's term of office. Only 2,126 price notifications were received by the Government from July 1967 to June 1970 (505 of these coming during its last six months in office, when the Government was most concerned about the electoral consequences of rising prices); and of the price increases it examined, the Government rejected only 110, and modified only 245. On the basis of the DEA's estimate of three million price changes a year, it appears that the Labour Government directly affected a grand total of 355 price changes out of nine million.[38] Labour's failure – or refusal – to control prices was a major factor in producing the new period of wage militancy.

One of the most notable aspect of this new militancy was that it included (and to some extent was led by) low paid, traditionally unmilitant workers, whose relative position had not improved under the incomes policy.[39] The main money wage gains made under the policy were through productivity agreements in 1968, entailing increased effort and a loss of defensive practices; and although the value of these increases had been diminished by rising prices and taxes, their effect on workers in industries with lower productivity growth (or where productivity could not be easily measured) was to lead them to reject the criteria of the policy in framing their wage claims and adopt instead the TUC strategy of securing target minimum earnings levels designed to benefit low paid and especially women workers. Moreover, whereas the Government had discriminated against the public sector in terms of sending wage (and price) references to the Board, a good deal of the labour unrest in 1969–70 occurred among public employees, manifesting itself in a number of bitter and protracted strikes.[40]

The incomes policy's failure on income redistribution was most graphically displayed in 1969 in the NBPI's Report, *Top Salaries in the Private Sector and Nationalized Industries*.[41] The salaries in question ranged from £7,000 to £13,000 on average but the Board found that the *percentage* increase from 1965 to 1968 had been significantly below that of all employees generally. It concluded, without regard to the absolute increases to which even a small percentage increase in these high incomes gave rise, that the incomes policy had been redistributive, although it admitted that this may have been offset by the growth of investment incomes or capital gains received by board members and senior executives. It was primarily concerned with the imbalance between top incomes in the nationalized industries and the private sector, however, and recommended an increase for the former of up to 60% over three years, a recommendation immediately accepted by the Government. Mrs Castle attempted to justify this increase as *consistent* with the incomes policy by calculating it in percentage annual terms back to 1964 and by contending that the application of percentages to vastly different incomes was valid on the grounds that the unions themselves favoured the percentage principle in order to maintain differentials. At the same time, however, she tried to justify the increases as valid *exceptions* to the policy on 'productivity' grounds, necessary to provide 'headroom' so the nationalized industries could compete with the private sector for capable senior managers.[42] The problem with the 'consistency' argument, however, was that the incomes policy had not normally allowed such retrospective increases; her calculations did not take account of the 'zero norm' applicable since July, 1966; and the TUC itself had made a deliberate effort to get away from the percentage principle by casting its own norm in money terms in order to benefit the low paid. As for the 'productivity' argument, the Government and the Board had refused to apply it to workers, explicitly rejecting as inflationary the idea that higher paid workers should receive increases in pay so there would be 'headroom' for rises to provide 'initiative' for low paid workers.

At the time, Stanley Orme, joined by backbench MPs from every section of the Party, had seen as 'absolute nonsense' Mrs Castle's 'endeavours to fit these increases within the tortuous criteria of the prices and incomes policy'.[43] But with this case, the central element of Labour's 'egalitarian' incomes policy in fact received its fullest expression, by proving that the policy itself was not concerned with income redistribution between classes but only to narrow income differentials within the working class, what we have called the doctrine of 'socialism in one class'. The failure of the policy in this latter respect was certainly partly the product of union insistence on retaining differentials, but this took place in a context where, according to the Government's 1968 earnings survey,[44] 80% of all workers earned between £15 and £33 a week, an extremely narrow range within which to effect income redistribution as compared with the massive disparities between working class incomes and those of other classes. The Government's corrective to the imbalance between top salaries of private and public board members and managers was found in applying the standards of the private sector to the public sector. The alternative solution of lowering top salaries in the private sector by controls or nationalization was not considered at all by the Board, nor, it seems, by the Government. Indeed in a classic example of what Bachrach and Baratz have called a 'non-decision', the one member of the Board, Jim Mortimer, who believed that the top salaries in question were objectively too high, did not bother to raise the alternative solution in the course of the Board's deliberation, anticipating that it would not be considered seriously by the rest of his colleagues or by the Government.[45]

In replying to criticisms from Labour MPs that the Government's acceptance of the Report had destroyed the basic principles of the incomes policy, Mrs Castle's Under-Secretary, Harold Walker, had been more candid. 'It is not a primary function of the Government's prices and incomes policy to redistribute incomes. Social and fiscal policies have their role to play in this, and they are doing it.'[46] But as the previous chapters have indicated, one of the main causes of the political breakdown of the incomes policy agreement between the TUC and the Government lay precisely in the fact that the TUC's hopes of gaining a stronger influence in such broader areas of economic decision-making had been dashed by the Treasury's repeated refusal to adopt to any significant extent the fiscal and social policies canvassed by the TUC. Indeed, H. A. Turner and Frank Wilkinson have shown, in their study of workers' net real incomes (i.e. disposable incomes after price *and* tax increases), that fiscal policy proved to be one of the major causes of wage militancy and rejection of the incomes policy. While corporate profits *before* tax, under the pressure of international competition and rising money wage costs, fell as a percentage of aggregate wages and salaries from 41.6% in 1949–52 to 39.5% in 1957–60 to 37.2% in 1965–8, the effect of taxation was to redistribute income from employment to non-employment incomes so that *after tax* corporate profits rose as a percentage of wages and salaries from 25% in 1949–52 to 28.7% in 1957–60 to 30.2% in 1965–8.[47] This was partly a product of direct state subventions to private industry through capital tax exemptions and investment allowances. It was also a product of the Labour Government's maintenance of a nominally progressive tax system which – as increased money earnings pushed low paid workers into the tax system for the first time, and higher paid workers into higher tax brackets – actually led to the burden of taxation falling increasingly on the working class and especially on the lower paid members of that class. The result was that the increases in money wages received under the Labour Government were not only diminished by rising prices (heavily induced by regressive indirect taxes used to deflate the economy) but also by rising direct taxes, so that net real income of the typical male manual worker (i.e. married with two children) rose by the negligible amount of 0.5% a year on average, despite an average annual growth in productivity of 3%. This fiscal policy operated in tandem with the incomes policy: when wage restraint succeeded in 1966–7, the tax effect was small; when it failed to some extent, as it did in late 1968, tax receipts were allowed to rise instead. Nor was there much compensation for stagnating real disposable income in the provision of collective social benefits by the Labour Government, as orthodox fiscal policies restricted the growth in social expenditures. Although total social security spending did increase under Labour, this was mainly the product of a rising demand for benefits in terms of more old people and more unemployed.[48] Overall, taking account of education and health benefits as well as family allowances, national insurance and public welfare, the ratio of benefits received to taxes paid fell for all families throughout the sixties and fell most steeply for the typical wage-earning family of two adults and two children.[49]

The Labour Government's ability to secure trade union cooperation in wage restraint, at least in the sense of their refraining from wage demands high enough to compensate for inflation and taxation, had produced stagnation in working class living standards. But as had been the case in 1948–50, there were evident temporal limits on the integrative potential of the Labour Government in this respect. At a time when Labour's incomes norm still stood at zero, with a ceiling of $3\frac{1}{2}$%, wage settlements in the last quarter of 1969 involved annual average increases of 7 to 8%, based on demands for often twice that amount. Real wage and salary earnings increased by 3.4% in the second half of 1969 as a result, and although prices in the first half of 1970 jumped by over 4%, the continuing trend of wage militancy compensated for this, yielding a total rise in real earnings of just over 5% in the last twelve months of the Labour Government, almost double the average annual increase over the four previous years.[50] Real net income increased for the typical annual wage earner by 1.3% annually over 1969 and 1970, compared with the 0.5% of the previous four years. Moreover, as the militancy of the low-paid extended into 1970, these increases gave 'a distinct preference to the lower paid'.[51]

It is important to note that the union leadership did not so much lead their members into the wage explosion of 1969–70 as rush after them in the new militancy. This was seen not only in the high proportion of strikes which were unofficial, but in such trend-setting disputes as the London dustmen's strike in the autumn of 1969, where the TGWU, NUPE and GWMU were aiming for an increase of only 15s a week when unofficial strikes began on the basis of demands for a $14\frac{1}{2}$% increase. Under very great pressure from their members, the TGWU made the dispute official and was reluctantly followed in this by the other unions. John Torode pointed out at the time that the 'unions might well have been faced with a breakaway union. Feelings were as high as that. It is to their credit that the union generals saw sense in time and went chasing after their members'.[52] Similarly, the TUC General Council did not actually abandon its Incomes Policy Committee until February 1970, by which time it was not only clear that the number of claims being submitted for vetting had slowed down to a trickle, but that the TUC's own norm had become irrelevant in the new industrial situation.[53] The fact, however, that union executives refused to go on counselling wage restraint was in itself an important facilitating factor in the wage explosion, and brought substantial organizational gains to the unions. At a time of high, indeed increasing, unemployment, membership rose by 9.4% in 1969–70, which not only compensated for the losses of 1966–7, but involved an increase one-third larger than over the whole of the previous two decades.[54] (Notably, the last substantial increase in union membership occurred in 1951, after the unions had rejected the 1945 Labour Government's wages policy). The growth in membership was not, of course, equally spread across all unions. The TGWU, whose industrial policies were fairly open to the rank and file militancy of the period, showed the most dramatic increases in membership, while the GMWU, with Lord Cooper continuing to cast dire prophesies against a 'free-for-all', experienced not only stagnating membership, but a high degree of internal strife, seen especially in the Pilkington's strike of 1970.[55] In general terms, however, the new militancy certainly facilitated a strengthening of the trade unions, after the loss of membership and disunity which resulted from cooperation in wage restraint, to an extent which allowed the unions to carry through a more aggressive industrial posture into the first years of Conservative Government.

But if the unions moved towards a realistic industrial strategy in 1969–70, *politically* the contradiction between a militant union movement and its allegiance to the integrative Labour Party persisted, as union loyalty to the Labour Party was reaffirmed in the context of the 1970 election. To be sure, this was facilitated to some extent by the actions of the Government in its last months in office. The CIM Bill was published without including statutory controls on wages, and the second version of the Industrial Relations Bill was introduced in Parliament containing some of the beneficial provisions of *In Place of Strife*, although neither actually was enacted before the election. And the fact that the Government refrained from applying the statutory powers contained in Part II of the Prices and Incomes Act helped to assuage the unions' ire at its reintroduction in December. But these were small concessions to unity, given the dissension which had but recently racked the Party–union relationship, and it was clear from the Party's 1970 election manifesto that the underlying causes of this dissension had not been swept away. The manifesto carefully avoided explicit mention of incomes policy, but its main proposal for 'greater price stability' was as before placed on 'wage increases . . . (being) linked to increases in production'. The 'invaluable work' of the NBPI was lauded and was to be continued by the CIM. 'Progress' was still seen to depend on the policies of 'the very large firms', who, unlike 'Tory Party doctrine' did not reject 'planning', and who would be 'accountable to the community' through the CIM which would 'report on costs, prices and efficiency and . . . stimulate competition'. This tired eulogy to the mixed economy was enveloped in the Party's 'purpose to develop a new relationship with both sides of industry in which the forward plans of both Government and Industry can be increasingly harmonized in the interests of economic growth'.[56] A jaded observer might have been moved to suggest that in place of a change in policy, the Labour Party was offering a change in the nomenclature of state agencies.

Such an approach to the election could not of course overcome the divisions and disillusion of the preceding years. DEP officials warmly welcomed in April 1970 a suggestion from Victor Feather that a new 'practical voluntary' incomes policy could be developed, but Hugh Scanlon adamantly opposed 'the resurrection of an incomes policy on either a compulsory or voluntary basis'.[57] Nevertheless, on the basic question of supporting the Labour Government's re-election there were no divisions among the union hierarchy. Even the TGWU's much vaunted decision to vet its Parliamentary panel in light of its sponsored MPs support of anti-union legislation came to naught, as the union continued to sponsor almost all of its MPs (including a number of Ministers) who had consistently supported the incomes policy. The union did withdraw 'official' sponsorship of George Brown, but provided him instead with a 'special grant' of £500 towards constituency expenses in his unsuccessful bid for re-election. That there was little question that this kind of support would be forthcoming had in fact been made clear at the 1969 Party Conference by Hugh Scanlon, who despite his refusal to cover over the incomes policy dispute introduced a resolution pledging the unions to securing the re-election of the Government. He gave three reasons: 'firstly, the Labour Party is the only effective working class party in the country; and secondly, by its endeavours a large number of people have a materially better standard of life than they otherwise would have had'. And finally, because the Conservatives 'will seek probably to please their business masters with some bloodthirsty threats against organized labour masquerading as union reform . . . and if for no other reason we will do our best, through our journals, through any propangada means, through meetings, to ensure that this Labour Government is returned'.[58]

There was considerable logic in this position. The Conservative Party's industrial and social programme in 1970 was manifestly anti-union and anti-egalitarian in content. Yet as Scanlon himself had pointed out in the course of the incomes policy debate, the claim that the Labour Party was an effective working class party or that it had raised substantially workers living standards was simply not credible to a significant proportion of workers given their experience under the Labour Government. The fact that the majority of working class voters returned to Labour in the 1970 election can only be seen as the product of the same factors that influenced the support of the union leadership – the strength of traditional party identification, combined with apprehension at the consequences of Conservative victory. Yet precisely because the British working class was not faced with a political alternative to match its industrial militancy in 1970, the Conservatives were able to take advantage of the effects which the Labour Government's policies had on its own supporters to capitalize on working class abstentions in the lowest voter turnout since 1935; so that as the 1970 election study had concluded 'the outcome can be seen as the reluctant decision of just enough electors that the Conservatives were, marginally, the lesser of two evils'.[59]

Such was the sad denouement to the hopes and aspirations which had produced the 1964–70 Labour Governments. But if the British working class had failed to fashion an adequate political complement to wage militancy in 1969–70, the possibility remained strong in the eyes of many Party and union activists that, given the acute strains which the Party had experienced and the enhanced strength of the left in the PLP, the Party conference and the National Executive, a transformation of the Labour Party might yet mark the years in opposition in the 1970s. Hope, indeed, springs eternal. Although the full implications of recent events cannot yet be fully grasped, it is necessary before moving to the conclusion to this study, to examine, albeit briefly, the various trends in the Labour Party which have emerged since 1970. And to do this, we have to take into account not only the experience of 1964–70, but the conflict between the labour movement and the Conservative Government of 1970–4, which set the immediate context for recent developments in the Labour Party.

The Heath Government and the unions

The strategy with which the Heath Government took office was designed to effect an important shift of direction for the quasi-corporatism of the new group politics. Whereas the state had earlier for the most part accepted the unions as they had been formed historically as free voluntary associations, and tried to modify their behaviour by the incorporation of union leaders in managing the mixed economy, the new Conservative Government initially rejected this approach in the context of a revitalized *laissez-faire* policy. It sought instead to redefine legally the goals of the unions and sanction those unions which conformed with those goals as legitimate and those which didn't as illegitimate. The inroads this made into the liberal principle of free association was marked by the fact that the Government's Industrial Relations Act reserved the term 'trade union' only for those unions sanctioned by a State Registrar with significant authority over the content of union rule books. Tax exemptions and legal immunity from breach of contract were now limited only to registered trade unions. A litany of 'unfair industrial practices' was legally established and administered by a new system of industrial courts. All collective agreements became legally enforceable except where express provision was made to the contrary and it became an 'unfair industrial practice' to induce anyone to strike during the life of such a contract. A sixty-day cooling off period and strike ballots could be ordered to defer major strikes. Above all, the unions were liable to severe fines, and ultimately to deregistration, not only for their official 'unfair' actions, but for the actions of their members. And while the unions were obliged to take 'all practicable action' to discipline their members if they were to avoid prosecution for unofficial activities, they were not permitted to discipline their members for refusing to take part in official activities which the state deemed 'unfair', or to be more precise, illegal.[60]

The primary aim of the Act was not to destroy trade unions, as was often alleged in the course of the labour movement's struggle against it, but rather to define, codify and back by state sanctions the obligations of the unions to employers and the state, including primarily the obligation to discipline unofficial strikes. Andrew Shonfield, who now found his 'Note of Reservation' to the Donovan Report embodied in legislation, described the philosophy of the Act as follows: 'there is nothing much wrong with British industrial relations which a few effective unions exercising more authority over their members could not remedy. The present system gives the unions the soft option of disclaiming responsibility for the actions of powerful workshop groups while in fact letting them determine wages and working conditions under the umbrella of official union protection'. Unlike Labour's attempt to deal with this (essentially decentralized and democratic) development by focusing mainly on unofficial strikers, the Conservatives were going 'to compel the union leadership to stand up and be counted'.[61]

The Conservative's strategy proved to be anything but a viable one, however. It was conceived and introduced in a period when union members were already highly mobilized for industrial action, not just in a few militant sectors but far more generally. Moreover, the union leadership was itself much more conscious than at any time since the war of the costs which stifling rank and file militancy entailed for them. Whereas Labour's proposed penal clauses were pre-emptive, anticipating the wage and strike explosion, the Conservative legislation to get union leaders to control unofficial strikes was more a matter of locking the proverbial barn door after the horse had bolted. The number of large official strikes had dramatically increased relative to unofficial strikes between 1969 and 1971, long before the Industrial Relations Act came into operation. Taking 1962–4 as the base year of 100 in an index of days lost through strikes, the number of official strikes rose from 152 in 1967–9 to 837 in 1969–71, while days lost through unofficial strikes rose from 269 to 428 over the same period.[62] The attempt to put a lid on this trend at a time of rapidly accelerating food prices and a property speculator's dream-come-true in terms of land and housing prices, had the effect of spurring rather than attenuating this union militancy.

The trade union movement's response to the legislation was even more unified and determined than it had been in 1969, and the first years of the Conservative Government evinced a degree of class conflict unmatched since the 1926 General Strike. Massive demonstrations, a number of one-day political strikes and a large TUC 'educational' campaign mobilized rank and file support against the Bill as it passed through Parliament. The TUC mapped out a policy of 'non-cooperation', whereby unions were 'strongly advised' not to become registered, or to sign collective agreements which would be legally binding, or to cooperate with the industrial courts and the state agencies administering the legislation. What union leaders had refrained from saying under Labour, was now openly declared by the TUC General Secretary himself: 'Unions and workpeople have learned from experience that when the cry "The National Interest" goes up, it means everybody but them.' [63]

The union campaign could not prevent the passage of the Act, but it did render it inoperable within three months of its full implementation in February 1972. This was again less due to the stand of the leadership itself than to the actions of their militant members. Although the policy of non-cooperation had been a radical departure for a union leadership weaned on maintaining ties with the state, to work from within, at all costs, there remained considerable disagreement among union leaders on whether to engage in political strikes, or disobey the courts when the law was applied, and initially at least, whether to expel from TUC membership those unions who did register under the Act. And when the Act was first applied against the official work to rule on the railways and the unofficial dockers boycott against container work outside dock areas (at lower pay), the General Council advised that the unions concerned should appear before the National Industrial Relations Court and comply with its rulings.[64] The railway unions therefore administered a compulsory membership ballot applied under the Act; and the TGWU, having already been fined £55,000 on the presumption by the Court that the union was responsible for the dockers' actions in the absence of TGWU representations to the contrary, agreed to put its case before the Court. But these were only apparent victories, for in substance the application of the Act proved disastrous in both cases as the union rank and file (reflecting a new spurt in militancy which accompanied the highly successful miners' strike of early 1972 [65]) made nonsense of the Act.

The Act was based on the premise that union leaders succumbed to a militant minority of shop stewards. To their dismay, the Government found they were dealing with majorities, not minorities, of rank and file trade unionists. The railway workers voted 6 to 1 in favour of the work to rule, leaving the Government with little alternative but to back down and pay up. Even more significantly, the fines on the TGWU had no effect on the dockers who instead extended their boycott in defiance of the Court. The Court of Appeals found the drafting of the law faulty, and upheld the TGWU's refusal to discipline the shop stewards involved, and the direct intervention of the Government in the due process of law was needed to defuse the industrial situation when the NIRC logically followed this decision by applying the Act directly to the shop stewards. When five of them were gaoled, the Government was faced not only with a national dock strike, but something much more serious. As Ken Coates has described it:

> factory after factory debated whether or more often, when, to join in, so that in short order the TUC General Council had resolved a total General Strike must be quickly called if the dockers were not released. Quite clearly the union leaders felt that if the TUC did not call such a stoppage, there was real possibility that it might take place without being called, and that sort of mass-movement might be very difficult to call off. But shaken as the union spokesmen showed themselves, the forces of authority were more troubled still. The Law Lords met as a final Court of Appeal under unprecedented pressures. They reversed the Appeal Court judgement that the union was not responsible for the actions of its officers, in this case the shop stewards. With great speed, the official solicitor reappeared, and in no time the dockers were out of prison again, reiterating their defiance of the NIRC to millions of television viewers. In the circumstances, it was transparently clear that there was no question of the TGWU taking 'disciplinary' action against

its members, whether it was held legally responsible or not.
This was the climax of the struggles against the new
law.[66]

While it is not particularly fruitful to engage in speculation about
what would have happened if the Government had not placed the
Act on ice, as it virtually did for the rest of its term of office, it *is*
fairly clear that it would have required extensive use of police powers
to gaol, not five, but thousands of trade unionists. In order for legal
sanctions to have operated effectively, at least passive acceptance of
the legitimacy of such sanctions was needed, and for this to be created
an invaluable ally was the union leadership, an ally the Government
did not have. Moreover, what a general strike of even short duration
would have entailed for a weak yet highly integrated British economy
in the 1970s cannot be easily calculated, but its effects would clearly
have been much more damaging than that wrought fifty years earlier.
Such a strike might well have been defeated, given the lack of preparation and enthusiasm for it on the part of the union leadership,
but it is fairly obvious that the assertion of extensive authoritarian
powers were needed to make the Industrial Relations Act work.
There is no evidence that the Government considered such an option;
in any case, it is clear that they had little support for doing so from
their own class. Indeed, the policy of abandoning the consensus
orientation had disturbed large and important sections of the capitalist class from the beginning and on the day of the gaolings *The
Times* reflected this unease in pleading for a reversal of policy in the
form of a return to bargaining between the Government and the
unions on incomes policy.[67]

The débacle of the summer of 1972 led the Heath Government
back to incomes policy in yet another attempt to 'sign away the
class war' now that the attempt to outlaw it had failed. To those
familiar with the previous history of this policy, the comings and
goings of Ministers, CBI and TUC leaders at Chequers and Downing
Street from July to November 1972 produced a distinct feeling of
déjà-vu.[68] It was not surprising that the union leaders jumped at the
chance of re-opening consultations with the Government. It will be
remembered that the majority of the unions in 1969 rejected a
statutory incomes policy but had still endorsed 'a genuinely voluntary' one. The General Council had not decided, upon the Conservatives' election in 1970, to leave Whitehall for Trafalgar Square
– they had been pushed out. And now that they were invited back
in, they went, looking, as is their wont, for moderate gains not revolutionary ones. Nevertheless, what the Heath Government's attempt

to re-establish the quasi-corporatism of the new group politics indicated was not only its disadvantages as compared with Labour in this project but also the accumulating instability of the new group politics. Whereas the incomes policy discussions in 1964 had been marked by 'enormous goodwill' and an 'anxiety to cooperate with the Government' on the union side, the 1972 discussions took place in an atmosphere coloured both by the bitter rancour of the preceding confrontations, and by the kind of suspicion of the Government which had not been applied to Labour. The Conservative proposals for voluntary price controls in 1972 were no less vague than Labour's had been – indeed they had proved much more capable of obtaining CBI cooperation in voluntary price restraint – but the General Council insisted on statutory price controls not so much because of their demonstrated effectiveness under Labour, but because it was 'a question of policy commitment on the part of the Government'.[69] Moreover, throughout the previous incomes policy, the General Council had accepted Labour's insistence on equivalence of treatment for prices and wages; they now insisted on voluntary wage restraint and statutory price restraint.

Unable to buy the unions' cooperation as cheaply as Labour had done, the Conservative Government allowed the talks to break down and introduced a statutory wage and price freeze (from November 1972 to April 1973) and followed this by two further phases of a statutory policy operative to October 1974. The Government pursued Labour's strategy of presenting the statutory policy as provisional pending TUC agreement to a 'voluntary tripartite' policy, which it claimed to prefer.[70] This had the effect of at least inducing the General Council to maintain consultations on each phase of the policy, in the hope that statutory wage powers would be lifted, although, as the AUEW contended in demanding that all consultations be broken off, this helped to legitimate the idea of wage restraint in the eyes of trade unionists.[71] Nevertheless, the TUC abjured the kind of direct role it had played in administering Labour's incomes policy, and it refused to sit union representatives on the new Pay Board and Price Commission. Even this was not enough to maintain effective control over the movement, however, and the General Council's rather passive policy of non-cooperation was explicitly repudiated by a Special Congress in March 1973. This Congress went on to pass a resolution which required the General Council to lead a one-day general strike against the statutory incomes policy.[72] Although the TUC leadership undertook this task with evident lack of enthusiasm, it nevertheless was the first official political strike in Britain organized by the TUC in half a century.

The Conservative's statutory policy did have its effect on workers' real incomes. Whereas real earnings of male manual workers had increased by 7.4% in 1971–2, this plummeted to 1.1% in 1972–3.[73] The fragility of the policy was fully revealed, however, in the context of the economic crises of the winter of 1973–4, and particularly in the miners' strike, which was for the Heath Government what the seamen's strike was for the Wilson Government in 1966 in terms of a critical challenge to the incomes policy. Nor was the immediate response, in declaring a state of emergency and attributing the unrest to communist influence in the union, much dissimilar. But whereas Wilson had just received an enormous popular mandate and could count on the support of the General Council for a statutory wage freeze, Heath's mandate was running out and he had already played all his cards with the TUC. The General Council did pledge that other unions would not use a miners' settlement as a basis for their own claims, but the Government did not believe that the TUC had the degree of influence over their members to make this stick.[74] At any rate, Heath was not inclined to try, and instead resorted to calling a general election on the clear class conflict issue of the unions versus the state.

It was an election which not only provided the final indignity to those analysts of post-war British society who had not so long before confidently predicted the disappearance of the class issue from the electoral arena, but also stood as an admission by the Conservative Party of its own failure to secure for British capitalism the industrial stability which had so long been sought from quasi-corporatist policies. Indeed, after the election, at least one Conservative MP seemed to heave a sigh of relief at the opportunity this gave his Party to drop in Labour's lap once again this immense problem. 'It is on the trade union question of pay and prices and industrial relations that the Tory dilemma is apparently acute', Ian Gilmour wrote in *The Times*, observing that while Labour could electorally 'make great play of its co-called social compact . . . the Conservative Party is in no position to make any similar fraudulent claim'. But he saw 'trade union reforms as more of a Labour Party problem than a Conservative one . . . If groups standing behind the main parties abuse their position, the party concerned suffers.' And as the Conservative's own contribution to ensuring that 'the social democrats in the Parliamentary Party' would 'shift the unions off the pitch and into the stands where they belong', he advocated that the Conservatives abandon any pledge to bring back even a 'much improved version' of the Industrial Relations Act. This would make it easier for the Labour Party itself 'to bring the unions to heel' by not forcing it to side with the unions against the Act, and thus avoid its real task, which he clearly perceived as similar to that of the Conservatives – 'to heal the country – not divide it'.[75]

Labour 1970-4: a new beginning?

To what extent did changes in the Labour Party in the 1970–4 period render invalid such expectations of Labour's integrative role? The years of majority Labour Government had left the Party marked by the conflict between its leadership and its trade union base, and this was reflected in the early post-1970 election period by extensive demoralization at the constituency level.[76] These effects were unlikely to be countered by reasserting the same formula in the same way, and this gave the Labour Left, its voice already strengthened in the unions, the PLP and the NEC, the opportunity of having significant impact on the future direction of the Party. It is true that it is always easier for the Party leadership when in opposition to portray itself as the champion of working class interests, and the policies of the Conservative Government made this even easier. But whereas this took place earlier in a situation where the leadership had considerable room for manoeuvre, allowing it to preserve a high degree of continuity between its policy in Government and that in opposition, the Labour leadership was in the unpalatable position in the early 1970s of having to reverse gears suddenly and openly. For unlike the situation after the 1951 defeat, Britain's largest unions now were associated with the left of the Party, and it was the centre and the right who found themselves on the short end of the block vote at Party Conferences. The alignment between the Left and the unions not only reversed the previous Labour Government's stand on restrictions on free collective bargaining and Common Market entry but also sought to recast the Party's approach to the mixed economy. This was particularly reflected at the 1972 Party Conference, which passed a resolution (by 3.5 to 2.5 million votes) put by the Shipley CLP which committed the Party to a large extension of public ownership run on the principle of workers control and management. It set forth the need for 'a socialist plan of production, based on public ownership, with minimum compensation, of the commanding heights of the economy', including specifically major monopolies, land, the building industry and finance houses.[77] This radicalism was nurtured not only by a reaction against the failures of the past, but also by the situation of heightened class conflict in which it took place. 'We are all Clause IV men, now,' Ian Mikardo exulted,[78] and Tony Benn accurately caught the mood: 'the crisis that we inherit when we come to power will be the occasion for fundamental change and not the excuse for postponing it.' [79]

Yet the tremendous difficulty that attends attempts to transform the Labour Party were again demonstrated during this period. Despite the inclusion of a few Tribune Group MPs in Labour's front bench, there were no major changes in the Party leadership. Moreover, resolutions from CLPs which would have required MPs and Ministers to abide by Conference resolutions on penalty of expulsion or debarment from renomination, were either kept off the Conference agenda or remitted to the NEC, which with the support of the Left refused to bind the PLP in this way.[80] The implications of this became fully apparent when Mr Wilson insisted on the Parliamentary Committee's right to exclude from the Party Manifesto a commitment contained in the NEC's major policy document of the period, to take controlling interest in twenty-five of Britain's largest companies.[81] After the demoralization of the first years in opposition, and as the prospects of a new election drew nearer, the Party leadership began to reassert its continuing commitment to the mixed economy, and it was able to obtain endorsement from the 1973 Conference that it should not be bound by the Party Conference on this matter. The Conference also passed a resolution which rejected 'the concept of shopping lists for industries and companies for social ownership' and overwhelmingly defeated a resolution which sought to specify the 1972 Shipley resolution by reference to the need for the nationalization of 250 major monopolies.[82]

In accordance with this, the 1974 election manifesto limited itself to proposing the nationalization of whole industries which were for the most part unprofitable and failing (the docks, shipbuilding and aircraft); profitable industries were not to be nationalized but the state would acquire an interest in individual firms in a restricted number of sectors (pharmaceuticals, machine tools, construction, road haulage). Labour's three main new proposals for state intervention – 'planning agreements' between the state and private firms on long term investment and pricing policies, a National Enterprise Board to invest in profitable sectors, and the creation of supervisory boards in industry on which trade unionists would hold half of the seats – each bore a striking similarity to the kind of state intervention which had proved successful in other capitalist societies. The first resembled the more *dirigiste* planning found in France; the second, the state holding companies in Italy; the third, workers participation in management structures in Germany. To be sure, the introduction of these measures could be a significant advance over

the previous Labour Government's National Plan and would provide a basis for much more information on private sector operations
than was available before. But the crucial question of what is to be
done with this information, and of the intentions of Labour Ministers in this respect, is most likely to be answered in terms of Dennis
Healey's pledge as the new Chancellor of the Exchequer after the
1974 election: 'Her Majesty's Government has no intention of
destroying the private sector or encouraging its decay, we want a
private sector which is vigorous, alert, imaginative – and profitable.' [83]
Even Mr Benn, who pressed ahead with developing the policies outlined in the manifesto against considerable opposition inside the
Cabinet, made it clear that although 'a lot of people were talking as
though the Labour Party had decided to wind up the mixed economy,
that was not true'.[84]

What must in fact be understood about Labour's apparent shift
to the left since 1970 is that it has taken place within the orbit of the
dominant integrative ideology. In the context of the class conflict
which characterized the period, Labour has sought to present itself
again as the true embodiment of national unity and purpose, thereby
patching up its nation–class synthesis which had threatened to come
unstuck so badly in the late 1960s. The prime basis for Labour's
opposition to the Industrial Relations Act was that it divided the
nation, that it was a 'militants charter', which would undermine
responsible union leadership. Wilson's indictment of the Conservatives was that 'they have consistently regarded the world of industrial
relations as a battleground for ideological confrontations, as part of
a wider political conflict'.[85] And far from providing the leadership
to win such a wider political conflict, he complained of the Conservative's own inadvertent fostering of revolutionary tendencies in
the working class:

> the growth of shop floor power, industrial militancy, part
> of it spontaneous and part of it capable of being created
> by unscrupulous unofficial leaders ... is the central fact of
> the 1970's ...
>   Faced with this new and dangerous development ... the
> court of the right hon. Gentlemen opposite shows as much
> understanding in the revolutionary situation as the court of
> Louis XVI or Nicholas II or King Farouk.[86]

The Party's role in the struggle against the Conservative legislation
was by no means one of directing this 'revolutionary' industrial situation into revolutionary political channels, but one of quieting the
unions' response to it. Faced with those militant union actions which

alone rendered the Act unworkable, the Labour leadership consistently urged the unions to obey the law and not take direct strike action against it.[87]

The touchstone of Labour's policy throughout its years in opposition was in fact to re-establish a 1963-type agreement on voluntary wage restraint, to refashion what the 1974 election manifesto came to call a 'new social contract' to 'rescue the nation from the most serious political and economic crisis since 1945'.[88] The embers of the late 1960s had not yet cooled before the Labour leadership readdressed itself to this task, at first cautiously, but progressively with more boldness. The task was not an easy one. A resolution at the 1970 Party Conference emphasizing 'the need for an incomes policy', was endorsed by the NEC, but defeated by 3.1 to 2.8 million votes. The TGWU's Harry Urwin, warning that trade unions were 'always the first victims of a corporate state', believed that 'a voluntary policy of wage limitation would essentially lead to a demand for statutory intervention to control those who would not conform to the voluntary policy', in a society still ruled by 'the profit motive and the stock exchange gambling'.[89] Similarly, Hugh Scanlon promised to 'talk about a Socialist incomes policy when we own the means of production, distribution and exchange', but refused to engage in talks with the PLP and NEC which preempted the real issue by being structured around incomes policy.[90]

The Party leadership was not frightened off, however. Mrs Castle maintained her belief that the question of social ownership was not *a priori*, and that incomes policy 'leads to the heart of a socialist society'.[91] James Callaghan, amidst a demand 'that the unions . . . disown completely, and refuse to follow the largely self-appointed unofficial leaders who try to usurp the functions of union officials', also called on the unions to take 'a fresh, unprejudiced look at a new form of voluntary incomes policy'.[92] Harold Lever even suggested that if a Labour government's commitment next time to full employment and economic growth led to a 'voluntary policy on incomes [which] is not effective, then we will have no choice but to move to a statutory one'.[93] But this was dangerous talk, and in general Labour leaders studiously avoided the question of coercion – in the aid of encouraging talks on a voluntary policy which the majority of the General Council had not rejected.[94]

In January 1972, the Labour Party preempted the Conservative's own unsuccessful attempt at a voluntary incomes policy by establishing a new *Liaison Committee* with the TUC. The Statements issued by this Committee (composed of General Council, NEC and PLP representatives) formed the basis for Labour's claim to have framed a 'new social contract'. The first Statement in July 1972 committed Labour to abolishing the Industrial Relations Act and to establishing a conciliation and arbitration service funded by government but independent of economic policy considerations.[95] The second Statement in February 1973 saw the Labour leadership largely accept the analysis of the TUC *Economic Reviews*. It contended that wages and salaries were 'very far indeed from being the only factor affecting prices', and saw the key to fighting inflation as 'a wide-ranging, permanent system of price controls'. It promised large-scale income and wealth redistribution including the long-elusive wealth tax, as well as 'the development of new public enterprise and effective public supervision of large private corporations' to induce greater investment and higher productivity and deal in this way with Britain's real problem – high costs *per unit of output*. But while these statements were full of references to 'union cooperation', what was pointedly missing was any reference to incomes policy or wage restraint. All they expressed was the hope that the other policies outlined would engender 'the strong feeling of mutual confidence' needed to facilitate 'the first task' of the next Labour Government – a 'wide-ranging agreement' with the TUC.[96]

The lack of specificity on incomes policy was not due to any lack of preparation by the Labour leadership. As early as August 1972, Harold Wilson presented in some detail the outlines of an incomes policy.[97] But the wariness of the trade union leadership to recommit themselves specifically to wage restraint solely on the basis of Labour's promises, ensured that the 'new social contract' remained extremely vague. The 1972 Party Conference did pass a resolution (by 3.4 to 2.6 million votes) calling on the NEC and TUC 'to formulate a prices and incomes policy' but in view of the Liaison Committee's failure to do this, the only successful resolution at the 1973 Conference which mentioned incomes policy did so in the negative sense of ruling out 'any wage restraint or incomes policy designed to solve the problems of the economy by cutting the standards of living of workers', and combined this with a call for extensive nationalization measures.[98] The difference from 1964 was frankly stated in the 1974 election manifesto:

> After so many failures in the field of incomes policy – under the Labour Government but even more seriously under the Tory Government's compulsory wage controls – only deeds can persuade. Only practical action by the Government to create a much fairer distribution of national wealth can convince the worker and his family that 'an incomes policy'

is not some kind of trick to force him, particularly if he works in the public service or nationalized industry, to bear the brunt of the national burden. But as it is proved that the Government is ready to act – against high prices, rents and other impositions falling most heavily on the low paid and on pensioners – so we believe that the trade unions *voluntarily* (which is the only way it can be done for any period in a free society) will cooperate to make the whole policy successful. We believe that the action we propose on prices, together with the understanding with the TUC on the lines which we have already agreed, will create the right economic climate for money incomes to grow in line with production. That is the essence of the new social contract which the Labour Party has discussed at length and agreed with the TUC.[99]

The February 1974 election gave Labour the opportunity of once again using its ties with the unions as an electoral asset to an integrative political party. The frequently alleged claim that the Party was under the control of Marxists and union extremists was belied not only by Wilson's appeal to the miners (unsuccessful) and the railwaymen (successful) to call off their strikes during the course of the election campaign, but also by the proof he offered that he too was prepared to stand up to 'union extremists', citing his action during the 1966 Seamen's strike.[100] This, together with the repeated pledge to strengthen the hand of union moderates, must be seen as evidence of how Labour continues to act to restrict working class consciousness. But there was no question that Labour's effectiveness in this, in terms of concrete policies for union integration, was more limited than at any time since the war. It was notable in this respect that what particularly upset *The Times* at the time of the 1974 election was not so much Labour's nationalization proposals, which the Party leadership assiduously played down, but 'the absence of any substantial agreement with the TUC'.[101] And while Len Murray, now General Secretary of the TUC, pledged that a Labour Government 'will find us responsible, although it will place a heavy burden on our shoulders',[102] the tenuous nature of the social contract could not be covered over. This was particularly reflected in a televised exchange between Harold Lever and Hugh Scanlon. Lever set off again on George Brown's infamous tightrope between voluntarism and coercion, suggesting that, 'in the last resort, if necessary', a statutory incomes policy with 'the assent of the Trade union movement' might be needed to make wage restraint stick. Scanlon replied that 'no compulsory wage restraint [by a Labour Government] would be acceptable to the trade union movement'.[103]

The lack of credibility of Labour's social contract was seen electorally in February 1974 in the Party's poorest showing since 1935: its percentage of the total vote fell from 48.7% in 1966 to 43.8% in 1970 to 38% in February 1974.[104] The minority Labour Government, in the context of repealing much of the Industrial Relations Act, abolishing the Pay Board, introducing food subsidies, and inheriting from the Conservatives the price-related threshhold wage increases induced by rampant inflation, was able to obtain General Council assent to zero real income growth in the context of the economic crisis. But the union leadership has been particularly insistent that Labour divest itself of the legacy of 1964–70 by probing the limits of social reform to a much greater extent. In any abstract sense, this would not appear too difficult given the absence of much probing by the previous Labour Government. But the economic weakness of British capitalism suggests that any major attempt at wealth and income equalization, together with the reintroduction of free collective bargaining, may run fairly rapidly into the problem of securing a 'vigorous and profitable' private sector to which Labour remains committed and on which the future of British capitalism depends. The instability of the quasi-corporatism of the new group politics over the past three decades has been a function of the impossibility of establishing a real balance of power and resources between the classes; and although Labour has been forced – in order to maintain its ability to integrate the unions – to adopt a policy of redressing the imbalance to a degree unequalled since 1945, the capacity of British capitalism to sustain this appears to be very restricted, as the economic crisis accumulates in intensity with each successive phase. The narrower the limits of social reform, the greater the reluctance of the capitalist class to grant concessions, the more likely is Labour, on the basis of past form, to turn to the working class for sacrifice in the name of the national interest.

Conclusion

This study of the Labour Party's relationship with the trade union movement since 1945 has endeavoured to show the extent to which the Labour Party has performed the functions of an integrative party in the British political system. The integrative element of its ideology, while by no means ubiquitous throughout the Party, has had its concrete expression in the economic and industrial policies of Labour governments, suggesting that this is in fact the effective and dominant ideology of the Labour Party. Labour's frame of reference is not primarily focused within the orbit of the working class's subordinate position in British society, involving questions of how to increase that class's solidarity, extend its economic and political power, defend it against loss of limited gains already made. These considerations are not absent from Labour's conception of its role, but they are confined within a national frame of reference – a concern for national unity shared in common with Britain's dominant classes – in which the aim of making the British economy viable is paramount. It is, to quote Tom Nairn, the 'nationalization of class',[1] from which Labour, wearing the twin hats of both national and class leadership, presumes to claim that its national concerns embrace the needs of the working class as well.

Analyses which begin with the premise that Labour is primarily a socialist party and a channel of working class representation and aspirations, and confine themselves to the attempt to explain Labour's consistent 'failure' to be 'socialist' when in government – whether in terms of the entrenched powers of the ruling class, or opportunist and middle class leadership, or even the limitations of a parliamentary strategy – must inevitably fall wide of the mark. For to a very large extent, what are seen as Labour's failures are really its successes. The function of the Labour Party in the British political system consists not only of representing working class interests, but of acting as one of the chief mechanisms for inculcating the organized working class with national values and symbols and of restraining and reinterpreting working class demands in this light. The Labour Party, in other words, acts simultaneously as a party of representation *and* as a major political socialization and social control agent, mediating between nation and class. In a generalized way, by upholding the values of the nation, parliament, responsibility, against the values of direct action, revolution or 'sectional' interests, it is performing a socializing role which both legitimates existing society and militates against the development of a revolutionary political consciousness on the part of the working class. In this respect, it is not so much transforming values as acting to maintain values to which the working class has already been exposed, and usually absorbed, from other institutions of political socialization such as the family, the educational system, the church, the media, and even the Conservative Party; although the credibility of the Labour Party as 'our' institution in working-class consciousness, gives it certain advantages in this regard. But when the Labour Party mobilizes popular support in the name of these values in a particular instance by portraying the demands of a union or group of unofficial strikers as 'sectional' and contrary to the 'national interest', it is acting as a highly effective agency of social control against the objective expression of working class dissent.

Labour's performance of its integrative role against the continued expression of industrial class conflict in the post-war period has an important bearing on those analyses which explained the 'deradicalization' of social democracy in terms of the emergence of a new political culture of consensus produced by the security of the welfare state and post-war affluence. These analyses were characterized by a crude determinism which argued from the premise that if the superstructure (the Labour Party) changed, the causes must lie in the economic base (the effect of broad socio-economic changes on the values of the working class). What they did not consider, apart from vastly exaggerating the egalitarian effects of post-war development in terms of income and power redistribution between the classes, was the possibility that the Labour Party itself might be an independent factor in inculcating the working class in general and the trade union leadership in particular with national values consistent with consensus. Rather than merely assume that political culture determines political structures, one must examine the extent to which political culture is formed by political structures. Frank Parkin has observed of social democracy:

> To see the party simply as a receptacle for the political
> views of its supporters is really to underestimate its potential

influence in shaping the social consciousness of the subordinate class and in providing its members with a distinctive
moral framework for interpreting social reality. If, as so many
observers suggest, there has occurred a marked decline in
working class radicalism in the post-war period, this may be
due at least as much to changes in the nature of the party as
to changes among its supporters.[2]

This insightful view of social democracy's socializing role has become somewhat current in recent years.[3] But our study suggests that
it is important not to fall into the error, as Parkin himself seems to
have done, of accepting the view that, the post-war period does in
fact constitute a fundamental break with the past either in terms of
any basic change in the nature of the Labour Party or in terms of any
real success in closing the fissures of class conflict. Indeed, as we have
argued elsewhere,[4] one of the main failures of many post-war analyses
of British social democracy was their insufficient understanding of the
Labour Party's ideology in the pre-1945 period. For although the
Party's integrative ideology was certainly strengthened and enhanced
after 1945, it was by no means a new development. It was previously
seen not only in the Party's rejection of the concept of class struggle
at its founding conference, not only in the national posture of both
the ill-fated Labour Governments in the inter-war period, but even
in Labour's programmes in opposition which repeatedly reaffirmed
that Labour was a national rather than simply a class party, a view
which we have seen was proclaimed with the full authority of the
Party's general secretary at the height of Labour's victory in 1945.
Informative in this regard is Tawney's view of the Labour Party in
the earlier period : 'It soothes the dog when it ought to be educating
him to know burglars when he sees them, and to fly at their throats
. . . In a party which appeals to men, not to follow habits, but to
break them, such an attitude is fatal.'[5] The complex factors which
would explain what led the organized working class to align itself
with an integrative party *in the first place*, cannot be examined here.
But if the political consciousness of the trade union leadership at
the turn of the century let it forge an alliance with a political party
inclined to promote class harmony rather than class conflict, what
must be appreciated is that in its turn that political party has helped
to maintain that political consciousness *throughout this century*. In
placing such emphasis on the guiding ideology of the Labour Party,
it has not been our intention to minimize other factors which are
often employed to explain Labour's integrative orientation, such as
the Michelsian organizational and psychological explanation of the

'iron law of oligarchy' which divorces leaders' interests from their followers, or the reliance on leaders from middle class backgrounds, or the independence of the parliamentary party from conference. But these factors are of greater value in explaining the deradicalization of working class parties with a revolutionary Marxist ideology than the integrative Labour Party, and even then they cannot explain the profound differences in ideology and programme which continue to separate social democracy from Communist Parties in the West.

If Labour's integrative orientation was enhanced in the post-war period, this did not reflect so much a basic change in the nature of the Party, but rather related to the fact that its greater electoral success gave the Party more opportunity of putting its effective ideology into practice at a time when changes in post-war capitalism generally provided social democracy with a larger and more obvious role in administering the society. What must be understood in this regard is that the integrative functions of the Labour Party, in terms of their precise content, are not determined by the Party alone, but by the capitalist system within which it is content to operate (and, to be fair, change somewhat from within) and its needs at a particular historical moment. What exactly is deemed to be 'in the national interest' and what sacrifices the working class is asked to bear in its name is conditioned by the state of the British economy and the perceptions of correct national policy widely accepted by industrial, financial and political leaders of the British upper classes with whom the Labour Party seeks to find a basis for cooperation, as well as by the process of 'non-decision' whereby possible alternative policies are not even considered by either working class or upper class leaders. And, to a very large degree, the *extent* as well as the precise nature of the contribution the Labour Party is able to make to national unity, economic viability, and working-class integration will be determined by these factors as well; so that, if Labour's national integrative posture was more fully elaborated in the post-war period, it is in this context that we discover why.

It was British capitalism's continual need for respite from wage pressure in the post-war period which underlay the Labour Party's enhanced integrative role. Beset by large sections of industry which were undercapitalized and highly inefficient, by a comparatively slow rate of economic growth, by a marked dependence on external trade and thus susceptible to pricing itself out of international markets and to recurrent balance of payments deficits, British capitalism has been particularly vulnerable to increased labour costs. Since mass unemployment is both an inefficient and politically dangerous solution, an incomes policy involving the trade unions voluntarily engaging in wage restraint is greatly desirable, if profit margins, the motive force for economic growth, are not to be unduly squeezed between labour costs on the one hand and international competition on the other. Increased state intervention in the economy, in the form of social welfare reforms, indicative economic planning, the extention of trade union representation in national decision making arenas, was undertaken as we have seen, from Beveridge on, by both Conservative and Labour Governments with the consideration of inducing union co-operation in wage restraint always an uppermost factor in the policy equation. This was a form of state intervention not opposed by capitalist interests, but promoted by them, although particular groups might quibble about the necessity or extent of certain elements of this intervention. Given the fact that the ideological basis of this 'new group politics' rested on a 'harmony of interests' conception of society, it might have been thought that the Conservative Party was best suited to introduce it. Yet it was Labour which repeatedly proved the better candidate for the operation.

This was partly because Labour, unlike the Conservatives, was not encumbered by a tradition of *laissez-faire* and an explicit bias towards business, which badly got in the way of Conservative forays into the kind of state intervention needed by modern capitalism. Moreover, Labour found itself in the post-war period in a political climate which appeared to allow it to give programmatic effect to its own ideology of class harmony without apparently contradicting the ideas of state intervention and economic planning which informed its socialism. In the pre-war period the class cooperation principle had always rested uncomfortably with Labour's socialist programme. As Beer has pointed out, public ownership in the pre-1945 period had been 'advocated on various grounds: to equalise wealth, to eliminate the political power of private wealth, to promote democracy in industrial life. But the principal case for it was the need for public control of the economy.'[6] Yet the burning question of how this was to be introduced with the agreement of the capitalist class, as the ideology of class cooperation, and the gradualism and parliamentarism which rested on it, required, was largely avoided (although the answer was implied in party programmes which proposed nationalization of only select industries or parts of industries which for the most part were failing and thus which the capitalist class as a whole could be relied upon to give up). In the post-war period, however, Labour found the capitalist class generally prepared to accept state intervention and planning and to cooperate in it. Labour's ideology and its programme could now be fused. In the context of indicative planning and the welfare state, it was no longer necessary for a party such as Labour to continue to emphasize nationalization: indeed it appeared that to do so was not only to confuse means with ends, but to miss the opportunity of putting Labour's class cooperation ideology into practice. The problem with doing this before had been seen to lie in the misconceived self-interested, rather than community-oriented, views of the capitalist class. These views had now apparently changed, at least in the eyes of Labour leaders who as early as the late 1940s, as we have seen, thought they saw around them an efficiency-oriented managerial capitalism which had come to understand the evils of the unrestrained market and the need for cooperation with the state and with the unions. No doubt, not only the economic vicissitudes of the British economy, but also Labour's own moderate attack on its unplanned nature made some contribution to the more open reception on the part of Britain's traditional ruling classes to ideas of state intervention and planning. As such, Labour leaders might well believe that the long-standing Fabian goal of educating the ruling classes to socialism was at hand. In any case, the system had changed (or so it seemed), the goal of class harmony in the national interest could now be grasped ('we are all socialists now') and the Labour Party, unencumbered by an out-moded *laissez-faire*, could meet the challenge.

It was in this way that the *logic* of Labour's traditional, integrative ideology, which remained fundamentally unaltered in the post-war period, carried the Party into an enhanced integrative role in British capitalism. The key to its playing this role of course remained the allegiance of the organized working class. That is, at the same time as Labour was elaborating its integrative functions through its promotion of indicative planning and incomes policy, seeking to effect a compromise between the various classes by promulgating a higher national interest, its very successes in this regard depended primarily on its structural ties with the trade unions. In the expectation that under a Labour Government the interests of the working class would take precedence over the interests of other classes, in the hope that the influence of the trade union leadership in economic decision-making would become not only formal but effective, as well as out of sheer emotional loyalty to the political arm of the labour movement, the trade unions were prepared to participate directly in developing and operating an incomes policy. Despite the fairly common expectation in the 1950s and early 1960s that declining working-class allegiance was the foundation of Labour's elaborated integrative posture, it was in fact the continued salience of working class political identification which facilitated the Party's performance of its integrative role.

Conversely, a significant element in Labour's appeal to other classes lay not so much in jettisoning commitments to increase the state's role in the economy as in Labour's ability to retain working class loyalty and promise wage restraint at no greater cost than the Conservative Government had itself proposed to incur in its unsuccessful attempt at economic planning and incomes policy. Labour's structural ties with the unions were not an electoral liability, but an electoral asset, particularly for a Party whose commitment to state intervention seemed to provide a better fit with the needs of modern capitalism than that of the Conservatives.

With a virtuosity that only comes with practice, the Labour Party leadership in the early 1960s played both possible interpretations of the planning and incomes policy theme, one to each audience. They proved their mettle as integrative politicians in this period, performing with much greater finesse and aplomb than they had when, moved by much the same ideological and economic exigencies, they had rather stumbled into indicative planning and wages policy in the late 1940s. But once in Government again, they had to actually write the score, not just interpret the theme. There is no need to recap here what earlier chapters have covered. The story is largely told in the disappointment of trade union expectations of extensive influence in the framing of economic policy; in the operation of incomes policy as wage restraint in the context of the abandonment of even indicative planning; in the extreme reluctance of the Labour Government to engage in price and profit controls; in the readiness with which the Government dropped the voluntary principle upon which the incomes policy was founded and thus challenged the unions' view of themselves as free agents in collective bargaining. Labour's incomes policy of 1964–70, like the wages policy of 1948–50 before it, was not designed to facilitate the planning and redistribution of incomes as part of a larger design to transcend the existing economic system, although as such it was likely to have been able to draw on the support of significant sections of the trade union movement. It was concerned rather to further the integration of the trade unions into the existing political and economic system by obtaining from the trade unions a more explicit acceptance of their responsibilities to society; to induce them to control their members more competently and, to a large extent, to define the unions' role as 'legitimate' interest groups and guide by statute their actions 'in the national interest'.

An overview and a contrast between Labour and Conservative success in restricting the growth of working class incomes since 1948 may be seen from the following table from the work of H. A. Turner and Frank Wilkinson, who have themselves come to the conclusion that 'it almost appears . . . as if the objective economic-historical role of the British Labour Party is to do (no doubt despite itself) those things to the workers that the Conservative Governments are unable to do'.[7]

Rates of growth in gross money,
real and net real income, men manual workers

Annual compound rate of growth	Gross money income	Net Real Income[b]
	%	%
1948–52	6·9	0·7
1952–56	7·2	3·5
1956–60	5·0	2.1
1960–64	5·5	1·3
1964–68	6·6	0·5
1968–70	10·0	1.3
1970–74[a]	12.5	1·8

[a] estimated

[b] Gross money income discounted by price inflation and by the effect of direct taxation computed for the average wage earner married with two children.

SOURCE: 1948–70: *Do Trade Unions Cause Inflation?* (see n. 7), Table 2, p. 66. 1970–74: Frank Wilkinson 'The Outlook for Wages' in Cambridge Economy Policy Group, *Prospects for Economic Management, 1973–1977*, Ch. 8, Table 2, pp 8–12.

In the period of the 1948–50 wages policy, the major factor in reducing the growth of working class incomes was rising prices as the Labour Government undertook its flight from economic planning in the 'bonfire of controls'. But this was complemented by an explicit decision by the Labour leadership that it could not compensate for this by a redistributive fiscal policy of 'fair shares' without damaging the incentive to invest on the part of the capitalist class, on which the 1945 Labour Government increasingly relied to achieve economic growth. Under the Labour Government of 1964–70 both price inflation and fiscal policy combined to restrict working class incomes, with an even sharper effect despite an average annual growth in industrial productivity of over 3% in 1964–9. The stagnation of workers' real incomes, as contrasted with the increases when the Conservative Party was in office was essentially the product of the Labour Party's greater political resources in terms of socialist and planning rhetoric and the traditional loyalty of the working class to the Party, so that it was able to secure union cooperation in wage restraint. This did

242

not have to entail lower money wage increases *per se*, although in particular crisis years like 1948–9, 1956–7, 1961–2 and 1966–7, a Labour Government was far more likely to secure wage restraint than a Conservative Government. What it essentially involved was ensuring that the trade unions refrained from developing an adequate industrial response (in the absence of an adequate political response) which would involve wage demands large enough to compensate for the effects of inflation and taxation on working class living standards.

The source of this distortion between promise and performance in the operation of the new group politics under a Labour Government essentially lies in the fact, that contrary to the claims by pluralist theorists like Beer that a 'new balance of power between the classes' had been established in the post-war period,[8] the pivot of power in British society continued to rest with Britain's capitalist class. Beer identified three sources of the 'unrecognizably transformed power position of the unions'[9] – the state's need for their expert advice on the formation of policy, for their acquiescence or voluntary agreement to administer state policies, and for their approval and legitimation of state policy in the eyes of their members. Yet what we have seen as characteristic of the new group politics was how governmental policies were repeatedly framed either without first securing the advice of the unions, or after having explicitly rejected their advice. This was seen in the Cripps wage freeze of 1948, in the Conservative pay pause of 1961, and throughout the various phases of Labour's statutory incomes policy from August 1965 on. It was not their advice, but their acquiescence and approval which were studiously courted, usually after the fact. The advice on which Labour acted in introducing deflation and statutory wage restraint and abandoning the indicative plan for economic growth was that of the CBI, the City and Britain's foreign creditors, in light of the latter's immediate concern to protect the pound against devaluation. Indeed, even when the advice on which Labour acted proved faulty in the extreme as devaluation eventually was forced on the Government, Labour had to continue to promote private business incentive to foster economic growth. For insofar as the logic of class cooperation ruled out command planning, it also largely ruled out a redistributive fiscal policy. The orthodox fiscal policy of the Government was not forced on it, therefore, but rather was produced by an interpretation of the national interest which was common to both Labour and business leaders.

As Cripps had done in 1948, the architects of Labour's economic policy in 1964–70 repeatedly made the rather simple point that redistribution of the national wealth would not itself produce a high standard of living for the whole of the British working class. Yet this in itself cannot stand as an argument against a much more egalitarian society. What ruled out the latter was the *necessity* for inequality within a society which needs economic growth indeed, but seeks to achieve it within capitalist structures. To have raised questions about the extent to which this indicated that British capitalists were still self-interested rather than community-oriented, would have entailed, however, a major shift of direction of which Labour Governments have proved ideologically incapable throughout this century. And the consequence of operating within the dominant interpretation of the national interest is the grotesque distortion of Labour's social reform policies. This was seen in our study as Labour orthodox fiscal policy underlined the innately conservatizing effects of incomes policy, which by its very nature in tying wage increases to productivity growth, seeks to remove the question of inter-class income differentials from the concern of the unions, the main economic forces for redistribution within capitalism. Wage claims based on comparability and profitability by definition raise questions about inequality in the social structure, while productivity bargaining eliminates this. The distorting effect all this produced in terms of Labour's need to be seen to pursue social reforms for the working class, was not the abandonment of the equality theme altogether, but the transference of it, in the context of incomes policy, to a concern with narrowing income differentials within the working class. This is what we have called the doctrine of socialism in one class – seeking to concentrate workers' concerns with inequality, not on the highly privileged, but on others in a similar class situation to their own. And even this policy was in turn distorted by its operation in a capitalist society. For except in the case of intra-firm differentials, the wages foregone by well organized workers in high profit and high productivity firms and industries are not transferable in the absence of a directive economic plan to workers in low paid, low profit and low productivity firms and industries. Thus the final result of Labour's 'national' policy of linking the theme of equality to that of economic growth within capitalism was to proclaim the existing distribution of income between the classes as legitimate, while declaring illegitimate the infinitely narrower differentials within the working class, about which neither the trade unions nor the Labour Government were able to do much via an incomes policy.

There can be little doubt that Labour's historical envelopment in a national, integrative ideology has been oriented towards making the achievement of social reform easier, given the traumas and difficulties entailed in social revolutions. It would be invidious and misleading to suggest that individual Labour leaders would not prefer a more equal distribution of wealth and income or a society somewhat less subject to the need to promote business incentive. The problem, however, is that when Labour's nation–class synthesis is translated into concrete policies in a class stratified society, both the concepts of national interest and of social reform become highly problematic. In terms of Labour's paramount concern to find a basis for compromise between working class and ruling class interests, the latter's position of dominance in the economy as well as its preponderant influence in the civil service, the judiciary and the media, inevitably comes to structure Labour's own definition of the national interest and to distort its aim of social reforms. What is primarily missing in both Labour's integrative ideology and pluralist theories of British society such as Beer's (which indeed bear a very close resemblance to each other), is an understanding of how the location of integration and the new group politics within a capitalist society inclines state interventionism towards policies that accord with the inner dynamic of such a society – the profit motive – to the enhancement of the class from which this dynamic stems and to the detriment of the working class. The 'new social contract' in this context is a contract not only between unequals but one in which the guarantor of the contract – the state, even under a Labour Government – is not and cannot be disinterested and neutral between the classes.

One very important insight contained in Samuel Beer's examination of the 'new group politics' is that it is a contemporary expression of corporatism. The corporatist idea arose in the nineteenth century in reaction to the competitive and individualist ethos of industrial capitalism and to the class conflict and revolutionary socialism which was its by-product. Although corporatism has exhibited many variants, the common theme was a desire to re-establish among the new collectivities of capital and labour that had been formed under the principle of free association of liberal democracy, the conception of mutual rights and obligations which were presumed to have united the medieval estates in a stable society. Corporatist programmes have perceived the nation state as the supreme collective community organically embodying the unity of economic groups and social classes through a universal scheme of vocational organization which would have the right of representation in national decision-making and a high degree of functional autonomy, but which would have the duty of maintaining the functional hierarchy and social discipline consistent with the needs of the nation state as a whole. In this way

Conclusion

an organizational pluralism was combined with the major premise of corporatism, societal unity.[10]

The question which has never been satisfactorily answered in corporatist thought is how this new collective unanimity is actually going to come to replace the conditions which corporatism opposes – the competition and class conflict of modern capitalist society. The most famous – or rather infamous – embodiments of corporatist practise in the twentieth century answered this question decisively – by the use of force. Both Fascist Italy and Nazi Germany established corporate states whose main aim was to repress both political and industrial class conflict. The indigenous voluntary organizations of the working class were the first to be smashed to this end, and were replaced by 'corporations' created by state fiat which in theory possessed autonomy in industry but which in fact were instruments of fascist repression, solidifying capitalist authority relations within industry. As Nigel Harris has observed, the fascist examples indicated that 'the harmony which it is assumed is intrinsic to society – if the squabbling cabals can be swept away – can in practise only be reproduced by the use of force. And the use of force directly contradicts the assumption of an intrinsic harmony . . . Corporatism assumes what it is designed to create, and destroys what it seeks to create by pursuing the only practicable means available: coercion.' [11] Our study has been concerned, however, not with fascism but with an implicit attempt to establish corporatist structures within the confines of the liberal democratic state, and this 'quasi-corporatist' project greatly limits the possibilities of coercion. Rather than the institutionalization of corporatist structures by abrogating the rights to free association through the destruction of trade unions and their replacement by bodies created by the state, quasi-corporatism has involved inducing existing voluntary associations, and primarily the trade unions via an incomes policy, to act as agencies of social control over their members.

This quasi-corporatist project has exhibited a basic characteristic, however, which is too often ignored by pluralist theorists of the new group politics, that is, a high degree of instability. In the absence of the underlying social harmony which is needed if trade union leaders are not to be repudiated by their members for their voluntary cooperation in wage restraint, corporatist structures and policies have proved difficult to establish in the first place, and much more difficult to protect from breakdown once established. While the Labour Party with its integrative ideology and working class loyalty has been quite successful in overcoming this problem for limited periods, it has nevertheless not proved able to prevent the recurrent breakdown of the quasi-corporatism embodied in incomes policies. Both in 1948–

50 and in 1964–70, the breakdown of incomes policy occurred, not after Conservative Governments were elected, but while the Labour Government was still in office. For as the burden of quasi-corporatism fell heavily on the working class, Labour's national-class synthesis came unstuck to a significant extent, revealing the contradiction between Labour's integrative ideology and its working class base when that ideology is translated into concrete policies. The unions themselves eventually came under particularly heavy internal pressure both in terms of a decline in union membership and in terms of an increase in rank and file militancy which posed a challenge to the incumbent leadership's cooperation with the integrative policies of the Labour Government. As the consensus between the Party and union leadership increasingly frayed and was combined with a significant degree of working class alienation from the Labour Party, the political expression of class conflict in British society became located largely within the Labour Party itself. This exhibited itself as both a defensive reaction by the unions against the consequences of the economic policies of the Labour Government and, to a lesser extent, as a challenge to the Party leadership's view of the Labour Party as a national party committed to managing a capitalist economy rather than as a working class party committed to extending public ownership and control and to raising working class living standards.

In this context, what we have observed in this study is how, even within liberal democracy and even when social democracy translates working class loyalty to its party into loyalty to the nation, the basic dilemma of corporatism – coercion in the name of harmony – comes to rear its ugly head. Indeed, we have seen that, from the point of view of the breakdown of incomes policy under rank and file militancy, both the Labour Government and the employer organizations recognized the limitations of voluntarism virtually from the beginning when establishing the incomes policy in 1964–5, and it was largely in anticipation of this breakdown that Labour turned, only three months after the voluntary policy was inaugurated, to statutory reinforcement. To avoid the direct state interference which this entailed, the union leadership responded by formalizing and extending its own policy of restraint, thus further enmeshing itself in corporatist structures. But this was accepted by the movement only under the explicit threat of the enforcement of statutory powers, making the distinction between voluntarism and coercion a highly tenuous one. Insofar as Labour maintained that its statutory policy was temporary, produced only by immediate economic exigencies, the Party leadership was able to withstand internal party pressures, aided by the passive acquiessence of the union leadership. Yet as the instability of quasi-corporatism became more and more apparent, there developed an increasing tendency on the part of the state to look to permanent statutory controls over the right to strike itself. And when Labour finally proposed such permanent controls via *In Place of Strife*, it was faced with a highly mobilized labour movement, which the union leadership was forced to lead (or risk losing control over the movement). In this situation, with the crucial link with its working-class base endangered, the PLP and the NEC had little recourse but to side with the union leadership against the Labour Government. The Government was not forced to abandon its integrative orientation, but it did have to fall back on the TUC's ability and willingness to control its members as well as on the temporary statutory incomes policy, both of which proved inadequate to stem rank and file militancy. Thus while Labour's structural ties with the unions were the condition of its success as an integrative party in the quasi-corporatist state, the defeat which Labour suffered on the penal clauses was indicative of the extent to which Labour's ties with the unions can also act as a structural constraint on its ability to act out its integrative role.

If permanent coercive measures were needed to establish the stability of quasi-corporatism within the liberal democratic state, it was the Conservative Party, free from the internal party contradictions which such an effort entailed for Labour, which appeared best suited to do it. Yet the failure of the Conservative's Industrial Relations Act suggests that the instability is not related to the contradictions of social democracy alone, but is endemic to the quasi-corporatist project itself. The importance of liberal democracy for capitalism lies in the guarantee of legal and political equality which makes the wage contract appear as an exchange between equals, with the state as the guarantor of that equality. As C. B. Macpherson has explained, 'the market economy, with its concentration of capital ownership and its distribution of rewards in accordance with the marginal productivity of each of the contributors to the product, maintained a massive inequality between owners and workers'. But, individual legal and political freedom under liberal democracy allows capitalism to appear 'as the system in which production is carried on without authoritarian allocation of work or rewards, but by contractual relations between free individuals (each possessing some resources be it only his own labour-power) who calculate their most profitable course of action and employ their resources as that calculation dictates'.[12] Trade Unionism does not alter the essential nature of the system. Indeed, by allowing free combinations of workers and free collective bargaining, the liberal state further obviates the apparent disjuncture between market inequality and legal equality. Nor does state interference in the economy itself essentially modify the system. The provision of welfare benefits and the use of fiscal policy alter individual calculations of most profitable action in the wage contract, but as Macpherson goes on to point out: 'This need not affect the mainspring of the system, which is that men do act as their calculations of net gain dictates.' [13] However, when the state seeks, through a statutory incomes policy or through direct legal controls over unions, to restrict the implementation of workers calculations *vis-à-vis* the wage contract, it runs the risk of directly connecting the state with the maintenance of that socio-economic inequality which otherwise seems to emerge as the ineluctable product of free individuals engaging in a free market. This tends to identify the state rather than the market as the fulcrum of society and thus brings out the inconsistency between legal and political equality guaranteed by the state and socio-economic inequality protected and maintained by the state. The social and material hierarchy embodied in a capitalist society may thus be revealed, not as the product of competition and exchange, but as the product of force and power.[14] The inequality evident in the policies produced by the new group politics, which rests on the myth of equality in negotiations and bargaining between the classes and their interest groups under the aegis of a neutral state, can be seen by workers as due to the failure by the unions or social democracy as effective representatives. Consequently, the latter are not unlikely to bear the blame themselves for their moderation in making political and economic demands. However, a legally established quasi-corporatism – administered by the courts, above politics and group bargaining – may in turn reveal a basic inequality in the system in the form of a bias on the part of the state itself against the working class. This is not unlikely to yield even greater instability, for rather than repudiate their own organizations, workers will tend to challenge the state, at least by refusing to abide by the law.

To meet the challenge posed by a working class united against the operation of laws that contradict the freedoms of unions as voluntary organizations, coercive measures have to go far beyond the immediate field of industrial relations. To have made the Industrial Relations Act operable, the extensive use of police powers would have been necessary, and probably would have involved limiting the rights to mobilize opposition through free speech and assembly. It would likely have entailed, in other words, the abrogation of liberal democracy itself. That the Heath Government backed off from such a venture must partly be seen as a product of the historical self-identification of Britain's political leaders and the capitalist class itself with the principles of liberal democracy. More important still, however, must have been the risks such a venture entailed for a capitalist society with a large working class prepared to defend its indigenous organizations and itself highly conscious of the value of political freedom.

The intra-party divisions that spring from the contradiction between Labour's integrative ideology and its working class base, and the instability which appears to be endemic to the quasi-corporatist project are both expressions of the class tensions and conflicts which persist in modern capitalism and which are reflected in the behaviour of trade unions. It has all too often been noted that trade unions are but institutional reflections of capitalist society, which do not seek to overthrow it but, operating within its domain, seek to regulate conflict through collective bargaining and the incorporation of union leaders in industrial and political decision-making arenas. But whether applauded or lamented, this is a highly one-dimensional view of trade unionism, which ignores its dialectical nature. For while unions may not deal with primal causes, they remain working class organizations which cannot but act as oppositional elements to the authority and class relations of modern capitalism.

The simple observation that trade unions mainly confine themselves to economic demands, tells us little in itself. As Richard Hyman has recently written, 'the level of demands which can be accommodated varies according to the economic context. In some contexts, *any* demands for improvement are unrealisable, and in any situation, there will be some points in excess of which demands are intolerable.' [15] We have seen that in the context of British incomes policy, trade union cooperation on wage restraint was secured on the basis of a promise of consistent, if moderate, annual increases in real wages – a promise which was not fulfilled. And for even those elements of the union leadership which were most committed to quasi-corporatism, this failure to 'deliver the goods' placed considerable limits on their freedom to cooperate in wage restraint. Nor, it should be remembered, was the incorporation of the British trade union leadership ever monolithic. In noting the role played by Deakin or Woodcock or Carron in restraining wage demands, supporting Labour's income policies at party and union conferences, and promoting collaboration with the state, one must not forget the counter-tendencies supplied by Cousins or Scanlon or Jones in their resistance to wage restraint, in their disparagement of indicative planning as opposed to socialist planning based on extension of public ownership, and in their support for union democracy in the form of a greater shop-floor role in wage bargaining and policy formation.

Although the stance of these union leaders on these questions has often been ambivalent, it has at least helped to reinforce rather than restrain rank and file or shop steward militancy, not only within their particular union, but by 'demonstration effect' in unions led by moderates as well.

Indeed, insofar as the union leadership has been close to monolithic on any issue related to quasi-corporatism, it has been in their commitment to voluntarism. This has reflected a suspicion, held even by moderate union leaders, and gained from historical experience, that the state is not necessarily to be trusted to act in a neutral fashion between employers and workers on the question of wages. This insistence on voluntarism is not simply a product of what is often seen as a structural defect of the British union movement – that it is less centralized and cohesive than its counterpart in Sweden or West Germany.[16] The ability of the TUC to frame policies for the movement and apply them vigorously and successfully was seen in the non-registration campaign against the Conservative's Industrial Relations Act, where 32 unions actually were expelled from the TUC. The refusal, indeed the inability, of the TUC to undertake this kind of disciplinary role on behalf of the wage restraint and anti-strike policies of the state, stands in sharp contrast to their action in maintaining the movement's cohesion and solidarity *against* these state policies. The reason for this difference in behaviour lies in the fact that union leaders are aware – or are at least often rudely woken up to the fact when they forget it – that their power base, unlike the leaders of fascist 'corporations', is their membership not the state. And what a statutory policy does is precisely to reduce the trade union leadership's options *vis-à-vis* their membership, undermining their flexibility of response to their members' demands. They may indeed engage in wage restraint policies, but if the flexibility that voluntarism gives them of 'running after their members' is removed, they themselves run a much greater risk of being repudiated by their membership.

The key to union integration within capitalism really lies in the integration of the working class itself. And although the union leadership may help in this process, it cannot be the determining factor. Any explanation of the instability of quasi-corporatism must deal ultimately, therefore, with why wage demands arise at the base. One of the most grievous errors one can make in this respect is to see wage demands under conditions of mass impoverishment as a necessary product of capitalism, but to see wage demands in modern conditions as greedy and arbitrary. Wage demands derive from the location of workers within the capitalist system itself, and this is equally true of the 'affluent' worker as of his pre-war counterpart. To quote Marx:

> Capital and Labour behave in a way like money and goods; if one is the general form of wealth, the other is only the substance which aims at immediate consumption. But capital, with its restless striving after the general form of wealth drives labour out beyond the limits of its natural needs, and thus produces the material elements needed for the development of the rich individuality, which is just as universal in its production or consumption, and whose labour thus itself appears not to be labour anymore but a full development of the activity in which the natural necessity has disappeared in its direct form; since the place of natural needs has been taken by needs that are historically produced.[17]

What has in fact happened in capitalist societies since World War II, aided by the development of a massive advertising industry, has been a vast and continuing 'expansion of needs', which has in turn produced a necessary demand on the part of labour for increased wages. And as is implicit in Marx's formulation, these needs are not simply material. For capitalism also has produced among many workers the *technical ability* to control production, but remained closed to the possibilities of realizing this potential; a potential which the incorporation of trade union officials in state agencies or the boards of nationalized industries, in no way realizes. As Andre Gorz has put it:

> [Wage] demands translate the desire to be paid as much as possible for the time being lost, the life being wasted, the liberty being alienated in working under such conditions: to be paid as much as possible not because the workers value wages (money and all it can buy) above everything else, but because, at the present stage of union activity, only the price of labor power may be disputed with management, but not control over the conditions and nature of work.[18]

Thus whether wage demands represent a need for material goods, or as Gorz suggests 'a distortion and a mystification of a deeper demand', they are inherent in modern capitalism. Insofar as material needs can be fulfilled through higher wages at any given historical moment, they are replaced by new ones created by capital. This is a positive development as well as an ongoing process which maintains industrial conflict between workers and their employers, who while creating the needs generally also seek to minimize labour costs in their own enterprise. And while this conflict is inherent in capitalism itself, in a weak, inefficient and undercapitalized economy such as post-war Britain's, the wage demands which advertising and consumerism induce and which workers' alienation from the control of production reinforces, need not be very great to yield economic crisis. Although the answer may be sought in wage restraint policies and anti-strike legislation, this runs the risk of creating only greater frustration among workers still trying to satisfy their recently expanded needs. We have seen that even moderate union leaders, in the long run, can ignore this frustration only at the cost of declining union membership and considerable intra-union conflict, at which point they usually go running after their members.

If the trade unions have necessarily reflected the conflict inherent in capitalist society and, in the British case at least, thereby helped to render unstable the economy and quasi-corporatist political structures required by it, the critical question that must be asked of the outbreak of industrial militancy since the late 1960s is what its consequences for political change are. It is true that industrial militancy does have a clear political character. The dissatisfaction with existing social relations is inherent in wage claims of 25, 30 or 40%; in the expectation by dockers or car-workers or miners that they be paid as much or more than groups high above them in the status hierarchy; in occupations of factories shut down in accordance with the law of profit; in the large number of strikes challenging managerial prerogatives. But this militancy retains a non-political veneer by virtue of the fact that it arises from separate segments of the working class at different times, and arises moreover in the absence of a generalized and explicit rejection of the economic and political structures in which these social relations are embedded. This is indeed an inherent limitation of trade unionism: demands for a 40% increase in the income of the working class as a whole, and for workers' control over production, cannot be effectively expressed industrially, but only politically, and although we have seen in recent years a number of overt and official political strikes for the first time since the TUC left Trafalgar Square for Whitehall in the aftermath of the General Strike, these actions have been hesitant, sporadic and defensive. Without a political party which would maintain and give focus to industrial militancy, it is not unlikely to be dissipated in yet another phase of quasi-corporatist policies, or, if not, to be met by a more fully authoritarian challenge than the British labour movement has yet faced.

It has been a central argument of this study that one of the crucial factors in explaining the 'missing link' between industrial militancy and the development of a revolutionary political consciousness has been the trade unions' ties with the integrative Labour Party. When the leader of the political arm of the labour movement laments the translation of industrial militancy into a wider political conflict, he is manifestly continuing Labour's traditional tendency to see the organized working class as a sectional interest group without claim to ruling the society, and to reinforce the working class's conception of itself as a subordinate class rather than a hegemonic one. Yet to point out the failure of the Labour Party to change fundamentally its role in this respect, as the previous chapter has suggested is the case, is not in itself to deny the possibility that the Party can change. It has in no sense been the argument here that the integrative ideology has been ubiquitous in the Labour Party. Indeed, to say that it is dominant necessarily implies that it dominates over something else. That something else is the Labour Left, which has repeatedly challenged the integrative premises and policies of the Labour leadership. It simply will not do, as Tom Nairn has done in his otherwise brilliant examination of Labour's national orientation, to dismiss the Labour Left as merely the soulful, Christian conscience of the Party, 'which opposes the right, not in the name of class, but in the name of the true nation', as a weak moral force consumed by 'pious delusions' of a New Jerusalem, recoiling from power lest it sully its 'religious nature (laicized as "ethical socialism" or not)'.[19] This characterization may apply to Cripps who could subsist on 'radish tops and orange juice' and expect British workers to do the same, and is clearly intended to apply to Michael Foot. But it is a ridiculous caricature of the Labour Left as a whole. The Tribune MPs in 1964–70 were in no sense a group of frustrated parsons: over half were militant ex-trade unionists. One cannot ignore Eric Heffer's belief that: 'There can be no neutrality in the class struggle. Either one is for the workers or against them.' And when Heffer urges that the Labour Party 'becomes a class party at every level', and that 'the theory of class struggle should be a cornerstone of our ideology',[20] he may be deluded about the likelihood of this transformation, but his premises are nevertheless in sharp contrast with the integrative ideology.

It is not surprising that many who reject the dominant ideology should work to change the Party from within. The Labour Left is in this respect at least not far different from the British Communist Party, which continues to see Labour as the main political vehicle of the working class, and but for the refusal of the Labour leadership to allow it, would have long ago met its goal of affiliation to the Labour Party. Thus while the political socialization of union leaders like Jones and Scanlon was also influenced by the Communist Party and Marxism, the Communists' own view of Labour has played a reinforcing role in tying such union leaders to social democracy, especially as the Communist Party's waning political (although not industrial) influence was felt in the post-war period and no other real alternative was available outside the Labour Party. It is not being suggested here that the Labour Left is ideologically indistinguishable from the extra-Labour Left, but that the former finds its strength in a social base not unknown to the latter. As evidenced by their repeated success in constituency balloting for NEC positions, the Labour Left has a real base among party activists. Moreover, militant trade unionists have historically gravitated towards and made common cause with the PLP Left. There was a direct correlation between the Bevanite struggles in the Labour Party and the opposition inside the trade unions to the union bureaucracy in the 1950s. And the main link between left-wing trade union leaders and the PLP during the 1964–70 period was the Tribune Group not their sponsored MPs.

Having said all this, what distinguishes the Labour Left from the extra-Labour Left, and how do we explain its failure to recast the Party's orientation? Two main factors are operative here, both of which have served to tie the Labour Left, against its will no doubt, to the dominant ideology of the Party. The first is the Left's acceptance of the doctrine of Parliamentarism. On this Labour has indeed been extensively united from its inception. It is true that during the 1930s, the Labour Left through the Socialist League questioned the assumption that a parliamentary majority was enough to secure a socialist transformation, but the question was largely forgotten in the context of the war and Labour's 1945 victory, and virtually sunk without trace among the concerns of the Labour Left in the post-war period. For the Right, this complete acceptance of a parliamentary strategy is a natural corrollary of the belief in class harmony. Parliamentary government represents the highest pinnacle of achievement for the British nation, the institutional expression of rational debate within the rules of the game, and the setting for Labour's aim of defining the national interest in conjunction with Britain's dominant classes. For the Left, however, the total acceptance of parliamentarism involves a direct contradiction with the view of irreconcilable class conflict. It stands as a barrier to fostering alternative forms of action, even when they are taken up in the trade union movement, and acts as a counter to the development of a coherent theory of the state in a capitalist society. Without such a theory, not only the Labour Left's supporters, but even those leaders of the Left who attain Cabinet positions themselves, are unprepared for the disappointments which regularly attend purely electoral victories in a capitalist society. We have observed in this study how the Tribune Group's primary occupation with parliamentary victories and defeats led it to take upon itself the task of preserving the unity of the PLP rather than force that responsibility on the Labour leadership. Similarly, the Left's unwillingness to embarrass the Party on the principle of opposition to direct action incapacitated it for providing much support, let alone leadership, to mass demonstrations against *In Place of Strife*. This was repeated again in the context of the Conservatives' Industrial Relations measures. Thus while Eric Heffer has indicated his belief that the political strikes were justified and the main source of effective opposition to the Act, the inconsistency between his responsibility to the PLP and direct action led him, in his own words, to 'duck the issue', although it 'embarrassed' him 'no end'.[21] The concern with parliamentarism has also affected the left-wing union leadership's ability to undermine the control of the parliamentary leadership over the Party. In an important speech at the time of the 1971 Party Conference, Jack Jones indicated his union's concern with ensuring that its parliamentary panel contained more MPs with active union backgrounds, but he emphatically rejected the notion that the unions should instruct their MPs on how to vote.[22]

A second, and even more important factor in the Labour Left's lack of success in changing the Labour Party, lies in its refusal to come to terms with the deep-rootedness of the class harmony orientation. The Left has generally seen this orientation as an aberration from the Party's origins: the Party and its leadership are not basically misdirected, but just not socialist enough, or reformist enough, or prepared enough, or close enough to the grass roots. The Left's task is to fill in the missing quantities by reminding the leadership of the Party's socialist traditions. The acceptance by the Labour Party of the mixed economy in the 1950s is seen by Eric Heffer as a period of 'utter folly' caused by the opportunist casting about for middle class support by non-socialist middle class leaders.[23] Any direct link between the Party's original rejection of the concept of class struggle and the policies of the 1950s is omitted. The great victories for the Left have been associated mainly with purely symbolic issues such as retaining Clause IV or electing a leader who is prepared to dot his speeches with socialist rhetoric or quotations from Nye Bevan. The fact that these victories turn into even greater disappointments rests on the Left's failure to realize that it is, as Eric Hobsbawm has put it, 'quite as easy to justify a moderate policy in socialist as it is in liberal or conservative phrases: the former may be even more effective'.[24] The rhetoric of socialism or public ownership or even industrial democracy, as has now become all too obvious, does not necessarily have much in common with a commitment to bring the working class to power. In this sense, the Right has understood the 'basic principles' of Labour far better than the Left. Anthony Crosland correctly noted that Labour's founders had not seen the Party as an 'essentially proletarian and one-class party', and he drew inspiration from Labour's 'fundamental socialist principle' that 'a "classless" society will never be achieved through a wholly class-orientated instrument. The object must be to present ourselves as a broadly-based national people's party.' [25] Indeed, in any battle cast in terms of Labour traditions, the Right has far more to draw on than the Left. By treating the problem before it as merely one of bringing the Party to its original principles, the Labour Left has mistaken its task and underestimated the difficulty of achieving it. For the task involves recasting fundamentally the ideological basis of the Party by wrenching Labour out of its tradition rather than glorying in it. 'Until the Labour Party recognizes it is not Socialist', Tawney wrote after the 1931 debacle, 'it is not likely to become Socialist'.[26]

Given the problems of the Labour Left and the tremendous difficulty of changing the Labour Party through it, a necessary pre-condition for the development of a revolutionary political consciousness in the working class would appear to be a break between the trade union movement and the Party. But while such a break is not out of the question, should the conditions of the late 1960s repeat themselves, it would certainly be unwarranted to look forward to an immediate rupture. It could conceivably come about 'MacDonald-style', that is, at the instigation of an integrative leadership this time able to retain the support of the parliamentary Party. But despite some wishful glances in this direction by certain Gaitskellites in recent years, the leadership has remained united behind Wilson's sanguine understanding that this would leave the Party 'uneasily poised between the Liberals and the Bow Group' without a mass base. It could come about through the union leadership following Briginshaw's action of 1968, and calling for a 'new political alignment', but this is unlikely at present for a number of reasons. First of all, the whole of the union leadership is by no means united in opposition to Labour's integrative policies *vis-à-vis* the unions, let alone the ideology on which these are based. Secondly, such a break would not take place in a political vacuum in which calculations with regard to the Labour Party alone are relevant. The unions are faced with a party system in which the Conservative (or Liberal) 'threat' is constantly present. And the unions' ability to secure from a Labour Government the repeal of Conservative measures harmful to union interests (even if this carries the unions no further than they were before these measures were introduced) is an important factor to be taken into account in any calculation of advantages and disadvantages in breaking with the Labour Party.

The most important factor militating against a break, however, remains the depth of loyalty of the union leadership, and indeed most union activists, to the Labour Party. The role that the Party has played as the major political socialization agent of union activists has nurtured the view of the Labour Party as the unique political expresion of the British working class. These activists created the Labour Party, and without their support an effective alternative party cannot be maintained. Indeed, the long history of Labour's retention of working class political allegiance, despite open and bitter conflicts, suggests that once electoral mass mobilization of the working class occurs, is institutionalized in the configuration of a political participation through a social democratic party, and crystallizes itself over a period of a half-century, as it has in Britain, a political mould is formed which becomes exceedingly difficult to break. Even under conditions of industrial militancy and economic crisis, the possibilities of working class *remobilization* seem quite limited in the face of loyalties formed at a crucial phase of working class political development and the inertia which inevitably attends their perpetuation over a significant period of time. In his speech at the time of the 1971 Party Conference, Jack Jones told a story of a man who was asked after 50 years of marriage if he had ever considered divorce: 'Divorce – never. Murder – often.' This, Jones explained, was how the trade unions felt about their marriage to the Labour Party.[27]

Nevertheless, to point out the difficulty of remobilization is not in itself a sufficient argument against the attempt insofar as the possibility of changing Labour from within seems even more daunting. Certainly the magnitude of the task is obvious – the whole history of the Party has to be overcome. And the fact that fewer and fewer revolutionary socialists now enter the Labour Party even further lessens the chances of change from within. At the same time, it is fairly clear that Labour's integrative role will only continue to be performed with an intensification of the attendant strains and conflicts which the Party's ties to the organized working class have repeatedly produced. To the end of re-establishing its credibility as a working class as well as a national party, Labour has adopted a more radical programme for social reform within capitalism. But the capacity of British capitalism, and the willingness of its dominant classes, to sustain such a programme is highly questionable, and the trade union movement has recently shown itself averse to undertaking limitations

Conclusion

on its bargaining freedom without concrete evidence that extensive social reforms are in fact forthcoming. In a situation of class conflict in the industrial sphere and severe weakness in the economy it has proved difficult, in other words, for Labour to re-establish effectively the basic condition of its success, that ideological synthesis in which it appears as the true expression of the nation as a whole as well as of the working class. This is a situation of real crisis for the Labour Party. And in view of the functional role Labour has played in the integration of the working class, to speak of the crisis of the Labour Party is, to a significant extent, really to speak of the crisis of British capitalism itself.

Appendix 1
Public opinion and incomes policy, 1965–1968

Various national public opinion surveys focussed on the prices and incomes policy under the Labour Government. For comparative purposes over time, the question asked most consistently was by Social Surveys (Gallup Polls) Ltd. between 1965 and 1968: 'Do you think the Government's Prices and Incomes Policy is a good thing or a bad thing?' (Up to January 1966 the question was worded slightly differently: 'Do you think that the Prices and Incomes Policy agreement as being discussed by Mr Brown is a good thing or a bad thing?'). The following table, computed from the Gallup Political Index and data supplied to the author by Gallup, gives some indication of the changing public attitude to the policy during these years, particularly in the crucial months of July to September 1966 which proved to be the turning point in the public's response to the policy.

Percentage of respondents

Attitude to Policy	1965			1966				1967		1968		
	Jan.	*Apr.*	*Sept.*	*Jan.*	*July*	*Aug.*	*Sept.*	*Mar.*	*July*	*Apr.*	*June*	*Dec.*
Good thing	41	47	47	46	43	48	37	45	33	39	35	26
Bad thing	13	11	13	14	20	23	34	24	32	32	33	38
Qualified answer	7	9	8	11	12	14	11	13	12	12	15	14
Don't know	39	33	32	29	25	15	18	18	17	17	17	23

It will be seen from the table that the intensive propaganda barrage that accompanied the introduction of the policy had the effect of making the policy more popular, although even in the early period outright support for the policy did not rise above 50%, at least in response to this direct question. In the aftermath of the seamen's strike, but before the freeze of 20 July 1966, a marginal fall in the policy's popularity was discernible. Immediately after the freeze, with the prospect it raised for price stability and the demands it made for rallying behind the Government during a severe economic crisis, there was a heavy fall in the number of 'don't knows', while the percentage of respondents who saw the policy as a 'good thing' rose to its highest point during the life of the policy, although it was significant that the percentage who thought the policy a 'bad thing' also increased. By the end of September 1966, as it became clear that the freeze was mainly effective on wages, support for the policy dropped off sharply.

The one main deviation from the trend away from support for the policy indicated by the table appears in March 1967. However, an NOP survey in the same month found that 52% thought the Government would have been wrong to continue with wage restraint for a further year, as opposed to 37% in favour of the idea. (*Daily Mail*, 22 March 1967). It was this poll which seems to have been most attuned to the trend for by July Gallup as well found that support for the policy had fallen drastically. In June 1968 there again seems to have been some increase in support as Mrs Castle placed renewed emphasis on price control, but this too dissipated very quickly and by December 1968 (the last time the question was asked) only one-quarter of all respondents thought the policy was a 'good thing'.

Appendix 2
1968 survey of trade union opinion
on incomes policy

The survey was conducted by the Centre for Television Research, University of Leeds, in July 1968. Its main purpose was to discern the influence of the mass media on various levels of union membership. I am indebted to Dr Jay Blumler for making the data on incomes policy, which has not previously been used, available to me.

The sample was drawn from membership in the AEF, NALGO, SOGAT and GMWU in Leeds; it was found that despite the GMWU's official support for the policy, its members were no more disposed to the policy than those in the AEF, although both were more favourable to it than SOGAT members whose union leadership had opposed the policy consistently since the summer of 1965. It was the white-collar NALGO membership, whose occupations were the most 'middle-class' (in terms of status rather than income) who responded more favourably than other trade unionists at this time to the incomes policy. The difficulty of making even a TUC policy viable, was indicated by the fact that only 13% of the rank and file, 16% of shop stewards and 24% of officials considered helping the TUC to run its policy a top union priority.

The following table is a summary of the findings.

Trade union opinion on who should operate an incomes policy

Category and number in sample	Unions/ Management only	TUC	Govt	Both TUC and Govt
	%	%	%	%
Rank and file (360)	61	5	4	23
Shop stewards (235)	64	12	2	21
Branch officials (51)[a]	43	20	—	35
Full-time officers (38)	50	24	3	21
AEF (173)	61	15	3	19
NALGO (155)	45	9	3	38
GMWU (191)	59	11	3	24
SOGAT (165)	74	6	3	13

[a] The percentage of Branch officials who favoured an incomes policy is probably unduly high because no SOGAT branch officials were included in the survey, although in each other category it was the SOGAT members who were most in favour of untrammelled union-management negotiations.

Appendix 3
Economic indicators

The following tables are offered as an overall guide to economic indicators during the period of the 1964–70 Labour Government's incomes policy.

Table I shows changes in the rate of growth, unemployment, wage rates, wage and salary earnings and retail prices during each discrete phase of the incomes policy. (The longest phase, that covered by the 1968 White Paper and extending from April 1968 to December 1969, is divided into two sub-periods.) The percentage increases reflect changes from the average for the quarter preceding each period to the average for the final quarter of the period. Hourly wage rate figures are based on the DEP's index of basic hourly rates of manual workers; earnings figures are based on the DEP's monthly index of weekly average wage and salary earnings in all industries and services, and are seasonally adjusted. The data was presented in this useful fashion by Allan Fels, in his *The British Prices and Incomes Board* (Cambridge 1972).

Tables II, III, and IV were derived from data presented originally in the NEDO's *Productivity, Prices and Incomes, A General Review*, published annually in conjunction with the incomes policy for the years 1966 to 1970. The figures presented for a given year in one Review were sometimes adjusted in subsequent Reviews, and wherever possible the most recent data presented in the Reviews for any of the years in question have been used in these tables.

Table II indicates the effect of rising prices on average money earnings during successive half-yearly periods from 1964 to 1970. Apart from the period covering October 1964 to October 1965, the NEDO presented the data in terms of average changes over two quarters, thereby minimizing the effect of fluctuations in the monthly figures.

Table III details the annual percentage change in employment incomes (wage rates, wage earnings, salary earnings) and non-employment incomes (gross trading profits of companies, self-employment incomes, rent income, dividend income, and the surpluses of public corporations.) It is important to bear in mind that the annual average figures often conceal fluctuations which took place within a given year, as shown in Table II with regard to earnings particularly during the 1966–7 period of freeze and severe restraint.

TABLE I *Some economic indicators under each phase of the incomes policy*

| | % increase at annual rates | | | | % of civilian labour force |
	Gross domestic product	Hourly wage rates	Earnings[a]	Retail prices	Unemployment
Policy phase					
Apr. 1965–June 1966	1·2	7·4	7·6	5·1	1·28
July 1966–June 1967	2·0	2·8	1·7	2·5	1·82
July 1967–Mar. 1968	4·6	9·2	8·8	2·8	2·30
Apr. 1968–Dec. 1969	3·4	4·5	7·6	5·5	2·35
Jan. 1969–Dec. 1970	1·5	5·6	8·3	5·1	2·32
Jan. 1970–June 1970	1·8	12·6	13·6	8·8	2·44
Apr. 1965–June 1970	2·1	6·5	7·3	4·7	1·99

[a] Seasonally adjusted.

SOURCE: Allan Fels, *The British Prices and Incomes Board*, Cambridge 1972, Tables 3.1 and 3.2, pp. 29–31.

TABLE II *Real earnings, percentage change, half-yearly*

	Oct. 64–Apr. 65	Apr. 65–Oct. 65	Q4 65–Q2 66	Q2 66–Q4 66	Q4 66–Q2 67	Q2 67–Q4 67	Q4 67–Q2 68	Q2 68–Q4 68	Q4 68–Q2 69	Q2 69–Q4 69	Q4 69–Q2 70
Average money[a] earnings (wages and salaries)	4·8	3·5	4·0	0·5	1·2	4·6	3·5	4·4	3·2	4·9	6·1
Retail prices[b]	3·8	1·0	2·7	1·1	1·4	0·7	3·8	1·7	3·6	1·5	4·3
Average real[c] earnings (wages and salaries)	1·0	2·5	1·3	–0·6	–0·2	3·9	–0·3	2·7	–0·4	3·4	1·7

[a] GB, all employees (seasonally adjusted). [b] UK (not seasonally adjusted) [c] Calculated by NEDO by dividing the index of earnings by the index of retail prices, no allowances for taxation.

SOURCE: NEDC, *Productivity, Prices and Incomes, A General Review*: 1966, Tables 12 and 16; 1967, Table 4; 1968, Table 10; 1969, Table 6; 1970, Tables 4, 6 and 20.

TABLE III *Annual percentage change in domestic incomes*

	Average 1960–4	1964–5	1965–6	1966–7	1967–8	1968–9	1969–70
Employment incomes							
Weekley wage rates	4·1	4·7	4·7	3·8	6·7	5·2	13·5
Weekly wage earnings[a]	6·1	8·5	5·8	4·0	8·2	7·8	12·9
Average salary earnings[b]	6·0	8·4	4·3	4·6	6·3	7·7	12·2
Non-employment incomes							
Gross trading profits (companies)[c]	4·9	3·7	−4·9	6·6	0·4	−5·5	0·4
Surpluses of public corporations[c]	9·2	7·6	3·1	7·3	18·8	6·7	−4·6
Self employment incomes[c]	3·4	5·4	0·4	4·2	3·8	4·4	5·6
Rent	6·8	9·0	8·2	8·1	8·9	10·1	11·2
Dividends on ordinary shares[d]	(	7·3[e]	)	−5·9	2·5	6·6	−3·0
Preference dividends and interest payments[d]	(	10·5[e]	)	13·2	15·6	14·3	7·1

[a] October to October for 1964–5 and 1969–70.
[b] October to October for the whole period.
[c] Before providing for depreciation, but net of stock appreciation.
[d] Dividends and interest payments are an allocation of total corporate income. They are not entirely incomes of individuals as part is received by the public sector, part goes overseas, and part goes into life assurance and superannuation funds.
[e] Average 1961–6.
SOURCE: NEDC, *Productivity, Prices and Incomes, A General Review*: 1966, Tables 1 and 18; 1967, Tables 1 and 2; 1970, Tables 1 and 2.

TABLE IV *Components of total domestic income percentage shares*

	Average 1960–4	1965	1966	1967	1968	1969	1970
Income from employment[a]	67·8	68·1	69·5	68·9	69·2	70·3	71·9
Self employment income[b]	8·3	7·7	7·6	7·9	7·9	7·8	7·5
Rent	5·6	5·6	6·0	6·2	6·5	6·8	6·9
Gross trading profits (companies)[b]	15·0	14·9	13·7	13·9	12·3	11·0	10·1
Surpluses of public corporations[b]	3·3	3·6	3·5	3·3	4·0	4·1	3·5

[a] Including Force's Pay and Employers National Insurance Contributions.
[b] Before Depreciation but Net of Stock Appreciation.
SOURCE: NEDC, *Productivity, Prices and Incomes, A General Review*: 1966, Table 17; 1967, Table 2; 1970, Table 3.

Table IV presents the shares of total domestic income in each of the years of the 1964–70 Labour Governments. It indicates general trends in pre-tax distributions, and as such it is important to note that while the share of trading profits in total domestic income declined over the whole period, this does not mean that total income declined or that the post-tax share of profits declined. As was suggested in Chapter 8, the effect of fiscal policy was to redistribute income to the benefit of corporate profits. Moreover, non-trading company income showed a high rate of increase, especially after devaluation, reflecting higher interest rates and a sharp increase in income from abroad.

Appendix 4
Interviews

Les Allen (*Head of the TUC Incomes Policy Committee Secretariat 1965–8*) at *NGA Headquarters, 8 July 1971.*

Lord Balogh (*Adivsor to the Prime Minister 1964–8*) at *the Reform Club, 14 October 1971.*

Richard Briginshaw (*General Secretary, NATSOPA*) at *NATSOPA Headquarters, 28 Sepember 1971.*

Ron Brown MP (*Chairman, PLP Productivity, Prices and Incomes Subject Group*) at *the House of Commons, 4 August 1971.*

Rt Hon. Barbara Castle MP, *at the House of Commons, 6 December 1971.*

Richard Clements (*Editor of Tribune*) at *Tribune offices, 15 November 1971.*

Lord Cooper (*General Secretary GMWU*) at *GMWU Headquarters, 19 November 1971.*

John Cousins (*TGWU official*) at *Transport House, 4 May 1971.*

Allan Fisher (*General Secretary NUPE*) at *the 1971 Labour Party Conference, Brighton, 5 October 1971.*

Rt Hon. Michael Foot MP, *at the House of Commons, 5 August and 11 November 1971.*

Rt Hon. Douglas Houghton MP, *at the House of Commons, 3 August 1971.*

Tom Jackson (*General Secretary UPW*) at *UPW House, 21 July 1971.*

Clive Jenkins (*General Secretary ASTMS*) *ASTMS offices, 1 April 1971.*

Hugh Jenkins MP, *at the House of Commons, 29 July 1971.*

Jack Jones (*General Secretary TGWU*) at *Transport House, 29 September 1971.*

Russell Kerr MP, *at the House of Commons, 4 November 1971.*

Alex Kitson (*TGWU official and Labour Party NEC Member*) at *1971 Trades Union Congress, Blackpool, 8 September 1971.*

W. E. J. McCarthy (*Former DEP Official and Research Director, Royal Commission on Trade Unions and Employers' Associations*) at *the 1971 Trades Union Congress, Blackpool, 7 September 1971.*

Ian Mikardo MP, *at 24 Palace Chambers, London, 17 November 1970.*

Jim Mortimer (*Full-time Member NBPI, 1968–70*) at *London Transport Headquarters, 31 March 1971.*

Lionel (Len) Murray (*TUC General Secretary*) *at Congress House, 8 December 1970 and 21 January 1971.*

Tony Murray (*Labour Party Research Department, Secretary to NEC Finance and Economic Policy Committee 1962–7*) *at the Economist Intelligence Unit, 21 July 1971.*

Stan Newens MP, *at the Labour Party Conference, Brighton, 8 October 1971.*

Stanley Orme MP, *at the House of Commons, 27 July 1971.*

Terry Pitt (*Secretary, Labour Party Research Department*) *24 November 1970 and 13 May 1971.*

Arthur Probert MP (*PPS to Frank Cousins, 1964–6*) *at the House of Commons, 4 August 1971.*

Giles Radice MP (*formerly Research Head, GMWU*) *at the 1971 Trades Union Congress, Blackpool, 7 September 1971.*

Bert Ramelson (*Communist Party Industrial Organizer*) *at the 1971 Labour Party Conference, 6 October 1971.*

Ernest Roberts (*AEU Assistant General Secretary*) *AEU Headquarters, 10 March 1971.*

Regan Scott (*Former Editor, TGWU Record*) *at the London School of Economics, 16 March 1970.*

Rt Hon. Edward Short MP, *at the House of Commons, 8 December 1971.*

John Stevens (*TUC Incomes Policy Committee Secretariat 1968–70*) *at Congress House, 24 September 1971.*

Rt Hon. Michael Stewart MP, *at the House of Commons, 2 August 1971.*

George Woodcock (*TUC General Secretary*) *at the Commission on Industrial Relations Headquarters, 17 June 1971.*

Notes

INTRODUCTION

1 Labour Representation Committee, *Report of the Conference of Labour Representation*, London 1900, p. 21.
2 See Leo Panitch, 'Ideology and Integration: The Case of the British Labour Party', *Political Studies*, vol. XIX, no. 2, 1971, pp. 184–200.
3 Ramsay MacDonald, *Socialism and Society*, 6th edn, London 1908, p. 144.
4 Tom Nairn, 'The Left Against Europe?', *New Left Review*, no. 75, September–October 1972, pp. 44–5.
5 A. Shonfield, *Modern Capitalism, the Changing Balance of Public and Private Power*, London 1965, p. 219.
6 V. Foa, 'Incomes Policy: A Crucial Problem for the Unions', *International Socialist Journal*, January 1964, p. 264.
7 S. H. Beer, 'The Comparative Method and The Study of British Politics', *Comparative Politics*, vol. 1, no. 1, 1968, p. 32.
8 S. H. Beer, *Modern British Politics*, London 1965, p. 395: cf. pp. 319–31.
9 *The Times*, *The Guardian*, 17 December 1964.
10 Martin Harrison, *Trade Unions and the Labour Party since 1945*, London 1960, pp. 165, 346.

CHAPTER 1

1 Trade unions had been represented on only one Government Committee in 1931; this number had grown to twelve in 1939 and sixty in 1948–9. For accounts of the integration of the unions into governmental decision-making, see V. L. Allen, *Trade Unions and The Government*, London 1960, pp. 32–4 and passim; Eric Wigham, *Trade Unions*, London 1969, Ch. 1; Ministry of Labour, *Industrial Relations Handbook*, HMSO 1961, pp. 16ff. See also PEP, *British Trade Unionism*, London 1948, and D. F. MacDonald, *The State and Trade Unions*, London 1960.
2 Cmd. 6284.
3 Quoted in Barbara Wooton, *The Social Foundations of Wages Policy*, London 1954, p. 113.
4 John Corina, *The Labour Market*, London 1966, p. 12. Cf. Murray Edelman & R. W. Fleming, *The Politics of Wage–Price Decisions*, Urbana 1965, p. 181, and W. K. Hancock & H. M. Gowing, *British War Economy*, London 1949, Ch. 15.
5 Some flavour of the discussion in Britain along these lines can be had from Barbara Wooton, *Freedom Under Planning*, London 1945, esp. Ch. 8; F. Zweig, *The Planning of Free Societies*, London 1942; and Evan Durbin, 'The Importance of Planning' (1935) in his *Problems of Economic Planning*, London 1949, pp. 56–7.

268

6 Cmd. 6527.
7 'Planning Full Employment', *The Times*, 23 January 1943. It has been
the subject of considerable debate among economists as to whether this
inflationary pressure results directly from the effect of rising wage rates
upon production costs and thus prices, or whether it is the result of too
high a level of demand to which high wages give rise. The literature is
extensive. For a good analysis of the various economic theories that
influenced policy decisions in the post-war period see J. C. R. Dow,
The Management of the British Economy 1945–60, Cambridge 1964,
Ch. 12. Cf. B. C. Roberts, *National Wages Policy in War and Peace*,
London 1958, pp. 13–18 and William Fellner *et al. The Problem of
Rising Prices*, OEEC 1961, pp. 12–13.
8 Sir W. Beveridge, *Full Employment in a Free Society, a Report*, London
1945, p. 200.
9 Roberts (n. 7 above), p. 64.
10 S. H. Beer, *Modern British Politics*, London 1965, pp. 200–1.
11 Continuing Government consultation with the trade unions took place
through the National Joint Advisory Council, the National Production
Advisory Council for Industry, and later through the Economic Planning
Board and the Development Councils. Formal contact via the Party was
maintained through a liaison committee between the National Council
of Labour and the Government.
12 Morgan Phillips, *The Labour Party, The Party with a Future*, May
1945, p. 1. This was reiterated shortly after the election. See the section
'A Truly National Party' in *The Rise of the Labour Party*, Labour
Discussion Series, no. 1, 1945, pp. 15–16.
13 Hugh Dalton, *Practical Socialism for Britain*, London 1935, p. 165.
Douglas Jay, *The Socialist Case*, reprinted with Attlee introduction
London 1947, pp. 240–1. E. F. M. Durbin, 'The Importance of Planning', (n. 5 above), p. 57. For Durbin's rejection of the idea of the class
struggle, see his *The Politics of Democratic Socialism*, London 1940, pp.
171ff.
14 For the hostile Fabian attitude to trade union methods see J. Melitz,
'The Trade Unions and Fabian Socialism', *Industrial and Labour
Relations Review*, vol. 12, no. 4, 1959.
15 'We have approximately the same shortage now as we had all through
the War years . . . I managed it [then] by having before me the actual
industrial requirements as set forth in contracts and I was able to put
before the country from time to time and before the trade unions where
the most urgent needs existed. I cannot see that being done at all now
on the production side . . . with the very inadequate facts before me as
chairman of the Manpower Committee I cannot really do the job.' Letter
to Attlee, 15 November 1945: from Francis Williams, *A Prime Minister
Remembers, The War and Post-War Memoirs of the Rt. Hon. Earl
Attlee*, London 1961, p. 126.
16 *Economic Survey for 1947*, Cmd. 7046, pp. 28–9. By far the best discussion of the various technological, social and institutional limitations on
manpower planning in post-war Britain is D. J. Dewey, 'Occupational
Choice in a Collectivist Economy', *Journal of Political Economy*, vol.
LVI, no. 6, 1968, pp. 465–79.
17 Attlee's opposition was indicated in an interview with V. L. Allen. See
Allen (n. 1 above), p. 283.
18 TUC, *Statement of Policy on Problems of Production, a Report of a
Conference of Executives of Affiliated Organizations*, 6 March 1947, p. 4.
19 *1946 LPCR*, p. 177.
20 *1947 LPCR*, pp. 143–57.
21 See *Economic Survey for 1947*, Cmd. 7046, pp. 5–9 and the lesser known

White Paper on European Cooperation, Cmd. 7572, 1948, preface and pp. 1–2.

22 Quoted by A. A. Rogow. *The Labour Government and British Industry, 1945–51*, Oxford 1955, p. 41. See also Herbert Morrison, *Economic Planning*, a speech to the Institute of Public Administration, London, October 1946, p. 11, and *Government and Parliament*, London 1954, pp. 299–310.

23 R. D. Henderson & D. Seers, '1949: Forecast and Fact, a Critique of the Economic Survey for 1949', Oxford Institute of Statistics, *Bulletin*, vol. 12, nos. 1 and 2, 1950, pp. 7–8. For a similar criticism by the TUC General Council see *1947 TUC Report*, p. 222. Cf. in this regard an interesting paper by the Information Division of the Treasury and the Reference Division of Central Office of Information, *Economic Controls in Britain*, April 1951.

24 Douglas Jay, 'Plans and Priorities' in *The Road to Recovery*, Fabian Society Lectures, Autumn 1947, pp. 15–16.

25 M. Harrison, *Trade Unions and the Labour Party since 1945*, London 1960, p. 224.

26 *1945 TUC Report*, p. 368.

27 See Morrison, *Economic Planning* (n. 22 above), p. 9.

28 TUC, *Interim Report on Post-War Reconstruction*, 1944, p. 25.

29 Ibid. p. 30.

30 TUC, *Statement of Policy on Problems of Production*, 6 March 1946, p. 11; cf. *1946 TUC Report*, pp. 224–9.

31 *1946 TUC Report*, p. 176.

32 *1947 LPCR*, p. 144.

33 'It is significant', Arthur Deakin argued in a speech against a wages policy in 1946, 'that this demand for a declaration on wage policy only came with the advent of our Labour Government. Those of us who have to deal from day to day with wage claims know with what ability the employers backed up that suggestion . . .' *1946 TUC Report*, p. 421.

34 Quoted by W. Singer, 'Wage Policy in Full Employment', *Economic Journal*, vol. LVII, 1947, p. 450.

35 'The needs of the present situation are such that it is not sufficient for the Trade Union Movement to adopt a negative policy of not embarrassing the Labour Government, but rather a positive attitude of strengthening the Labour Government by the development of a production and wages and prices policy.' L. J. Gregory, *1945 TUC Report*, p. 343. The General Council's position was: 'No responsible authority has attempted to set out in any detail the meaning of the phrase "National Wages Policy"'. TUC, *Statement of Policy* (n. 30 above), p. 10.

36 *1946 TUC Report*, p. 229.

37 *1947 TUC Report*, esp. p. 432.

38 *Keep Left*, New Statesman Pamphlet, April 1947, p. 21. *Keep Left's* own preferences for manpower planning were to create a tighter system of controls over materials in order to direct them away from inessential industries and to introduce a 'negative direction of labour' by suspending replacements in essential industries, and by varying real incomes by the selective supply of consumer goods to workers in essential industries and discrimination in taxation according to industry and occupation. It also argued that this Wages Policy should be combined with a 'National Profits Policy' which would set differential real profits to match differential real wages; taxation should be used to discriminate between profits in various industries according to their priority as well as between distributed and undistributed profits in general. The pamphlet expected that these measures would help to reduce the resistance of that 'decreas-

ing group' of trade union leaders who were opposed to a national wages
policy.
39 *A Statement on the Economic Considerations Affecting Relations Between Employers and Workers,* Cmd. 7018.
40 The convertibility crisis of 1947 is the key to the austerity policy followed by the Labour Government in the following years. At Bretton
Woods in 1945, the American loan was secured on the condition that
sterling be made convertible, although this was intensely resented in
Britain. When, on 15 July 1947, convertibility was instituted, Britain
became the only country in Europe to have a fully convertible currency.
In view of the dollar shortage and the extensive post-war demand for
consumer goods, which America alone was able to produce on a large
scale at the time, this solitary British position was fraught with dangers.
A massive capital flight from sterling to dollars occurred, and by 20
August, when convertibility had to be repealed, $3,600m of the $5,000m
credits extended to Britain by the US and Canada had been exhausted.
See Dow (n. 7 above), pp. 21ff.
41 See V. L. Allen (n. 1 above), pp. 288–9.
42 For an account of the meetings between the TUC and the Government
in the fall of 1947 see TUC, *Prices, Wages and Exports,* Report to
Special Conference of Trade Union Executives, 24 March 1948.
43 Ibid. pp. 47–8.
44 446 *HC Deb.* 4 February 1948, cols. 1829–31, and Cmd. 7321.
45 446 *HC Deb.* col. 1834.
46 448 *HC Deb.* 12 February 1948, col. 680.
47 *Economist,* 7 February 1948, p. 210. The Communist *Daily Worker* also
appreciated the significance of the *Statement,* if in less moderate terms.
Its headline on 5 February read: 'Attlee Declares War on Wages', and
it featured a report that Cripps had made it clear to the Cabinet that
any rise in wages would be matched by a reduction in food subsidies.
48 Beer (n. 10 above), p. 205.
49 Its determination to cooperate was evidenced by its overlooking the
petulance of Cripps who, at a meeting with London members of the
General Council to discuss the policy, '. . . opened the meeting by
explaining the purpose of the (White) Paper, then pushed it across the
table and departed from the meeting before any discussion could take
place.' V. L. Allen, *Trade Union Leadership,* London 1957, p. 127.
50 *The Times,* 6 and 12 February 1948. Cf. 1948 *TUC Report,* pp. 289ff.
51 447 *HC Deb.* 12 February 1948, col. 6.
52 See TUC, *What the TUC is Doing,* Spring 1948, p. 5.
53 *The Times,* 12 March 1948.
54 T. E. M. McKitterick, *Wages Policy?* (with a preface by George Isaacs,
Min. of Labour), Fabian Society 1949.
55 The Orders covered items like umbrellas, walking sticks, metal office
equipment and pencils. Cf. Beer (n. 10 above), p. 206 and *Economist,*
24 April 1948, p. 683.
56 Dow (n. 7 above), p. 35.
57 *General Council Report to Special Conference of Trade Union Executive Committees,* 24 March 1948, p. 51.
58 Allan Flanders, *A Policy for Wages,* Fabian Tract 281, July 1950, p. 7;
see also Allen, *Trade Unions and the Government* (n. 1 above), p. 281;
Roberts (n. 7 above), pp. 57–8; Edelman & Fleming (n. 4 above), p. 182.
59 *The Times,* 24 February 1948. After the statement was endorsed by the
affiliated unions, *The Economist* wrote that 'it is only the lack of perspective endured by a close preoccupation with crisis economics . . .
which prevents a general recognition that this endorsement is a landmark in trade union history. Who, twenty years ago, could have

imagined a conference of trade union executives in any circumstances, accepting the general principle of a wage stop? The trade union mind has travelled – on previous form – a long way.' 2 April 1948, p. 536. Of course not all of the press was content with the limitations the trade unions had accepted. 'Candidus' in the *Daily Sketch* expressed a more basic demand: 'There are no trade unions in Russia and when the Revolution occurred in 1917 the trade union leaders were among the first to be executed, which was a thoroughly well-deserved fate.' 19 February 1948.

60 Dudley Seers, 'The Levelling of Incomes', *Oxford Institute of Statistics, Bulletin*, vol. 12, no. 11, October 1950, p. 289. For a similar view of the success of the 1948 restraint policy see Wm. Fellner *et al.*, *The Problem of Rising Prices*, OEEC 1961, p. 61. The above statistics are taken from the following sources: G. D. N. Worswick & P. H. Ady, *The British Economy 1945–50*, Oxford 1952, Table 6, p. 330; D. J. Robertson, *The Economics of Wages and the Distribution of Income, 1938 to 1958*, London 1960, Table 9, p. 142: Allan Flanders, 'Wage Movements and Wage Policy in Post-war Britain', *The Annals of the American Academy of Political and Social Science*, vol. 310, March 1957, Table I, p. 89.

61 See *The Times*, 24 March 1948, and 9 April 1948; *Special Conference Report* (n. 57 above), pp. 10–11; and F. J. Bayliss, *British Wage Councils*, Oxford 1962, pp. 96–7.

62 Quoted in *The Times*, 13 March 1948.

63 See Deakin's speech to the special conference, *Report* (n. 57 above), p. 31 and Allen, *Trade Union Leadership* (n. 49 above), p. 132.

64 *1948 TUC Report*, p. 503; for Deakin's defence of profit margins see *Special Conference Report* (n. 57 above), p. 30; and *1948 LPCR*, p. 142.

65 *1947 LPCR*, p. 137.

66 *1948 TUC Report*, pp. 861–2.

67 See Colin Cooke, *The Life of Sir Stafford Cripps*, London 1957, pp. 367–78; and *1948 LPCR*, p. 108.

68 R. A. Brady, *Crisis in Britain*, London 1950, p. 563. Brady estimated that among the leaders of the Labour Party, only Aneurin Bevan, John Strachey and Harold Laski excepted themselves from this view. See the 1949 Labour Party document, *Labour Believes in Britain*, April 1949: 'Unless there is economic necessity, there is no reason for always socializing whole industries.' (p. 12).

69 447 *HC Deb.* 12 February 1948, col. 636.

70 456 *HC Deb.* 17 September 1948, cols. 454–5.

71 *1948 LPCR*, p. 200.

72 *1949 TUC Report*, p. 480.

73 See Harrison (n. 25 above), p. 342, and Edelman & Fleming (n. 4 above), p. 160.

74 Thus when the Conservative Government began to interest itself in a wage policy in 1956, Macmillan intimated that he too would like to be invited to the TUC. He received a scathing reply (to thunderous applause) from Frank Cousins: 'What does he think it is – a Film Festival? We will welcome a Chancellor of the Exchequer, but . . . we will wait for a Labour Chancellor of the Exchequer.' *1956 TUC Report*, p. 400.

75 *Daily Herald*, 24 February 1948.

76 See Wigham (n. 1 above), p. 110; Harrison (n. 25 above), p. 248, and B. Hennessy, 'Trade Unions and the British Labour Party', *American Political Science Review*, vol. XLIX, 1955, pp. 1050–60.

77 The position of these MPs was enunciated by Jennie Lee who, after citing large profits in the engineering industry, said: 'I am not for one moment suggesting that these excessive profits are a large fraction of our total wealth, but they are a spectacular thing. They are the part of our

social economy which make life impossible for the reputable labour and trade union leader when he goes among his own men and women in industry.' 447 *HC Deb.* 12 February 1948, col. 618.

78 For the list of signatories see *The Times*, 12 February 1948. An incomplete account of this revolt is in Robert J. Jackson, *Rebels and Whips*, London 1968, p. 53–4.

79 J. M. Burns, 'The Parliamentary Labour Party in Great Britain', *APSR*, vol. XLIV, no. 4, 1950, p. 861.

80 See *Daily Herald*, 12 February 1948, and Allen, *Trade Union Leadership* (n. 49 above), p. 147. In marked contrast, business groups made extensive use of Tory MPs in their negotiations with the Government on the policy. See Beer (n. 10 above), p. 206, n. 4.

81 P. Belcher (Tobacco Workers Union), *1948 TUC Report*, p. 490.

82 See esp. K. C. J. C. Knowles, 'The Post War Dock Strikes', *Political Quarterly*, July–September 1951, pp. 266–90. A Survey of the 1949 Dock Strikes produced the following responses to the question of the dockers' satisfaction with their union set up. 'We don't run the Trade Union; its the bloody Union that runs us.' 'The Union is supposed to represent the men, but they don't support the strikes.' 'While the Labour Government is in you can't have official strikes because most of the Union officials have got positions in the Government and they've forgotten about the men.' *Mass Observation Bulletin*, New Series no. 31, January 1950.

83 *1948 TUC Report*, p. 339.

84 *1949 TUC Report*, p. 443.

85 They were joined by Morgan Phillips, who called for a campaign against communism in the trade unions and received the support of the Government, especially Ernest Bevin. See two articles by the Labour Correspondent of *The Times*, 'Communism in the Trade Unions', 9 and 10 February 1948; cf. TUC General Council, *Defend Democracy, Two Statements of Policy*, TUC Pamphlet, 1948.

86 With regard to the 1948 Special Conference Ian Mikardo wrote of the 'sterile, negative anti-Communism which the platform offered as their own answer to a pointed, relevant and constructive debate'. 'Apart from being an insult to the conference, this was a tactical blunder of the first magnitude, because it suggested that the communists can poll a two million vote in the trade unions – a suggestion which is arrant nonsense.' *Tribune*, 2 April 1948.

87 See *The Times*, 9 March 1948, *Tribune*, 12 March 1948 and R. T. McKenzie, *British Political Parties*, 2nd edn, London 1963, pp. 495–6.

88 Barbara Castle MP, *1949 LPCR*, p. 161. Cf. *Keeping Left*, New Statesman Pamphlet, November 1949, and G. D. H. Cole, *Labour's Second Term*, Fabian Tract 273, London 1949, esp. p. 6. This frustration was reflected as well in the numerous grievances raised at Party and union conferences at the time with regard to the nationalized industries, particularly with regard to the lack of worker participation, the amount of compensation paid in a period of austerity, the high salaries of Board members and managers, and the appointment of previous owners to the Boards. For a gauge of the dissatisfaction see the results of a questionnaire sent by the TUC Economic Committee to its affiliated organizations, *1948 TUC Report*, pp. 212–20.

89 *Daily Worker*, 9 November 1949.

90 Flanders (n. 58 above), p. 9; cf. TUC, *Trade Unions and Wages Policy*, Report of a Special Conference of Trade Union Executive Committees, 12 January 1950, Appendix.

91 Ibid. p. 29. The tone of the dissidence was caught by one delegate particularly: 'I want to say that none of the women cleaners in the Civil

Service will agree to have their wages frozen. Last year, we tried to get
a rate of 2s. an hour for our work, and all we got offered was Sir Stafford
Cripps farthing and we told him what he could do with it . . . We feel
that this idea of freezing wages should be applied to some of the higher
ups, but if you ask us to live on our present wage, then the answer is
NO, and if that is being awkward, then I will say that we did not vote
in the Labour Party in 1945 in order for our position to be made worse.'
(p. 30).

92 *Tribune*, 26 May 1950.

93 *1950 TUC Report*, pp. 467ff.

94 *1950 TUC Report*, pp. 467ff.

95 *1950 LPCR*, p. 195. It is a marked failure of Robert McKenzie's *British
Political Parties* that he does not take account of the NEC's preventative
action at this Conference. Had they faced the wage restraint question
straight on, the platform would undoubtedly have been defeated. This
failure is the remit of McKenzie's too rigid separation between the
annual TUC and the Party Conference. The two cannot be as easily
separated as he imagines. It is also notable that two other major works
on the Party and the unions, Harrison's *Trade Unions and the Labour
Party* and Stephen Haseler's *The Gaitskellites* (London 1969), pay hardly
any attention to the defeat of the General Council at the 1950 Congress.
Indeed, Haseler gets his facts wrong and writes that the opposition to
the wage freeze was defeated at the Congress (p. 25, n. 4).

96 See A. T. Peacock & W. J. L. Ryan, 'Wage Claims and the Pace of
Inflation (1948–51)', *Economic Journal*, vol. LXIII, 1953, pp. 385–92.

97 See Oxford Institute of Statistics, *Bulletin*, March 1950 to March 1951
inclusive, esp. Seers, 'The Levelling of Incomes', October 1950, pp.
271–2. Cf. Richard Titmus, *Income Distribution and Social Change*,
London 1962, esp. p. 198, Rogow (n. 22 above), pp. 126–7, 199–200, and
Worswick & Ady (n. 60 above), Ch. 8.
The large rise in profits was largely undistributed, although dividend
restraint fell by the wayside with wage restraint in 1950. There were
various means of evading dividend limitation, however, especially by
the issue of bonus shares, which allowed companies to pay a large total
dividend while declaring a lower dividend rate. Increased undistributed
profits also reflected themselves in the rising value of shares, and since
no capital gains tax was operative at the time, this amounted to tax-free
income for recipients of capital transactions. In its taxation policies, the
Government discriminated sharply between distributed and undistributed profits to encourage company savings to finance investment. To
this end it began to represent undistributed income as 'belonging' to
no one income group. National Income White Papers in 1949 and 1950
introduced this subtle change by presenting their data on the distribution of personal incomes *excluding* undistributed profits, whereas
earlier they had included them. As Dudley Seers pointed out at the time,
this was a tactic which revealed the distribution of personal spendable
income at a given moment, but concealed the more fundamental real
distribution of resources between the classses.

98 See Ministry of Labour *Gazette*, November 1950, p, 336 and December
1960, p. 462.

99 See John Corina, 'Wage Drift and Wages Policy', *Economics*, Spring
1963, pp. 284–93.

100 University of Liverpool, *The Dock Worker*, Liverpool 1954, p. 132.

101 Allen, *Trade Unions and the Government* (n. 1 above), p. 291. Cf. pp.
264–5, for the changes in trade union representation inside the Government.

102 Harrison (n. 25 above), p. 298. Harrison noted that as early as 1947 the

NUPE conference was asked to 'view with grave concern the attitude adopted towards the trade unions by the Labour Party' including 'the growing indifference to trade union delegates at Party meetings' (p. 116).

103 See the *Tribune* pamphlets *Going Our Way* and *One Way Only*, 1951.
104 *Going Our Way*, p. 14. The differences between the 'Deakinites' and the 'Bevanites' on policy matters were of course greater than the Bevanites admitted at this time. Bevan was in favour of a national wages policy, but in the context of automatically tying wages to rises in the cost of living, increased controls and further redistribution of income. Source: Personal interview with Michael Foot; cf. Donald Bruce, 'Communication or Compulsion', *Tribune*, 19 April 1968.
105 Discussions with John Corina, based on his unpublished D.Phil. thesis, 'The British Experiment in Wage Restraint', Oxford University 1961.
106 See the White Paper *Control of Dividends*, July 1951. Cmd. 8318.
107 *Labour*, The TUC Magazine, vol. I, no. 3 (Revised Series), November 1950, pp. 75–6. For the proposals current at the time, see Flanders, *A Policy for Wages* (n. 58 above), pp. 15–31. Cf. George Darling, MP, 'A Suggestion for the Chancellor', *Tribune*, 15 December 1950.
108 In what can only be described as a startling instance of dramatic foreshadowing, Les Cannon, then a young Communist ETU delegate to the 1949 TUC, attacked the General Council for its 'class collaboration with monopoly capitalists' in the wages policy: 'I am quite a young man and I am sure that there are many ghosts of my age hanging behind the members of the General Council. I only hope my ghost does not haunt me in a similar fashion in twenty years time.' See *1949 TUC Report*, p. 355. Under the Labour Governments of 1964–70, Les Cannon, having shed his communist affiliations and beliefs and taken over the leadership of his union, became one of the staunchest union supporters of the second edition of Labour's wages policy.

CHAPTER 2

1 See the Annual Report of the Economic Committee in the TUC Reports and especially the overall review of a decade, 'The Economic Situation', Appendix A, *1959 TUC Report*, pp. 485–511. Cf. W. J. McCarthy, *The Future of the Unions*, Fabian Tract 339, September 1962, pp. 23–4.
2 See V. L. Allen, *Trade Unions and the Government*, London 1968, p. 34.
3 Sir Vincent Tewson, 'Relationship of the Trade Union Movement to Government and Industry' in *Trade Unions Today*, British Institute of Management, 1953, p. 4; for Deakin's similar views see V. L. Allen, *Trade Union Leadership*, London 1957, pp. 138–9.
4 *1952 TUC Report*, pp. 79, 484. Cf. similar motions and debates in the 1953, 1954 and 1955 TUC *Reports*. These resolutions, although defeated, consistently secured $2\frac{1}{2}$ to 3 million votes.
5 *1952 LPCR*, p. 136.
6 G. D. H. Cole, 'The Labour Party and the Trade Unions', *Political Quarterly*, vol. 24, no. 1, 1953, p. 22.
7 At the same time the Party explicitly ruled out a return to an extensive system of price controls. A resolution calling for this at the 1954 Conference was defeated by 3,758,000 votes to 2,132,000 votes and the NEC's position was stated baldly as: 'Labour's policy on price control is retention of controls only where goods are in short supply.' *1954 LPCR*, p. 179.
8 J. A. Monk, 'Trade Union Leadership', *Political Quarterly*, vol. 27, no. 1, 1956, p. 73. The early and mid 1950s were marked by an outpouring of literature on a wages policy. But as one review of this literature pointed out: 'a new conception of wages policy cannot be drawn up without establishing a national profits policy in the context of a more

coherent national economic policy. If there is a thread of agreement among the writers here considered, it is that the problem of wages cannot be solved without deciding the general distribution of the whole national income.' PEP, 'New Writings on Wages', *Planning*, vol. XXI, 1955, p. 275.

9 *1952 TUC Report*, pp. 283–5 and *1954 TUC Report*, p. 290; B. C. Roberts, *National Wages Policy in War and Peace*, London 1958, p. 144; and A. Flanders, 'Wages Movements and Wage Policy in Post-War Britain', *The Annals of the American Academy of Political and Social Science*, vol. 310, 1957, pp. 91–4.

10 Cmd. 9725, March 1956.

11 For a detailed account of these events see H. A. Clegg & R. Adams, *The Employers' Challenge*, Oxford 1957.

12 See Robert Carr, 581 *HC Deb.* 6 February 1958, cols. 1475–7 and Ian Macleod, ibid. col. 1380.

13 See *Council on Prices, Productivity and Incomes, First Report*, HMSO, February 1958; *1958 TUC Report*, pp. 280–1; and K. C. J. C. Knowles, 'Wages and Productivity' in Worswick & Ady (eds.) *The British Economy in the 1950s*, Oxford 1962, pp. 511–35.

14 Harold Wilson, *Remedies for Inflation*, a series of articles in *The Guardian*, November 1957, reprinted as a Labour Party pamphlet, 1957, p. 14.

15 *Plan for Progress, Labour's Policy for Britain's Economic Expansion*, July 1958, p. 37.

16 'Congress asserts the right of Labour to bargain on equal terms with Capital and to use its bargaining strength to protect workers from the dislocations of an unplanned economy.' *1956 TUC Report*, p. 398.

17 Ibid. pp. 399–400.

18 R. H. S. Crossman, *Memorandum on Problems Facing the Party*, NEC, 26 April 1950. Unpublished, in NEC files.

19 See Stephen Haseler, *The Gaitskellites*, London 1969, pp. 145–6. Butler & Rose, *The British General Election of 1959*, London 1960, esp. p. 70; and R. Miliband, *Parliamentary Socialism*, 2nd edn, London 1972, Ch. 10.

20 *1956 TUC Report*, pp. 490–1.

21 See esp. *1958 LPCR*, pp. 150ff.

22 Party Political Broadcast on behalf of the Labour Party, 'Prices, Wages and Employment', 29 April 1958: in BBC archives.

23 547 *HC Deb.* 25 July 1957, cols. 635–8; *1958 LPCR*, pp. 145–6; *Remedies for Inflation* (n. 14 above), p. 14.

24 581 *HC Deb.* 6 February 1958, col. 1415.

25 *1958 LPCR*, pp. 165–6.

26 See A. Glyn & B. Sutcliffe, *British Capitalism, Workers and the Profit Squeeze*, London 1972, pp. 39, 58.

27 John Corina, 'The Pause as Incomes Policy Strategy: 1961–2', unpublished paper, pp. 1–2. This study, based on primary sources, is the fullest study to date of the events surrounding the pay pause. Other accounts can be found in S. Brittan, *Steering the Economy, The Role of the Treasury*, London 1970, Ch. 6; Edelman & Fleming, *The Politics of Wage–Price Decisions*, Urbana 1965, pp. 186ff; V. L. Allen, *Militant Trade Unionism*, London 1966, pp. 63–9; A. Shonfield, *Modern Capitalism, the Changing Balance of Public and Private Power*, London 1965, pp. 107ff; T. L. Johnson, 'Pay Policy after the Pause', *Scottish Journal of Political Economy*, vol. 9, 1962, pp. 1–16; and The Times, *Towards a National Incomes Policy* (pamphlet), London 1962.

28 Wm. Fellner *et al.*, *The Problem of Rising Prices*, OEEC 1961. For an indication by the Government of the influence this report had on it, see

NIC, *Memorandum of Evidence submitted by HM Government, Scottish Builders and Plumbers Agreement*, January 1963 (unpublished, in the Library of Political and Economic Science). The Cohen Council also now reversed its earlier position and recommended a 'money incomes policy' to apply to profits as well as pay. *Council on Prices, Productivity and Incomes, Fourth Report*, July 1961, p. 24.

29 Ibid. p. 64. For criticism of the Report by the Joint Trade Union Advisory Committee to the OEEC, see *Trade Union Affairs* No. 4, Autumn–Winter 1964, pp. 94–104.

30 Corina (n. 27 above), p. 18.

31 *1962 TUC Report*, p. 244.

32 General Council Statement, 20 July 1961, *1961 TUC Report*, p. 258. This criticism was not confined to the TUC, of course. See the NIESR submission to the NEC, *Scottish Builders and Plumbers Agreement, Memorandum of Evidence*, February 1963.

33 See *1962 TUC Report*, pp. 367, 468–71. The four NIC reports, all based on *post hoc* references by the Government had no effect on the size of the settlements and their contribution was limited to their effect on public opinion. See H. A. Clegg, 'The Lessons of the NIC', *New Society*, 11 March 1965, pp. 7–9.

34 General Council Statement, 24 January 1962.

35 Corina (n. 27 above), p. 32.

36 *1962 TUC Report*, pp. 276–9.

37 *1963 TUC Report*, p. 390.

38 '. . . we have learnt from bitter experience over the last ten years in talking to ministers, all kinds of ministers, that the attitude they take up in relation to our criticisms is a defensive one. They seek to justify what they have done, they seek to explain away difficulties that might have arisen. They do not open out . . . they tend to be circumspect.' *1962 TUC Report*, p. 369.

39 General Council Statement, 24 January 1962.

40 NEDC, *Conditions Favourable to Faster Growth*, HMSO 1963, p. 51.

41 *1963 TUC Report*, p. 492–5.

42 See FBI, *Profits and the National Incomes Commission*, 24 July 1963; and *The Times*, 'Profits and Pay Yoke Opposed by FBI', 25 July 1963; cf. FBI *In Search of a National Incomes Policy*, 11 March 1964.

43 *1964 TUC Report*, pp. 306–7. An account of this meeting is to be found in the USDAW Journal, *The New Dawn*, vol. 20, no. 15, 16 July 1966, pp. 455–6.

44 *1963 LPCR*, p. 189.

45 See Butler and King, *The British General Election of 1964*, London 1965, p. 36. In 1964, 48% thought there was 'a class struggle in this country', while 34% thought there was not.

46 See Richard Rose, *Influencing Voters*, London 1967, p. 256.

47 *1962 TUC Report*, pp. 371ff.

48 In the early sixties Gaitskell founded the XYZ Society where Labour leaders and economists met with sympathetic City men. This contact with the City grew as the election approached. See 'Labour and the City' *Socialist Commentary*, April 1964, pp. 13–14.

49 See Morgan Phillips, *Labour in the Sixties*, 1960, Part II, 'The Party and the Unions'; cf. Crosland, *Can Labour Win?*, Fabian Tract 324, 1960, pp. 17–18.

50 *1961 LPCR*, p. 155.

51 Ibid. p. 106.

52 Ibid. p. 98.

53 Until the Conservatives' action only the nominal left of the Party had insisted on putting planning first. See Crossman's *Labour in the Affluent*

Society, Fabian Tract 325, 1960, and Wilson's 'A Four Year Plan for
Britain', *New Statesman*, March 1961. In contrast Morgan Phillips's
Labour in the Sixties (n. 49 above) did not put planning at the top of its
priorities, and Crosland's *Can Labour Win?* (n. 49 above) in fact contended that Britain's economic stagnation was a poor issue in that it was
too abstract and attacked the Tories on their own ground (p. 19).
Significantly, when Crosland reissued his pamphlet in 1962, this argument was omitted. See *The Conservative Enemy*, London 1962, esp.
p. 159.

54 'Election Agenda', *Socialist Commentary*, May 1962, p. 5, emphasis in
text.

55 612 *HC Deb* 3 November 1959, cols. 862, 872–3: This was Bevan's last
speech in the House of Commons and is still widely referred to in the
Labour Party; in fact the problem as outlined by Bevan was chosen by
Harold Wilson as an introduction to his *The Labour Government,
1964–70, A Personal Record*, London 1971, although the political failures
that Bevan outlined were not quoted.

56 *1963 LPCR*, p. 191.

57 See esp. *1962 TUC Report*, pp. 296–8; TUC, *Sweden: Its Unions and
Industrial Relations*, May 1963; and Jack Cooper *Industrial Relations.
Sweden Shows the Way*, Fabian Research Series 235, 1963.

58 See Guy Routh, *Occupation and Pay in Great Britain 1906–1960*, Cambridge 1965, esp. Table 147, p. 104.

59 See Richard Titmuss, *Income Distribution and Social Change*, London
1962.

60 R. J. Nicholson, *Redistribution of Income: UK Income and Wealth
Series X*, International Association for Research in Income and Wealth,
1964, pp. 121–35; and R. J, Nicholson, 'The Distribution of Personal
Incomes', *Lloyd's Bank Review*, no. 83, January 1967, pp. 11–21. Cf.
Robin Blackburn 'The Unequal Society' in Blackburn and A. Cockburn,
The Incompatibles, London 1967, pp. 15–55; J. E. Meade, *Efficiency,
Equality and the Ownership of Property*, London 1964 and John Hughes
'The Increase in Inequality', *New Statesman*, 8 November 1968.

61 The 1963 and 1964 TUC debates on the question showed this to be the
major preoccupation. See *1963 TUC Report*, pp. 393ff; and *1964 TUC
Report*, pp. 446ff, esp. the speeches by Jim Mortimer of DATA and Les
Cannon of the ETU, pp. 446–9.

62 See *1961 LPCR*, pp. 64–5, 94–7, and debate on Industrial Relations in
652 *HC Deb*. 29 January 1962, cols. 720–833 and especially Brown's
speech cols. 832–3.

63 663 *HC Deb*. 26 July 1962, vol. 1742. Insofar as the idea of incomes policy
was seriously canvassed before this, it was by a group of intellectuals on
the left of the party who saw it as an opportunity to enfuse Labour with
a radical social policy 'which would probe the limits of reform within
capitalism'. See John Hughes and Ken Alexander, *A Socialist Wages
Plan, the Politics of the Pay Packet*, Universities and Left Review
Pamphlet 1959, and the heated debate it produced between John
Turner, John Corina, Michael Kidron and the authors, 'A Polemic
on the Wages Plans' in *The New Reasoner*, Autumn 1959, pp. 73–106.
The pamphlet had little immediate impact on the party or the unions.,
but the political atmosphere of the pay pause made a subsequent
pamphlet more timely: see Hughes and Alexander, *Trade Unions in
Opposition*, Fabian Tract 335, 1961.

64 663 *HC Deb*. 26 July 1962, col. 1742.

65 'We shall be partners in a great adventure. We shall consult – and I
mean consult, not present you with a diktat – we shall listen and we shall
say what in our view the national interest demands.' Harold Wilson,

1964 TUC Report, p. 384. The emphasis on consultation was so marked
in Callaghan's speech on planning and incomes policy to the 1963 Conference (*1963 LPCR*, pp. 198–201) that other Labour leaders were
reported as feeling 'that Mr Callaghan gave a little too strong an
impression that a Labour Government would be so cooperative with
the unions that it would constantly be consulting them and deferring to
them about economic policy. This is not how Labour leaders see the
future', Ronald Butt, *Financial Times*, 4 October 1963.

66 *1962 LPCR*, p. 219.
67 On this committee sat Ian Mikardo, Callaghan and Wilson, and among
its co-opted members were the economists, Thomas Balogh, Nicholas
Kaldor and R. R. Nield. Most were long-standing enthusiasts for an
incomes policy. See especially Balogh's *Planning for Progress*, Fabian
Tract 346, 1963, and his 'Planning in Britain', *International Socialist
Journal*, vol. 1, no. 4, 1964, pp. 387–406.
68 Personal interviews with Len Murray, and with Tony Murray, then
secretary to the Party's Finance and Economic Policy Sub-committee.
69 Personal discussions with participants. Cf. Edelman & Fleming (n. 27
above), and *1963 TUC Report*, pp. 267, 399.
70 'To curb inflation we must have a planned growth of incomes so that
they are broadly related to the annual growth of production. To achieve
this a Labour Government will enter into urgent consultations with the
Unions and employers' organizations concerned.
    'Unlike Selwyn Lloyd's notorious "pay pause", Labour's incomes
policy will not be unfairly directed at lower paid workers and public
employees; instead it will apply in an expanding economy to *all* incomes;
to profits, dividends and rents as well as to wages and salaries.' *The New
Britain*, p. 12.
71 *The Times*, 9 July 1963.
72 Harold Wilson, Birmingham, 14 January 1964 in *The New Britain:
Labour Plan, Selected Speeches*, London 1964, pp. 9, 18–19; cf. the
speeches at Swansea (25 January 1964) and Edinburgh (21 March 1964),
pp. 28–9, 52–3; and Callaghan's TV Debate with Maudling, *The Times*,
25 February 1964. In response to the contention by the Prime Minister
that there was no difference between the Labour Party's and the Government's approach to incomes policy and his suggestion that Wilson
give more help in keeping wage demands 'within bounds', Wilson
countered indignantly: 'Is he not aware when asking for my help in
talking to the unions that last July at the conference of the Transport
and General Workers Union I made an appeal for an incomes policy?
Is he further aware that at the Labour Party conference this was passed
by an overwhelming majority, involving all the unions? Will the right
hon. Gentleman agree that it is impossible for his Government to make
these appeals?' 690 *HC Deb.* 25 February 1964, col. 235.
73 *The Times*, 13 April 1964.
74 See James Margach, *Sunday Times*, 6 October 1963.
75 *1963 TUC Report*, pp. 393ff.
76 *1964 TUC Report*, Composite Resolution 6, p. 446.
77 *The New Britain*, pp. 12–13.
78 NEC, *Working Party on Taxation*, 'Report on Taxation and Incomes
Policy', April 1964, pp. 7–8 (mimeographed).
79 *Financial Times*, 31 January 1964.
80 *1964 TUC Report*, p. 384.
81 'Time is Not on Our Side', *Socialist Commentary*, April 1964, p. 7.
82 See especially, John Boyd's reaction in the *AEU Journal*, May 1964,
p. 158, where he questioned Gunter's suitability to be Minister of
Labour.

83 Harold Wilson, *1964 TUC Report*, p. 383.
84 Harold Wilson, Swansea, 25 January 1964, *Selected Speeches* (n. 72 above), p. 19.
85 *Tribune* in the pre-1964 period was a strong supporter editorially of an incomes policy. See 'Planning and the Unions', *Tribune*, 6 September 1963.
86 *1963 LPCR*, p. 198. Cousins' approach to planning was outlined at the 1961 TUC. 'We do not endorse either the French idea or the German co-determination idea . . . Selwyn Lloyd's idea of planning was planning by advice and planning by example, not planning by directive. We said "If you are going to have planning in an orderly society there has to be a directive". You will notice when the employers endorsed his proposal they made it clear they endorsed it provided there was no compulsion.' *1961 TUC Report*, p. 385.
87 *1964 TUC Report*, p. 446.
88 *Economist*, 3 October 1964, p. 17.
89 P. Gibson, Croydon Central CLP. *1963 LPCR*, p. 195. Cf. David Marquand, 'Was Mr Gibson Right?' *New Society*, 25 December 1969, p. 1022.

CHAPTER 3
1 DEA, *Broadsheets on Britain*, no. 1, 'The Need for a Prices and Incomes Policy', June 1965.
2 See United Nations, *Incomes in Post-War Europe*, Geneva 1967, Ch. 3, pp. 2–4.
3 See esp. *Minutes of Evidence to the Royal Commission on Trade Union and Employers' Associations*, nos. 1–69, 1966 and 1967 (hereafter cited as *Minutes of Evidence*), DEA, no. 18, 25 January 1966, p. 649.
4 TUC, *Productivity, Prices and Incomes, Report of a Conference of Executive Committees of Affiliated Organizations*, 30 April 1965, pp. 32–3, (hereafter cited as *Conference of Executives*, 1965). Cf. *The Guardian*, 6 November 1964.
5 See *The Administrators*, Fabian Tract 355, 1964, esp. p. 9 and George Brown, *In My Way, The Political Memoirs of Lord George-Brown*, London 1971, pp. 95–6. An additional reason often mentioned in Labour Party and DEA circles, was that Wilson, who was against giving Brown the Foreign Office, needed to set up a position in Government for Brown equal to his position of influence in the Party.
6 See DEA *Progress Report No. 1*, January 1965.
7 DEA *Progress Report No. 1*, January 1965.
8 Brown (n. 5 above), p. 100 and S. Brittan, *Steering the Economy: The Role of the Treasury*, London 1970, p. 311.
9 *Financial Times*, 17 October 1964.
10 For the history of these developments see *British Industry*, no. 3, February 1965, p. 10; and CBI *Annual Report*, pp. 5–6.
11 H. A. Clegg, *How to Run an Incomes Policy*, London 1971, pp. 47–8.
12 See CBI, *Minutes of Evidence* (n. 3 above), First Memorandum, November 1965, and *Selected Written Evidence to the Royal Commission on Trade Union and Employers' Associations*, Para. 70, p. 264, 1968.
13 George Brown, 701 *HC Deb*. 4 November 1964, cols. 221–4. When the Government introduced an emergency package on 26 October to meet the balance of payments crisis, it resorted to an import surcharge rather than physical import quotas as the main element in the package, despite the fact that, as the Prime Minister pointed out, the latter would have incurred less criticism abroad since technically quotas were permitted in GATT and EFTA trade agreements. See Harold Wilson, 701 *HC Deb*. 3 November 1964, cols. 77–8. One Labour Minister was reported as say-

ing at the time: 'I don't think people realize . . . how vital it was from the point of view of the philosophy of a Labour Government that we used the surcharge on imports rather than quota restrictions. To win that battle so early, to avoid returning to all the business of controls, that really mattered.' Quoted in Henry Fairlie, 'Labour Learns the Facts of Life', *Sunday Telegraph*, 29 November 1964. The one member of the Cabinet who consistently opposed this approach was Frank Cousins. But, as Wilson has revealed, Cousins was battling not only against most of his Cabinet colleagues but against the Prime Minister himself. 'In the forties I had tried to maintain in being an attenuated form of wartime price controls, when President of the Board of Trade, but this had become increasingly difficult as the economy became more consumer-orientated and new lines for export were being designed daily. The view of my colleagues responsible for these matters confirmed my view of the impracticality of the idea.' (i.e. of Cousins' advocacy of a strict control on all significant prices). Harold Wilson, *The Labour Government 1964–70*, London 1971, p. 245.

14 See Andrew Shonfield, 'Labour Britain', *Listener*, 2 March 1966; Eric Moonman, *Reluctant Partnership: A Critical Study of the Relationship between Government and Industry*, London 1970; and Henry Brandon, *In the Red*, London 1966, p. 115.

15 One DEA official ventured the opinion that the CBI spent more time inside the DEA in the first ten months of Labour Government than it had spent inside Government Departments in the previous ten years.

16 John Laing, BEC president, quoted in *The Guardian*, 18 March 1965.

17 See D. Butler & D. Stokes, *Political Change in Britain*, London 1969, Chs. 4 and 5.

18 Sir Harry Douglass, *1965 TUC Report*, p. 488.

19 See Richard Rose, 'Class and Party Divisions', *Sociology*, vol. 2, no. 2, 1968, p. 431; and D. Butler & A. King, *The British General Election of 1964*, London 1965, pp. 235–7.

20 Butler & King (n. 19 above), p. 236.

21 Conversely the proportion of members of the Cabinet that were university educated rose from 30% and 37% in 1924 and 1929 respectively to 50% in 1945, to 57% in 1964 and finally to 83% in 1969, and the largest proportion of the 1964–70 Cabinets were Oxford graduates. See Rose (n. 19 above), p. 132 and Butler & Stokes (n. 17 above), pp. 153ff. Cf. Jean Bonner, 'The Four Labour Cabinets', *Sociological Review*, vol. 6, 1958, pp. 37–48.

22 Personal interview with George Woodcock; cf. *Conference of Executives*, 1965 (n. 4 above), pp. 39–40.

23 J. Corina, 'Can an Incomes Policy be Administered?', *British Journal of Industrial Relations*, vol. V, no. 3, 1967, p. 301.

24 701 *HC Deb.* 10 November 1964, col. 1043.

25 Quoted in *The Guardian*, 26 November 1964.

26 *Minutes of Evidence* (n. 3 above), no. 18, 25 January 1966, p. 674.

27 Woodcock, *Conference of Executives*, 1965 (n. 4 above), p. 35.

28 Ibid. p. 11. Cf. *Railway Review*, May 1965, p. 12.

29 710 *HC Deb.* 7 April 1965, col. 536.

30 Cmd. 2577, February 1965.

31 'I am making it plain that my desire and that of everyone who has been associated with us in this exercise, and all of those who want it to succeed, is that it should operate on a voluntary basis and that all parties on both sides of industry, as well as in Government, should be willing and ready to participate fully and to accept decisions that are made.' George Brown, introducing the White Paper, *The Guardian*, 12 Febru-

ary 1965. Cf. Harold Wilson, 708 *HC Deb.* 16 March 1965, cols. 247–8 (Written Answer).

32 In 1965, as far as the General Council was concerned, 'compulsion could not be envisaged or countenanced in relation to unions engaged in the process of collective bargaining'. *Conference of Executives*, 1965 (n. 4 above), p. 17.

33 D. A. V. Allen, Deputy Under-Secretary of State, DEA, *Minutes of Evidence* (n. 3 above), no. 18, pp. 672–3.

34 Of course from the beginning the Government was faced with the problem that these organizations might not have the power to secure compliance with the policy. This was one of the major considerations in appointing at this time the Donovan Commission to enquire into the functions of trade unions and employers associations. See DEA, *Minutes of Evidence* (n. 3 above), no. 18, p. 653. On the Donovan Commission and its relation to the incomes policy see Ch. 7 below.

35 See *Conference of Executives*, 1965 (n. 4 above), p. 9.

36 See *British Industry*, no. 1, 8 January 1965, p. 9.

37 *Conference of Executives*, 1965 (n. 4 above), p. 12.

38 'Persuasion before the Strongarm', *The Guardian*, 12 February 1965.

39 *Conference of Executives*, 1965 (n. 4 above), p. 12.

40 Cmnd. 2577, Paras. 2–4.

41 *The Guardian*, 4 February 1965.

42 Cmnd. 2639, April 1965.

43 Ibid. Paragraph 15.

44 The singular attempt by the Parliamentary Labour Party to insert itself into the early development of the policy concerned a move to strengthen this 'social justice' aspect. A private member's bill, *The Emoluments of Top Management (Disclosures and Regulations) Bill*, was moved by Peter Shore and obtained the support of 53 Labour MPs from all sections of the Party. The Bill was designed to provide for the disclosure (to a Higher Incomes Council) of the salaries and expense accounts of some 20,000 people who were at the head of quoted public companies and the larger public enterprises. The Bill was not by any reading a radical egalitarian measure: its supporters explicitly agreed that there should be high rewards for the income recipients in question, but they sought to subject these incomes to an element of public control. The Government, however, refused to support the Bill. See 703 *HC Deb.* 26 February 1965, cols. 462–874.

45 Quoted in *The Times*, 24 May 1965. Cf. Brittan (n. 8 above), p. 314.

46 It was an ironic, but endemic aspect of the incomes policy that Jones was given a salary of £15,000, which nevertheless represented for him 'a substantial financial sacrifice'. (George Brown, quoted in *The Times*, 18 March 1965). This was an increase of 20% over the salary which the Chairman of the NIC had received. Writing of the NIC, but with pointed reference to the NBPI, to which he was appointed himself in 1966, H. A. Clegg pointed out that such salaries were an additional source of dissatisfaction to the unions: 'They invited comparison with the much lower wages and salaries on which the commission would have to pronounce judgement. Thus the commission could be represented from the outset as a body of men paid large salaries to tell trade unionists (who had no intention of listening to them) that they ought not to have been granted wages increases.' 'The Lessons of the NIC', *New Society*, 11 March 1965, p. 7.

47 *The Times*, 25 March 1965. He was joined in his criticism by McGarvey of the Boilermakers and Gormley of the NUM. But in view of the General Council's endorsement of the appointment, the matter was dropped apart from a motion against it at the 1965 USDAW Conference

which was quickly crushed without a vote. *The Times*, 28 April 1965. But cf. *1965 LPCR*, p. 231.

48 See Aubrey Jones, 'The Soviet Challenge', in *Science and Society*, Eight Oxford Lectures, Conservative Political Centre 1962, pp. 30–8. Cf. Brown (n. 5 above), pp. 103–4.

49 Aubrey Jones, *Industrial Order*, Forum Books, London 1950, pp. 24–9. For the consistency with which these views were held see his *The New Inflation*, London 1973, esp. p. x.

50 Ibid. pp. 27–8, 31–2.

51 Jones, quoted in *The Times*, 20 March 1965.

52 Brown, speech to NALGO Annual Conference, *The Guardian*, 9 June 1965.

53 *TGWU Record*, February 1965.

54 *The Guardian*, 4 February 1965.

55 *Daily Worker*, 2 April 1965.

56 A Left Wing amendment to this resolution to the effect that the Government would secure trade union cooperation only by strict control of prices and profits and the absence of wage restraint was defeated by 37 votes to 14 amid executive attacks on 'Communists' who paid lip service to a Labour Government but worked against it. See *The Times*, 28 April 1965.

57 See p. 40 and p. 257, n. 108 above.

58 *Conference of Executives* (n. 4 above), pp. 21–2, 42.

59 Ibid. p. 33.

60 Quoted in *The Times*, 25 April 1965.

61 *Conference of Executives* (n. 4 above), pp. 28–30.

62 Ibid. p. 32.

63 See *The Times* and *The Guardian*, 25 March 1965.

64 TGWU officials interviewed, including those opposed to the policy, affirmed this was the case in 1965.

65 See A. J. Corfield, 'Incomes Policy', *TGWU Record*, July 1965, p. 20. It is significant that Jack Jones used the quotation again at a Fabian Meeting at the 1971 Labour Party Conference with regard to the possibility of resurrecting an incomes policy.

66 TGWU *Minutes of Evidence* (n. 3 above) no. 30, 15 March 1966, pp. 1206–7. Cf. TGWU *Our View on Incomes Policy*, 1965, p. 4.

67 Jack Jones, letter to *Socialist Commentary*, June 1967, p. 28. Cf. his 'The Low Paid Worker', *Socialist Commentary*, April 1967, pp. 15–17.

68 Ibid.

69 See Corfield (n. 65 above), p. 21.

70 Nicholas, *Conference of Executives* (n. 4 above), pp. 44–5. Cf. TGWU *Record*, 'Incomes Policy and the Profits Jungle', September 1966, pp. 5–7.

71 Woodcock, *Conference of Executives* (n. 4 above), pp. 66–7.

72 See the speeches by Jim Mortimer (DATA), pp. 40–2; Clive Jenkins (ASSET), pp. 48–9; and George Elvin (ACTAT), pp. 57–60; and Jenkins' list of 'preconditions' for supporting the policy, in *Tribune*, 30 April 1965. These unions took the forefront at the time in the campaign against the policy. They began publishing a series of pamphlets against the policy beginning with a counter-document to the Declaration of Intent, *The Declaration of Dissent* in August 1965. This was followed later in the year by a second pamphlet, *Five Unions Speak . . . In Defence of Trade Union Rights*, 1965.

73 See *The Guardian*, 30 April 1965 and the NALGO Executive Statement, quoted in *Labour Research*, June 1965, p. 91.

74 George Doughty, General Secretary of DATA, *Minutes of Evidence* (n. 3 above), no. 36, 17 May 1966, pp. 1552–3 [emphasis added]

CHAPTER 4

1 Ministry of Labour *Gazette*, May 1965, p. 245.
2 Quoted in *The Times*, 4 June 1965.
3 DEA *Progress Report*, no. 14, February 1966. Cf. Brown 716 *HC Deb.* 22 July 1965, col. 1809.
4 *Minutes of Evidence to the Royal Commission on Trade Union and Employers' Associations*, nos. 1–69, 1966 and 1967. DEA, no. 18, 25 January 1966, p. 651.
5 NUR *Minutes of Evidence*, no. 17, 18 January 1965, pp. 634–5.
6 NBPI, *General Report*, April 1965 to July 1966, Cmnd. 3087, p. 25.
7 Reported in *Sun*, 27 April 1965. Cf. George Brown, 720 *HC Deb.* 17 November 1965, cols. 1185–7.
8 DEA *Minutes of Evidence* (n. 4 above), p. 651.
9 *The Times*, 25 April 1965.
10 Ray Gunter, quoted in *The Times*, 5 June 1965.
11 Quoted in *The Times*, 5 July 1965.
12 717 *HC Deb.* 28 June 1965, col. 590.
13 717 *HC Deb.* 2 August 1965, cols. 1192–3.
14 Cmnd. 2695.
15 See NBPI, *General Report* (n. 6 above), pp. 9–10; and *Daily Telegraph*, 28 June 1965.
16 See Brown, 710 *HC Deb.* 7 April 1965, col. 536.
17 *1964 TUC Report*, p. 383.
18 717 *HC Deb.* 27 July 1965, cols. 228–41.
19 See Harold Wilson, *The Labour Government, 1964–70*, London 1971, pp. 131–2; Brandon, *In The Red: The Struggle for Sterling, 1964–66*, London 1966, pp. 85ff; and the interview with Aubrey Jones in *The Banker*, August 1966, p. 515. At the time this aspect of the Government's discussions with the US Treasury remained a carefully guarded secret. They were first revealed in *The Economist*, 18 December 1965, p. 1300. I have been able to confirm this picture from personal interviews with members of the Cabinet at the time.
20 The following account of this meeting is based on a number of sources: personal interviews with some of the participants; *1965 TUC Report*, pp. 465–73 and 564–7; *Observer*, 'Black Days at Brighton', 12 September, 1965; *Sunday Times*, 'Brass Tacks at Brighton', 5 September 1965; *The Times*, 3 September 1965; Wilson (n. 19 above), pp. 132–3; and Brandon (n. 19 above), pp. 102–8.
21 *1965 TUC Report*, p. 469.
22 *The Times*, 4 September 1965.
23 *1965 TUC Report*, p. 468.
24 These tactics allowed the Woodworkers, for instance, to support the incomes policy and the General Council's Supplementary Report since the resolution at their own conference, which had repudiated their executive's support for the policy, had merely 'opposed all forms of wage restraint, where prices and profits were allowed to rise'. See *The Woodworkers Journal*, July 1965, pp. 139–40 and October 1965, pp. 147–8; and the speech by J. Marshall, *1965 TUC Report*, pp. 480–1: 'It is time that some of us in this hall realized where our loyalties really lie.'
25 *Observer*, 12 September 1965.
26 See *1965 LPCR*, p. 238. Cf. *The Times*, 30 September 1965; for Carron's repudiation of the AEU vote see *The Times*, 12, 13 October 1965.
27 *1965 LPCR*, pp. 229–31, 247; and the exchange of letters between the movers of the motion and the NEC, published in *Tribune*, 14 January 1966, where the NEC made clear this distinction. The NEC at this time

endorsed the Government's approach to incomes policy, the main exceptions being Jack Jones and Ian Mikardo. When the NEC met with the Cabinet at Chequers to discuss the Labour programme before the 1966 election, only Jones raised the matter of the proposed legislation, and not more than a few minutes was devoted to it in the course of a whole day's discussion. See *The Times*, 7 February 1966.

28 *Prices and Incomes Policy: An 'Early Warning' System*, Cmnd. 2808. Unlike the earlier White Papers, this one did not indicate TUC and CBI agreement, but only that the document had been drawn up in discussions with these organizations.

29 John Davies, CBI *Minutes of Evidence* (n. 4 above) no. 6, 23 November 1965, pp. 323–3.

30 *The Times*, 21 October 1964.

31 *The Times*, 12 November 1965.

32 *1965 TUC Report*, pp. 313–15, 457. Unlike the notification system to the Government via the CBI, the TUC scheme did not exclude claims covering fewer than 1,000 workers on the grounds that this might be prejudicial to lower paid workers. Of the first 500 claims notified to the TUC, over half were concerned with less than 1,000 workers. Nevertheless three-fifths of the $5\frac{1}{2}$ million workers involved in total were covered by 3% of the claims.

33 By December, the TGWU had notified 75 claims, by July, 280. There are various interpretations adduced to explain this cooperation. Many of the Government's incomes policy advisors believed the TGWU was attempting to 'sabotage' the Committee by flooding it with claims. (See *The Times*, 21 October 1965). A diametrically opposed explanation has been offered by Tony Cliff – that the TGWU notifications indicated how even 'Left' union leaders 'are trapped completely by procedure'. See *The Employers' Offensive*, London 1970, p. 187, n. 47. Both of these interpretations are wide of the mark. The problem for the policy was not too many notifications, which gave the TUC a 'bank' of information on wage bargaining it never before had, but to get unions to accept TUC advice. The Committee would have preferred others unions, who supported the policy, to be so punctilious in their notifications. Nor did the submission of claims itself indicate that the TGWU's opposition was mere rhetoric, any more than the AEU's very few notifications prove that Carron was not 'trapped by procedure'. Certainly an important factor was that both Nicholas and Ellen McCullough (then Head of Research in the union and responsible for notifications) were strong Labour Party loyalists and were showing their desire to help the Government in this way. But the main consideration was that cooperation gave the union a number of tactical advantages, while not interfering with the prosecution of claims. Certain TGWU Regions – especially London – were very loyal to the Government and expected their claims to be notified. By doing so, the union leadership was able to soften some of their criticisms of union policy. Also, by notifying so many claims, the union was able to argue both to their own members and other unions that it was pursuing actively its members' interests. Finally, it allowed the TGWU to claim that many of the unions who supported the policy were being hypocritical in not submitting many claims while the TGWU accepted the democratic decision of the majority. This was an important tactical consideration at a time when the TGWU was very isolated from the other large unions in opposing the incomes policy. It reasoned that it had a better chance of converting other unions to its position if it played by the TUC rules while continuing to pursue its wage claims. Similar considerations led ASSET and DATA to submit most of their claims to the Committee.

34 See *1965 TUC Report*, p. 313; and *The Times*, 20 January 1966.

35 *The Times*, 7 January 1966.

36 H. A. Turner, 'The Progress of Incomes Policy'. *Progress, The Unilever Quarterly*, vol. 52, no. 292, 2/1967, pp. 38–9.

37 Woodcock claimed in the summer of 1966 that the restraining effect of the TUC's scheme had amounted to $2\frac{1}{2}$–$3\frac{1}{2}\%$ on national claims, but this is extremely suspect. This figure was not based on any analysis of claims and settlements by the Incomes Policy Secretariat. and the Head of the Secretariat from 1965 to 1968, Les Allen, believed that the effect of the TUC alone on the level of claims was 'negligible'. Personal interviews with Les Allen and George Woodcock.

38 See D. A. V. Allen, DEA *Minutes of Evidence* (n. 4 above), pp. 657–8.

39 The Board itself was least happy about this kind of reference; it most emphatically did not want its role to be one of conciliation and arbitration. See *Wages in the Bakery Industry (Interim)*, Report No. 9, Cmnd. 2878, 1966, p. 3.

40 Allen (n. 38 above). The one case of a union refusing to cooperate with a reference was that of the TGWU in the busmen's reference in March 1966.

41 *The Times*, 5 May 1965.

42 *The Times*, 5 May 1965.

43 NBPI, *General Report* (n. 6 above), p. 19.

44 NBPI, *Official Handbook*, June 1968, p. 3. Cf. Aubrey Jones, 'The National Board for Prices and Incomes', *Political Quarterly*, vol. 39, no. 2.

45 See Report no. 8, *Pay and Conditions of Service of British Railways Staff*, Cmnd. 2873, January 1966; and Report no. 9, *Wages in the Bakery Industry*, (Interim) Cmnd. 2878, January 1966.

46 See in this regard Allan Fels, *The British Prices and Incomes Board*, Cambridge 1972, esp. pp. 107–23.

47 Wilson, *The Labour Government* (n. 19 above), p. 199.

48 DEA submission to NBPI, quoted in internal NBPI 'Steering Brief on the Industrial Civil Servants reference', 26 November 1965, pp. 11–12. (Unpublished, in the possession of the NGA).

49 Report no. 11, *Pay of the Higher Civil Service*, January 1966, Cmnd. 2882.

50 Report no. 3, *Prices of Bread and Flour*, September 1965, Cmnd. 2760.

51 Bakers' Union Executive Resolution, quoted in V. L. Allen, *Militant Trade Unionism*, London 1966, p. 130.

52 Report no. 3 (n. 50 above), p. 11. Cf. *Labour Research*, November 1965.

53 Report no. 17, *Wages in the Bakery Industry*, June 1966, Cmnd. 3019, p. 20.

54 Fels (n. 46 above), pp. 224–5. The TUC had no influence on the Board decisions in this respect: the Board refused to show draft reports to the TUC until the day before publication, and Aubrey Jones was careful to ensure that the Board remained at arms length from the TUC even with regard to the appointment of trade unionists to Board panels.

55 *General Report* (n. 6 above), p. 10.

56 The only modifications were to bring forward the introduction of the 40 hour week and the $3\frac{1}{2}\%$ increase by one month to March and September 1966 respectively. See the accounts in *Railway Review*, January and February 1966, V. L. Allen (n. 51 above), pp. 27–9 and Wilson (n. 19 above), pp. 208–11. This case is a good example of how the incomes policy served to induce wage restraint by delaying settlements apart from its effects on reducing their size. The NUR had experienced only an $8\frac{1}{2}$ month delay in respect of their 1964 claim between the time the written claim was presented and when the pay-award was made. This

time, the claim was presented in April 1965, and after the reference to the Board and negotiations with the Government, they accepted a delay of the pay award until September 1966, an interval of 16 months. The wage freeze of July 1966 then further delayed the increase for another six months. I am indebted to John Corina for first drawing this to my attention.

57 Wilson (n. 19 above), p. 208.

58 Ministry of Labour Letter to NBPI, 26 October 1965, in NBPI internal memoranda in the possession of the NGA.

59 Wilson had formulated his election strategy a month earlier. See Wilson (n. 19 above), p. 215.

60 This had particularly been the case at the AEU delegation meeting at the Labour Party Conference where no less than three AEU sponsored MPs, Fred Lee, Austen Albu, and Charles Pannell, together with the AEU member of the Labour Party NEC, John Boyd, appealed to the delegation to give its support to the incomes policy. See *The Times*, 30 September 1965.

61 When Foot spoke on economic affairs at the 1965 conference, he concentrated on the need for steel nationalization, but did not mention at all the incomes policy or the legislation. In contrast, Stan Orme focused exclusively on an attack on the proposed legislation. In a personal interview, Foot explained that it was Cousins' resignation which influenced him to oppose the incomes bill when it was finally introduced in early July 1966, and that it was the wage freeze later that month which finally convinced him to oppose the incomes policy. On Dickens' support of the legislation at first, see Eric Heffer, *The Class Struggle in Parliament*, London 1973, p. 285. Dickens and Foot were in fact close to the views expressed at the time by John Hughes and Ken Alexander: 'The TUC anxiously debated the Government's intention to legislate for advance notice of wage claims and price increases. But we welcome this development: had the Government accepted the need for "teeth" earlier, the incomes policy would be more securely established now.' 'Prices and Incomes', *Tribune*, 10 December 1965. The division inside the Labour Left was seen when Royden Harrison and Michael Barratt Brown, who together with Hughes and Alexander had earlier published articles in *Tribune* urging the Left to support the policy (see particularly Harrison's 'What divides the Left on Incomes Policy?' *Tribune*, 28 May 1965), parted company with Hughes and Alexander at the end of 1965, and accused them of discrediting 'Socialist incomes strategy by failing to distinguish it from present government policy'. *Tribune*, 14 January 1966. Richard Clements, *Tribune*'s Editor, had earlier reflected some of the TGWU's criticisms of the policy (see 'How Private Industry Sabotages the Nation', 28 May 1965) but it was not until the turn of the year that the paper editorially opposed the legislation. See 'How the Union Leadership Has Let Down the Rank and File', 31 December 1965.

62 Personal interviews with Short, Orme, Atkinson, and Foot. At the time this was not revealed publicly except for an obscure allusion to the incident by Ian Mikardo in *Tribune*, 8 October 1965. Cf. Butler & Pinto-Duschinsky, *The British General Election of 1970*, London 1971, p. 4, and Heffer (n. 61 above), pp. 53–4.

63 See Wilson (n. 19 above), p. 199, where Wilson makes the election timing in this regard perfectly clear. Cf. Brandon (n. 19 above), p. 118.

64 See *Economist*, 18 December 1965, p. 1300.

65 *Prices and Incomes Bill*, Bill 77, *Parliamentary Papers*, 1965–6, vol. II, para. 14(4), p. 15.

66 *The Times*, 11 March 1966.

67 712 *HC Deb.* 11 May 1965, col. 285

68 *The Times*, 9 July 1965. At the Labour Party Conference he astonished some of his fellow Ministers by sitting with the TGWU delegation on the floor of the hall.
69 See 'The Trade-Union Tycoon at Westminster', *The Times*, 14 February 1966; and *TGWU Record*, July 1965, pp. 5–6.
70 See Wilson (n. 19 above), p. 245.
71 *The Times*, 3 March 1966.
72 When the Bill was reintroduced in July, he wrote to Wilson: 'Just before the General Election you gave me to understand that you would help to break down the shibboleth of a belief that what we needed to secure economic recovery was sufficient power in the hands of the Government to compel the unions to accept without question the decisions of the Board for Prices and Incomes. Unfortunately, you did not maintain that view.' Quoted in Margaret Stewart, *Frank Cousins, A Study*, London 1968, p. 141. Although Wilson maintains that he gave him 'the chance gracefully to withdraw at the time of the election' (Wilson (n. 19 above), p. 245), a number of Cousins' associates with whom I have spoken have confirmed Cousins' belief that the legislation would not be reintroduced. Indeed, Wilson at the time sent a draft of the Election Manifesto to Stanley Orme, drawing his attention to the fact that it did not contain a reference to statutory controls on wages.
73 *Time For Decision*, p. 7.
74 Quoted in *The Guardian*, 11 March 1966.

CHAPTER 5
1 Address to Delegates, *69th Annual Congress*, Aberdeen, 22 April 1966, p. 12.
2 David C. Smith, 'Incomes Policy' in R. Caves and Associates, *Britain's Economic Prospects*, London and Washington 1968, p. 133. Cf. R. S. Bodkin, *et al. Price Stability and High Employment: The Options for Canadian Economic Policy, an Econometrics Study*, Special Study, no. 5, Economic Council of Canada, Ottawa 1967 and DEP, *Prices and Earnings in 1951–69; an Econometric Assessment*, HMSO, May 1971.
3 See NEDC, *Productivity, Prices and Incomes, A General Review*, 1966, p. 33ff and Michael Artis, 'Fiscal Policy for Stabilization', in Beckerman, *The Labour Government's Economic Record 1964–70*, London 1972, p. 298, Table 8.11.
4 Joan Mitchell, 'Why We Need a Prices Policy', *Lloyd's Bank Review*, April 1969, p. 14. Cf. NBPI, *Second General Report*, August 1967, Cmnd. 3394, pp. 20–1.
5 See *The Seaman*, Special Edition, no. 1, 20 May 1966, p. 3. Cf. *The Seaman*, May 1966, pp. 81–3, and August 1966, pp. 107–8. The best account of the 1966 Seamen's strike is Paul Foot, 'The Seamen's Struggle' in R. Blackburn and A. Cockburn, *The Incompatibles: Trade Union Militancy and the Consensus*, London 1967, pp. 169–209.
6 See esp. Wilson, 731 *HC Deb*. 14 July 1966, col. 1733.
7 Quoted in Wilson, *The Labour Government 1964–70*, London 1971, p. 230; and Foot, 'Seamen's Struggle' (n. 5 above), p. 187.
8 729 *HC Deb*. 14 June 1966, cols. 1243–7, and *1966 TUC Report*, p. 127.
9 730 *HC Deb*. 20 June 1966, cols. 1612–17.
10 730 *HC Deb*. 28 June 1966, col. 1616.
11 *The Seaman*, Special Edition, no. 7, July 1966.
12 Wilson (n. 7 above), pp. 240–1
13 *The Seaman*, Special Edition, no. 7, July 1966 and December 1966, p. 183.
14 Gallup Political Index and Social Surveys (Gallup Polls) Ltd. files.
15 *The Guardian*, 26 June 1966.
16 Quoted in *Tribune*, 8 July 1966 and *The Times*, 20 October 1967.

17 *1966 TUC Report*, p. 124.
18 The General Council concentrated in its consultations with the Government mainly on altering certain details so that the legislation would be as 'inoffensive to trade unionists' as possible. See *1966 TUC Report*, p. 439. The only changes of significance from the February Bill were: (*a*) that the TUC was allowed to assume liability for notifying those claims submitted to its Incomes Policy Committee; and (*b*) that the Government was empowered to make standing references to the NBPI and thus keep certain cases under continuous review. An additional change was that dividends (which had increased by three times as much as hourly earnings in 1965) were now included in the early warning system. Although clearly designed to mollify the unions, this was little more than a symbolic gesture since a penalty of only £50 was provided for failure to notify, and since the rules of the stock exchange already required immediate disclosure of companies' dividend decisions.
19 *The Times*, 4 July 1966, reprinted in Stewart, *Frank Cousins, A Study*, London 1968, pp. 140–3.
20 731 *HC Deb.* 14 July 1966, cols. 1789–94.
21 Editorial, 'Mr Cousins' Departure', 4 July 1966.
22 Of the 363 Labour MPs elected in 1966, 132 were trade union sponsored. For a complete list of the signatories see *The Times*, 14 July 1966.
23 See NUM *Annual Conference Report*, Scarborough 1966, Resolution 30; and *The Times*, 7 July 1966.
24 My understanding of these events has been enhanced by my interviews with some of the participants and by conversations with Peter Jenkins who interviewed most of the participants at the time. The best account of the 1966 crisis is Brittan, *Steering The Economy, The Role of the Treasury*, London 1970, pp. 329–39. But also see Insight, 'How the Bubble Burst', *The Sunday Times*, 24 July 1966; William Davis, *Three Years Hard Labour*, London 1968, pp. 83–95; D. Butler & M. Pinto-Duschinsky, *The British General Election of 1970*, London 1971, pp. 8–13; and R. Williams (ed.), *May Day Manifesto*, London 1968.
25 See Wilson, *Labour Government* (n. 7 above), pp. 249–61.
26 *Sunday Times*, 3 July 1966. The idea of a wage freeze had never been ruled out in principle by the Government in the sense that devaluation had. It had been raised as a planning option inside the Treasury in September 1965, and again in May 1966 when the Treasury began to have doubts that the deflationary measures of the Budget were adequate. The DEA opposed the idea of a wage freeze and in any case it had not been very actively considered and was not discussed by the Cabinet. In June 1966 the idea had begun to gain some currency publicly as a policy alternative, and *The Sunday Times* of 3 July featured an Opinion Research Centre poll which listed a wage freeze 'for a year or so' among a group of possible 'sacrifice measures' which might have helped to put 'this country on its feet', and found that 69% said they would accept a freeze in this context.
27 See F. W. Paish, 'The Limits of Incomes Policies', Part I of Paish & J. Hennessy, *Policy for Incomes?*, Institute for Economic Affairs, 1968, esp. p. 23ff. After the freeze was announced, Callaghan, while at The Hague for a Group of Ten finance ministers and central bankers meeting, said that a successful wage freeze was not necessary to restore balance of payments equilibrium since the deflationary tax and credit measures would themselves bring this about. The freeze would only 'give us something over the top toward our objective'. *New York Times*, 26 July 1966, p. 43.
28 See 723 *HC Deb.* 20 July 1966, cols. 627–38.
29 See George Brown, *In My Way, The Political Memoirs of Lord George-Brown*, London 1971, pp. 115–16.

30 *The Times*, 21 July 1966.
31 See the Solicitor-General, *HC Official Report*, Standing Committee B, Session 1966–7, vol. III, Prices and Incomes Bill, 4 August 1966, cols. 725–8.
32 *Prices and Incomes Standstill*, Cmnd. 3073. For the full text of, and a narrative guide to, the legislation, see W. Sergeant & E. Roydhouse, *Prices and Wages Freeze*, London 1966.
33 See Anthony Howard, 'How Walter Mitty Joined the Bulldog Breed', *Observer*, 31 July 1966.
34 See 733 *HC Deb*. 3 August 1966, cols. 492–610.
35 See Ministry of Labour *Statistics on Incomes, Prices, Employment and Production*, no. 24, March 1968, Table E.5, p. 77.
36 General Council Statement, 27 July 1966, *1966 TUC Report*, p. 325.
37 See Brown, *HC Official Report* (n. 31 above), 4 August 1966, cols. 457–8, and 733 *HC Deb*. 10 August 1966, cols. 1831–2.
38 Personal interview with Michael Stewart.
39 See Robert McKenzie, 'Laying the Socialist Ghost', *Observer*, 30 July 1966, and William Rees-Mogg, 'Let Us Face the Future', *Sunday Times*, 5 August 1966.
40 See *Observer*, 24 July 1966.
41 For the text of the Statement see *Tribune*, 29 July 1966. This alternative policy was further elaborated when a working committee of six university economists and 21 MPs published the pamphlet, *Beyond the Freeze, a Socialist Policy for Economic Growth*, in September 1966. The pamphlet accepted an incomes policy which it recognized 'inevitably involves the abrogation of bargaining power by the organized labour movement', on the conditions that there be a system of socialist economic planning including an increase in the rights of workers to run their own industries.
42 The figures are based on reports and lists published in *The Times* and *The Guardian*, the day following the vote, and checked against the division lists in Hansard.
43 See 732 *HC Deb*. 20 July 1966, col. 640.
44 See 733 *HC Deb*. 9 August 1966, cols. 1550–1665.
45 *HC Official Report* (n. 31 above), col. 331.
46 John Biffin, ibid. col. 44.
47 Ibid. cols. 1381–2.
48 Ibid. cols. 149–50.
49 733 *HC Deb*. 9 August 1966, col. 1606.
50 See the report of his speech to the Tribune Group, *Financial Times*, 9 August 1966.
51 General Council Statement in *1966 TUC Report*, p. 326.
52 See Peter Jenkins, 'TUC learn little from Chancellor', *The Guardian*, 19 July 1966 and *1966 TUC Report*, p. 307. The TUC did not counsel devaluation.
53 *1966 TUC Report*, pp. 321–3.
54 Ibid. p. 459.
55 Ibid. p. 326; 'The Wage Freeze: Woodcock's Role', *Tribune*, 12 August 1966; and personal interview with George Woodcock.
56 *The Times, The Guardian*, 28 July 1966.
57 *1966 TUC Report*, pp. 325–6.
58 Ibid. pp. 322, 261–2.
59 Ibid. p. 326.
60 732 *HC Deb*. 27 July 1966, col. 1852 [emphasis added] The CBI had, in fact, reacted more cautiously. Although its first response on 20 July was that the Government was finally 'grasping the nettle', it refrained from endorsing the freeze until 3 August after it had received assurances that

there was likely to be a 'reasonable construction' of the price rules by the Government. See *The Times*, 21 July 1966; *Financial Times*, 26 August 1966 and *CBI, 1966 Annual Report*, p. 12.

61 On 20 July, Cousins had announced that his union would not take official strike action, although it would not discourage unofficial action. The major strikes during the freeze period were mainly associated with redundancies caused by the deflation, particularly in the car industry. In general, the few strikes that occurred against pay being frozen were unofficial and small. Working days lost in stoppages fell from 1,788,000 in the first half of 1966, to 612,000 in the second half. In the first half of 1967 the figure rose again to just over 1 million, but the number of days lost over the full twelve months of freeze and severe restraint (1,678,000 from July 1966 to June 1967) was considerably less than over the previous twelve months (2,703,000 from July 1965 to June 1966). Ministry of Labour *Gazette*, August 1967, Table 133, p. 701.

62 *Railway Review*, 30 September 1966.

63 See *Sunday Times*, 4 September 1966, and *The Guardian*, 5 September 1966.

64 See Insight, 'Cashing the Last Reserves of the old Labour Loyalty', *Sunday Times*, 4 September 1966. Cf. *AEU Journal*, August 1966, p. 317; and Ken Coates, 'The State of the AEU' in *The Crisis of British Socialism*, Nottingham 1970, esp. p. 170. Subsequently, the AEU's Final Appeal Court, considering appeals from four branches against Carron's action, found that the executive had been wrong to usurp the voting rights of the union delegation and should also have recalled the National Committee. However, since the Appeal Court did not meet until mid October, these rulings had no effect on AEU voting at either the TUC or the Labour Party Conference. A more immediate remedy was tried by branch officials of the GMWU and NUM; they sought High Court injunctions restraining the leaders of the unions from casting their votes in favour of the freeze at the TUC. On 7 September, the day of the TUC vote, the Court rejected the GMWU application and postponed the NUM case, but in any event the ruling was made after the Congress vote on the freeze had already taken place.

65 *1966 TUC Report*, pp. 475–84. The discrepancy between the two votes was mainly the result of the ETU's decision to cast its votes both against the TGWU motion and the Report on the grounds that the ETU supported the legislation in principle, but could not endorse a policy which held up agreements made before the freeze, particularly its own 3-year agreement in electrical contracting. Cf. *The Times*, 8 September 1966, and *The Electron*, December 1966, p. 244.

66 *1966 TUC Report*, pp. 466–7, 474–5, and *Sunday Times*, 4 September 1965.

67 *1966 TUC Report*, pp. 476–7; *Tribune*, 9 September 1966; and USDAW's *The New Dawn*, vol. 20, no. 20, 24 September 1966, p. 617.

68 Quoted by Matthew Coady, 'Brothers Grim at Blackpool', *New Statesman*, 9 September 1966, p. 338.

69 See Clive Jenkins, 'Trade Unionists and the Wage Freeze', *Tribune*, 29 July 1966. For the union's general criticism of the 20 July measures see ACTAT *et al.*, *The Bad Package, or how the Government sticks to its guns – almost everywhere*, London 1966. ASSET was in a better position to challenge the freeze in this way than most unions in that a high proportion of its members had individual contracts of service with their employers.

70 Sources: personal interviews with Clive Jenkins, Russell Kerr, MP, and Ian Mikardo, MP. In the event only one junior Minister, David Ennals, publicly resigned from the union. See *Tribune*, 9 September 1966.

71 See *Financial Times*, 30 September 1966, *The Times*, 2 October 1966, and 737 *HC Deb.* 5 December 1966, cols. 1081–1192, 399–400.

72 Personal interviews with Michael Stewart and Les Allen. Cf. Stewart, 748 *HC Deb.* 13 June 1967, col. 335; and *1967 TUC Report*, p. 321.

73 *1966 TUC Report*, p. 395–8 [emphasis added]. Bevan, however, had not called for disciplining, but for a closer attunement by the political leadership to the problems of the rank and file. See above, Ch. 2, pp. 54–5.

74 *Daily Telegraph*, 12 September 1966, and *Tribune*, 16 September 1966.

75 'Labour's New Opportunity', *New Statesman*, 9 September 1966, p. 337. Cf. 'What Frank Should Have Said', *New Statesman*, 8 July 1966.

76 'How Labour blundered into Socialism', *New Statesman*, 16 September 1966, p. 378, and 'From Freeze to Socialism', *New Statesman*, 21 October 1966, pp. 73–5.

77 *Tribune*, 16 September 1966.

78 733 *HC Deb.* 9 August 1966, col. 1605.

79 *1966 TUC Report*, p. 464.

80 See Ian Mikardo, 'Fairy Stories about Labour's wage planning', and Eric Heffer, 'Trade Unions, Socialism and Freedom', *Tribune*, 30 September 1966. Mikardo was responding to the use of *Keep Left* quotations by Crossman and Paul Johnson, the editor of the *New Statesman*, to buttress their case. Heffer defended his position by quoting from a speech by Lenin on 30 December 1920, where Lenin described the Soviet State as 'a workers state with bureaucratic distortions' : 'Our present state is such that the entirely organized proletariat must protect itself and we must utilize those workers organizations for the purpose of protecting the workers from their own state, and in order that the workers may protect our state.'

81 *Tribune*, 16 and 23 September 1966.

82 'The Unfinished Argument', *Socialist Commentary*, October 1966, pp. 3–4.

83 At the NEC meeting of 27 July, Jack Jones and two right wing trade union leaders, Boyd and Chapple, had criticized the Government's measures, but the NEC had supported the Government even to the extent of defeating Jones' proposal that the press statement after the meeting indicate that some concern had been expressed. See *The Times*, 28 July 1966.

84 *1966 LPCR*, Appendix I, p. 298.

85 Ibid. pp. 211, 244.

86 For the exact voting figures on the long and complex list of resolutions see ibid. p. 248.

87 Ibid. p. 251.

88 Ibid. pp. 255–73. The AEU vote was also cast for a resolution against Government support of American policy on Vietnam and this motion was also passed by 3,851,000 to 2,644,000. This account of the AEU's voting behaviour is based on the following sources : 'How the Left Could Fight Again', *Sunday Times*, 9 October 1966; *Financial Times*, 6 October 1966; Coates (n. 64 above), pp. 171–2; and personal interviews with Ernie Roberts, Assistant General Secretary, AEU and Lewis Minkin of Manchester University who has conducted a study of voting behaviour for his forthcoming major work on the Labour Party Conference.

89 Quoted in *Financial Times*, 7 October 1966. For the general principles involved see Robert McKenzie, *British Political Parties*, 2nd edn, London 1963, pp. 485–6, 510ff and Ralph Miliband, 'Party Democracy and Parliamentary Government', *Political Studies*, vol. 2, 1958, pp. 170–4.

90 *The Guardian*, 29 August 1966.

91 734 *HC Deb.* 25 October 1966, cols. 907–8.

92 Ibid. cols. 965–7; *The Times* and *The Guardian*, 26 October 1966.
93 A resolution to this effect was endorsed by the PLP on 2 November 1966. See *Observer*, 30 October 1966, and *The Times*, 3 November 1966.
94 *Tribune*, 4 November 1966.
95 Andrew Roth, *Parliamentary Profiles*, 27 October 1966.
96 *Tribune*, 28 October 1966.
97 For the debates and division lists see the relevant entries in 737–46 *HC Deb.* 5 December 1966 to 3 May 1967.
98 Personal interview with Les Allen; See Stephen Fay, 'Secret TUC Share in Pay Control', *Sunday Times*, 11 June 1967; Michael Stewart, 748 *HC Deb.* 13 June 1967, col. 335, and Fred Lee, 751 *HC Deb.* 24 July 1967, Written Answers, cols. 61–2.
99 See NBPI, *Second General Report* (n. 4 above), p. 23.
100 Stephen Brown, CBI, *1966 Annual Report*, pp. 5, 13.
101 NEDC, *1966 General Review*, pp. 3, 22–6, and *1967 General Review*, p. 11.
102 *1966 TUC Report*, p. 398.
103 See D. Robinson, 'Low Paid Workers and Incomes Policy', *Bulletin of the Oxford University Institute of Economics and Statistics*, vol. 29, no. 1, 1967, esp. pp. 8 and 25; and Ronald Butt, 'Social Policy and Wage Structure', *Financial Times*, 2 December 1966.
104 *1967 TUC Report*, p. 138. The General Council deliberately decided at this stage not to define 'lowest-paid' workers in any precise terms, although later, in April 1967, it did finally endorse the £15 minimum.
105 See Peter Jenkins, 'Union right to bargain . . .', *The Guardian*, 19 September 1966; Bernard Ingham, 'TUC says own body could vet wages', *The Guardian*, 29 September 1966; and Samuel Brittan, 'What Will Happen After the Freeze?', *Financial Times*, 3 October 1966. I have been able to confirm the above account in an interview with Michael Stewart. At the time these discussions were in progress, Aubrey Jones suggested to the Donovan Commission that a similar committee should be set up to legitimate the use of Government compulsory powers based on NBPI judgements. But while arguing that this would 'underpin the legal powers' he admitted that the Government would retain the final power of decision. *Minutes of Evidence*, NBPI, no. 51, 4 October 1966, pp. 2189–2204.
106 Ian Coulter, 'TUC: 3-Way Plan breaks down', *Sunday Times*, 27 November 1966. Another was reported to have said: 'It's the Government's document. Let them get on with it. Let them stew in their own juice.' Quoted in *Financial Times*, 18 November 1966.
107 *Prices and Incomes Standstill: Period of Severe Restraint*, Cmnd. 3150.
108 *1967 TUC Report*, pp. 319–25.
109 'The Board cannot hope to execute the policy alone. It is in a sense the final court needing screening procedures in advance of it. The preliminary screening bodies are two: the TUC Vetting Committee and the various Government Departments.' *Second General Report* (n. 4 above), p. 20. Cf. Stephen Fay, 'How the TUC's Vetting system has worked', *Sunday Times*, 25 June 1967.
    Beginning in January 1967, monthly meetings between Woodcock, Stewart, Aubrey Jones and John Davies of the CBI were held to discuss which cases should be referred to the Board. See *Financial Times* and *The Guardian*, 11 January 1967.
110 NBPI Reports, no. 25, *Pay of Workers in Agriculture in England and Wales*, Cmnd. 3199, January 1967, and no. 27, *Pay of Workers in Retail Drapery, Outfitting and Footwear Trades*, Cmnd. 3224, March 1967.
111 NBPI Report, no. 29, *The Pay and Conditions of Manual Workers in Local Authorities, the National Health Service, Gas and Water Supply*,

Cmnd. 3230, March 1967, p. 32 [emphasis added]. Although the Board's proposals for productivity and incentive schemes were wide ranging and welcomed by the unions, the Board itself had criticized the standards of management in these services, and in fact by 1971, four years later, only one-third of full-time local authority workers were on any form of incentive schewe. See *TGWU Record*, June 1971, p. 14 and TGWU, *Local Authorities Manual Workers Wages Application*, July 1971, p. 11.

112 H. A. Clegg, *How to Run an Incomes Policy and why we made such a mess of the last one*, London 1971, p. 29. On the various and conflicting standards used by the Government, see Roy Hattersley, 743 *HC Deb.* 15 March 1967, col. 644, and 744 *HC Deb.* 4 April 1967, Written Answers, col. 30.

113 Minutes of NBPI Meetings, 2 and 6 March 1967 and Memorandum from A. A. Jarratt, Secretary to the Board, to Aubrey Jones, 1 March 1967, in possession of the NGA. Cf. Report, no. 29 (n. 111 above), pp. 40–1.

114 NBPI Report, no. 23, *Productivity and Pay During the Period of Severe Restraint*, Cmnd. 3167. The one significant modification to these guidelines made by the Board in its final report in June 1967 was that such agreements did not need to reduce prices but only contribute to stable prices. See NBPI Report, no. 36, *Productivity Agreements*, Cmnd. 3311, June 1967.

115 *The Times*, 22 December 1966. Cf. David Basnett (then National Industrial Officer, GMWU), 'Productivity Bargaining', *Socialist Commentary*, May 1967, pp. 13–15.

116 NBPI Report, no. 24, *Wages and Conditions in the Electrical Contracting Industry*, Cmnd. 3172, paras. 15–21 and Appendix B. Cf. NBPI Report, no. 120, *Pay and Conditions in the Electrical Contracting Industry*, Cmnd. 4097, June 1969, para. 24; ETU, *Further Submission to the Royal Commission on Trade Unions and Employers Associations*, 24 January 1967 and *Memorandum by ETU and NFEA to NBPI*, 11 August 1966 (unpublished, in the possession of the NGA).

117 National Federated Electrical Association, *64th Annual Report*, 1965, pp. 10–11.

118 Clegg (n. 112 above), pp. 36–7.

119 Ibid.

120 Report no. 24 (n. 116 above), para. 47.

121 National Incomes Commission, *Report on Agreements of February–March 1963 in Electrical Contracting*, Cmnd. 2098, July 1963, paras. 183–5.

122 NBPI, *Steering Brief*, Annex C, 4 August 1966, pp. 22–3 (unpublished, in the possession of the NGA).

123 NBPI Reports, no. 26, *Prices of Standard Newsprint*, Cmnd. 3210, February 1967; no. 23, *Prices of Compound Fertilizer*, Cmnd. 3288, March 1967; no. 33, *The Remuneration of Milk Distributors (Interim)*, Cmnd. 3244, March 1967. Insofar as the Board did attempt to keep profits down in this period, it was with regard to financial institutions, see Report no. 34, *Bank Charges*, Cmnd. 3292, May 1967.

124 *Second General Report* (n. 4 above), p. 7.

125 See NEDC 1967 *General Review*, pp. 32–5.

126 I am indebted to the Department of Trade and Industry for supplying this information.

127 747–8 *HC Deb.* 13 June 1967, Written Answers, cols. 267–84, 405–6.

128 DEA, *Broadsheets on Britain*, no. 2, July 1965.

129 NEDC *1967 General Review*, Table 4, p. 11, cf. Appendix 3 below.

130 *Second General Report* (n. 4 above), p. 6.

131 NEDC *1967 General Review*, p. 12.

132 *Second General Report* (n. 4 above), p. 6.

133 Source: Gallup Political Index and Social Surveys (Gallup Polls) Ltd. Cf. Appendix 1 below.

134 *Allen v. Thorn Electrical Industries Ltd; Griffin v. Receiver for the Metropolitan Police District, Court of Appeals, Civil Division (Lord Denning MR) June 12, 13, 14/1967/2 All ER*, pp. 1137–45.

135 Editorial, 'Faults of Drafting', *The Times*, 15 June 1967. The 1967 Prices and Incomes Act closed the loophole, but only had effect on legal proceedings started after 5 June 1967.

136 *The Guardian*, 12 July 1967. For the full speech see *TGWU Record*, September 1967, pp. 1–23.

137 *Employment and Productivity Gazette*, November 1970, Table 2, p. 1024; *Ministry of Labour Gazette*, December 1960, p. 42 and November 1950, p. 366; and TUC *Annual Reports*. I am indebted to George Bain of Warwick University for supplying me with his compilations of trade union membership statistics.

138 TUC, *Incomes Policy, Report of a Conference of Executive Committees*, 2 March 1967, p. 17 hereafter cited as *Conference of Executives, 1967*.

139 Alfred Dulson, quoted in *The Times*, 2 February 1967. The union reaffiliated to the Labour Party in 1969.

140 See *Railway Review*, 18 November 1966, p. 10; and *The Guardian*, 11 November 1966. One District of USDAW noted of branch reports: 'A recurring factor in the reports was the intimation that some branches were seriously considering withholding affiliation fees to their local Labour Party as a protest against what they considered to be the anti-trade union attitude of the Government.' *The New Dawn*, vol. 21, no. 5, May 1967, p. 156. Fifteen branches of the TGWU put motions on the agenda for the 1967 union conference urging dissociation from the party or withdrawal of financial support. See *The Guardian* and *Daily Telegraph*, 14 July 1967.

141 *Report of the Chief Registrar of Friendly Societies*, 1969, Part IV, p. 16; and M. Harrison, *Trade Unions and the Labour Party since 1945*, London 1960, pp. 32–3.

142 See *1967 LPCR*, pp. 7–8, 37 and *1968 LPCR*, p. 11. For a region by region survey of the CLP morale and attitudes to rising prices and to incomes policy see Eric Silver & Dennis Barker, 'Eighteen Months to solve price problem', *The Guardian*, 9 June 1967. Cf. Francis Flavius, 'Why Labour's rank and file still hold the key', *Tribune*, 18 August 1967.

143 See Butler & Pinto-Duschinsky (n. 24 above), p. 21, and *1967 LPCR*, pp. 13–18.

144 'The Lost Labour Vote', *Socialist Commentary*, February 1969, p. 20.

CHAPTER 6

1 'Today a new harmony sounds from the celestial spheres', Harold Wilson told a Labour Party rally at Swansea. 'In industry, the City, the financial columns – above all in the foreign exchange markets – there is a new spirit of optimism and confidence . . . And the price of freedom from crisis, from stop–go is the abandonment of a free-for-all in incomes.' Quoted in *The Guardian*, 4 February 1967.

2 See Callaghan, 745 *HC Deb.* 17 April 1967, col. 208; cf. Stewart, 743 *Deb.* 22 March 1967, col. 1718.

3 *Prices and Incomes Policy after 30th June, 1967*, Cmnd. 3235, 22 March 1967.

4 744 *HC Deb.* 11 April 1967, cols. 889–90.

5 John Davies, quoted in *Daily Telegraph*, 16 March 1967, cf. CBI 1967 *Annual Report*, pp. 17–18.

6 Source: personal interviews with Les Allen and Michael Stewart, cf. *1967 TUC Report*, pp. 330–5; H. A. Clegg, *How to Run An Incomes Policy*, London 1971, p. 57.

7 *1967 TUC Report*, p. 325.

8 TUC, *Incomes Policy, Report of a Conference of Executive Committees*, 2 March 1967, hereafter cited as *Conference of Executives, 1967*: Woodcock, pp. 23–4. 'We ask to be allowed to do a job no man in his right senses would try . . . Why we should be made supplicants for something that will kill the whole goddam lot of us if it goes on long enough I don't know.' Woodcock, quoted in *The Times*, 10 February 1967.

9 In a speech on 3 March, Wilson suggested as a long-term proposal that Government and industry should estimate each year a 'National Dividend' – i.e. the total production available for consumption – and that the predetermined workers share of this should be distributed according to priorities set under the TUC's new scheme. It was an extremely vague proposal, which was immediately repudiated by both Woodcock and Davies. Wilson, *The Labour Government 1964–70*, London 1971, p. 449, *Sunday Times*, 5 March 1967.

10 *Conference of Executives, 1967* (n. 8 above), p. 25; *The Guardian*, 1 March 1967.

11 See esp. Cannon, Boyd and Allen, *Conference of Executives, 1967* (n. 8 above), pp. 33, 43, 50.

12 Personal interview with Michael Stewart. The arguments inside the Cabinet were widely leaked to the press at the time. See especially the articles by Peter Jenkins in *The Guardian*, and John Bourne in *The Financial Times*, throughout January, February and March 1967.

13 See p. 166.

14 The speech is reprinted in full in *The Post*, 15 April 1967.

15 See *The Times*, 18 April 1967 and 748 *HC Deb*. 13 June 1967, col. 332.

16 *The Times*, 10 July 1967. In light of the furore this statement created, Crossman claimed that he had meant unemployment rather than legal penalties as the 'medicine', but the damage had already been done.

17 750 *HC Deb*. 10 July 1967, col. 205.

18 Ibid. col. 218.

19 See *The Times*, 2 February 1967, *The Guardian*, 14 and 25 February 1967.

20 On 20 April, the Scottish TUC voted overwhelmingly to repudiate the Government's incomes policy and on 26 April, Carron lost control of the AEU National Committee, which voted by 26 to 25 against the 'coercive legislation'. This was followed by similar decisions at most other union conferences which at the same time continued to support a voluntary incomes policy.

21 *Daily Mail*, 22 March 1967.

22 See the report of the PLP meeting in *The Times*, 18 April 1967.

23 *1967 TUC Report*, pp. 326–31. Cf. Frank Cousins, 'We can't have TWO plans for WAGES!'. *Sunday Citizen*, 19 March 1967.

24 See esp. Alf Allen *Conference of Executives* (n. 8 above), p. 43.

25 Woodcock, ibid. p. 25.

26 Quoted in *The Times*, 6 June 1967.

27 *Financial Times*, 7 June 1967. Woodcock, in a personal interview, explained that he took this action because he sympathized with the Government's problems, believed that Labour MPs were exaggerating the dangers of the Bill, and did not want to place the General Council in the position of seeming to be indebted to the PLP's opposition to the legislation.

28 See *The Times*, *The Guardian*, 14 June 1967 and 748 *HC Deb*. 13 June 1967, cols. 439–42. The Government's majority was 53. The Bill's

passage through its final stages was enhanced by the fact that this time
the Government packed the Labour side of the Standing Committee on
the Bill with backbench loyalists.

29 See *The Guardian, Financial Times,* 14 July 1967.

30 The Government responded to sharp public criticisms of the increases
by announcing that all future major price increases proposed by the
nationalized industries would be referred to the NBPI. Paradoxically,
this had the effect of further reducing the Board's capacity to examine
private sector prices.

31 *1967 TUC Report,* pp. 527–43. The TGWU motion was seconded by
Robert Willis of the NGA who resigned as the trade unionist on the
NBPI in August.

32 *1967 TUC Report,* pp. 506. 546–8; cf. *Financial Times,* 2 September
1967.

33 Ibid. pp. 518–19.

34 Ibid. p. 507.

35 Personal interview with Laurence Daly. Cf. Wilson (n. 9 above), p. 430.

36 *1967 LPCR,* pp. 163–201. It was significant in this connection that
Tribune MPs polled very strongly in the election to Constituency section
of the NEC and the two vacant seats were filled by Frank Allaun and
Joan Lestor, who had abstained on the legislation in the Commons.

37 *1967 TUC Report,* p. 521. Cf. *AEU Journal,* November 1967, pp. 453–4.
On the bitter conflict between the two factions during the election, see
John Berny & Stephen Fay, 'Left or Right for the Unions?', *Sunday
Times,* 5 February 1967; cf. *Engineering Voice* throughout 1966 and
1967, which was widely read in the union and a key factor in Scanlon's
victory.

38 See Hugh Scanlon, 'The Role of Militancy, Interview', *New Left
Review,* no. 46, November–December 1967, esp. p. 7.

39 See the speeches by Ray Gunter reported in *The Times,* 17 October,
The Guardian, 19 October and *Sunday Telegraph,* 29 October 1967.

40 The Chancellor may not have foreseen, however, the small rise in retail
prices in the second half of 1967, which meant that real wages increased
considerably after their fall during the standstill. See NEDC, *1967
General Review,* p. 11, and Appendix 3 below.

41 754 *HC Deb.* 7 November 1967, col. 375.

42 *1967 General Review,* p. 2.

43 S. Brittan, *Steering the Economy: The Role of the Treasury,* London
1970, p. 354. Brittan provides the best account of events leading to
devaluation. Cf. W. Davies, *Three Years Hard Labour,* London 1968,
Chs. 8–10; W. Beckerman, *The Labour Government's Economic Record,
1964–70,* London 1972, pp. 61–4; and Wilson (n. 9 above),
Ch. 23.

44 *1968 LPCR,* p. 136.

45 Letter of Intent, 755 *HC Deb.* 30 November 1967, col. 650.

46 *1968 LPCR,* p. 165.

47 In reply to a letter from the TUC in 1969, asking whether it would 'be
fair to say that the IMF can lay down conditions in certain circumstances for making further arrangements', Jenkins answered: 'all drawings on the IMF are conditional in the sense that they are considered
by the Fund in the light of the member's fiscal and monetary policies,
and its cooperation with the Fund's principles and purposes, as embodied in the Articles of Agreement. Drawings are made in ''tranches''
of a member's quota in the Fund. Part of the quota is paid in gold.
Drawing within what is known as the gold tranche – that is to say drawings which do not exceed the currency equivalent of the gold portion
of a member's quota – are effectively automatic. Drawings in ''higher''

tranches involve closer consultation. The recent drawings by the United Kingdom in 1964, 1965, and 1967, have been in the higher tranches, and so would be any new drawings.' Roy Jenkins to Victor Feather, 5 June 1969, *TUC Economic Committee Minutes*, June 1969.

48 Roy Jenkins: 'Even if the IMF had never been heard of does anyone seriously contend that excessive wage and salary increases could not fritter away the competitive edge of devaluation over a year or so? . . . It needs no IMF to tell us these facts.' 755 *HC Deb*. 5 December 1967, col. 1200; The Government had no illusions that its policy would not produce conflict with the unions, on the other hand. Indeed, one un-identified 'member of the Government' wrote that 'the international cover we need for sterling could not have been obtained without a tremend-ously visible tug of war between Government and unions'. 'Cloth Caps or Hornrims, by a member of the Government', *The Guardian*, 30 September 1968.

49 DEP, *Gazette*, November 1970, p. 1024.

50 NEDC, *General Reviews*, 1966–8; cf. Appendix 3 below.

51 See *1968 TUC Report*, p. 345.

52 TUC, *1968 Economic Review and Report of Conference of Executives*, March 1968.

53 *1968 TUC Report*, p. 374. Although the DEA and NEDC prepared another 'planning document' in the course of 1968, it was emphasized that this was not a plan, and it committed the Government to no par-ticular course of action, projecting three possible targets of economic growth. See *The Task Ahead, An Economic Assessment to 1972*, HMSO, February 1969.

54 756 *HC Deb*. 18 January 1968, col. 629.

55 For the history of the Government's battle against the TGWU in the bus industry, see Tony Topham, 'Municipal Busmen, Productivity and the Incomes Policy' in Coates *et al.* (eds.) *Trade Union Register*, London 1969, pp. 201–10 and Andrew W. J. Thomson, 'Collective Bargaining Under Incomes Legislation: The Case of Britain's Buses', *Industrial and Labour Relations Review*, April 1971, pp. 384–405.

56 Lord Carron, for instance, responsible for the 1968 engineering claim, disdainfully refused to specify the claim to the Committee. *Minutes of TUC Incomes Policy Committee*, 21 February 1968.

57 TUC, *1968 Economic Review*, pp. 98–104, 142–3.

58 Ibid. p. 136.

59 Ibid. p. 116.

60 761 *HC Deb*. cols. 263–6; and *Productivity Prices and Incomes Policy in 1968 and 1969*, Cmnd. 3590, April 1968. For the first time the delaying powers took precedence over the Government's statutory obligation to enact Wage Council awards.

61 See *1968 TUC Report*, p. 362. Cf. Brittan (n. 43 above), p. 381 and *DEA Progress Report*, no. 39, April 1968, p. 2.

62 See Barbara Castle, 'A Socialist Incomes Policy', *New Statesman*, 25 September 1970, pp. 356–7; W. De'Ath, *Barbara Castle, A Portrait from Life*, London 1970, p. 42; and Peter Jenkins, *The Battle of Down-ing Street*, London 1970, pp. 1–5.

63 Differences remained between the unions on the question of the TUC's voluntary policy. The AEU Conference passed by 46 to 6 a resolution against the legislation and the Government's policy, and also rejected by 36 to 24 the TUC scheme. See *The Times*, 1 May 1968, *The Guardian*, 8 May 1968. On the other hand, USDAW similarly rejected the Government's approach, but supported the TUC. See *The New Dawn*, vol. 22, no. 6, 1968, pp. 163–4 and *The Guardian*, 30 April 1968. The GMWU reflected the extent to which even the most loyalist of the

union executives had moved on to the defensive when it refrained from putting to its conference in May a special report on the need for an incomes policy as it had done in previous years. Nevertheless, Cooper admitted that if he were an MP he would vote for the legislation to save the country from the Tories. See GMWU *1968 Congress Report*, pp. 306–11.

64 *Report of the Chief Registrar of Friendly Societies*, 1969, Part IV, p. 16. This was partly due to contracting out: in the AEU the number contracted out increased from 240,000 in 1966 to 325,000 in 1968, at a time when union membership fell by 65,000; and in the UPW the number contracted out rose from a steady figure of around 5,000 (3%) up until 1965 to 7,000 by the end of 1967 and to 8,600 (4.7%) by mid 1968. In addition there was the phenomenon of what Martin Harrison (*Trade Unions and the Labour Party since 1945*, London 1960, p. 46), earlier called 'voluntary non contribution', i.e. members not contracting out officially, but simply refusing to pay the political levy. This would seem to explain the situation in the TGWU and GMWU whose official figures showed a slight decline in the number contracted out, while the number actually contributing to the political fund fell drastically: in the TGWU from a high of 1,454,000 in 1965 to 1,295,000 in 1967, a fall of over $11\frac{1}{2}\%$, whereas total membership fell by only 3%; and in the NUGMW from 780,000 in 1965 to 715,000 in 1967, although membership fell by only 13,000. These figures are taken from the unions' annual returns to the Chief Registrar, with the exception of the UPW figures which are from the Minutes of the UPW General Purposes Committee, 1960–70.

65 *1970 LPCR*, p. 57.
66 *Financial Times*, 16 March 1968.
67 On the CLPs, see the special report, 'Disillusion in the Labour Party', *The Times*, 21 February 1968.
68 D. Butler & M. Pinto-Duschinsky, *The British General Election of 1970*, London 1971, p. 35.
69 *Financial Times*, 21 March 1968.
70 'My Reply to Barbara Castle', *Tribune*, 24 May 1968.
71 *Financial Times* and *The Guardian*, 9 May 1968.
72 Quoted in *Financial Times*, 13 May 1968.
73 *Tribune*, 9 February 1968. For Scanlon's similar use of his influence, see *Tribune*, 3 May 1968. Cf. Michael Foot, 'Credo of the Labour Left – Interview', *New Left Review*, no. 49, May–June 1968, pp. 23–4.
74 The AEU executive, in an effort to combat contracting out circularized all branches and districts with copies of a pamphlet, *Political Levy*, to which they required all members wishing to contract out to have their attention drawn. See *Executive Council Report to 50th AEU National Committee*, 1968, p. 149.
75 Personal interview with Bert Ramelson, National Industrial Organizer of the Communist Party.
76 *The Times*, 12 March 1968. For a survey of the same approach taken by other union leaders see Arthur Sandles, 'How the unions pay the piper without calling the tune', *Financial Times*, 18 July 1968. The AEU and DATA conferences in 1968 did however pass resolutions similar to the 1967 TGWU resolution on union sponsorship. This led to the resignation of the DATA MP, Will Howie, from the union in July 1968.
77 *1968 TUC Report*, p. 354.
78 Quoted in *Financial Times*, 16 and 31 May 1968.
79 *Financial Times*, 14 May 1968.
80 See *The Times, Financial Times*, 22 May 1968 and 765 *HC Deb.* 21 May 1968, cols. 419–30. Although the rebels now included a number of

centre and right-wings MPs (including Shinwell) only 13 of the 35 were union sponsored (as opposed to 15 of the 32 who abstained on Second Reading in 1967).

81 *Gallup Political Index*, no. 98, June 1968, and Social Surveys (Gallup Poll) Ltd. files.

82 767 *HC Deb.* 25–6 June 1968, cols. 343–40; *The Times*, 26 June 1968; *Financial Times*, 27 June 1968.

83 767 *HC Deb.* 27 June 1968, col. 875.

84 Clive Jenkins, *1968 TUC Report*, pp. 506–7.

85 NBPI, *Third General Report, August 1967 to July 1968*, Cmnd. 3715, p. 67.

86 'To postpone wage increases to the tune of 1% is to reduce effective demand by something approaching £100 million. If that were the only achievement of the policy, it would not be a minor one.' Roy Hattersley, 765 *HC Deb.* 21 May 1968, col. 414.

87 See NEDC, *1968 General Review*, pp. 18–20; and DEP, *Gazette*, May 1971, Table 8, p. 439.

88 NBPI, *Third General Report*, pp. 10–11.

89 *Gallup Political Index*, nos. 99 to 100, July, August 1968. *Daily Telegraph*, 28 July 1968; and Social Surveys (Gallup Polls) Ltd. files, and Appendix 1 below.

90 The poll was conducted by Conrad Jameson Associates in June and the representative sample inclined towards company directors to ensure that decision-makers were sufficiently represented. The results were publishd in *The Times*, 13 August 1968.

91 The general findings of this survey, conducted in Leeds in July 1968, are in Jay Blumler & Alison F. Ewbank. 'Trade Unionists, the Mass Media and Unofficial Strikes', *BJIR*, vol. VIII, no. 1, March 1970, pp. 32–54. The data on incomes policy were not used by the authors however, for which see Appendix 2 below.

92 See Richard Briginshaw, 'We're Sitting over Dynamite', *Daily Express*, 5 July 1968.

93 *1968 TUC Report*, p. 553. Perhaps the best comment on union attitudes to TUC wage vetting was a song sung at unofficial Congress festivities to the tune of the popular song 'Congratulations': 'Cap-it-u-lation, and ab-dic-a-tion./ – that's the slogan of our great centenary. /There's hesitation and vacillation,/ and we're going to change our name to PIB. /If you've a wage claim and want some help to get it, /When you know the boss is trying to upset it, /Bring it along to Congress House – and we will vet it,/ and then forget it, inefficiently.' Quoted in *Observer*, 8 September 1968.

94 *Financial Times, The Guardian, Daily Telegraph*, 30 September 1968.

95 *1968 LPCR*, pp. 123–5.

96 *1968 LPCR*, pp. 137–8.

97 Ibid. p. 153.

98 The NEC endorsed this motion with the reservation that a return to wartime price controls in the absence of rationing, utility schemes and detailed controls of production, was impossible, ibid. pp. 125–6, 149. As in previous years the 30 CLP incomes policy resolutions on the agenda were mainly critical of the prices policy but in 1968 half of these also demanded that the penal clauses over wages be dropped. An indication of the effect which a left-wing leadership in both the AEU and TGWU could have on the Labour Party Conference, if not on the Parliamentary Party, was seen when a radical CLP resolution, entirely out of spirit with the dominant ideology of the Labour Party over the previous twenty years, was defeated by only 300,000 votes (3,282,000 to 2,921,000). It declared 'that the policies of the Government have been and are

dictated by the monopolies and big financial interests . . . only by taking into public ownership the 500 monopolies, private banks, finance houses and insurance companies now dominating the economy . . . can the Government effectively develop the resources of our country for the benefit of the people' (p. 127).

99 McKenzie, *British Political Parties*, 2nd edn, London 1963, p. 505.
100 Quoted in *Financial Times*, 3 October 1968.
101 *1968 LPCR*, p. 152.
102 See *Financial Times*, 30 May 1968 and *Sunday Telegraph*, 3 June 1968.
103 *TUC Incomes Policy Bulletin*, 1968–9; and *Minutes of TUC Incomes Policy Committee*, 1968–9.
104 Home Policy Sub-Committee, *Incomes Policy after 1969, the Problems of Labour's Economic Strategy*, February 1969, p. 6 (unpublished).

CHAPTER 7

1 See *The Times*, 27 September 1968.
2 For the statistics on official and unofficial strikes and the development of shop-steward influence and local bargaining, see *Royal Commission on Trade Unions and Employers Associations 1965–8, Report*, Cmnd. 3623, esp. Chs. 3 and 4, hereafter cited as *Donovan Report*; W. E. J. McCarthy, *The Role of Shop Stewards in British Industrial Relations*, HMSO 1966; W. E. J. McCarthy & S. R. Parker, *Shop Stewards and Workshop Relations*, HMSO 1968; *Written Evidence of the Ministry of Labour to the Royal Commission on Trade Union and Employers' Associations*, 1965, pp. 36–43; H. A. Turner *et al.*, *Labour Relations in the Motor Industry*, London 1967; H. A. Turner, *Is Britain Really Strike Prone?* Department of Applied Economics Occasional Paper, no. 20, Cambridge 1969; W. E. J. McCarthy, 'The Nature of Britain's Strike Problem', *BJIR*, vol. 8, no. 2, 1970, pp. 224–36; and M. Silver, 'Recent British Strike Trends: A Factual Analysis', *BJIR*, vol. 11, no. 1, 1973, pp. 66–104.
3 *Written Evidence of the Ministry of Labour* (n. 2 above), p. 3.
4 CBI, 'First Memorandum', November 1965, in *Selected Written Evidence to the Royal Commission on Trade Unions and Employers' Associations*, HMSO 1968, Para. 63, p. 262.
5 *Minutes of Evidence to the Royal Commission on Trade Union and Employers' Associations*, nos. 1–69, 1966 and 1967: CBI, no. 22, 8 February 1966, p. 808.
6 *Fair Deal at Work*, Conservative Political Centre, April 1968.
7 This assessment is based on personal interviews with individuals close to both the Ministry and the Commission at the time.
8 *Donovan Report* (n. 2 above), pp. 131–2. Cf. pp. 52–3.
9 Ibid. p. 128.
10 Ibid. p. 130.
11 Ibid. pp. 112–15.
12 Ibid. pp. 40ff.
13 Ibid. pp. 137–8; cf. pp. 128–32. Allan Flanders, who had an important influence on the Donovan Report, explicitly suggested this: 'it is extremely important that the parties should first gain confidence in the tribunal before it is given any compulsory powers. I would have said this is the natural mode of development'. *Minutes of Evidence* (n. 5 above), no. 62, 6 December 1966, p. 2785.
14 Ibid. pp. 288–9.
15 Ibid. p. 289.
16 Ibid. p. 215.
17 See *1968 TUC Report*, pp. 204–6 and TUC, *Action on Donovan*, October 1968.

18 CBI *1968 Annual Report*, pp. 7–8, 34–6.

19 'Strikes in the Motor Industry: Call for Legal Action', Letter to the Editor, *The Times*, 24 September 1968, from W. B. Batty (Ford), D. L. Highland (Vauxhall), Lord Rootes (Rootes) and Donald Stokes (British Leyland). Relations between certain motor industry leaders and the Government were particularly close. Stokes was an advisor to the Government on arms exports as well as deputy director of the IRC, and was made a Life Peer. George Cattell, director of manufacturing at Rootes, was appointed Director of Manpower and Productivity Services at the DEP in June 1968.

20 *1968 LPCR*, p. 299.

21 Wilson, *The Labour Government 1964–70*, London 1971, p. 591.

22 In accord with an agreement by the participants at the time, little has been revealed about the details of this meeting. See, however, Butler & Pinto-Duschinsky, *The British General Election of 1970*, London 1971, p. 39, and Roy Hattersley, 'Could Barbara Have Won', *New Statesman*, 4 September 1970, pp. 263–4. My own understanding of Mrs Castle's position has been aided by personal interviews with a number of the participants.

23 See Peter Jenkins, *The Battle of Downing Street*, London 1970, pp. 31–2.

24 Gallup Political Index and Social Surveys (Gallup Polls) Ltd; and Jenkins (n. 23 above), p. xiv.

25 'Role of the Commission on Industrial Relations', an interview with George Woodcock, *Employment and Productivity Gazette*, vol. LXXVII, no. 2, 1969, pp. 116–18 [emphasis added].

26 *In Place of Strife: A Policy for Industrial Relations*, January 1969, Cmnd. 3888.

27 Barbara Castle, 779 *HC Deb*. 3 March 1969, col. 42.

28 The main elements of modern sociological pluralist and functionalist theory had been outlined for the Donovan Commission in a Research Paper by Alan Fox, *Industrial Sociology and Industrial Relations*, HMSO 1966. Cf. L. A. Coser, *The Functions of Social Conflict*, London 1956.

29 *In Place of Strife* (n. 26 above), pp. 5–6.

30 Ibid. para. 14, p. 8.

31 Ibid. p. 10.

32 See *Minutes of Evidence* (n. 5 above), nos. 20, 22 and 23, February 1966, esp. pp. 806–8 and 898–9; and *1966 TUC Report*, pp. 370–1.

33 See George Brown, 731 *HC Deb*. 14 July 1966, cols. 1751–2. It is interesting to note that Gallup found in July 1966, when public opinion support for the incomes legislation was still high, that on the possibility of fines under the legislation being deducted from pay-packets, 58% of respondents *disapproved*, including 60% of Labour supporters and 70% of trade unionists: Social Surveys (Gallup Polls) Ltd files.

34 *In Place of Strife* (n. 26 above), p. 29.

35 TUC Economic Committee *Minutes*, 8 January 1969.

36 TUC, *Economic Review 1969, Report of Conference*, February 1969, p. 6.

37 Peter Jenkins (n. 23 above), pp. 35–8; and interviews with Barbara Castle and Richard Crossman in *Decision-Making in Britain, The Labour Decision on Industrial Relations*, transcriptions of BBC Open University Film Programme, 1971, 3 February 1974.

38 'Role of the Commission on Industrial Relations' (n. 25 above), p. 116.

39 This account of the General Council's initial response is based on personal interviews with members of the General Council.

40 Lord Cooper, quoted in *Financial Times*, 14 May 1969.

41 *1969 TUC Report*, pp. 205–8.

42 *Decision-Making in Britain* (n. 37 above), pp. 4–5, and Jenkins (n. 23 above), pp. 38–9.

43 David Watt, 'Barbara Castle's delayed time bomb', *Financial Times*, 24 January 1968; Jenkins (n. 23 above), p. 85; and personal interviews conducted by the author.

44 *1969 TUC Report*, p. 209.

45 Barbara Castle in *Decision-Making in Britain* (n. 37 above), p. 11.

46 *The Times*, 20 February 1969.

47 *1969 TUC Report*, pp. 225–8.

48 See Victor Feather in TUC, *1969 Economic Review, Report of Conference*, p. 71.

49 Quoted in *The Times*, 3 February 1969.

50 It was significant in this regard that a study of trade union opinion in Leeds in July 1968 had found that while 47–57% of GMWU, SOGAT and NALGO stewards endorsed the idea of legal penalties against unofficial strikers, only 27% of AEF stewards did so. See Blumler and Ewbank, 'Trade Unionists, the Mass Media and Unofficial Strikes', *BJIR*, vol. VIII, no. 1, 1970, p. 45.

51 See H. Benyon, *Working For Fords*, London 1973, p. 281.

52 Ibid. pp. 280–1.

53 There were, to be sure, special conditions at Ford which strengthened the shop stewards' position: particularly the fact that earnings (based on the day-rate system) lagged far behind the Midlands car industry (based on payments by result).

54 Benyon (n. 51 above), pp. 267–8.

55 Fred Silberman, 'The 1969 Ford Strike', in K. Coates *et al.* (eds.) *Trade Union Register*, London 1970, p. 224.

56 Jenkins (n. 23 above), p. 60.

57 Quoted in *The Times*, 26 February 1969. Fred Silberman has written that 'what troubled Fords was that the strike had been made official, that the two main unions were openly against them and on the side of their militants . . . The important point is that one of the most skilled and experienced personnel directors in Britain saw the trade unions *as a vital part of the company's control machinery over its employees.*' Silberman (n. 55 above).

58 Quoted in Jenkins (n. 23 above), p 61.

59 *Socialist Commentary*, April 1969, pp. 3–4.

60 *The Guardian*, 14 April 1969.

61 *The New Dawn*, March 1969, p. 83.

62 See 772 *HC Deb.* 6 Nov. 1968, cols. 895–902; *Tribune*, 15 Nov. 1968.

63 See E. S. Heffer, *The Class Struggle in Parliament*, London 1973, p. 100. A Times News Team survey of 75 trade union MPs found 45% in favour of a Government imposed cooling-off period, but 33% opposed, and only 32% actually in favour of legislation putting such a proposal into effect. *The Times*, 8 January 1969.

64 See Jenkins (n. 23 above), pp. 71–3.

65 See 779 *HC Deb.* 3 March 1969, cols. 39–166; *The Times*, 4 March, and *Daily Telegraph*, 5 March 1969.

66 *The Times, The Guardian*, 19 December 1968.

67 *The Guardian*, 7 January 1969.

68 Home Policy Sub-Committee, *Incomes Policy after 1969*, February 1969, p. 2.

69 Ibid. p. 1.

70 *The Times*, 26 March 1969.

71 For the best account of this NEC meeting and the response it engendered see Jenkins (n. 23 above), pp. 78–84.

72 In March, Gallup found that 71% were in favour of legal intervention

in unofficial strikes 'harmful to the national interest', *Gallup Political Index*, no. 107, March 1969.

73 *Decision-Making in Britain* (n. 37 above).

74 CBI, *Annual Report*, 1969, pp. 30ff.

75 See *The Times*, 20 January 1969 and Robert Carr, 779 *HC Deb.* 3 March 1969, cols. 60–1.

76 781 *HC Deb.* 15 April 1969, cols. 1003–5, 1175–89

77 Barbara Castle, 781 *HC Deb.* col. 1186.

78 Ibid. cols. 1186–7.

79 Ibid. col. 1187, and Harold Wilson (n. 21 above), p. 642.

80 Quoted in *The Times*, 18 April 1969.

81 The most sophisticated sections of the national press well understood this facet of the Government's proposals: *The Financial Times* envisaged that the bill 'might well prove difficult to enforce in practice', and saw it as 'of more symbolic than practical importance'. Editorial: 'Spanner in the Works', *Financial Times*, 21 May 1969.

82 *The Times*, 18 April 1969.

83 *The Times*, April 29 1969.

84 General Council *Minutes*, 23 April 1969, and *1969 TUC Report*, pp. 211–12.

85 See Jenkins (n. 23 above). p. 122.

86 Such demands were made at the USDAW, GMWU, and TGWU conferences in the spring. See *The Times*, 31 March 1969.

87 *Tribune*, 18 April 1969.

88 *Socialist Commentary*, May 1969, pp. 3–4.

89 'The Labour Back-Bencher', *Political Quarterly*, vol. 40, no. 4, 1969, pp. 460–1. Cf. Eric Moonman, MP, *Reluctant Partnership: A Critical Study of the Relationship Between Government and Industry*, London 1970, pp. 45–6.

90 Quoted in *The Times*, 16 April 1969.

91 See n. 88 above.

92 See in this regard the letter by Peggy Duff, *et al.* 'Tribune's sham war?' *Tribune*, 2 May 1969.

93 *The Guardian, Financial Times*, 29 April 1969.

94 Jenkins (n. 23 above), p. 117.

95 Personal interview with Douglas Houghton; cf. *The Guardian*, 8 May 1969, and Peter Jenkins (n. 23 above), p. 119.

96 *General Council Minutes*, 23 April 1969, p. 113 and *1969 TUC Report*, p. 212.

97 *The Guardian*, 29 April 1969.

98 Personal interview with Richard Briginshaw; cf. *Tribune*, 11 April 1969.

99 Quoted in *Morning Star*, 5 June 1969.

100 There had been signs as early as March that the General Council had come to doubt the efficacy of their incomes policy strategy. See TUC Economic Committee *Minutes*, 12 March 1969, and 11 February 1970; and *1969 TUC Report*, pp. 419–21.

101 *Programme for Action*, Report of a Special TUC, 5 June 1969, para. 82, cf. the excellent profile on Feather, 'The Workers Voice', *New Statesman*, 28 February 1969, p. 289.

102 *Programme for Action* (n. 101 above), p. 4; and General Council *Minutes*, 15 May 1969, p. 122.

103 General Council *Minutes*, 15 May 1969, p. 123.

104 Ibid. pp. 121–2.

105 The following account of these discussions is mainly based on the TUC's own minutes (circulated among General Council members) of its meetings with the Prime Minister, Mrs Castle and DEP officials, each entitled *TUC Proposals on Industrial Relations, Report of a meeting between*

the Prime Minister, First Secretary of State and the General Council, hereafter cited as *Report of Meeting*. Cf. *1969 TUC Report*, pp. 212–25.

106 Peter Jenkins (n. 23 above), in particular tends to give this impression; see his Chs. 7 and 8.

107 George Woodcock, 'To Reason and Persuade', *Financial Times*, 31 May 1968.

108 *Programme for Action* (n. 101 above), pp. 39–40 and *1969 TUC Report*, pp. 216–17.

109 *Programme for Action*, para. 24, p. 8, and *Reports of Meetings* (n. 105 above), 12 May, p. 3, and 11 June, p. 11.

110 *Report of Meeting* (n. 105 above), 12 May, p. 6.

111 *Programme for Action* (n. 101 above), esp. para. 42.

112 *Report of Meeting* (n. 105 above), 12 May, pp. 4–8.

113 Ibid, p. 8.

114 *Report of Meeting* (n. 105 above), 21 May, pp. 4–10.

115 *The Times*, *The Guardian*, 21 May 1969.

116 General Council *Minutes*, 15 May 1969, p. 123; John Boyd, 'The AEF vote row', *Tribune*, 30 May 1969; and Eric Wigham, 'Britain's hydra-headed union', *The Times*, 23 May 1969.

117 *The Times*, 4 June 1969.

118 See *Tribune*, 6 June 1969.

119 It rejected the penal clauses by 8,252,000 to 359,000 votes; accepted that some provisions of the White Paper were 'in principle' useful by 8,608,000 to 144,000 votes; and accepted the TUC's own plan by 7,908,000 to 846,000 votes.

120 Quoted in Jenkins (n. 23 above), pp. 141–2. Jenkins suggests here that the Government tried to sabotage the unanimity of the Congress vote in order to give itself grounds for rejecting the TUC plan as incapable of working. On 3 June, the DEP sent a letter to Feather detailing a long list of objections to the TUC plan, thereby implying that the Government was going ahead with the bill and inviting left-wing union leaders to withdraw their support from the General Council. Feather, however, did not show the letter to the General Council until after the Congress vote. General Council *Minutes*, 5 June, pp. 137–9.

121 *Report of Meeting* (n. 105 above), 9 June, pp. 4, 7.

122 *Report of Meeting* (n. 105 above), 18 June, p. 9.

123 *Report of Meetings* (n. 105 above), 11 and 12 June, p. 10.

124 Ibid. p. 4. Wilson includes the comment himself in his *Labour Government* (n. 21 above; p. 656), but puts it even more bluntly in terms of a 'master–servant' relationship.

125 Ibid. Appendix A.

126 Ibid. p. 2, and *Report of Meeting*, 18 June, p. 11.

127 Peter Jenkins (n. 23 above), pp. 151–2.

128 Ibid. p. 115, and *The Times*, 10 May 1969.

129 Peter Jenkins' account (pp. 152–4) of this Cabinet meeting has been confirmed as being substantially correct in my own interviews with Members of the Cabinet.

130 Personal interview with Douglas Houghton. Cf. Jenkins (n. 23 above), p. 155, and Moonman (n. 89 above), p. 46.

131 Jenkins (n. 23 above), Ch. 8; Butler & Pinto-Duschinsky (n. 22 above), p. 44; Heffer (n. 63 above), pp. 131–6.

132 *Report of Meeting* (n. 105 above), 18 June, p. 4.

133 Personal interviews with Tom Jackson and Lord Cooper.

134 *Report of Meeting* (n. 105 above), 18 June, p. 4.

135 See Wilson (n. 21 above), p. 658.

136 The Bridlington Congress of 1939 had supplemented Rule 12 with a

series of decisions relating to disputes between unions over membership recruitment. The general acceptance of these 'principles' as well as Rule 12 was seen in the fact that out of 1,000 awards made by the General Council Disputes Committees in the 3 subsequent decades, there had been only one clear case of disobedience. See TUC, *Trade Unionism, Evidence to the Royal Commission*, 1966, pp. 21–2 and *Report of Meeting*, p. 3.

CHAPTER 8

1 TUC Economic Committee *Minutes,* 11 June 1969. Cf. *1969 TUC Report*, pp. 435–6.

2 T. Topham, 'The Labour Government's Incomes Policy and the Trade Unions', in K. Coates *et al. Trade Union Register*, 1970, p. 117. Topham's study of the politics of incomes policy in the last half of 1969 was by far the best analysis of any one particular stage of Labour's incomes policy.

3 *Report of Meeting*, 18 June, p. 12 [emphasis added].

4 General Council *Minutes*, 25 June, p. 147 [emphasis added]: cf. *Programme for Action*, Report of a Special TUC, 5 June 1969, p. 97.

5 'Report of a meeting between the Economic Committee and the First Secretary of State for Employment and Productivity', 24 July 1969, p. 5. in Economic Committee *Minutes*, 13 August 1969.

6 Ibid. p. 4.

7 *1969 TUC Report*, p. 563.

8 The General Council in February had sought legal advice on the implications of simply removing the wage and salary provisions from Part II, but by June it had dropped this idea, apprehensive that the Government would expect the TUC to match statutory price powers with voluntary wage restraint of a kind that would simply expose the vacuous exercise in which the TUC's Incomes Policy Committee was by that time engaged. TUC Economic Committee *Minutes*, February, June and August, 1969.

9 *1969 TUC Report*, pp. 561–7.

10 *Agenda for a Generation*, p. 5, original emphasis. Although the NEC had refused Mrs Castle's suggestion for a study group on incomes policy on the grounds that this would imply acquiescence in the continuation of the legislation, the NEC had appointed a study group charged with examining over-all economic strategy. That group's report, published in August as *Labour's Economic Strategy*, concentrated on impressing on the Government the need for price reductions and a wealth tax. But it did so in the context of arguing that this would make 'the more stringent parts of incomes policy . . . more palatable'. And while suggesting that the central task of ensuring that incomes did not outstrip productivity growth would fall to the trade union movement itself, the report explicitly acquiesced in the activation of Part II (pp. 53–5).

11 *1969 LPCR*, pp. 259–60.

12 Ibid. p. 260.

13 Ibid. p. 269.

14 Harry Urwin, *1969 LPCR*, p. 137.

15 Ibid. p. 195.

16 See above Ch. 7, p. 191.

17 790 *HC Deb.* 6 November 1969, col. 42.

18 *Productivity Prices and Incomes Policy after 1969*, Cmnd. 4237, 11 December 1969, p. 12.

19 'Report of a meeting between the Economic Committee and the Secretary of State for Employment and Productivity', 2 December 1969, in TUC Economic Committee *Minutes,* December 1969, pp. 4–5.

20 Report of 2 December Meeting (n. 19 above), p. 4; cf. *1970 TUC Report*, pp. 155–6.
21 See Rodney Cowton, 'Price rise gesture to CBI', *The Times*, 10 December 1969.
22 These figures are based on data supplied to the author by the Department of Trade and Industry.
23 *The Times*, 12 and 18 December 1969.
24 See esp. Brian Walden's attack on this 'irrelevant, irritating, sham order which is nothing more than a gesture'. 793 *HC Deb.* 17 December 1969, col. 1405.
25 Quoted in *The Times*, 29 October 1969.
26 See *The Guardian*, 21 November and 5 December 1969.
27 See Topham (n. 2 above), pp. 120–2.
28 *The Times, The Guardian*, 18 December 1969. Gormley received an OBE in the January awards list.
29 Quoted in Topham (n. 2 above), p. 122. Cf. Houghton's speech during the Commons debate, 793 *HC Deb.* 17 December 1969, cols. 1916–20. In a personal interview Houghton told the author he acted in this way because his views coincided with those of the Government on incomes policy, and because he was anxious not to give the impression that he was always 'against the Government'.
30 See *The Times*, 13 December 1969, and E. S. Heffer, *The Class Struggle in Parliament*, London 1973, pp. 145–6.
31 See *The Times*, 12 and 17 December, and the speeches by Mrs Castle and Roy Jenkins, 793 *HC Deb.* 17 December, esp. cols. 1379, 1476.
32 Quoted in John Torode, 'Prince Philip and George Brown', *Socialist Commentary*, December 1969, p. 20.
33 Quoted in *The Times*, 17 December 1969.
34 See 793 *HC Deb.* 17 December 1969, cols. 1477–82 and *The Times*, 18 December 1969; 15 of the 29 abstainers were Trade Union MPs.
35 See DEP *Gazette*, May 1971, p. 439. Approximately half the days lost in 1970 took place *before* the June election.
36 NEDC, *1969 General Review*, Table 6, p. 10. Cf. Appendix 3 below.
37 Michael Artis, 'Fiscal Policy for Stabilization', in Beckerman, *The Labour Government's Economic Record 1964–70*, London 1972, p. 279.
38 Data supplied to the author by the Department of Trade and Industry.
39 On the basis of the DEP's six-monthly earnings survey, the NBPI calculated that between April 1965 and April 1969, the average weekly earnings of male manual workers in the lowest paid quarter of all industries surveyed increased by the same amount as the average for all industries – i.e. by 6.3%. And this did not take into account the higher marginal rates of taxation these money increases occasioned for lower paid workers. See NBPI, Report no. 169, *General Problems of Low Pay*, Cmnd. 4648, April 1971, Table F, p. 15.
40 See R. J. Liddle and W. E. J. McCarthy, 'The Impact of the Prices and Incomes Board on the Reform of Collective Bargaining', *BJIR*, vol. 10, November 1972, pp. 416–19; and NBPI Report no. 170, *Fifth and Final General Report July 1969 to March 1971*, Cmnd. 4649, April 1971, p. 3.
41 Report no. 107, Cmnd. 3970, March 1969.
42 781 *HC Deb.* 3 April 1969, col. 659.
43 Ibid. col. 664.
44 See DEP *Gazette*, May 1969, pp. 401–2.
45 Personal interview with Jim Mortimer; and see Peter Bachrach and Morton Baratz, 'Decisions and Non-Decisions: an analytic framework', *APSR*, vol. 57, September 1963, pp. 632–42.
46 780 *HC Deb.* 26 March 1969, col. 1625.

47 H. A. Turner & F. Wilkinson, 'The Wage–tax spiral and labour militancy' in Dudley Jackson *et al. Do Trade Unions Cause Inflation?*, Cambridge 1972, Table 11, p. 81. Despite some disagreement in the relevant literature, based on different methods of calculation, as to the exact pre- and post-tax profits situation in the 1960s, there appears to be general agreement that taxation had the effect of at least arresting, if not reversing, the decline on pre-tax profits. For a good review of the literature, see G. J. Burgess & A. J. Webb, 'The Profits of British Industry', *Lloyd's Bank Review*, April 1974, pp. 1–18.

48 See J. C. Kincaid, *Poverty and Equality in Britain*, London 1973, pp. 68–87; A. B. Atkinson, 'Inequality and Social Security', in P. Townsend & N. Bosanquet, *Labour and Inequality*, Fabian Society, 1972, pp. 12–26; and P. Townsend, 'The problem of social growth', *The Times*, 9–12 March 1971.

49 See Turner & Wilkinson (n. 47 above), pp. 83–4.

50 NEDC, *1969 General Review*, Table 6, p. 10 and Appendix 3 below.

51 Turner & Wilkinson (n. 47 above), p. 78. The NBPI's *General Problems of Low Pay* (Report no. 106, Cmnd. 4648, 1971, pp. 14–16), drew opposite conclusions on the effect of the new militancy on the relative position of the low paid, but its analysis stopped in April 1970, when many of the salient agreements were still in the process of settlement. See John Hughes, 'The Low Paid', in Townsend & Bosanquet (n. 48 above), pp. 162–73, and TUC, *Inflation*, December 1970, Annex A.

52 'Don't Blame the Dustmen', *Socialist Commentary*, November 1969, pp. 24–5. Cf. Mike Taylor, 'The Revolt against Low Pay in the Public Services', *Trade Union Register 1970*, pp. 198–212.

53 The Incomes Policy Committee was replaced by a Collective Bargaining Committee simply designed to secure information on negotiations and settlements but with no wage-vetting functions. During 1969 the TUC received only 202 wage claim notifications in contrast with the already diminished 351 in 1968. TUC, *Incomes Policy Bulletin*, nos. 14–41, January 1968 to February 1970; Economic Committee *Minutes*, January and March 1970; and *1970 TUC Report*, pp. 458–9.

54 See G. S. Bain & R. Price, 'Union Growth and Employment trends in the UK, 1964–70', *BJIR*, vol. 10, no. 4, 1972, pp. 366–81, who suggest that 'the opposition put up by the unions to income restraint encouraged workers to see them as the main instrument for improving terms and conditions, with the result that they turned to them in large numbers in 1969–70'. (p. 375).

55 See T. Lane & K. Roberts, *Strike at Pilkington*, London 1971.

56 *Now Britain's strong, let's make it great to live in*, Labour Party, 1970, pp. 3–9.

57 *The Times*, 16 and 21 April 1970.

58 *1969 LPCR*, pp. 301–2.

59 D. Butler & M. Pinto-Duschinsky, *The British General Election of 1970*. London 1971, p. 346. Labour lack of credibility on the wage–price issue was a central plank in the Conservative campaign. Edward Heath: 'Do you really think – knowing as you do the history of a Labour Government's double-talk on wages – do you really believe that, under a new Labour government, the wage increases granted by both private industry and the state would in fact be paid in full? . . . When we are elected on 18 June, we are not going to have a compulsory wage freeze.' Speech at Birmingham Town Hall, 3 June 1970, quoted by John Torode, 'Year of the Good Old Incomes Policy', *New Statesman*, 1 January 1971, pp. 4–5. Of course, apart from its 1970 Industrial Relations Act, the Conservative Government introduced its own statutory wage freeze two years later.

60 For a discussion of the details and implications of the Act, see K. Coates, 'Converting the Unions to Socialism', in M. Barratt Brown & K. Coates (eds.) *Trade Union Register: 3*, Nottingham 1973, pp. 9–43; cf. K. W. Wedderburn, 'In Place of Consultation', *The Times*, 6 October 1970; V. L. Allen, *Defeat the Bill, an exposure of the Tories' Attack on Trade Unionism*, TGWU pamphlet, n.d.; and TUC Educational Service, *Industrial Relations Bill, Notes and Diagrams*, n.d. The Conservatives' rationale for the Act was presented most cogently in its *Industrial Relations Bill: Consultative Document*, October 1970, reprinted in full in *The Times*, 6 October 1970.

61 Andrew Shonfield, 'A Bill with a clear philosophy', *The Times*, 6 October 1970.

62 See Michael Silver, 'Recent British Strike Trends, A Factoral Analysis', *BJIR*, vol. 11, March 1973, Table 2, p. 89.

63 Victor Feather, introduction to the TUC's *Reason, The Case against the Government's proposals on Industrial Relations*, 1970, p. 2. On the TUC's policy of non-cooperation, see *Report to the Special Trade Union Congress*, 18 March 1971, Annex, *1971 TUC Report*, pp. 341–77.

64 See *1972 TUC Report*, pp. 83ff.

65 See J. Hughes & R. Moore, *A Special Case? Social Justice and the Miners*, London 1972.

66 K. Coates (n. 60 above), p. 18.

67 *The Times*, 23 July 1972. For a discussion of these demands for incomes policy and the view, reflected in *The Financial Times*, that a General Strike 'might divide the nation more deeply than at any time since, perhaps, 1688, and that whoever won, it might take generations to clean up the mess', see Anthony Barnett, 'Class Struggle and the Heath Government', *New Left Review*, vol. 77, 1973, esp. p. 15.

68 See TUC, *The Chequers and Downing Street Talks*, 1972, pp. 1–2.

69 Ibid. p. 17.

70 See the White Papers, *The Programme for Controlling Inflation: The Second Stage*, Cmnd. 5205, January 1973, and *The Operation of Stage Two*, Cmnd. 5267, March 1973.

71 See *1973 TUC Report*, pp. 512–15.

72 Ibid. p. 281.

73 Data supplied by Frank Wilkinson in advance of the second edition of Jackson *et al. Do Trade Unions Cause Inflation?* The sharpness of this decline was mainly the result of increased inflation: the increase in money earnings only fell from 15.4% in 1971–2 to 13.9% in 1972–3. Despite the policy's inability to stem what was by then a virtually rampant inflation, it is interesting to note that the Conservative policy was somewhat more *dirigiste* on prices than Labour's had been. During Phase Two of the policy, for instance, from April to November 1973 alone, the Price Commission received 1,130 applications for price increases, of which 524 were approved in full, 281 modified and 325 withdrawn or rejected by the Commission. See Price Commission, *Report for the Period 1 September–30 November 1973*, and *Report for the Period of 1 June–31 August 1973*, HMSO 1973.

74 On the TUC offer and the Government's rejection of it, see John Whale & Eric Jacobs, 'Three Warnings Held Heath Back', *Sunday Times*, 20 January 1974.

75 Ian Gilmour, 'How Mr Heath could establish Industrial Harmony', *The Times*, 3 May 1974.

76 See in this regard Malcolm Dean's excellent survey of the Labour Party, 'Is Labour Dying', a series of four articles in *The Guardian*, 18–21 January 1971.

77 *1972 LPCR*, pp. 173–9.

78 Ibid. p. 190.
79 *1973 LPCR*, p. 187.
80 See *1972 LPCR*, pp. 109–10 and *1973 LPCR*, pp. 14–16, 189.
81 See *1973 LPCR*, p. 167, and *Labour Programme for Britain*, 1973, pp. 33–4.
82 *1973 LPCR*, pp. 171–88.
83 Quoted in the *Daily Telegraph*, 17 May 1974.
84 *Guardian Weekly*, 3 August 1974.
85 See *1972 LPCR*, p. 76.
86 808 *HC Deb.* 15 December 1970, cols. 1233–5.
87 See esp. Harold Wilson's and Reg Prentice's comments regarding the dockers, in 841 *HC Deb.* 25 July 1972, cols. 1551–90. The leadership's attitude was well reflected in the *New Statesman's* front-page attack on the TGWU and AUEW for undertaking political strikes: 'The Mindless Militants', 12 March 1971.
88 *Let Us Work Together – Labour's Way Out of the Crisis, The Labour Party Manifesto 1974*, pp. 1–2.
89 *1970 LPCR*, p. 224.
90 Ibid. pp. 121, 223.
91 Barbara Castle, 'A Socialist Incomes Policy', *New Statesman*, 25 September 1970, pp. 356–7.
92 James Callaghan, 'The Way Forward for the Trade Unions', *AUEW Journal*, vol. 38, no. 1, 1971, pp. 2–3.
93 Harold Lever, 'Cooperation – the fairer way to fight inflation', *The Times*, 27 January 1971.
94 In May 1971, Wilson joined those elements of British capitalism who had been calling since the election for a return to incomes policy, in predicting the Heath Government would 'before long' itself have to negotiate such a policy with the unions: 'it is becoming inconceivable that national economic policies will be developed which do not contain, as a significant element, some form of incomes policy'. On the tricky question of coercion, he did not rule this out in principle, but for pragmatic reasons: 'the lessons of our experience is such that a [statutory] freeze can only be of short duration . . . before anomalies make it totally unworkable and, as they do, discredit not only the policy, but even the system of society in which it operates'. Speech to an international symposium on labour relations in New York, quoted in *The Times*, 5 May 1971.
95 *Statement on Industrial Relations*, July 1972, reprinted in *1972 LPCR*, Appendix 1.
96 'Economic Planning and the Cost of Living', February 1973, reprinted in *1973 TUC Report*, pp. 312–14.
97 See 'My Cure for Inflation', *Sunday Times*, 6 August 1972. Wilson proposed a new board ('not necessarily statutory'), prices-related threshold agreements, and pay norms expressed in cash terms rather than percentage increases to benefit the low paid. He even resurrected his 1967 *National Dividend* proposal whereby the Government, the CBI and the TUC would annually agree on the allocation of the likely increase in national income among their members and public expenditure. See p. 296, n. 9.
98 See *1972 LPCR*, p. 264, and *1973 LPCR*, p. 115.
99 See n. 88 above (pp. 9–10).
100 On Wilson's appeals to the unions on strike see *Daily Telegraph*, 7 and 12 February 1974; on his reference to the seamen's strike, see *The Times*, 14 February 1974.
101 Editorial, 'An Election About Survival', *The Times*, 23 February 1974.
102 Quoted in *The Times*, 14 February 1974.

103 Quoted in *The Times*, 21 February 1974.
104 See Opinion Research Centre, *Changes in Voting Behaviour 1970–1974*, mimeo, London, n.d.; and Louis Harris International, *Harris Polls and the General Election on 28th February, 1974*, mimeo, London, n.d.

CONCLUSION

1 T. Nairn, 'The Left Against Europe', *New Left Review*, no. 75, 1972, p. 43.
2 F. Parkin, *Class Inequality and Political Order*, London 1971, p. 99.
3 In addition to Parkin see Tom Nairn (n. 1 above); and Barry Hindess, *The Decline of Working Class Politics*, London 1971.
4 Panitch, 'Ideology and Integration: The Case of the British Labour Party', *Political Studies*, vol. XIX, no. 2, 1971.
5 R. H. Tawney, *Equality*, 4th edn, London, p. 19.
6 S. H. Beer, *Modern British Politics*, London 1965, p. 190.
7 D. Jackson *et al. Do Trade Unions Cause Inflation?*, Cambridge 1972, p. 76.
8 Beer (n. 6 above), p. 216.
9 Ibid. p. 211.
10 Significant elements of corporatism, particularly the theory of organic unity, are to be found in both Labour and Conservative Party thought, see especially J. R. Macdonald, *Socialism and Society*, 6th edn, London 1908, and David Clarke, 'The Conservative Faith in the Modern Age', in Conservative Political Centre, *Conservatism 1945–50*, (London 1950). For commentaries on this see Panitch (n. 4 above); Nigel Harris, *Competition and the Corporate Society*, London 1972, esp. Ch. 4; Beer (n. 6 above), esp. Chs. 1 and 3.
11 Harris (n. 10 above), p. 72.
12 C. B. Macpherson, 'Politics: Post-Liberal Democracy' in Robin Blackburn (ed.), *Ideology in Social Science*, London 1972, pp. 28–9.
13 Ibid. pp. 29–30.
14 Anthony Barnett has made the same point in his discussion of the Conservative Government's Industrial Relations Act. See 'Class Struggle and the Heath Government', *New Left Review*, no. 77, 1973, pp. 36–8.
15 Richard Hyman, *Marxism and the Sociology of Trade Unionism*, London 1971, p. 40.
16 Beer subscribes to this view; see *Modern British Politics* (n. 6 above), p. 421.
17 *Marx's Grundrisse*, trans. David McLellan, London 1971, p. 95; cf. the translation by Martin Nicolaus, London 1973, p. 325.
18 A. Gorz, *Strategy for Labor*, Boston 1967, p. 36.
19 Nairn (n. 1 above), pp. 48–9.
20 Eric Heffer, *Class Struggle in Parliament*, London 1973, pp. 272, 279, 283.
21 Heffer (n. 20 above), p. 232.
22 'Trade Unions and the Labour Party', speech to Fabian Society Meeting, Brighton, 4 October 1971.
23 Heffer (n. 20 above), p. 279.
24 E. J. Hobsbawm, 'Trends in the Labour Movement', in *Labouring Men*, London 1964, p. 330.
25 A. Crosland, *Can Labour Win?* Fabian Tract 324, 1960, p. 20.
26 'The Choice Before the Labour Party', *Political Quarterly* (1932), quoted in Royden Harrison, 'Labour Government: Then and Now', *Political Quarterly*, vol. 41, no. 1, 1970, p. 78.
27 'Trade Unions and the Labour Party' (n. 22 above).

INDEX

A page number followed by a note number in brackets indicates that there is a quoted passage on the page but that the person quoted is not referred to by name except in the note.

Index

Index

Index